MYSORE MODERN

Mysore Modern

. . . .

Rethinking the Region under Princely Rule

Janaki Nair

University of Minnesota Press

Minneapolis

London

An early version of chapter 1 was published as "Tipu Sultan, History Painting, and the Battle for Perspective," *Studies in History* 22, no. 1 (2006): 97–143. A previous version of chapter 5 was published as "Drawing a Line: K. Venkatappa and His Publics," *Indian Economic and Social History Review* 35, no. 2 (1998): 179–210. An earlier version of chapter 6 was published as "Devadasi, Dharma, and the State," *Economic and Political Weekly* 29, no. 50 (1994): 3157–67. A prior version of chapter 7 was published as "Prohibited Marriage: State Protection and the Child Wife," *Contributions to Indian Sociology* 29, nos. 1 and 2 (1995): 157–88.

Published by the University of Minnesota Press
111 Third Avenue South, Suite 290
Minneapolis, MN 55401-2520
http://www.upress.umn.edu

Library of Congress Cataloging-in-Publication Data

Nair, Janaki.
Mysore modern : rethinking the region under princely rule / Janaki Nair.
    p.   cm.
Includes bibliographical references and index.
ISBN 978-0-8166-7383-4 (hc : alk. paper) — ISBN 978-0-8166-7384-1 (pb : alk. paper)
    1. Karnataka (India)—Politics and government.   2. Karnataka (India)—History.   3. Karnataka (India)—Social conditions.   4. India—History—British occupation, 1765–1947.   I. Title.
DS485.M9N345 2011
954'.87—dc22

                                                                    2011017082

To the memories of Shankar Lallapura,
Jugnu, Vijaya, and Mohammad Moeinuddin
and briefly shared journeys through Mysore/Karnataka

For Devayani

Contents

Acknowledgments

I HAVE WRITTEN THIS BOOK to consolidate an understanding of the meanings and consequences of indirect rule under colonialism and the legacies for modern India. I have previously focused on the histories of marginal groups and popular practices (whether those of industrial workers, women, or a range of social groups in the city), so my concerns in *Mysore Modern* represent a significant departure. I hope it will demonstrate that a history of the practice of power and of the ruling elites need not be elitist and instead may illuminate, without extolling, the practice of a "monarchical modern" form of state power and its death throes.

I accumulated many debts over the period in which I was writing the book, too numerous to acknowledge in full. I enjoyed a hospitable and constructively critical environment at the Centre for Studies in Social Sciences, Kolkata, where most of these chapters were written and presented. I am indebted to G. Arunima, Ramesh Bairy, Gautam Bhadra, P. K. Datta, William Glover, Thomas Metcalf, Tapati Guha Thakurta, and an anonymous reviewer for detailed suggestions on how to improve the manuscript. Raziuddin Aquil, Clare Arni, B. S. Bhooshan, Robert del Bonta, Sheela Gowda, Aya Ikegame, the late Mohammad Moienuddin, Balan Nambiar, N. Pushpamala, and A. R. Vasavi have been more than generous with their time and resources. Thanks, too, to Ann Ninan and Devika.

I extensively consulted collections at the Divisional Archives, Mysore; the Karnataka State Archives, Bengaluru; the National Archives, Delhi; and the libraries of the Mythic Society, Bengaluru; the Centre for Studies in Social Sciences, Kolkata; and the University of California, Berkeley. G. Kumarappa at the National Library, Kolkata, provided invaluable assistance. To Abhijit Bhattacharya, Ranjana Dasgupta, and Kamalika Mukherjee, who never hesitated to help with illustrations, special thanks.

Several versions of this work were presented over the years at conferences and seminars at Calcutta University, the Centre for Studies in

Social Sciences, and Jadavpur University, Kolkata; the Indian Council for Historical Research and the National Institute of Advanced Studies, Bengaluru; Kannada University, Hampi; and M. S. University, Baroda; and to university audiences at Berkeley, Davis, Hyderabad, Minnesota, and Tokyo.

Putul Masi, Meena, and Manju freed me from domestic drudgery and made everyday life more comfortable. To Joyce, Kim, Paul, Rajashri, and Sushil, for keeping the faith, a special salute. To Jason Weidemann and all at the University of Minnesota Press who have been meticulous in their efforts to clean up the manuscript, I remain extremely grateful. Any mistakes that remain are my own.

I lost many close friends over these years, some of whom I remember in my dedication. To my own *mysuru hudugi*, who shared many of my journeys, travails, and disruptions but retained her good humor and poise, I offer this book as proof that at least some of my preoccupations have ended pleasantly.

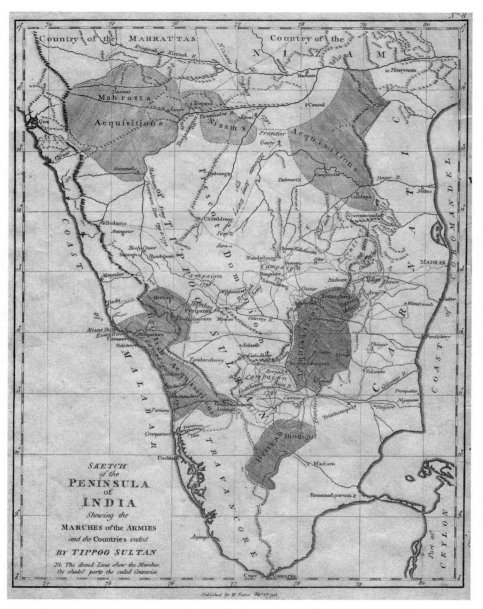

Figure 1. Mysore in 1793, at the end of the Third Mysore War, showing regions ceded by Tipu Sultan. Courtesy of the Clare Arni Collection.

Reconceptualizing the Modern, the Region, and Princely Rule

IS THE REGION, and especially one under indirect colonial rule, the necessary site from which to rethink Indian modernity? This is a theme that haunts the pages of this book, and justifies the long period that it covers, from the late eighteenth century to the mid-twentieth century. It was in this time that some of the most important institutions, modalities, and practices of the modern took root to become an important legacy for contemporary Karnataka. Questioning the temporality of Indian modernity disturbs the all-too-easy identification of the onset of colonial rule with the arrival of the "modern" and suggests that there are elements of the modern (as indeed the premodern) that may have persisted over different periods and given new meaning. It is now widely accepted that there was no single or homogenous modernity that reproduced itself throughout the world, whether through the spread of capitalist modes of production or forms of (bureaucratic) rationalism.[1] Neither in its origins nor in its effects was modernity uniform or homogenous, though it represented a rupture with modes of production, organization, and being that preceded it. The challenge of tracing the discrepant histories of Indian modernity is not to deny capitalist modernity's claim to universality but to highlight the limits of such universality and of the continuous production and staging of difference.[2]

Lest this work be seen as just another, if regional and late, variant of what has been normed as an account of the experience of colonialism's founding moments in India, it is important to spell out why areas of India that have long been considered only "regions" may be the appropriate sites from which to begin a reconceptualization of modernity "as a historically contingent combination of its constituent elements," be they new practices of production, governance, scientific cognition, education, or artistic and cultural creativity, which could draw on, while staging a decisive break with, material from preexisting conditions.[3] To suggest a new way of conceiving Mysore's uneven and discontinuous modernity, from the time of Tipu Sultan (r. 1782–99), the indefatigable opponent of British expansion in India, to the time when Mysore state was absorbed into Karnataka (1956), is to stress the important *sequential differences* between the historical experience of modernity in (and even within) western Europe and (especially) within India.[4]

A wide range of colonial, nationalist, and postindependence historians have found it imperative to claim Tipu Sultan as part of a national narrative, whether that is a narrative of conquest, resistance, nationalism, or historical reperiodization. Yet Mysore's subsequent history has been relegated to, and therefore neglected as, the history of the region, sustaining no further enquiry. If the historians and political theorists of Indian modernity have had to wrestle with the easy equation of a (European) particular with a universal truth, regions and groups on the subcontinent that marked a departure from the now familiar historical narratives of one regional modernity have labored under the further burden of explaining their lacks, even if some of these lacks attracted nationalist praise rather than opprobrium.[5] This work avoids the compulsion of having to compile or explain a laundry list of lacks for Mysore's failure to pass through the stages that have already been naturalized for other parts of modern India.

Rather, this book turns attention to the specific arrangements under indirect rule in Mysore that would take new and influential forms in the period of high colonialism (from the mid-nineteenth century) and incipient nationalism (the twentieth century), pioneering a "monarchical modern" form of power, that is, adapting the agenda of cultural renewal, modernization, and reform using the instrumentalities of state power refracted through the trappings of monarchy. Rather than explain Mysore's passages to modernity as irreducibly different or exceptional,[6] I emphasize the constituent elements of its modernity through several phases to draw out the consequences for wider understandings of modernity as a whole. Was there a progressive growth of administrative practices between the eighteenth and twentieth centuries, as K. N. Venkatasubba Sastri suggests?[7] Or was Mysore's modernity a discontinuous process that complicates our understandings of the meaning of power and authority under colonial rule, questions the meaning of good governance delinked from fundamental economic or social changes, and highlights the conditions that enabled a different route to social or cultural reform and indeed nation-ness?

Princely India and Its Historians

Although most historians of princely regimes in India are agreed that the British reconstituted princely power in ways that bore little relationship to its precolonial forms, assessments of indirect rule are varied. Mihir Kumar Ray, Ian Copland, and Michael Fisher focus on colonial imperatives and policy initiatives; Barbara Ramusack's broader survey, *The Indian Princes and Their States*, highlights both the legacies of the precolonial period that were preserved and the new and innovative ways in which the rulers came to terms with colonial rule and worked within the realms of circumscribed authority in large kingdoms or small principalities.[8] Comparative histories of some large princely states by Vanaja Rangaswami, Manu Bhagwan, and S. Chandrasekhar outline the different trajectories that were traced by princely states of similar resources and constraints.[9]

By far, the most nuanced insights on the nature of princely power and authority have emerged from monographs on individual princely states that take both official and nonofficial sources into account. Ranging from narratives of political and economic development in large states such as Hyderabad or Mysore to the questions of how region and religion shaped the texture of social and cultural, and therefore political, engagements in the making of modern Kashmir, these monographs have generated new perspectives of the meaning and depth of indirect rule in colonial India.[10]

Ethnohistorical monographs on the little kingdoms of the south, such as Puddukottai, Ramnad, and Shivagangai, made ambitious claims about the meaning of princely power under colonial rule. Nicholas Dirks characterizes the princely state of Pudukkottai as nothing more than a "hollow crown," the site for a theatrical display of power in the nineteenth and twentieth centuries.[11] Although Dirks points out that such hollowed power reached its apogee in the little kingdoms of south India, his formulations have been read as a compulsory framework for understanding all princely states.[12] Pamela Price makes a strenuous argument for "a continuing evolution of royal symbols and values under colonial rule" rather than a mere hollowing of power in other little kingdoms such as Ramnad and Shivagangai.[13]

Clearly, there are limits to generalizations that rest on the experience of smaller kingdoms. The most obvious distinction is one of scale, for the comparison between a little kingdom such as Puddukottai or Ramnad and a large regional power such as Mysore or Hyderabad is difficult to sustain. Possessing the space and resources to strike out in new and innovative directions even under the stifling conditions of colonial rule, many large states earned sometimes praise (e.g., Mysore and Baroda) and sometimes notoriety (e.g., Hyderabad and Kashmir) for their policies and programs from both colonial rulers and their own subjects. Second, even under conditions of indirect rule, the Mysore court with its pomp and splendor, far from being emptied of significance, was a highly contested site, which, along with modern civil social institutions, shaped and produced the loyalty and affection of subject populations. The desire of the sovereign to see and be seen emerged as a struggle over forms of self-representation as much as it sculpted new modes of spectation.

Manu Bhagwan has found "a comprehensive assault on the ideological soul of colonialism" in the policies and statecraft of Mysore and Baroda, suggesting that they successfully exploited the Idea of Progress to fashion a "non colonial modernity."[14] In Mysore, although resistance is more difficult to establish, bureaucratization, particularly after 1831, replaced forms of incorporative gift giving centered on the king. In other words, the meaning of kingship even within the same state did not remain stable or predictable under conditions of colonialism. Indeed, Mysore's emergence from the folds of a dynastic claim to power and its transition to a recognizable region was enabled by the success with which the bureaucracy produced a royal family in the place of a ruling dynasty.

Of the small body of historical works on modern Mysore, the earlier histories were quick to identify the modern period with the onset of British rule.[15] James Manor and Bjorn Hettne focused largely on the political-economic spheres of twentieth-century Mysore.[16] S. Chandrasekhar's two volumes of social history and some monographs marked out a different set of questions and sources.[17] Aided by a small but significant body of new research on Mysore,[18] this may be an opportune moment to ask, does the thematic of modernity, rather than colonial policy or administrative imperative, enhance our understandings of princely regimes in the nineteenth and twentieth centuries? What do the discrepant histories of realms such as the aesthetic-political, the social-legal, or the national-developmental tell us about the specific forms of power developed in princely states and the sculpting of subject populations? Do these cultural, social, and political transformations signal another route to the modern?

An Indigenous Modern Reversed?
The Early Nineteenth-Century Princely Order

In his 1930s assessment of the Sultanat-i-Khudadad (God-Given Government) of Tipu Sultan, Mahmud Khan Mahmud Banglori noted:

> When Tipu Sultan captured power, he turned his attention to the unity of the Muslims, and unity of the communities of Hindusthan. He gave full attention to industry and trade, so that Hindusthan was not dependent. It is this determination of Tipu Sultan to unite Muslims/Indians, and make them self sufficient, that made the East India Company an opponent. This opposition kept him busy. Despite this, Mysore made progress in ways unsurpassed in past and future.[19]

Burton Stein traces the vigorous transformation of Mysore into a new system of fiscalism to finance the continuous wars of the late eighteenth century to Haidar Ali (r. 1761–82), who developed a form of centralized authority to be perfected by Tipu Sultan.[20] In his effort to mop up the resources of the state to fund the wars, Tipu replaced tax farmers with a systematized bureaucracy staffed by *amildars* (revenue officers in charge of *taluks*, administrative divisions of groups of villages) under provincial governors, or *asafs*, and further instituted a series of well-documented measures, such as the resumption of *inams* (revenue-free land grants) enjoyed by Brahmans and temples, the organization and training of the military, and plans for a navy; the establishment of military industries; the encouragement of indigenous production; state intervention in retail trade; and state monopoly of the sandal, betel nut, cardamom, and pepper trades.[21] Venkatasubba Sastri noted that Haidar Ali and Tipu Sultan drew at least two lessons from the European presence in India: that force, not dharma (righteousness), is the basis of authority in a heterogeneous society and that the state should regulate the economic life of the country.[22]

Tipu Sultan was not alone among the southern Indian rulers of the eighteenth century in introducing these aggressively new measures; Raja Martanda Varma's expansion of Venad Kingdom into Travancore State (between 1734 and 1752) similarly involved the reorganization of the army on European lines and monopoly over the pepper, timber, and cardamom trades, models that were also followed by the neighboring Cochin State.[23]

Yet Tipu Sultan experimented with new definitions of kingship and state power that were similar to, but also significantly departed from, other South Indian models.[24]

If Tipu Sultan's Mysore represents an example of the indigenous routes to the modern pioneered by innovative though absolutist rulers, what came afterward in Mysore? Following Sastri, we might ask if there was an attempt to renew the notion of *rajadharma* (kingly duty) in the interregnum between early British control (1799) and direct British rule (1831). In the first two decades of his rule, Krishnaraja Wodeyar III (r. 1799–1868), despite severely curtailed power, attempted to forge a less centralized mode of governance that would lend it an aura of legitimacy independent of colonial rule. The quest for legitimacy was urgent because, as Governor-General Wellesley knew only too well, the Haidar-Tipu period had "subsisted for such a length of time as to have nearly extinguished the hopes of the Hindoo family," though he chose the Wodeyar family in 1799 because it would "be more acceptable to the Hindus who form the majority of the province."[25] In contrast to what happened in Tanjore, Arcot, or Awadh, a ruling Muslim dynasty was replaced with a forgotten Hindu one and fashioned from principles markedly different from those devised for other Indian states.

The administration of the reinvented kingdom of Mysore was first placed under the Maratha Brahman Purnaiya (*Dewan*, or chief minister, from 1799 to 1811), who had served both Haidar Ali and Tipu Sultan and survived the regime change.[26] Entrusted with the twin tasks of bringing "stability" to the war-torn province and promptly paying the subsidy, Purnaiya was quick to win the praise of his real masters.[27] His extractive mode of revenue collection, with none of its improving characteristics, soon resulted in complaints about the extortions of the new regime.[28] Even the Nagar peasants, when launching their rebellion of 1831, were haunted by the memory of better times: "While we were under the dominion of the family of Caladi Sivappa Naik, who governed this country for many years and also in the days of Nawab Bahadur Tippoo, we were in a state of happiness."[29] The return of Mysore to "Hindu" rule did little to bind peasant loyalty to the king.

If anything, colonial rule in Mysore as elsewhere was inaugurated by a series of revolts and peasant uprisings that had been singularly absent in the time of Tipu Sultan. *Paleyagaras* (warrior chieftains) attempted to wrest away control of their territories that had been absorbed by the Mysore rulers. Dhondia Wagh's guerilla war, begun just a month after the fall of Tipu, drew disgruntled peasants, demobilized soldiers, and unemployed Muslims to an army that posed the most serious challenge to British control over Mysore.[30] Rebellions continued until 1804,[31] and would resurface as full-blown resistance in Nagar in 1831. "Mohammedan" disaffection, meanwhile, flowered on the eve of the rebellion at Vellore.[32]

On the other hand, the Mysore army came to the British East India Company's aid in the Maratha wars and served as a granary during the time of acute food scarcity in 1804–6 in British and Maratha territories.[33] Little wonder that Lewis Rice concluded in the late nineteenth century that Purnaiya's "system of government was no doubt absolute; and . . . the accumulation of surplus revenue presented itself to him, as a prime end to be attained. It may be questioned . . . whether he did not . . . enrich the treasury at the expense of the State, by narrowing the resources of the people."[34] Apart from swelling the land and excise revenues, Purnaiya's "absolutism" drew from the colonial state and was markedly different from Tipu's vision of new interventionist roles for the state. Colonial rule, on the other hand, had quickly resulted in deurbanization following the decline of manufactures, in the decline of agriculture, and in damaging changes to systems of trade and commerce.[35]

Experiments with the Art of Governance

Despite its ambiguous legacies, Purnaiya's regime was considered to have given Mysore "good governance."[36] Of what did this consist? Burton Stein points out that the practice of granting inams to Brahmans, temples, and *mathas* (monastic institutions) was renewed in the 1790s by the new British administration of Thomas Munro in the ceded districts (from Bellary in the west to Cuddapah in the east) in an attempt to recall patterns of South Indian kingship.[37] Purnaiya lost no time in creating a circle of faithful beneficiaries through "unauthorised *khyreat* [missives of wellbeing] to Brahmans."[38] Similarly, Krishnaraja Wodeyar III's art of governance consisted of lavish patronage of Brahmans, temples, and mathas and the dispersal of power to the *amildars*. When questioned about the rapidly falling revenues and mounting personal costs four years after his assumption of direct rule, Krishnaraja Wodeyar III explained:

The late Dewan Poornia whose task lay only in the collection of
Revenue . . . was inattentive to the interests of the people. . . . The
whole of my attention is now earnestly employed in bettering the
conditions of my subjects, by which the public finances are now
improved and secured, and in promoting the general prosperity
of the country which is the first object of good government.[39]

Gift giving, without the expectation of returns, was central to the reconstructed kingship. The lustrous court of writers, artists, and musicians resulted in a steady rise of endowments to 265,683 Canteroy pagodas (C.P.),
and the Maharaja's personal expenditure had climbed to 508,598 C.P. in
1813–14 from 163,300 C.P. in 1809–10.

The period between 1812 and 1831 was in fact marked by a struggle between the Maharaja and the East India Company over who was the real
master, because the Mysore king exceeded the company's expectations in
his enthusiasm to recoup sovereignty. In 1821, Thomas Munro, governor of
Madras, acknowledged on a visit to Mysore that gifts were an important
attribute of sovereignty, because the "loss of much of their [the princes']
real power makes them more anxious to preserve forms that yet remain
of royalty."[40] Was Krishnaraja Wodeyar III striving to produce new and
splendid meaning out of limited resources, or was he just the "the native
knight who bore the British coat of arms"?[41] The compulsive gift giving,
seen by the British as a form of corruption, could not produce a recipro-
cal effect, given that the incorporation of parts of the Mysore territory
was no longer necessary. Yet it remained an important one-way transac-
tion, which, according to Aya Ikegame, was predicated on a concept of
kingly duty that lingered well into the twentieth century.[42] The revenue
farming (shirti muchalika) system (which conferred the amildari, or right
to collect revenue—including the civil charge—of a taluk on the person
"who agreed to collect a certain amount of revenue which was generally
larger than that of the previous year") was a way of expanding and gen-
eralizing what had been introduced in 1806–7 and was finally abandoned
in 1827.[43]

The size of the Mysore subsidy left no alternative to the tax farmer
system. This short-lived interregnum was neither a "harking back" nor
a sign of the future but represented a time between two well-developed
forms of modern state power, indigenous and colonial. Between the
practice of centralized power represented by Tipu Sultan and full-blown

colonial dominance was the attempt to craft a broadly semifeudal political order that would mask the true roots from which Wodeyar authority was derived.[44]

Although it was recognized in 1806 that "Mysoor exhibits to all the states of India a monument of British liberality, equity, and moderation," Krishnaraja Wodeyar III refused to be the man-king that the British hoped for, striving instead to create a glory drawn from his kinship to the gods.[45] By 1814, the colonial regime realized that the princely state alternative to the "corrupt and degraded Government of India"[46] or to such regional powers as Arcot, Awadh, and Tanjore was unworkable. The theology of gift giving, which combined elements of the material and the spiritual, seriously disrupted the new economic rationality of the colonial regime.[47]

Rebellions that broke out in Nagar in 1831 and soon spread to other parts of Mysore and the borders of Coorg and Malabar gave the East India Company ample reason to assume direct control of Mysore. The Maharaja was reduced to a stipendiary, receiving 100,000 C.P. per annum in addition to one-fifth of the revenue of the state.[48] Throughout the crisis, the colonial administration knew that by stressing maladministration, it could deflect the trenchant critique of colonial rule emerging in many parts of the Karnataka region.[49] In Mysore, as in the neighboring Canara, the peasants first petitioned the government, then gathered in *kootas,* or assemblies, demanding a radical restructuring of the revenue collection system and seeking relief.[50] Only the report of the committee to inquire into the peasant insurrection in 1833 admitted, though in passing, that Purnaiya's "good governance" might inevitably have led to "the detriment of the wealth of Mysore."[51]

Other than the timely payment of the subsidy, of what did the art of governance consist? The Mysore Maharaja was continually urged to be more assertive and forceful, truer to the capricious models of indigenous kingship: Resident Casamaijor complained in 1828 about the king's aversion to capital punishment and mutilation, "although the legitimacy of such an award is founded upon the practice, usage and laws of the native government of India."[52] As such, a style of kingship that sought to disperse power was doomed to come to grief under colonialism.

After 1831, as most narratives have it, the Maharaja turned his quest for legitimacy to the private realm and clung to every small vestige of authority within his kingdom. The privileged cultural realm under the patronage of the Maharaja was neither representational (in terms of the rulers being seen as the center of de facto kingship) nor aesthetic (for which the conditions of possibility emerged only in the late nineteenth century in Mysore). Suspended between the "cult value" of a representational regime and the emergence of "exhibition value," the artistic productions of the early nineteenth century could neither set themselves free from the economy of representing power nor embrace a newer economy abdicating it.[53] In the large collection of portraits or in the body of mural paintings, the king was seen in terms quite different from those surrounding his predecessor.

Every change in administrative style cut deeper into the threadbare power of Krishnaraja Wodeyar III. By 1867, he had learned an expensive lesson in the "art of governance." He rued his "twenty years of despotic power" in this *khureeta* (letter from royalty, delivered in a silk bag) to the Viceroy John Lawrence:

> I have learned that the possession of absolute power is a dangerous and undesirable possession for any man, and I have observed that . . . the British government is careful to entrust no such prerogative to any of its functionaries from the highest to the lowest. Every officer . . . even the monarch, is ruled and guided by law and order in financial, judicial and administrative affairs.[54]

This statement showed his willingness to be a *legal* king instead of a *divinely ordained* one, if his line was guaranteed safe lodging in Mysore. By this time, his tenacity in seeking the return of Mysore to his adopted successor was rewarded on condition that the new Maharaja would consent to being a reconstituted monarch.[55]

Direct British Rule and the Triumph of the Colonial-Modern

What model of governance, under the "improving" influence of Mark Cubbon (Commissioner 1834–61), found praise among the chronicles of the nineteenth century? Cubbon's administration, under the twin influences of utilitarianism and evangelicalism, combined the principle of accumulation with that of godliness.[56] The important difference was that, unlike his fellow Victorians, Cubbon had only a small clutch of economic "improvements" to report: the British administration took 25 years to reach the annual gross revenues of 1799–1810 Mysore, and only in 1860–61 did land revenue reach 1802–3 levels.[57]

Cubbon and Lewin Bowring (Commissioner 1862–70), the two important commissioners of Mysore, ensured that there could be no return to the dispersed practice of power of Krishnaraja Wodeyar III. Between 1831 and 1881, the bureaucracy was fashioned into an instrument of governance, and subjects were gradually rendered into a "population." The commissioners were content to ensure the regular extraction of revenues through a regime "more scientific, formal and rigid, governed by rules and regulations."[58] Following the death of Krishnaraja Wodeyar III, the colonial authorities wasted no time in asserting their absolute control over the kingdom of Mysore; the palace establishment was steadily dismantled and "rationalized," and the affairs of the young prince were brought under the strict tutelage of colonial masters. Major Elliot, who was entrusted with the task of reorganizing the palace in 1868, made the first move to assert that the state, rather than the king, was the patron of religious institutions, which was later systematized by the Muzrai Memorandum.[59]

When Chamarajendra Wodeyar X was "given back" his kingdom (1881), a fully reconstituted kingship was in place, parallel to and increasingly subordinated to the appointed administrative head, the Dewan.[60] Mysore city itself, now divested of its administrative associations since the administration had moved to Bangalore, became the abode of a diminished royalty. The link between the person of the king and kingship was severed, and the Maharaja was made even more beholden to the colonial authorities for his power. If there was one period of modern Mysore history that resembled the description of the "theatre state," it was the last quarter of the nineteenth century, when a formal split was achieved and maintained between the royal family and its duties and the administration of the state of Mysore.

Even at this time, it would be difficult to assert that the royalty was a largely privatized entity. Rather, the Mysore royalty, supported by a periodically revised but restricted civil list after the death of Krishnaraja Wodeyar III in 1868, became increasingly bureaucratized,[61] partnering with and often extending the dreams and schemes of an invigorated bureaucracy in its quest for regional economic development and redefined social relations.

It was in the relatively restrained reign of Chamarajendra Wodeyar X that the transition was made from Mysore as the realm of a ruling dynasty whose fortunes waxed and waned to Mysore as a *territorial unit* of which the ruling family was only a symbol. Strenuous efforts were made to imbue Mysore with a national identity, long believed alien to its people.[62]

Chamrajendra's recognition from participation at the Imperial Assemblage in 1877 that Mysore—despite its large size, unwavering loyalty, and immense monetary contribution to the British Indian government—did not command the respect of smaller, high-status Rajput states, led to a "Rajput Policy." He forged a "genealogical" link with the region of Dwarka, the birthplace of the epic hero Krishna, by seeking a marriage alliance for his son, Krishnaraja Wodeyar IV, with an antique Rajput state.[63]

Chamarajendra Wodeyar did not live to witness the fruit of these efforts, but he provided the territory of Mysore with a well-marked identity. He composed a "national anthem" and formally adopted the Gandabherunda (a mythical two-headed eagle that was among the important insignia of the Vijayanagara kings and was taken over by several successor vassal states, including Mysore) as the insignia of the Mysore royal house so that house could take its place in a new national order.[64] The "Rajput Policy," which reversed the logic of caste redefinition by marriage, took longer to bear fruit, and it was only in 1928 that the secretary of state suggested:

> Whatever may in fact be the position as regards the Kshatriya descent claimed by the ruling house of Mysore, Lord Birkenhead feels that since a claim to such descent has consistently been made, and the present Maharaja has married a Kathiawari Rajput lady, the suggestion that his Highness is, or might be, a Sudra, is likely to give offence . . . the GOI [Government of India] may think it well to take steps to secure that the Mysore House shall not be described as "Sudra" in official correspondence.[65]

The first census of Mysore, in 1881, which measured, enumerated, and (territorially) fixed its people as a body to be governed, was completed in the inaugural year of Chamarajendra Wodeyar's reign. In that year, the first Dewan of the refashioned state, C. V. Rangacharlu, inaugurated an "Assembly of Representative Raiyats and Merchants from all the Taluks of Mysore State." Convened as an annual meeting to coincide with the revived public celebration of Dasara after a fifty-year gap, it had, as Vanaja Rangaswami rightly notes, "the purpose of affording the people an opportunity for paying homage to the new rulers, a revival of the Durbar [royal assembly or court] in a new setting."[66] Yet at the time when the population was being constituted as the site for the exercise of governmental power, it was still the community that the government sustained and even created, so that the modalities of "governmentality" (here, following Michel Foucault, understood as individuation, normativization, and the disciplinary practice of power) remained curiously hybridized in Mysore, as in other parts of India. The composition of the assembly, even after limited principles of election were conceded, therefore represented "communities and interests," including new interests such as gold mining and newly defined communities such as the Adi Dravidas (earlier, Depressed Classes).

In its determined pursuit of governmental programs to reorder communal blocs and thereby enlarge the space of modernity, though often in contradictory ways, the Mysore bureaucracy was unusually interventionist. It strained to produce the civil social institutions adequate to the task of economic development by affirming and extending the use of community categories, revealing a new and unprecedented political rationality.[67] The Mysore state was committed, indeed obliged, to create the conditions for new forms of social life to take root.[68] Turning Mysore into a space of mobilizable resources, an *economy*, was the task undertaken by the upper levels of the bureaucracy with vigor, while the reconstitution of caste hierarchies was attempted within the only spheres of public life and employment then available, that is, government jobs and education.

The "Bourgeoisie's Political Intelligence" and the National-Modern in Mysore

Most accounts of the history of modern Mysore are agreed on the extraordinary success with which the Mysore bureaucracy transformed the state after 1881 to create a space of "enlightened" modernity.[69] The power and vision of its Dewans marked Mysore off from some of its equals in size and importance and from the petty principalities (such as the Rajput states) that were less hospitable to the modalities of democracy.[70]

Satish Deshpande has argued that "one of the dominant modes in which the Indian nation has been imagined is as a community of producers, as an economy."[71] He identifies three stages in the imagining of the modern Indian economy: first, a recognition that the economy is enslaved, calling for nationalist mobilization and effort; second, the Nehruvian stage, when "the newly liberated economy comes to be enshrined as the very essence of the emergent nation"; and third, the period of the 1980s and 1990s, when "the economy has a very uncertain status in the collective conception of the nation."[72] In Mysore, the bureaucracy succeeded in forging a sense of nation-ness primarily in the economic domain well before independence, though it refrained from any overt critique of colonial modernization. As the "repository of the bourgeoisie's political intelligence," the bureaucracy envisaged a role for the state to enter the domain of production "as a mobilizer and manager of investible resources."[73] Princely Mysore's industrial policy thus anticipated the ideals of Nehruvian development planning, the second of Deshpande's stages. Only when the colonial government thwarted Mysore's plans to build a car factory in 1940 did the bureaucracy voice open criticism of colonial rule.[74]

The Mysore state also displayed an entrepreneurial flair in putting in place institutional forms that would compensate for a marked disinterest in associational practices. Indirect rule in Mysore thus departed significantly from the better-known sites of both British and princely India in the colonial period.[75] The relative autonomy of the princely state assumes great relevance in such a discussion, because the Mysore bureaucracy was able to play a role far in excess of its British Indian counterparts. The bureaucracy at once represented the autocratic power of the colonizer and anticipated the moral-intellectual leadership of the nation. In its economic initiatives and in its deployment of the law, beginning from the late nineteenth century, the state addressed the most serious internal impediments to economic progress and capitalist development through administrative initiatives and economic incentives (for instance, in the development of joint stock companies to mobilize capital, in social measures to increase the indigenous population of Malnad, or in five-year plans [such as that of 1933–38] to develop the infrastructure of that region).

The upper echelons of the Mysore bureaucracy were drawn from a section of the Western-educated upper castes, largely Brahman, initially from the Madras Presidency and later from within Mysore itself.[76] The absorption of the Brahman into the new-style bureaucracy was accomplished with ease until the time when caste was once more visibilized to limit Brahman prospects.[77] The next step in recasting the bureaucracy was aided by the visions and initiatives of Krishnaraja Wodeyar IV, himself seeking to redefine the status of his Ursu clan within a national caste order. The gradual inclusion of men from the backward, though dominant, castes by the Maharaja was resisted by Dewan Visvesvaraya in the period 1912–18. The *Miller Committee Report* (1918), however, showed that state apparatuses could be realigned to transform society itself and questioned the unalloyed category of merit that would automatically reserve the jobs in the upper echelons for the Brahmans.[78]

Only a framework that recognizes the role played by the bureaucracy in lieu of an absent bourgeoisie permits us to make sense of the totality of legislative and administrative initiatives attempted in Mysore. At the same time, the molecular transformation of social relations in Mysore, for which the instrumentalities of the law were crucial, by no means effected a democratization of the social order, and may even have thwarted it. These points are better illustrated in the discussion that follows.

To the extent that the Mysore bureaucracy was not driven by a pursuit of democratic ideals, it was truer to the despotic colonial regime from which it derived its power and to the indigenous princely authority in whose name it ruled. In his exchanges with Jawaharlal Nehru at the height of the Congress movement in Mysore (1937–38), Dewan Mirza Ismail (Dewan from 1926 to 1940) "reiterated repeatedly that the Mysore Government stood for economic democracy above the political."[79] Here democracy implied self-sufficiency or independence:

> I had set before myself the ideal of a truly socialist state in Mysore. Explaining my policy in the course of my address to the Representative Assembly in 1936, I referred to the fact that the commercial enterprises we had embarked upon had laid us open in some quarters, to the charge of going too far in the direction of "state socialism.". . . In the great countries of the west, like England, the field of industry and commerce was pre-eminently one for the private entrepreneur, and any undue incursion into his preserves was looked upon as a violation of the doctrine of laissez-faire. On the other hand here in India, where private enterprise is proverbially unenterprising, and private capital notoriously shy, Governments have, perforce, to take a more active and practical interest in the problems of trade and industry than by merely passing a legislative measure regulating the hours of work here or amending laws there.[80]

In this sense, the bureaucracy anticipated the ideas of the nationalist elite both in its understanding of colonialism and in its muted critique of it. When Congress nationalism finally gained some ground in Mysore in the late 1920s and 1930s, its principal critiques were directed against the "authoritarian" nature of the Dewan's rule rather than the agenda of modernization as such, for it was the same terrain over which it sought to establish dominance.[81]

Mysore, one of five twenty-one-gun states, was fifth in area (29,475 square miles), and remained second in population of more than 550 states, large and small.[82] For at least half a century (1881–1930), successive Dewans showed that the massive Rs 3.5 million subsidy was a debilitating drain that impeded Mysore's progress and well-being. With the appointment of Dewans such as M. Visvesvaraya and Mirza Ismail, however, the state embarked on plans that would confront the British colonial government with some of its earlier promises and stake claim to greater economic autonomy, though usually only with limited success. The failure of Mysore to successfully negotiate the establishment of the automobile company in Bangalore was the climax of a long battle between the Dewans and the Government of India, leading to the resignation of Mirza in 1941.[83]

Commensurate with Mysore's "imagined economy" was the aspiration to universalize the legal form, though in uneven ways: the state apparatuses were not averse to entering, restructuring, and, in the process, reordering social relations, sometimes achieving a modicum of consensus; at other times, they overrode, as the Dewan thought fit, the will of the Mysore people and their representatives at the assembly.[84]

Initiatives aimed at recasting concepts of conjugality and the family did not emanate from or dissolve into the terms of discourse that have been elaborated by several social historians of British India.[85] A princely state under the titular leadership of the Maharaja could amend the personal laws of Hindus without invoking outcries as in British India. The state intervened in the regulation of practices such as infant marriage or the abolition of *devadasi* (temple dancer) services in temples and palaces. A considerable body of public opinion had been built up in the neighboring Madras Presidency but bore administrative fruit in Mysore. In its pioneering approach to two important domains, gender relations and caste disabilities, the Mysore bureaucracy developed techniques of governance that made political resolutions of social questions redundant. How does the Mysore experience rewrite the relationships among state, community, and civil society?

Mysore Modern: Governance in Lieu of Politics

There is an impressive list of firsts that most assessments of Mysore readily concede: not only did it have the first Representative Assembly (1881) and the first Legislative Council (1907); it was the first princely state to use

6749 1 104 1 6249   **

9780816673843 1080
MYSORE MODERN: RETHINKING TH   27.50t
10% off General Books   -2.75

Sub Total   24.75
Tompkins County Tax 4% Total   0.99
1 - NYS Sales Tax 4% Total   0.99

TOTAL   26.73**

Payware EF# 5**********0994   26.73
Authorization Code: 078517
Ref: 5414174S7

00262809O - Arjun Biddanda

15:31 12/05/13 Sale

1.1.104.6749.16776

Receipts required for returns/exchanges.
Texts & Course Materials must be
returned within 7 days. Textbooks
purchased after 10/4/13 may not be
returned. Tech Products must be
returned within 7 days; general
merchandise within 21 days with tags
attached. Clearance items are
nonreturnable. Open/ damaged packaging
will be charged a 20% fee

electric power to illuminate cities (Bangalore in 1905), found a state bank (1913), start a university (1916), found a chamber of commerce (1916), initiate a program of reservation for Backward Classes (1918), set up a Serum Institute (1929), fund birth control clinics for the general public (1930), send a trade commissioner to London (1930), and run an administrative training institute for Indian princes. Its policy of state aid to industries was not only the envy of south India but paved the way for the location of major public sector industries in the immediate postindependence period.[86]

Mysore's claim to being a model state is easily questioned: it barely equaled Madras and Bombay in general education and lagged far behind Cochin and Travancore, even though the state played an interventionist role in redressing perceived deficiencies that were acting as a drag on economic development.[87] M. Visvesvaraya's wide-ranging efforts emblematized this yearning, whether in founding the Economic Conference in 1911, the Karnataka Sahitya Parishat (later Kannada Sahitya Parishat) in 1915, and the Mysore Civic and Social Progress Association; instituting "efficiency audits" of the bureaucracy; or establishing exhibitions and clubs.[88] Such strenuous intervention in public life, which was relatively lacking in an associational culture beyond the caste associations, may not have had the desired results, though the public sphere was expanded in carefully controlled and sometimes undemocratic ways.

Mysore state thus absorbed the nationalist agenda, tending "to suffocate non-state institutions of civil society by theoretically equating the principle of public good with the institutional form of state control."[89] The language of development and change that animated its economic nationalism combined with the monarchical trappings to bind the population to the region of Mysore and win the pride and affection of its people. Indeed the museumization of Mysore city, after its long and uncertain existence through the nineteenth century, was a sign of the triumph of not just the refurbished monarchy but the new bureaucratic order.

However, even such interventions were not without contradictions. The resignations of Vivesvaraya in 1918 and Mirza Ismail in 1941 were not quirks of ambitious, reforming Dewans as much as sharp responses to the structural limits to modernizing the economy or society under conditions of colonialism. Both Dewans differed from the Maharaja on the principles on which state intervention was necessary and legitimate: Visveswaraya disagreed with Krishnaraja Wodeyar IV on state intervention for social change, and Mirza Ismail was disappointed in the failure of

Jayachamrajendra Wodeyar to support economic transformation. The former was unable to prevent the Maharaja from introducing the principle
of communal equality in government service following the issuance of the
Miller Committee Report, and the latter was unable to shake the Maharaja's
loyalty to the colonial regime on the question of shelving the prestigious
car factory project.

In matters that did not question the sovereignty of the colonial regime,
the bureaucracy undertook a programmatic, if molecular, transformation
of society through the instrumentalities of the law. The finesse with which
the state anticipated and absorbed the disruptive potential of the "communal" question as it was framed in twentieth-century Mysore once more
served to undermine the political nationalist cause and substitute the
rhetoric of good governance in its place. State intervention on questions
of caste and gender revealed the project of, and limits to, Mysore's pursuit
of modernity.

Caste and Community in Twentieth-Century Mysore

Political mobilization around a "sons-of-the-soil" movement (represented
at first by the movement against Brahmans from the Madras Presidency
dominating the Mysore bureaucracy in the late nineteenth century and
developing into a demand for proportional representation of Backward
Classes in public appointments from the early twentieth century) pre-
dated the restricted sphere within which nationalist politics took root in
Mysore in the 1920s.[90] The Brahmans of Mysore, however, did not hesitate to represent Depressed Classes in Bangalore and dominated the labor
unions, particularly in Bangalore, as well as the small but visible sphere of
radical political activities.[91]

However, caste associations were the registers on which progress—
educational levels, knowledge of English, or representation in public
services—could be written, to be measured and rectified by the state (and
sometimes communities themselves) through surveys or the use of census and other official data.[92] In other words, by the twentieth century,
caste had entered its governmentalized form through the readiness of
not just the communities themselves but the state and even the palace, to
enter into the correction of imbalances through a policy of reservations.[93]
Indeed, the emergence of a politics around "communal" questions, as
these activities were referred to at this time, though not in a pejorative

sense, was an imperative for those who did not enjoy such dominance and visibility in public services.[94] Caste was far from being the part of one's identity that had to be jettisoned in order to enter into the realm of the modern; in Mysore it was the very ground on which modernity was fashioned.

The role played by the state, the Mysore royalty, and the growing non-Brahman public sphere in foregrounding the question of caste as the principal ground of Mysore's modernity crucially reconceptualizes Indian history.[95] The Wodeyar rulers engaged in a process of revising the caste status of the Ursus (from which they were drawn) from Sudra to Kshatriyas as early as the seventeenth century, the time of Chikkadevaraja Wodeyar (1673–1704). By the nineteenth century, the production of genealogies rooted in mythology was just one way in which such revision was done. Anxieties about caste redefinition were heightened by the restoration of the Hindu dynasty and further enhanced under Chamarajendra Wodeyar with the integration of Mysore into the nation-space. The Ursus alternated between invoking the larger caste identity or that of the subcaste group as the situation demanded.[96] There was relatively easy conversion of this high (royal) ranking, particularly by the upper end of the caste hierarchy, into the new symbolic capital of Western-style education by the end of the nineteenth century.[97] Education became the cultural capital that enabled the transition of a "warrior" race to a modern, refined aristocracy.

Caste associations created the space for redefinition of the two dominant castes, Lingayats and Vokkaligas, through the establishment of educational institutions that ensured a higher degree of social mobility. In 1883, the Lingayats of Dharwar started the Lingayat Educational Development Fund, and the Akhil Bharatiya Veerasaiva Mahasabha was founded in 1904. In Mysore, the Lingayat Education Fund was set up in 1905, followed a year later by the establishment of the Vokkaligara Sangha. In 1918, the Maharaja himself commissioned a survey of the members of the Ursu caste living in villages in order to provide them with scholarships and hostels for education in Mysore city as a way of consolidating what was numerically a miniscule caste group.[98] Between 1923 and 1925, eighteen such caste associations were set up.[99] Mysore state also encouraged the equalization of caste-communities by allowing the Vokkaliga takeover of the Adi Chunchunagiri mutt in 1926.[100]

Not all community associations and agitations were given the same encouragement. Tagadur Ramachandra Rao worked hard to redefine the

Kanniyars as Sudra, not Panchama, demanding their admission to village schools and their right to draw water from village wells and intervening to resolve discriminatory practices in the factory setting.[101] Yet he did not get permission to launch the newspaper *Kaniyara Patrike,* a freedom that was readily granted to other caste groups.

However, Mysore pioneered a route to provide adequate representation of backward communities in the public service.[102] The state had adopted, though somewhat fitfully, some form of reservation in government jobs from at least 1874.[103] The appointment of the Miller Committee was an attempt to systematically institute a set of workable guidelines for reservations for non-Brahmans. Headed by Madras judge Sir Leslie C. Miller, the committee was set up in August 1918 and recommended that "at least half of the higher governmental posts, and two-thirds of the lower appointments" be filled with candidates from communities other than the Brahman, with due preference given to the Depressed Classes when qualified candidates were available.[104]

The *Miller Committee Report* is a breathtaking document if only for the optimism with which it proved that state intervention in the narrow field of government employment could redress long-standing social cleavages and divisions. The reservations were merely the starting point of an exposé of the extent to which the Brahmans (and small communities like the Mudaliars) were entrenched in institutional and governmental spaces. That the 1921 general order based on the *Miller Committee Report* did not yield dramatic results need not surprise us.[105] In the decades that followed, however, the visibility of the dominant castes in public life dramatically increased, and there was a confidence with which they translated social power into the institutional forms shaped by the nationalist politics of the region by 1937.[106] Krishnaraja Wodeyar IV favored giving Backward Classes such as Kurubars, Bestars, Kunchitigas, who had no representation in the services of the state, privilege over other Backward Classes. By this time, symbolic concessions had also been made to the Adi Karnatakas in recognition of their growing political presence in the state. One such concession was their admission to the Dasara durbar in 1936 in response to a plea from A. Subrahmanya Iyer of Mysore (and here again we may note the Brahman "speaking for" the Adi Karnatakas).[107]

The entire discourse on the new opportunities to be made available to caste communities in Mysore was gendered male, for it unquestioningly assumed that the proper subject of the community, and not just its leadership, was male. If the question of rights appeared only secondary in the discussion of communal equations in the state, with a number of demands for both material and symbolic gain being framed in terms of "entitlements," a far more direct invocation of rights was evident in discussions of the status of women. Why was the rhetoric of rights more appropriate to the discussion of women's status, especially when it appeared to produce once more a unified category (that is, Hindu society) that had so strenuously been dismantled by the discussions on caste? I suggest, however, that the question be reframed this way: were the women of Mysore, as subjects of reform, assigned the role of unifying what had been fractured on other registers?

State "Resolution" of the Women's Question

If caste became an important, and indeed sometimes the sole, ground on which modern institutional forms were imagined, produced, and sustained by the state, the "women's question" was the site at which Mysore bureaucrats and Congress nationalists alike felt free to declare their liberal credentials, often through illiberal and arbitrary measures. Elsewhere I have discussed the extension of Hindu women's rights to property in Mysore (1933) even before a similar act was passed in British India.[108] The issue was first raised when K. T. Bhashyam observed in the Legislative Council that "in Mysore, we have had it explicitly laid down by more decisions than one that sex is no ground of disqualification for inheritance." In order to facilitate the move toward judicial innovation on the matter, he introduced a draft bill called the Hindu Law of Inheritance Bill in 1928.[109] The government responded by appointing a commission headed by a senior judge, C. H. Chandrasekhara Aiyar, which included a token woman representative, K. D. Rukmaniamma, then a member of the legislature. The state's interest was in helping to provide uniformity in the application of Hindu law, which had become "unwieldy and ruinous." The committee pushed for decisive changes in Mitakshara law as it pertained to the rights of women.[110] The final bill, however, as one critic, H. C. Dasappa, had it, "seriously made an inroad into the existing rights of Hindu women. . . . Under the guise of giving them a few rights here and there, they have practically taken away the whole loaf.[111]

The state machinery was untroubled by the lack of women's "voice," so the invocation of the rhetoric of rights was neither an invitation to enter the male-gendered public sphere nor a reform of patriarchal family forms. It was of a piece with the arbitrary confidence with which the state made its moves through the early twentieth century: squashing a bill to permit the remarriage of widows in 1912, supporting the majority defeat of the bill to extend the franchise to women in 1921, and finally allowing the Widow Remarriage Bill to be introduced in Mysore in 1936, eighty years after the British Indian legislation.[112] Thus it was that the Mysore government was able to legislate for the rights of women to property on the one hand (through the passage of the Hindu Law as to the Rights of Women Act, 1933) and against immorality on the other (the passage of the Suppression of Immoral Traffic in Women and Girls Act of 1937). The rights discourse became more useful in the discussion of gender than in the discussion of caste, applying a general principle that in effect systematized law and even extended privileges to Hindu men. Yet rights and entitlements were both granted in the name of a renewed, modern Mysore.

Mysore Reconceptualizes the Modern

The first four chapters of this book argue for the necessity of reading the vast and varied cultural productions of Mysore between the late eighteenth century and the twentieth as a realm in which the triumphs and anxieties of precarious monarchies were staged. Analysis of cultural productions from such a long period of time attracts the rather obvious criticism that these chapters are straining to tell a well-known tale of princely regimes coming to terms with and surviving under the rubric of colonialism. Rather than seeing the artistic and architectural heritage of Mysore as illustrative of what is part of the historical commonsense of Mysore, I have attempted to note the ways in which these cultural productions spoke of both power and its absence, of strivings and victories, of resigned acceptance of the new political field of forces inaugurated by colonialism and crucial ways of defining spaces within those constraints. The realm of the visual was an important one on which the battles for supremacy and legitimacy were fought well into the twentieth century, sometimes through the adoption of, and other times by keeping at bay, modes of representation and spectation that formed part of the arsenal of the colonizers.

Chapters 1–4 discuss transformed styles of painting, architecture, and city planning at both Srirangapatna and Mysore as communications of (even truncated) power. Chapter 1, "Tipu Sultan's War Colors and the Battle for Perspective," discusses the ways in which a set of historical murals at the Dariya Daulat at Srirangapatna, executed in the time of Tipu Sultan, became the basis for colonial judgments of the failure of the artist to follow the rules of perspective, the quintessential sign of the "modern" in painting. How might the torrent of interest it generated—easy condemnation giving way to restoration and display—be read? I suggest less in terms of aesthetic achievements and more in terms of the new modes of representation and indeed spectation that were inaugurated in the late eighteenth century, of which the British triumph formed a small part.

Chapter 2, "An Illusion of Permanence: Visualizing Legitimacy in Mysore," takes further the argument that the realms of art and painting can be seen as important registers from which to attempt a reading of the political that may not always be confirmed by official sources, here the desire of the monarch to be seen in painting when his hold on the throne was most endangered. Chapters 3 and 4, "Srirangapatna: Capital City to Topography of Conquest" and "The Museumized Cityscape of Mysore," describe two parallel moments in the history of the old and new capitals of Mysore, when Srirangapatna was abandoned in favor of the city of Mysore. Although one site largely memorialized the death and defeat of Tipu and the victory of the British and presented a desolate remnant of its former glory, the other site, Mysore, long a neglected outpost, was made into a new and resplendent royal city long after the centers of administrative control had moved to Bangalore.

The next four chapters, largely focused on the twentieth century, discuss a different set of themes in the history of modern Mysore, including the use of the law and the language of development as instruments of social change. Chapter 5, "K. Venkatappa and the Fashioning of a Mysore Modern in Art," which deals with the career of the painter K. Venkatappa, serves as the bridge between the two sections, not just because it is concerned with the field of artistic production in twentieth-century Mysore but because it traces the relocation of Venkatappa himself (from Mysore to Bangalore). In the book, his life serves as an instance of a more general shift away from the preoccupations with kingship or legitimacy centered on the twin sites of Srirangapatna and Mysore and, with the interiors of the palaces, to the more public concerns and practices of a bureaucratic national-modern sensibility largely based in Bangalore. Chapters 6 and 7, "The Illicit in the Modern: Banning the Devadasi" and "The Licit in the Modern: Protecting the Child Wife," are focused on the different routes that were charted by the Mysore bureaucracy in recasting the family and renewing and recasting Hindu religious practices. Much as in other parts of India, the focus of such reform efforts was the status of women, but, as I have noted earlier, with important differences.

The last chapter, "Giving the State a Nation: Revisiting the Karnataka's Reunification," discusses the debates that convulsed Mysore in the very last stages of its 157-year existence. When the creation of the linguistic states became an unavoidable reality, unprecedented cleavages and loyalties came to the fore, leading to bitter divisions within and beyond the state legislature. I track the features of this legislative debate in the early 1950s, when history no longer sufficed as a resource for imagining the new state and questions of geography and the state's resources could be yoked to a program of economic development.

By way of conclusion to this inaugural discussion of Mysore's modern, let me recount an exchange between two of Karnataka's leading public figures. D. V. Gundappa recalls seeking permission from Dewan Visvesvaraya to start a new English newspaper in 1913:

> DVG: I have to select one out of a list of three names suggested by friends, "The People," "The Citizen," and "The Karnataka."
> DEWAN: Why not "Progress" or "Forward" or "Advance"? Some name suggestive of a new aspiration and a new spirit in the country?

> Neither list of names rules out the contexts of the other [says DVG]. But the difference in emphasis is noteworthy, the first list stressing political democracy and the country's historical heritage and the second breathing the gospel of material regeneration and the go ahead urge of modernism.[113]

When a unified Karnataka was proposed in 1956, however, both DVG and Visvesvaraya found themselves on the same side of a deep and bitter divide. They both made passionate arguments for the continuance of a remembered Mysore, one emphasizing its royal historical heritage and its impact on the nation-form and the other stressing a space where the modern had enjoyed a limited triumph. Both forms of the modern, they believed, stood threatened by the pressures of parliamentary democracy and the expansive aspirations of a developmental state. Though from different perspectives, both were as committed to the modern as they were wary of democracy.

Mysore's modern history, I have tried to suggest, can no longer be defined as a lack or as an absence against the broader canvas of Indian history but must be seen as a specific route to modernity under colonialism. Despite the well-known limits to its economic and political sovereignty, initiatives of the twentieth-century Mysore state were so broad ranging, penetrating, and ambitious as to recall not the contradictory "success" of colonial models of government but the promise of its early modern existence under Tipu Sultan. This is by no means another effort to minimize the scale and depth of the colonial rupture but is rather a way of emphasizing the specific marks of Mysore's political rationality, against which alone we may make sense of the cultural, legal, or political events and processes with which this book is concerned. By doing this, the historian may hope not to renew appreciation of the Mysore monarchy, as so many have done, but give it the burial it so richly deserves.

CHAPTER 1

Tipu Sultan's War Colors
and the Battle for Perspective

"THE BEGINNINGS OF MODERN MYSORE," said M. Shama Rao in 1936, "may be dated from the fall of Seringapatam on the 4th of May, 1799 to British arms."[1] The historian's certainty of the date on which modernity made its debut in Mysore agreed in important ways with the unrestrained exuberance of those British officials who announced the defeat and death of the East India Company's most formidable foe in India, Tipu Sultan. The military victory was initially acknowledged for what it was in the many exultant accounts that commemorated the success of British arms—the removal of the one stubborn obstacle to British control of India. Thus Colonel Beatson, who participated in the siege of 1799, said: "The fall of this capital placed the whole kingdom of Mysore, with all its resources at the disposal of the British Government, and extinguished the only power in India, which was deemed formidable, or in any wise disposed to second the dangerous views of the French."[2] The ideological refashioning of this military and political triumph as the inaugural moment of Indian modernity took slightly longer; a full-blown version emerged from the pen of Colonel Mark Wilks in 1811 in his magisterial history of Mysore:

> Thus terminated a dynasty composed only of two sovereigns, the first of whom had risen from obscurity to imperial power, and the last educated as a Prince, had fallen in the defence of a hereditary crown; resembling in some of the circumstances of its close, the fate of the Roman capital of the Eastern Empire, substituting, like that catastrophe, in place of the fallen dynasty, not only the power of a new Sovereign, but the influence of a new race, yet exhibiting the marked contrast of kindling, not quenching in its fall, the lights of science and civilization.[3]

Indeed, after this military victory historical representation itself became one of the earliest terrains on which the "light of science and civilization" was cast and was posthumously brought to bear on the very powers that had resisted the territorial ambitions of the East India Company.[4] The prodigious efforts of British officials to exorcise the ghosts of Tipu Sultan and celebrate their eventual triumph over an implacable enemy, however, simultaneously appeared as a virtuous restoration of the interrupted rule of a Hindu dynasty. The colonial power's urge to control and transform indigenous representational practices was quickened by the very success with which this indigenous power had adopted and deployed many modern techniques to its advantage. The repetitive and widely circulated British representations of Tipu's defeat and death, in writing and in pictures, were therefore crucial registers on which the battle for legitimacy was fought, a legitimacy that had been battered in Britain and yet to be established in India. Not for nothing did the instruments of the British triumph over India include "artistic (palette), cartographic (the dividers) and architectural (ziggurat at rear) elements," as in the title cartouche to James Rennel's first map, *Hindoostan*.[5]

What occurred in the wake of Tipu's defeat were not just the enormous political and institutional transformations that signaled the onset of colonial rule in India but the qualified triumph of a new scopic regime, one that was ocular centric and reconstituted the perceptual field in ways that privileged vision. The retinal image was produced by the most mechanical, least mediated, and indeed the least subjective or "sensuous" of sense organs, the eye. As Martin Jay reminds us, the "ubiquity of vision," especially when aided by instruments such as the telescope and the microscope, was among the hallmarks of the modern era.[6] The camera obscura aided the production of the objective ground of visual truth, upholding the fiction of realism. After its appearance in the 1500s, says Jonathan Crary, the camera obscura assumed "pre-eminent importance in delimiting and defining the relations between observer and world," to become the "compulsory site from which vision can be conceived or represented."[7]

Control of the memory and representations of the Haidar and Tipu regimes was therefore no mere reflection of the attempt to seize political and economic hold of what was clearly turbulent terrain but rather another vital register on which the triumph was staged.[8] The taking of Srirangapatna ranked in imperial iconography along with the Battle of Plassey as the founding moment of British rule: the Madras Government

House, built in 1802 by Governor Clive (1798–1803), boasted of two huge pediments that "were decorated with trophies of two conquests that laid the foundations of the Raj; the siege of Seringapatnam (1799) over the northern entrance, the battle of Plassey (1757) over the southern."[9]

However, I use the term *triumph of perspective* only advisedly, because perspectivalism, in its narrower sense of pertaining to a new visual order and also in its broader sense of connoting an abstract, quantitatively conceptualized rational history, was neither free of contradictions nor passively accepted. The triumph of perspective was therefore neither as decisive nor as final as the military triumph. It is this moment of flux that is traced here, when several elements of the new scopic regime were known and even experimented with, but within different modes of power, so perspectivalism could achieve its hegemony only well after the establishment of British rule.

The argument is divided into four parts. In the first I will discuss the enduring consequences of the ways in which early colonial accounts described the history paintings in Srirangapatna. In the second I consider the architectural and pictorial space of Dariya Daulat Bagh, or Tipu's summer palace in Srirangapatna, as a site that actively deployed evolving notions of legitimacy.[10] In the third section I consider some of the ways in which the establishment of the "objective" ground of (visual) truth, namely, the "point of view" in historical writing and the singular point of vision (or vanishing point) in pictorial space, began to challenge indigenous modes of representation as well as to claim the affections and pride of a skeptical British public. In the last section I turn briefly to the modes of spectation that were produced by the two sets of paintings and the consequences for the ways in which they were judged. The tensions between the two modes of seeing were resolved by a split in the modes of representation achieved by the emergence of a Mysore "traditional" style, which is discussed in chapter 2.

Perspective on a Decisive Victory

In September 1780, at a site about six miles northwest of Kanchipuram, the British army suffered what was described by Sir Thomas Munro as the severest blow that the English had ever sustained in India until then.[11] A British force of about 3,800 troops, including a few hundred Europeans, led by Colonel Baillie found itself surrounded on all sides by the troops of Haidar Ali and Tipu Sultan.[12] Expecting reinforcements from Colonel Hector Munro at Madras but aided only by a small force of 1,000 under Colonel Fletcher, the British contingent fought a short but fierce battle in which two tumbrels of ammunition exploded from shots fired by French and Indian troops directed by Commander Lallee. The British yielded to the onslaught of the combined troops of Tipu Sultan and Haidar Ali, close to 100,000 troops, in which Fletcher was killed and Baillie and Baird wounded and taken prisoner along with 200 other Europeans. Tipu Sultan's army, meanwhile, went on to take Arcot and Ambur by 1781 and won fine victories against Colonel Braithwaite near Thanjavur. Despite Haidar Ali's defeat by Eyre Coote in the battle of Porto Novo that year and his own setbacks at Wandiwasi, Tipu might have strongly countered the British forces had he not been forced to join the siege of Malabar and eventually withdraw altogether on hearing of Haidar Ali's sudden death in 1782.

The victory of the Haidari army at Polilur in 1780 was described by Tipu's court poets thus: "The Flash of his [Tipu's] sabre struck the army of Bailey like lightning, it caused Munro to shed tears, resembling the drops distilled from spring clouds."[13] Baillie, however, is purported to have tried to rob the victory of its shine by saying to Haidar Ali, "Your son will inform you that you owe your victory to our disaster rather than to our defeat."[14]

In the aftermath of Tipu's defeat, indigenous representations of the clash between the British and Tipu were too important to leave alone. British troops entering the town of Srirangapatna after the victory in 1799 were dazzled by the wealth to which, as victors, they had unrestrained access, and predictably looting and mayhem followed until they were brought under control a few days later.[15] The pictorial celebration of the early Mysore triumphs on the walls of Tipu's Dariya Daulat palace at Srirangapatna was among the treasures that were found.

Representations of battle in certain stylized forms have been known in South India since at least the tenth century in the form of "hero stones," or *virakallu*.[16] Since the sixteenth century, battle paintings have accompanied the accounts of victory: the Deccani *Tarif-i-Husain-Shah* is a vivid portrayal of an important turning point in history, the battle of Rakshasatangadi or Talikota between Bahmani Adil Shah and Ramaraya in 1565, in which the Bahmani Sultan triumphed.[17] These representations deployed a variety of devices to emphasize the valor of the victors. As Jennifer Howes points out in her discussion of the battle between Ramnad's Muthu Vijaya Raghunatha Setupati and the Maratha king Serfoji, in 1720, which was

Figure 2. Battle of Polilur, 1780, showing Colonel Baillie in the palanquin while Colonels Fletcher and Baird are on horseback. Detail of mural on west wall of Dariya Daulat, Srirangapatna. Tipu Sultan Museum, Dariya Daulat Bagh, Srirangapatna. Photograph by Clare Arni, 2008.

soon after memorialized in a painting on the walls of Ramalinga Vilasam at Ramnad, this could include a depiction of the warriors using bows and arrows to evoke memories of an epic fight.[18]

In the sixteenth and seventeenth centuries (under the sultanates of Ahmadnagar, Bijapur, and Golconda), powerful schools of miniature painting also began to develop. They drew from Mughal and Persianate styles, as well as Vijayanagar wall-painting conventions, developing distinctive elements that came to characterize the Deccani school of painting. But even well before the eighteenth century, other uses of pictorial space began filtering in and became some of the many options for local Indian artists. For instance, in the second quarter of the eighteenth century, the Hyderabad school of painting under the Asaf Jahis drew from the earlier Qutb Shahi traditions and Mughal styles to produce a significant contribution to the Deccani school, though it never reached the heights of its predecessors.[19] Following the conquest of the Deccan by the Mughals, these schools were fragmented and found patrons in smaller principalities located at Kurnool, Cuddapah, and Shorapur.

The authorship of the murals at Srirangapatna is shrouded in obscurity because there is no known reference to the commission. Indeed, the palace and its murals had "many lives" after the defeat of Tipu Sultan, so that what visitors to Dariya Daulat see today was at least partially altered over the past two centuries, as we shall see later. What follows is therefore based on readings of the extant work, drawing both on interpretations of palace mural traditions in South India and on Deccani or Mughal painting, as well as on the work of cultural historians who are attempting to rethink notions of South Indian kingship that were being forged in the eighteenth century, by Tipu Sultan among others.

Soon after the end of the Second Anglo-Mysore War and the signing of the Treaty of Mangalore in 1784, the Dariya Daulat (Summer Palace) was built on the banks of the Cauvery in Srirangapatna.[20] Set in a landscaped garden, it was one of three palaces on the island capital of Mysore Kingdom. The main palace, called the Lal Mahal, was to the northwest within the fort and was the chief residence of Tipu Sultan. Adjoining the Gumbaz, or Mausoleum of Haidar, at the southeastern end of the island was the modest but lavishly decorated palace in the Lal Bagh, a garden planted by Haidar Ali.

The Dariya Daulat was completed in 1784 in the first heady years of Tipu's reign. It is an oblong building mounted on a high basement, surrounded by deep verandahs, and built of wood, brick, and mortar. Set in the midst of an elegantly landscaped garden, on the north side of which wide granite steps lead to the river, it became a favorite retreat of Tipu Sultan: "He lived in turns," said Ramachandra Rao ("Punganuri"), an employee of Tipu's court, "in the fort [of Srirangapatna] and in this garden."[21] The palace itself, as well as the one in Bangalore, built on a similar pattern, is said to have imitated in style the palace of the Mughal governor Dilvar Khan at Sira, Tumkur District.

The most striking feature of the modestly sized building is the lavish decoration that covers every inch of the walls. The outer walls are covered with portraits and other figural compositions, whereas the inner walls are richly embellished with floral and leafy decorations and rich gilding. The south-facing building has, on its outer western wall, four panels that depict the warrior heroes preparing for and engaging in combat. One of the panels of the western wall commemorates the disastrous defeat of the British at Polilur. Measuring approximately thirty-one by seventeen feet, the mural is among the largest in India.[22] On the eastern wall is depicted a series of portraits, occasionally of rulers with whom Tipu may have held court or whom he wished to conquer, as well as some who came later (e.g., Krishnaraja Wodeyar III). Other murals refer to scenes from everyday life, ranging from portrayals of noblewomen and men in more contemplative moments to depictions of people of lower stations engaged in chores such as the maintenance and exercise of animals.

The work was executed by a group of local artists attached to the court who were clearly struggling with new vocabularies of artistic expression and experimenting with styles and forms that they had reason to encounter, if only in reproduction.[23] Itinerant artists from the flourishing schools in Cuddapah, Arcot, and Hyderabad may have offered some of their skills to the new ruler following the assumption of power by Tipu Sultan. However, no other commissioned works on paper exist except for an album of paintings of Indian sufi saints commissioned by Tipu in 1796.[24]

When the murals came to British attention after 1799, they were ridiculed as "caricatures." Francis Buchanan chose to say little about the painting itself, although, like several other British commentators, he was enamored of the technique for gilding used by the artists. Only indirectly did he refer to the murals' "lack of perspective" when he included a picture of a Brahman couple commissioned from the "finest painter of Seringapatam," which he considered self-explanatory.[25]

Nearly all later British writers who focused more or less entirely on the battle scene were openly dismissive of the work, not for its distortion of the facts of a well-known event but for its disregard of perspective. Thus Mark Wilks dismissed the paintings in a terse line: "The walls are covered with rude paintings of his [Tipu's] military exploits, and particularly the defeat of Colonel Baillie in 1780."[26] In 1833 Colonel Walter Campbell wrote a detailed description of the painting and was authoritatively cited throughout the nineteenth century and well into the twentieth:

> The subject of the painting is supposed to be the faithful representation of one of Tippoo's victories over the British troops. It exhibits a glorious contempt for anything like perspective or proportion; but what it lacks in correct drawing is amply made amends for by variety and brilliancy of colouring. Pink elephants, yellow men, and sky blue horses, with yellow feet and scarlet tails, are jumbled together in glorious confusion.[27]

Lewin Bowring referred to the "grotesque frescoes of the battles between [Tipu] and Col. Baillie," which he called a "mimic fight."[28] In a letter to friends from Srirangapatna written on November 27, 1868, Lady Bowring added:

> Everywhere [Tipu] is represented as complacently smelling a rose, either on horseback, in a palanquin, or mounted on an elephant, in the midst of the most dreadful carnage, in which of course the English are shown as getting the worst of it. The perspective is amusing, and legs, arms and heads are flying in every direction but on careful inspection, the corresponding bodies will be found somewhere.[29]

In 1927 Edmund Bull referred to "a certain flaring bombast in keeping with Tippoo's character [that] pervades the whole execution of this quaint design," whereas Constance Parsons referred to the "childish glee" with which Baillie's defeat was portrayed.[30] The well-worn critique of the picture's lack of perspective continued well into the 1930s, although Shivarama Karanth's disappointment was unconcealed when he compared the murals to works by two other European greats, Tintoretto and Michelangelo.[31] Mildred Archer classified the murals as "economically represented in a 'journalistic' style that has all the hallmarks of [East India] Company painting and

no resemblance to the Mysore school of painting."[32] Even the most detailed recent analysis of the work by an art historian has drawn heavily, and
uncritically, on colonial descriptions of the complex.[33]

The many "lives" enjoyed by the Dariya Daulat mural from the time
of its execution reflect shifts in power within Srirangapatna itself and less
often transformations in the name of "preservation."[34] Some changes may
have been made as early as 1791, as we shall see later. The palace murals
were restored by Colonel Arthur Wellesley, who occupied the palace as
Commissioner of Srirangapatna from 1799 to 1801.[35] In 1820, the original
painting of the Battle of Polilur was committed to paper by an Indian artist
and sent to England. More transformations, especially of the eastern wall,
occurred sometime in the nineteenth century, as is evident from Lord
Valentia's early account.[36] He said:

> I was mortified to see there a British officer, whom Tippoo said
> he always wished to have the command against. . . . *This person is
> represented more than once.* In one place he is drawing his sword on
> a woman, with a most threatening air and countenance. In another
> he is amusing himself with dancing-girls. In the same verandah are
> figures of natives of every cast and profession. These are very inter-
> esting, and I should much like to have had them copied had there
> been time. General Wellesley has had them retouched, as they were
> going rapidly to decay.[37]

These changes apart, the murals were often defaced. Tipu himself is
said to have ordered the whitewashing of the murals sometime before
1799.[38] Following Tipu's defeat, the face of Mir Sadiq, the Chief Dewan, in
charge of the Revenue and Finance Department and popularly associated
with the treachery that led to the British triumph, was disfigured wherever
it appeared on the mural.[39] Similarly, according to legend, the portrait of
Purnaiya, who served as Tipu's chief Mir Miran but stayed on to serve the
British, was defaced by the locals and replaced with a portrait of Krishna
Raja Wodeyar III by the Mysore Dewan P. N. Krishnamurthi (a descendent of Purnaiya) in the early twentieth century. The style of painting on
the eastern wall, however, strongly suggests a mid-nineteenth-century
re-rendering.

The most important refurbishing of the mural occurred in the mid-
nineteenth century in fulfillment of Dalhousie's Minute of 1854.[40] In that
year, the visiting Governor-General, appalled by the disrepair into which

the palace had fallen, insisted that it be preserved but not in memory of Tipu. Rather, this "purely Eastern Residence" deserved attention because of the glorious career of its later occupant, Arthur Wellesley:

> In all respects this structure is one full of interest, but it is most especially worthy of our reverential awe as the material object, which more than anything now remaining in India, most immediately and most vividly brings before us of this day the memory of that great man, with the early period of whose glorious career the East India Company must ever be proud to connect the history of its rule.[41]

The fate of Srirangapatna's other palaces—decay and demolition—was thus averted by the memory of one for whom Srirangapatna was only the springboard to greater and more spectacular victories at Waterloo, Arthur Wellesley, the Duke of Wellington. "It should" Dalhousie's minute continued, be "upheld nearly as possible in the condition in which it was left by Colonel Wellesley" and its paintings restored, "by the aid of persons still living who remember them in their completeness."[42] Further restorations took three years, from 1884 to 1887.[43]

The Dariya Daulat appears to have turned into a pilgrimage center for British visitors anxious to retrace Wellesley's victorious steps, of which we shall see more in chapter 3. A flight of steps to the river was constructed in the late nineteenth century.[44] In 1916, Mirza Ismail, then the Huzur secretary to Mysore's Krishnaraja Wodeyar IV, succeeded in getting five painters from the Mysore palace to "repaint" "the battle scenes facing the west" at Dariya Daulat.[45] The museum was established in 1959.

Putting "History" in Perspective

The battle scene alone aroused most interest and anxiety among British observers at the time and continues to dominate comments up to the present day.[46] Fewer scholars have attempted an interpretation of the palace and its paintings as a text of power, visually asserting a notion of kingship and authority that was yet to be fully fashioned. The timing of its establishment is of some value here, for the idioms of kingship that Tipu borrowed from the other South Indian Hindu traditions were clearly not as useful after 1792, when a stronger appeal was made to Islam. The battle panel cannot therefore be extracted from the larger whole of which it was a part, for what is represented on the walls of the Dariya Daulat is the universe that Tipu aspired to command. In other words, the setting and the paintings serve as an allegory of power within which the *representation of history* (the battle painting) was only a very small part.

To what extent does the Dariya Daulat mural draw on the changing idioms of southern Indian court painting? Mark Zebrowski speaks of the escapist mood of the Deccani courts, "where the Sultauns took more interest in leisure and the arts than in government or conquest."[47] Zebrowski also notes the Deccani obsession with princely portraits compared with hunts, court ceremonials or rituals (as in the Rajasthani miniatures), or historical events (as in the Mughal paintings); the portraits themselves became sterile with political stability.[48] One therefore needs to speculate on some of the other parallels that might exist within the realm of mural painting itself, an amplified grammar of power in Hindu South India.

Regarding the placement of the themes on the walls of the palace, Jennifer Howes, in her discussion of Ramalinga Vilasam, the audience hall of the Ramnad palace, suggests that the outer walls of the palace, in the context of eighteenth-century southern India, correspond to "the exterior realm of the kingdom." Other scenes that adorn the inner walls, of kingly intimacy, for instance, rather than suggesting a strict disjuncture between inner and outer, public and private, or even secular and religious, must be taken as "expressing the many facets of south Indian Kingship as it existed before the colonial period."[49] At Dariya Daulat a physical and conceptual distinction is made between the inner and outer walls that is similar to the distinction between the western and the eastern walls. The outer walls display the public world of the conquering hero, and it is striking that neither Haidar nor Tipu is portrayed in any other position than at war. The eastern and western walls reflect another difference. The display and celebration of valor on the battlefield adorns the western walls. The eastern wall portrays durbar scenes that are once more divided into two sections: one side (the right) consists of portraits of those whom Tipu encountered, wished to encounter, or even wished to conquer. The other side (the left) consists of scenes from everyday life.

The placement of the paintings reveals certain structural similarities with other South Indian palaces of the time, which constructed an ambulatory rather than fixed mode of spectation. The battle scene is encountered as one turns the corner from the south entrance, filling the lower right-hand corner of the western wall. Above it is placed a portrayal of the

Nizam preparing for battle. As one proceeds along the western wall, the two panels depicting the war processions of Haidar and Tipu appear. The southern and northern walls are profusely decorated with thin foliage and floral decorations. The eastern wall bears two sets of portraits, whose settings, unlike that of the battleground on the western wall, are largely urban, and the pictures are architecturally framed. The western and eastern walls are pierced by entrances over which hangs a *jharoka*, or audience balcony. The southern and northern walls have recessed bays with *jharokas* on either side, and they support a floor overlooking the main audience room.[50]

Taken together, the murals and the architecture of the palace produce an enhanced setting for a *darshan* (viewing) of the king as well as a record of his past exploits. Arthur Wellesley recognized only too well the importance of occupying the palace to assert the legitimacy of the new British rulers in 1799.[51] What real and imagined cosmos of Tipu Sultan is represented on these walls?

On the left-hand top panel of the western wall, facing south, Haidar Ali is shown as a powerful presence on his favorite elephant, Poon Ganj. He is in an elaborately designed howdah and is preceded on horseback by Mir Sadiq, the head of the Revenue and Finance Department, the most important officer of Haidar and Tipu's government, who offers his greetings. The lower panel, also facing south, shows Tipu in procession, dressed in rich blue brocade and mounted on a white horse that is decorated in style; he is accompanied by his commander in chief, Kamruddin Khan. He is preceded once more by Mir Sadiq and followed by Ghulam Ali Khan of the Ordnance and Garrison Department. He is also flanked by a guard of French soldiers, behind whom is Count Lallee, seated on a brown horse and waving a sword.

The top right panel, facing north, depicts the Nizam's war procession. The Nizam is on a white charger followed by two rows of six elephants whose howdahs are all empty. Below this, and arguably the focal point of the whole wall, is a depiction of the famous turning point of the Battle of Polilur in 1780, when Colonel Baillie's ammunition tumbrels exploded, sowing confusion and disorder among the British troops (see Figure 2). Haidar is once more placed above Tipu Sultan, and both are on elephants, moving toward the center of the action, along with their separate armies. Mir Sadiq now appears with Tipu, while Sayid Gaffur, formerly of the East India Company and now a trusted commander in Tipu's army, is seen in a clearing in the middle of the picture, accompanied by his standard bearer.

Figure 3. Tipu Sultan accompanied by Kamruddin Khan on the battlefield, facing Mir Sadiq, head of the Revenue and Finance Department. Popular historical memory of the purported "betrayal" of his master by Mir Sadiq has led to the defacing of his portrait, even in the present day. Detail of mural on west wall of Dariya Daulat, Srirangapatna, c. 1784. Tipu Sultan Museum, Dariya Daulat Bagh, Srirangapatna. Photograph by Clare Arni, 2008.

The main part of the action is near the center of this panel, which shows Colonel Baillie, seated in his palanquin, within a square of British troops, obviously distressed by the loss of the tumbrel (in the upper left-hand corner), which has scattered his men in confusion. The British troops, dressed in red coats, white trousers, and hats and shoes, are everywhere shown as dominated in the encounter with the Haidari army. Baillie is seen biting the back of his hand in consternation, while Colonels Baird and Fletcher are seen to his left on horseback.

The composition of the procession paintings as well as the battle scene conforms in many ways to the conventions of the Deccan school as it was developed in Ahmadnagar and Golconda, where Hindu and Muslim elements had become inseparable.[52] Mark Zebrowski has noted the "dramatic intensity typical of the Deccan" in his discussion of a seventeenth-century Golconda painting at Leningrad, which pictures a moving crowd with a skill that was rare among Mughal artists and reveals a (new) acquaintance with realist architectural settings and the vanishing point.[53] At Dariya Daulat, however, there is little recession of the figures at the top or bottom, and the panels are evenly lit. The cavalry is strictly aligned in rows of alternate brown and white to form large patterned surfaces. Foreground and background are not systematically distinguished; depth of field is suggested by the figures coming over the hills on the tufted ground.

Instead, definite strategies were used to pictorially establish hierarchies. Haidar, Tipu, and the Nizam are thus shown in the "strict profile" that Stella Kramrisch notes was the characteristic of Deccani paintings,[54] without the nimbus commonly used to portray the Mughal emperor. Deccani nobility is thus signified by the regal smelling of the flower, even when on the battlefield, and emphasized by the enhanced size of the animals. Tipu's horse is four times larger than the horses of the cavalry. At the same time, he is still in the shadow of his father, who is depicted on an elephant with a superior howdah. In these panels there appears to have been an attempt to idealize the nobility (to paraphrase Ebba Koch, who described late Mughal representational practices) and avert the possibility of producing an exact likeness. Indeed, "the standardized and idealized profile representation emphasized that the ruler and those in the state who mattered were above what is human, imperfect and subject to change."[55] Yet a certain resemblance to the real person was not avoided in the features without a fuller explication of character or mood.[56]

If anything, the regal demeanor of the rulers preparing for battle appears to deliberately contradict the logic of action in this mural, as in the depiction of the battle itself. Yet the battle mural displays an overall fidelity to the original event. Gulammohammed Sheikh, while describing a mid-nineteenth-century mural at Tambekarwada in Baroda, suggests that the style evolved by the artists can amount to an "informal realism."[57] I would like to adapt this term to describe the battle painting, where an "informal realism" lends credence to every detail of this British debacle. "Detail," conceded Edmund Bull, who was among the many British critics of the painting, "is scrupulously observed. The British square with the exploding tumbrels which mainly brought about the disaster is meticulously depicted."[58]

It is likely that the early nineteenth-century historian Meer Syed Hussain Kirmani offered a literal rendering of the painted mural, and throughout his account, the telescope is acknowledged as crucial in avoiding or causing defeat. At times, it is even used as a metaphor for scientific and rational thinking. In his account of the Battle of Polilur, Kirmani says:

> Lalli, the Frenchman, discovering with the telescope of his intellect and science, the position of the army's ammunition, fired a shot from a heavy gun at the Colonel's tumbrels, all of which had been collected at one place. By accident the ammunition blew up, and by the shock of the explosion, the bond of the union of the colonel's force, were broken up.[59]

In the mural, Lallee is indeed shown surveying the field with an enormous telescope while his footman steadies his horse in readiness, the tumbrel having already exploded.

The artists chose to portray all the British as clean shaven in contrast to their whiskered French counterparts.[60] Furthermore, though the Indian artist might have been accustomed to portraying his royal subjects in profile, "he snatches a frontal or three fourths view of an English face here and there and tries similar tricks elsewhere" (as did the artists of the Tambekarvada mural, whom Sheikh has described).[61] Clearly, the portraiture of the subaltern was more relaxed and permitted the use of the three-quarters profile, which was not part of the norms governing the representation of the nobility.

The work was also probably altered through the later addition of symbols depicting new political relations between the Mysore rulers and the

Nizam. Thus, in a long-favored popular interpretation, the Nizam's regality was undone by a symbolic representation of his decision to renege on his 1788 treaty with Tipu and join his forces to those of the Marathas and the English in 1791. He is interpreted in the oft-quoted museum caption as "coming like a bountiful white cow" and departing like a black boar. The portrayal of scenes on the right side of the eastern wall, which included recognizable historical figures such as Peshwa Balaji Rao II, the Raja of Tanjore, and Madikere Nayaka of Chitradurga, is far more relaxed and combines an uncoordinated architectural perspective with the older styles of portraying figures. Though the portraits are not identified, the various architectural styles serve as visual clues to the specific kingdoms or powers that are shown; kings from neighboring courts may have been set against a light-blue background, as at Ramnad, though the use of white marble pavilions is distinctive.[62]

The virtuosity of the artists who painted the murals is displayed in the elaborately patterned turbans, costumes, and architectural settings, which are many and varied on both walls. Shivarama Karanth suggested that the work on the eastern wall may represent an "example of a transitional stage between native and European styles experimented [with] here" and may even have been executed under the supervision of European artists in the service of Tipu Sultan.[63] However, it is more likely that this wall was substantially altered in each renovation, and indeed the style of the drapery strongly resembles that used in manuscript illustration under Krishnaraja Wodeyar III; a procession painting of the king bears a remarkable resemblance to some features of the Dariya Daulat mural.[64]

On the right-hand side of the eastern wall, scenes of leisure include many of animals being exercised and four representations of women. Here, too, the conventions of painting are more relaxed and there is a spirit of experimentation, with a more naturalistic rendering of the figures and a freer use of three-quarters and even full-front portraits. However, Tipu was averse to being portrayed as given to the pleasures of life. This was in striking contrast to his Hyderabad counterpart, Asaf Jah II, who commissioned a very large body of work, including several portraits of himself, always in a relaxed and pleasure-seeking mood; noticeably absent in those works was any portrayal of the Nizam at war or in the hunt.[65]

Taken together, the Dariya Daulat and its paintings function as an assertion of princely power using idioms that were known and deployed in other peninsular settings. At the same time, conscious choices were also

Figure 4. Scenes from the everyday life of Indian rulers and nobles. Detail of mural on east wall of Dariya Daulat, Srirangapatna, c. 1784. Tipu Sultan Museum, Dariya Daulat Bagh, Srirangapatna. Photograph by Clare Arni, 2008.

Figure 5. A portrait of Tipu Sultan of Mysore, as imagined in the early nineteenth century. Artist unknown; ink, gouache, and gold on paper; 38.4 x 30.0 cm. Courtesy of the University of California, Berkeley Art Museum and Pacific Film Archive, gift of Jean and Francis Marshall. Photograph by Benjamin Blackwell.

made about the spaces and themes to which new techniques would be applied. Rather than serving as the focal point of either the building or the paintings, then, the representation of the Battle of Polilur is subservient to the overall project of portraying a new power. Princely power is not represented as subject to the vagaries of historical events: here there is more than a hint of multiple time frames.

If the Tipu of the written word—in his letters and autobiography, in the several injunctions to his officers, and in his abundant collection of treatises on the correct behavior of the Sunni Muslim[66]—comes across as strictly conforming to the dictates of a proselytizing universal religion, the palace and its representational regime asserted a different notion of power and authority. Although an aura of piety was artistically achieved in the series of portraits of Muslim nobles at prayer or reading the Quran, Dariya Daulat appears to have combined representations of southern Indian kingship in the eighteenth century while protecting the image of the sultan as a conformist Muslim. As the available descriptions of the interior of Tipu's Lal Mahal and the Bangalore palace clearly indicate, figural representations were strictly avoided, although a distinctive use of the babri stripe and Islamic verses was achieved.

Visualizing Historic Battles

The quick condemnation of the painting at Dariya Daulat as caricature and the simultaneous denigration of Tipu's own writing by the British may have had something to do with the widespread circulation of images depicting British defeats in Mysore. Thus "MMDLT" (Monsieur De La Touche), the French officer who served in Haidar's army and wrote an account of the life of his court and his campaigns, described a cartoon produced at the end of the First Anglo Mysore War in 1769:

There was fixed to the gate of Fort St. George, called the Royal Gate, a design in which was seen Hyder Ali Khan seated under a canopy on a pile of cannon; Mr Dupre and the other ambassador (Boschier) being on their knees before him. Hyder held in his right hand the nose of Mr Dupre, drawn in the form of an elephant's trunk, which he shook for the purpose of making him vomit guineas and pagodas. . . . In the background appeared Fort

St. George, and on one of the bastions, the governor and council were drawn on their knees, holding out their hands to the nabob [Haider Ali].[67]

Wilks similarly referred to the caricatures that adorned the walls of Srirangapatna, which he claimed were hastily whitewashed on the eve of an expected siege of Srirangapatna in 1791:

> In one it was a tiger seizing a trembling Englishman; in another it was a horseman cutting off two English heads at a blow; in a third it was the nabob, Mahommed Ali, brought in with a rope around his waist, prostrating himself before an Englishman seated on a chair, who placed one foot upon his neck; but the more favourite caricatures are necessarily excluded from decorous narrative.[68]

Above all, the widespread circulation of reports and images of British defeat in Britain and the multiple narratives from British soldiers, some of them former prisoners of Tipu, led to many unsparing cartoons.[69] In *The Coming On of the Monsoons or the Retreat from Seringapatam,* James Gillray had Tipu spraying a retreating Cornwallis with urine when the British army was forced to give up the siege of Srirangapatna due to rains in 1791. Tipu is heard saying, "Now, my Lord, I'll *tip you* for the swamps."[70] British victory in 1792 sharpened Gillray's wit, and his droll cartoon mocking the "Nincumpoop's glee" is a good instance of this.

The fortunes of the British turned in the next year (1792), when Tipu was forced to sign the ignominious Treaty of Seringapatam, by which he surrendered half his territory (see Figure 1) and sent two of his sons as hostages in lieu of his debts to the British. Marshall notes the transformation of a terse dispatch from Cornwallis to the East India Company into a highly embellished account.[71] It led to an explosion of jubilant reports in the British press and quickened a somewhat sluggish British interest in history painting.[72] The 1792 treaty, in particular, became the subject of an entire series of history paintings of India.[73] "An Impartial [British] Observer" and admirer of Tipu Sultan noticed how quickly the "definitive treaty signed and sealed by Tippoo and delivered to Lord Cornwallis by one of the sons of the Sultaun, had already become the subject of historical painting; and different artists are concerned in the design."[74]

As Peter Marshall suggests, victory amounted to "a triumph for British humanity as well as for British armies."[75] Scenes of the surrender of power, rather than battle painting per se, called on the talents and intellectual abilities of the history painter proper. According to an early theorist, Jonathan Richardson, the history painter "must possess all the good qualities requisite to an Historian. . . . He must moreover know . . . the Habits, Customs, Buildings and c. of the Age, and Countrey, in which the thing was transacted." But history painting was no mere journalistic record and did not even require its practitioners to have first-hand experience of the place or time. By definition, history painting was the production of affect, calling for "an elevation of genius beyond what pure historical Narration does."[76]

Verisimilitude was thus subordinated to the production of affect, and the obsessive return to the theme of hostages in paintings affirms this. Although based on British eyewitness accounts, these paintings were as suffused with sentimentality as historical inaccuracy, and most appear to have been prompted by the purported eloquence of Ghulam Ali Khan, the lame *vakeel* (representative or ambassador), while handing over Princes Muizuddin and Abdul Khaliq to Cornwallis in 1792. Robert Home, the British painter who witnessed the handover of the hostages, reported:

> Lord Cornwallis . . . met the princes at the door of his large tent as they dismounted from their elephants and after embracing them, led them one in each hand into the tent. When they were seated on each side of his lordship, Gullam Ali, the Vakil, addressed him thus: "These children were this morning the sons of the Sultan my master; their situation is now changed and they must look up to your lordship as their father."[77]

Cornwallis is supposed to have replied that "he knew what the feelings of a father were, and that they should never want a father under his care."[78]

The hostage paintings are literal illustrations of the paternal qualities of empire, the loving relationship of the colonial masters to their new subjects. But there is also an active imagining of the Orient that accompanies these paintings and an invitation to its possession.[79] In his *Lord Cornwallis Receiving the Sons of Tipu Sultan as Hostages* (c. 1783–84), Robert Home, who, with A. W. Devis, was one of only two artists who actually visited India,[80] anchored the campsite in the Orient with the massive hulk of the elephants, with the central figures of George Kennaway, Cornwallis, the princes, and Ghulam Ali occupying a very small part of the whole tableau.

Home inserted himself into the painting, carrying a folder of paintings, in order to emphasize the authenticity of the narrative.

Further versions of the same event dramatized it through a variety of techniques, enhancing or reducing figures through the play of light and shade to portray the moment of triumph over an implacable foe and reducing the scene to its principal actors. In his *Lord Cornwallis Receiving the Sons of Tipu Sultan as Hostages* (1796–1805), Devis thus introduced, amidst the whiff of powder and grapeshot, the British flag and a multitude of British onlookers. The campsite yielded place to a generalized Oriental landscape in George Carter's version of the hostage handover (1792), although he portrayed only one hostage prince. Henry Singleton's version similarly used the Oriental setting, focusing on the innocence of the two hostages. Thomas Stothard took extraordinary liberties with historical narration by further sentimentalizing the scene, fusing, or perhaps confusing, two historical moments, the surrender of the two sons in 1792 and the final moment of Tipu Sultan's death in 1799.[81]

Mather Brown's hostage pictures quickly gained popularity. Brown, an American who had studied with Benjamin West on his arrival in London in 1781, deliberately shook free of documentary accuracy. In two small oil paintings that he exhibited in 1792, Brown borrowed from his master while innovatively drawing parallels between Tipu's fate in South India and the fates of the more venal British kings.[82] In *The Departure of the Sons of Tippoo from the Zenana* and *The Delivery of the Definitive Treaty by the Hostage Princes to Lord Cornwallis* he attempted to repeat his master's pictorial and commercial successes.[83] His version focused attention more closely on the key figures who were taken in fulfillment of the harsh treaty, the sons of Tipu Sultan, while the stiffly posed British literally look down on the treaty itself.

Brown was upbraided for the fanciful rendering of the young boys, who were portrayed in a sweetly effeminized way, and in his next execution he proudly reclaimed authenticity by getting the colors and style of the turbans right.[84] However, the Indians were by now receding into the darkness, so that in his more "accurate" version the eye is strongly focused on the conquerors, with Cornwallis himself looking into the distance rather than at the boys with any avuncular interest, while the Indians assume a servile position.

In contrast to the attention of the British historian and history painter to the moment of surrender were the unsentimental words of a contem-

Figure 6. Daniel Orme (following Mather Brown), Lord Cornwallis Receiving the Sons of Tipu Sultan as Hostages, 1793. Oil on canvas; 77.5 x 57.1 cm. A favorite theme of many British history painters (most of whom never visited India) was this 1792 turning point in the British battles for the control of Mysore. Victoria Memorial, Kolkata. C986/R1456.

porary historian, Ramachandra Rao ("Punganuri"), who said: "In the year Paridhavi month Chattra Suddha 5 (8th March 1792) Lord [Corn]wallis received these noble hostages; then he set out with them and proceeded by the road that goes through Madduri Chennapatnam."[85] Kirmani went even further by reducing the harsh treaty to an agreement between equals:

Agreeably to the request of the English Commander in Chief, Mazuddin Sultan and Abd-ul-Khalik Sultan, the sons of the Sultan, under the guardianship of Ghulam Ali Khan and Muhammad Raza Khutib, were appointed ambassadors and sent off to the General and these wise and learned envoys . . . cleared the royal roads of friendship and peace from the dirt and rubbish of suspicion and enmity.[86]

The extraordinary and even frenzied British production of paintings on Tipu's defeat has usually been discussed as a sign of "patriotism"[87] or even jingoism, though in history paintings artists attempted to avert such degeneration. Sudipta Sen confirms the "value of historical accuracy in the memorialisation of the moment of conquest and the British regicidal conscience."[88] But these descriptions fail to capture the cathartic element of the paintings, which becomes clearer when we consider the entire genre of Tipu paintings, including those that focused on the search for his body after the siege of May 4, 1799.[89]

There was active speculation in the early 1790s regarding Tipu's possible flight from Srirangapatna in the event of a British victory.[90] In 1799, British officers, led by General Baird, were surprised that he was not at the palace; Baird "severely threatened" the *killedar* (commander of the fort) and Tipu's family to yield him up but learned that he had been injured in battle near the gateway on the north face of the fort. Baird immediately proceeded to the place and found a pile of dead bodies:

> The number was so great, and the place so dark, that it was impossible to distinguish one person from another. The Sultaun's horse which had been shot and his palanquin were first discovered. *As it was a point of the utmost political importance to ascertain the fate of the sultaun* the bodies were taken out and particularly examined in the presence of the killedar who after some time, having pointed out that of the sultaun, it was put into a palanquin and carried to the Palace under the charge of a guard.[91]

The production of the series of paintings of this moment was also a political reaffirmation of the death of a valiant hero. When the historical narrative is under no such political compulsion, it may omit the dramatization of this moment altogether, as in Kirmani's unsentimental report.[92] However, in the hands of the history painters the event took on more than a political meaning, becoming the proof of Britain's triumph in India. Singleton painted *The Last Effort and Fall of Tippoo Sultaun* in failing light, with a clearly beleaguered Tipu facing the equivalent of a firing squad. The pictorial representations of the hostage taking were by this time so much part of the public imagination that it was possible for engravers to make them a reference on the margins of a painting as a chronicle of the British triumph foretold. Between two equally balanced forces, British and Indian,

Figure 7. The valiant and worthy hero Tipu Sultan, as imagined in his moment of defeat in 1799, was another favorite theme of late eighteenth-century history painters in England. Cornwallis receiving the sons of Tipu Sultan as hostages in 1792 forms a subnarrative of this painting, suggesting a defeat foretold. The Last Effort and Fall of Tippoo Sultaun, engraved by Walker after [Henry] Singleton, R.A. (1766–1839), published by James S. Virtue, London, ca. 1860. Hand-colored steel-plate engraving with a vignette below: "Tippoo's sons given to the English as hostages." From Nolan, The Illustrated History of the British Empire in India and the East. Robert J. Del Bontà Collection, E071. Photograph by Robert J. Del Bontà.

was Tipu's fight to the finish. These engravings had a long afterlife, symbolically undoing the many humiliations heaped by Tipu Sultan on the British.

Beatson's dramatic prose forms the basis for another more purposive portrayal of these events, a posthumous reclamation of General Baird's historical role in the "siege of Seringapatam," an honor that had been unfairly bestowed on Arthur Wellesley. In *General Sir David Baird Discovering the Body of the Sultaun Tippoo*, commissioned by Baird's widow in 1838,

David Wilkie deployed his skills as a portrait painter to reclaim honor for Baird, illustrating Beatson's tone:

He who left the Palace in the morning a powerful imperious Sultaun, full of vast ambitious projects, was brought back a lump of clay . . . and his palace occupied by the very man Maj. General Baird who about 15 years before, had been with other victims of his cruelty and tyranny released from near four years of rigid confinement, in irons, in a prison scarce 300 yards from the spot where the corpse of the Sultan lay.[93]

In this painting Baird appears in the manner of one who, not content with the discovery of the slain hero, vicariously participates in his death with drawn sword. The viewer is urged to look up at this British hero who is fully illumined by the flare and the lantern while encountering, just below eye level and in relative darkness, the body of Tipu Sultan.

David Wilkie's portrait of Baird in his moment of glory illustrates the many devices that were deployed in buttressing the truth claims of perspectivalism. Many, including the Duke of Wellington in 1838, are supposed to have praised Wilkie's portrait for its extraordinary fidelity to the original setting and to Baird himself. However, the artist's commission was to lionize Baird and undo his humiliation at the hands of Tipu Sultan, who had once been his captor. Depicting two different points of the Srirangapatna fort and two different moments in history within the two-dimensional space of a single painting called for an imaginative deployment of symbols. It took the form of a grating that recalled the light source of the dungeon to which he had been confined after 1780 along with other European prisoners.[94]

Not all the concerns of this period were exhausted by the series of works that were intended to produce "affect." After the storming of Srirangapatna, history painting assumed a pedagogical role through a careful reconstruction of the momentous siege. Robert Ker Porter's panorama called *The Storming of Seringapatam* was of epic proportions and was called the Great Historical Picture when it was first displayed in the exhibition room of the Lyceum on the Strand in 1800. It was done on "a scale of magnitude hitherto unattempted in this country," a work measuring 120 by 21 feet, occupying 2,550 square feet and arranged on curved screens.[95] The urgency with which Ker Porter painted this work (it was completed in

SIR DAVID BAIRD DISCOVERING THE BODY OF TIPPOO SULTAUN
AFTER THE CAPTURE OF SERINGAPATAM. 4TH MAY. 1799.

FROM THE PICTURE BY SIR DAVID WILKIE R.A. AT NEWBYTH HOUSE MID-LOTHIAN.

Figure 8. A posthumous reclamation of honor of the one who participated in the siege of Srirangapatna. Sir David Baird Discovering the Body of Tippoo Sultaun after the Capture of Seringapatam, 4th May 1799, *from the picture by Sir David Wilkie, R.A., engraved by M. Nargert, lithograph. Newbyth House, Mid-Lothan. From Archer,* Pictures and Royal Portraits Illustrative of English and Scottish History. *Robert J. Del Bontà Collection, E942. Photograph by Robert J. Del Bontà.*

the space of six weeks) clearly spoke of the need to provide visual props, in the time before the photograph, for the British people to participate (i.e., become eyewitnesses themselves) in the act of storming the impregnable fort of Srirangapatna. The flurry of activity was also prompted by the fact that "panorama painting in London around 1800 had become a potentially lucrative but highly competitive business."[96] But the painting was unintelligible without the explanatory booklet, which in turn was pieced together from "authentic materials," namely, various eyewitness reports and government documents and had formed the basis for Ker Porter's effort.[97]

As many as twenty life-sized portraits of British officers were included in this painting, which energetically featured the triumph of British military organization and technology (and the ubiquitous "glass," or telescope, was not forgotten). It was offered to the East India Company, which refused to purchase it, and was then destroyed in a fire, though not before it was engraved by John Vendramini in versions that were widely circulated throughout Britain and India.[98] Designed for an ambulatory viewer in its original version, in its flattened reprint it came close to resembling the multiple time sequences of the Srirangapatna mural without forsaking its claim to certain elements of perspectival realism.

Ker Porter, though not the originator of the English battle panorama, was easily its most celebrated popularizer.[99] He achieved popularity among a fee-paying London public, which repeatedly visited the Lyceum, for his "accurate portraits of the main participants" and his "objectivity," though many liberties were taken with the representation of Srirangapatna.[100]

Wilkie's large painting came as the last in a series of paintings on the Tipu theme for a number of reasons: for one, the genre of history painting itself had clearly degenerated, particularly with the emergence of photography, and, for another, perspective was reduced to a dispensable convention.[101] Edouard Manet's 1868 rendering, *The Execution of Maximilian,* by its deliberate reference to the pathbreaking work of Francisco Goya on the horrors of war, *The Shootings of July 3, 1808,* with nothing of its anguish, negated the genre in the most decisive fashion. Manet's indifference to the general rules for the achievement of perspective, his inversion of the traditional iconographies of the crucifixion, and above all the achievement of a painterly effect that subsists between two historical codes, the informational–journalistic and the traditional–experiential, were signs of the tectonic shifts within western European representational practices.[102] Within India, the sharp political break occasioned by the rebellion of 1857 produced a new set of concerns regarding the continuance of empire rather than its founding moments.

The career of Ker Porter's *Storming of Seringapatam* is therefore instructive, because it came to represent an authentic rendering of 1799. It quickly became the single most used image of Tipu's period in museums, textbooks, and myriad popular productions, shorn of the political context in which it had been born. In important ways, the new scopic regime had triumphed over indigenous representational practices.

History Painting and its Legacies

Exhibits within the Bangalore and Dariya Daulat palaces today prominently display prints from the Vendramini engraving of Ker Porter's panorama. A large collection of the engravings of "views" of the conquered territory, as well as the forts of Mysore and Malabar, is included in the display at Dariya Daulat. Along with the engraving of Henry Singleton's extremely fanciful 1800 rendering, *The Body of Tipu Sultan Recognized by His Family,* and his *The Last Effort and Fall of Tippoo Sultaun* (c. 1800), as well as the fine pencil portraits of Tipu's sons and some courtiers executed by Thomas Hickey between 1801 and 1805, these images have long circulated as reminders of the momentous defeat of Tipu Sultan.[103] Although the Srirangapatna murals may draw appreciation from the visiting public for their aesthetic qualities, British representations lay claim to the historical truth, as revealed in their placement in the palace museums at Srirangapatna and Bangalore, and even at the Dasara Exhibition in Mysore in 1929.[104]

Did the rule of perspective after 1799, then, become the "compulsory site from which vision [could] be conceived or represented"?[105] Did the conditions under which these conventions arose and flourished in Britain exist in India? The possessive version of perspective is outlined by John Berger in *Ways of Seeing,* particularly as a mode of representation that achieved its supremacy when the bourgeoisie was ascendant in Europe.[106]

Colonialism soon drew on another mode of understanding, reducing, controlling, and visually mastering a vast and unknown territory, the art of cartography. Kirmani noted the importance of cartographic knowledge to the enterprise of the British army, for which "Colonel Read obtained maps of the whole of the country by sending clever spies and able munshis [scribes] at great expense."[107] Alexander Beatson attempted the kinds of landscapes that would stand in for the detailed cartography that was to follow. As Barry Lewis has shown, these drawings were the "cameras and the remote sensing instruments of military intelligence and civil administration" in the late eighteenth century and the nineteenth, and instruction in drawing and perspective was part of the training of many military officers.[108] At least three artists were engaged after 1791 in drawing landscapes of the conquered territory. The best known of these were Robert Home, James Hunter, and R. H. Colebrooke.[109] Drawings of the Mysore countryside by A. Allen and engraved by J. Wells form the bulk of the views of forts that are on display at Dariya Daulat today.[110]

The arrival of cartography provided new tools for visual domination of the conquered territory. Narration and description, the twin bases of the new scopic regime, drew from diametrically opposed notions of visuality even when they were aided by mechanical tools for the enhancement of vision. As opposed to producing historical works and paintings that were ocular centric and embodied, the task of cartography was to describe territory in a disembodied way. The former privileges the corporealized eye, for which the camera obscura was the tool par excellence, while the latter privileges a view from nowhere, perhaps even a God's-eye view. The certainties of description were not "contaminated" by the interpretative pitfalls of narration, even when it was provided by an eyewitness, because "a *sketch map allows no opinion*."[111] Yet we know, following Mathew Edney's systematic study of colonial cartography, that "maps are constructs that combine numerous observations into an image of space *without perspective*, although they are then viewed by the individual in lieu of the world."[112] Moreover, the conventions of perspective, even as they were developed within Europe, were far from monolithic or singular, as both Svetlana Alpers and Martin Jay suggest.[113] Perspective is taken as consisting of multiple rather than singular modes of seeing, which is of greater explanatory value in the setting we analyze.

Such contemporary challenges to the power of perspective do not, however, undo the power that it enjoyed in the historical moment under discussion.[114] The insistence with which British encounters with the battle mural at Dariya Daulat emphasized its purported "lack of perspective" must be understood in the context not of its failures but in terms of *the very success with which it participated in historical truth-telling*, despite the use of a language and idiom that invoked a completely different set of rules and sensibilities. The Indian artist, K. G. Subramanyam reminds us, "has no traumatic obsession with whether he is conforming to [visual truth] or deviating from it, as realism does not hold for him any absolute value. . . . But when modern western artists came into contact with the arts of non-modern cultures they had to make a special effort to rationalize these to themselves."[115] Nevertheless, what was achieved in the panel on the Battle of Polilur did not require the techniques of perspective to make its claim to truth. The radical absence of "perspective" is therefore a less useful yardstick to judge Mysore's eighteenth-century traditions than degrees of borrowings between styles of painting and contrasting qualities of flatness and illusionism.

On the other hand, British history painting, as we have seen, despite its formal adherence to the laws of perspective, often constructed a narrative that departed from the historical truth in many ways, using other techniques and devices for the ends of producing affect. History was not available as a transparent resource for pictorial representation because painters actively intervened to produce narratives themselves. Formal rules alone could not ensure historical veracity. In her study of the career of realism in European painting, Linda Nochlin points out that the achievements of realism as a style and movement are to be distinguished from those of mere verisimilitude. She argues that "it was not until the nineteenth century that contemporary ideology came to equate belief in the facts with the total content of belief itself."[116] By the late nineteenth century, moreover, there was widespread recognition that the rules of perspective were a convention for achieving a visual effect, which could be, and indeed was, overthrown by the syntax of modernism. Western European modernism's indifference to and active repudiation of the laws of perspective succeeded in delinking the retinal correspondence between picture-making and the object.

Over time, however, the early British indictment of the Srirangapatna murals became entrenched, especially in India. Shivarama Karanth compared three sets of Indian murals in his work and expressed the highest admiration for those at a Jain *matha* at Sravanabelagola, which he admired for its "purely native" style compared with Dariya Daulat and the Narasimha Temple at Sibi, Tumkur District (done in the early nineteenth century). Artists who were succumbing to the attractions of Western art practices, without the necessary degree of control, were castigated.[117] Tipu's defeat signaled not just a loss of freedom but a retreat of "native styles which we find in Sravanabelagola and Sibi."[118]

Technically underskilled and unable to produce affect, the Indian painter deployed rudimentary skills; Karanth went on to point to the indiscriminate use of Prussian blue as indicative of the needless contamination of

styles occasioned by colonialism.[119] He thus inverted the Olympian dis-
missals of European commentators to speak of a different kind of incom-
petence on the part of Indian painters. Without entering into a discussion
of verisimilitude, he focused on the skills that had been lost before new
ones could be mastered.

However, it was not just in his comparison of styles that Karanth found
the Indian mural wanting but in the modes of spectation that it engen-
dered. The Tintoretto mural, says Karanth, "is housed in a hall that is
long enough to get a clear and full view of the panel in its entirety." Not
so the Srirangapatna mural, which is housed along a ten-foot-wide verandah, with a long-distance view of it further hindered by the existence of
sun screens.[120] Karanth stumbled on an important distinction between
two ways of seeing that may be summarized by the difference between
the "gaze" and the "glance." If British landscapes, battles scenes, and portraits invited the possessive gaze that John Berger and others have so well
documented, the Srirangapatna mural, in its setting and style, invited only
the act of glancing and did not function as a communication of the same
order. Neither did it lapse into a merely decorative function. Its purpose
was to present the visitor to the palace with a context within which to have
a glimpse of the ruler, to view the embodiment of a new princely authority,
a victor of many battles who aspired to craft an alternative to the then de-
funct Mughal monarch while inserting himself into the conventions of the
eighteenth-century Hindu monarchs of South India. The mural portrayed
the battle in all its historical particulars while subordinating it, through its
placement within a universe of symbols and representations, to an emerging and by no means fixed field of forces. In this an informal realism was
employed as an option.

Conclusion

How did a discussion that centered exclusively on the lack or presence of
perspective in Mysore's artistic practices succeed in characterizing Tipu's
Mysore as premodern or nonmodern? Why were British discussions of the
murals at Dariya Daulat so exclusively centered on a singular way of representing historical truth? I have suggested that the Dariya Daulat mural was
no less an engagement with the modern than were its "history painting"
counterparts in a narrative of victory that was attentive to the historical
detail and used an available repertoire of styles. In fact, when the conven-

tions of perspective began to gain ground, I suggest, not least because of the military and political successes of the British in India, representational practices came to be split decisively between a revived "Mysore (decorative) tradition" and new forms of realism that later crystallized around the photograph.

Well into the nineteenth century, there were signs that the skills and triumphs of the history painters of Srirangapatna were admired. One extant paper version of the Polilur mural from the nineteenth century is in the National Gallery of Scotland, executed by an Indian artist, probably at the instance of a British buyer. But a curious long scroll, cut into two segments, is on display at the Vadodara Museum and Art Gallery, titled *Battle between Raja of Tanjore and Nawab of Carnatic,* referring to the Carnatic Wars between the Maratha rump state and Mohammed Ali in the mid-eighteenth century.[121] Attributed to a Tanjore artist of the early nineteenth century, the scroll is an ingenious adaptation of the western wall of Dariya Daulat to the elongated pictorial space of a scroll. Approximately 1.5 by 20.0 feet in size, the scroll brings the four original panels of Dariya Daulat (and not the battle scene alone) into a single pictorial space with interesting effect. It places Haidar, Tipu, and the Nizam not in separate panels but in a sequence, thereby altering the meaning and order of the historical event itself, despite paying scrupulous attention to the particulars (for instance, the arrangement and the dress styles of layers of troops, which are quite distinct from those in the Srirangapatna mural). The wrong identification of the scroll could be attributed to a museum official or the previous owner, but the scroll itself is an innovative adaptation of a historical, and indeed historic, mural. The two known paper versions testify to the meanings of the "portability" of images during the nineteenth century, because once it was wrenched from its architectural setting, which communicated a specific notion of power, it could become an aesthetic object adapted to other tales of power.

CHAPTER 2

An Illusion of Permanence:
Visualizing Legitimacy in Mysore

A S SRINIVAS HAVANUR SAYS in his history of modern Kannada literature, Krishnaraja Wodeyar III, by virtue of being one of the longest-
reigning monarchs, joins the roll call of the Kannada region's heroic kings,
matching the Chalukyan Pulakeshi, the Rashtrakuta Nrupathunga, the
Hoysala Vishnuvardhana, and Vijayanagar's Krishnadevaraya. True, unlike the restored Wodeyar, these heroes won their laurels on the battlefield
as well as in their courts, but did he not wage a continuous struggle with
the British to maintain his right to the kingdom of Mysore?[1]

Unlike his predecessor, Tipu Sultan, whose cultural legacy was more
than overshadowed by his military, administrative, and economic innovations, Krishnaraja Wodeyar III was acknowledged for his lustrous "court,"
consisting of Sanskrit scholars who had taken refuge from a decaying
Peshwa order, a large and impressive band of musicians, and an accomplished array of artists.[2]

However, the cultivation of a court of practitioners of music, literature,
and art, for which nineteenth-century Mysore has been so critically acclaimed, was clearly in inverse proportion to the political powers that the
king enjoyed and was also in direct contrast to the paltry production of
the previous forty years. How reliable as an index of power are the cultural productions of late eighteenth- and nineteenth-century Mysore?
This cultural efflorescence, in portrait and mural painting, was not exclu-
sive to Mysore, as Indira Vishwanathan Peterson and Molly Aitken have
shown.[3] The nineteenth century saw an increase in the use of the portrait
as a "coin of exchange" in transactions between regional leaders and the
British as the former attempted to forge a new relationship to what was
emerging as the paramount power.[4] Mysore reconfigured this history in
significant ways, striking different paths through the nineteenth and twentieth centuries.

If the contours of the Mysore kingdom were in flux at the time of Haidar Ali and Tipu Sultan, no such uncertainty about the *territorial* limits of the Mysore kingdom remained after the British victory. Between 1799, when its borders were drawn up in the partition treaty with the Nizam and the Marathas, and 1956, when the new linguistic state came into being, the state of Mysore remained remarkably stable. Over this period of nearly 160 years, Mysore experienced relative internal and external calm that was only briefly threatened by the peasant rebellions of 1831–34.[5]

The *political* relationship between the Raja of Mysore and his colonial masters was another matter. Indeed, the cultural efflorescence was distinctly at odds with the new, precarious "monarchy" that took shape following the defeat of Tipu Sultan, because Krishnaraja Wodeyar III's occupation of the throne, especially after 1831, was dogged by uncertainty. In his attempt to recreate, though in very different ways, the glories of the Vijayanagar court during the periods of direct rule (1811–31) and indirect rule (1832–68), Krishnaraja Wodeyar III displaced the practice of power into the realm of the symbolic. How might we understand this production that occurred in the interregnum between a representational regime that, as "a regime of visibility," entered into an overall hierarchy of political and social power, and the emergence of an aesthetics, "a specific regime for identifying and reflecting on the arts," the emergence of art in the singular?[6] How do we name this expression of powerlessness except as a way of incubating the hope of a revived kingship?

The crisis about the continuance of the Mysore monarchy was largely resolved when an adopted successor to the Mysore throne was accepted in 1865 and the state returned to direct rule in 1881. Yet, far from disappearing with the emergence of the new stability, the displaced practice of power was marked off and institutionalized under the auspices of the Mysore bureaucracy. The new regime of visibility was driven as much by the compulsions of engaging with and shaping an emerging Mysore public as of representing a modern, and indeed model, region to which the royal family was a supplement.

This chapter reflects on the possible meanings and uses of kingly portraiture and the creation of "a Mysore style of painting" in the nineteenth century as it borrowed from both past and contemporary art practices while strenuously avoiding the adoption of Western or academic realist styles, in sharp contrast to the Tanjore and Travancore courts, which more enthusiastically and readily embraced European techniques, styles, and uses of color.[7] In addressing these questions I trace a series of transitions in the portraiture and mural traditions, including brief experiments with the "Company style." How, for instance, do the murals at the Jaganmohan palace (today Jayachamarajendra Art Gallery) compare with those at Dariya Daulat in communicating power or, more properly, the lack of it? Further, how do they compare with the murals of the twentieth-century Mysore palace, where styles based on photographic realism found full expression and fostered new modes of spectation among the members of the emerging Mysore public?

Artistic Practice and Displaced Political Power

As a creature of British rule, the "Rajah of Mysoor" retained all the formal authority that recalled a period of more active kingship.[8] He drew on existing and emerging idioms of monarchy, reviving older religiopolitical models from which Tipu Sultan had staged his famous break.[9] Far from wearing only a "hollow crown" vis-à-vis the paramount power, Mysore's king aspired to strengthen the bonds with his subjects via the modalities of a remembered sovereignty.

This vision of sovereignty was badly shaken when kingly authority was simultaneously threatened from below and above, that is, by both the people and the paramount power, during the Nagar rebellion of 1831. The period when Krishnaraja Wodeyar III withdrew to a reclusive life of restricted patronage was the time when the "monarch" was resigned to the prospect of the kingship and his line ending with his own death. As a stipendiary of the British, Krishnaraja Wodeyar III was left a small sphere of autonomy;[10] the cultural corpus alone connected the king with his ancestors and asserted his right to continue the dynasty, serving as a coin of exchange to cement the loyalty of the royal Ursus and negotiating his relationship to the colonial masters.

All this changed dramatically during the latter part of the nineteenth century and the twentieth century, when a thoroughly reconstructed monarchy was restored to the throne. After the rendition of 1881, relations between the British and the Mysore palace were firmly mediated by the figure of the Dewan, and the semifeudal political order yielded place to a more systematized rule by records. By this time, the administrative capital of Mysore state also moved to Bangalore, leaving Mysore city to develop its profile as the site of princely pomp focused on the royal family, supplementing the administrative power of the bureaucracy.

Although the increasing use of new technologies such as photography further altered the visual field, its effects in Mysore were once more quite distinct. The Mysore style of painting was all but abandoned as the productions of the palace were quickly adapted to the seductions and conventions of photographic realism. By the time of Krishnaraja Wodeyar IV (r. 1902–40), the Wodeyar family possessed a surety of tenure, successfully achieving a depth of historical distance while simultaneously representing the modernizing hopes and aspirations of the Mysore region.

The Invention of Mysore Traditional

In *Traditional Paintings of Karnataka,* S. R. Rao and B. V. K. Sastry organically link the period of Raja Wodeyar (1578–1617) to Krishnaraja Wodeyar III by suggesting that the term *traditional painting* connotes "a continuity of a time-honoured practice based on ancient concepts, themes, and rules of painting" through the treatment of largely religious and mythological themes.[11] Yet the authors also admit that all extant works of the "Mysore style" of painting belong to the period of Krishnaraja Wodeyar III, attributing the relative paucity of examples from previous epochs to the swift political changes of the late eighteenth century.[12] S. K. Ramachandra Rao also notes a strong line of continuity between the mural traditions of the medieval period and the nineteenth-century miniature and illustrative practices of Mysore, describing these as "traditional" while acknowledging the significant ways in which the artists of the time experimented with and used a range of emerging techniques and idioms.[13] Although the art of the Vijayanagar court might have been influenced by contact with the Portuguese, "in the area in and around Mysore, traditional painting continued almost in its indigenous phase, outside these influences."[14] The formal adherence of the Mysore painters to precolonial textual prescriptions is taken as testimony of this tradition despite the absence of examples from the earlier period, murals apart.[15]

The political instability of the eighteenth century scattered artists across the *samstanams* (small regional courts or estates) of the south, such as Kurnool, Gadwal, Shorapur, and Wanaparthy, some of whom joined the courts of Mysore and Tanjore by the turn of the nineteenth century.[16] Unlike artists of the Tanjore school, however, Mysore artists did not follow the styles set by the Golconda, Deccani, and Company schools, instead revealing a partiality to the tradition of the Rajasthani *ragamala* (a garland of melodic forms, frequently illustrated).[17] The Mysore court during the time of Krishnaraja Wodeyar III had such artists as Durgada Krishnappa (the grandfather of K. Venkatappa), Thippana (who conceived and executed the first *santanambuja*, a genealogy represented in the form of a lotus), Madhugiri Lingappa, Patala Nanjundappa, Venkatasubbu (who experimented with Company-style paintings), Kondayya, Anantamurti, and Sundarayya (the chief artist of the Jaganmohan murals), all from the Chitragara caste. That the Mysore court did in fact succeed in developing and sustaining a distinct and accomplished regional style by the middle of the nineteenth century is more than amply attested by the sometimes unfinished but high-quality illustrated manuscripts of the time, in addition to the ornately decorated *ganjifa* (playing cards) and mural paintings on palace and temple walls. The *Sritattvanidhi* is an example of one such effort, a Sanskrit work written in as well as translated into Kannada. It is a fifteen hundred-page manuscript illustrated with several hundred paintings.[18] In the *Swarachudamani* (an appendix to the *Sritattvanidhi*), a large compendium of *ragamalas*, illustrations of gods, goddesses, and mythological figures, is interspersed with instructions to painters regarding composition, placement, and color choice or mood.

Robert J. Del Bontà's discussion of a *Bhagavata Purana* manuscript similarly affirms the aesthetic achievements of the period. He asserts that the work, dated to the second quarter of the nineteenth century, "is in a purer Karnataka Style."[19] Suggesting that the Mysore artists achieved higher standards on paper than they did in murals, of which there is an impressive corpus, Del Bontà searches the idiom for markers of its adherence to an unadulterated past.[20]

Even the unsentimental prose of the Mysore Archaeological Department stresses the virtuosity of the nineteenth-century Mysore artists. Discussing a watercolor *Battle of Kurushetra* by Thippajee (or Thippanna), a report of the department identifies a "late Mysore style" that had peaked in the second quarter of the nineteenth century.[21] In these accounts the "Mysore traditional style" rose, peaked, and declined within the first three decades of the nineteenth century itself. What all the writers are agreed on was that the productions of the Mysore court represent a unique art historical moment.

Precolonial artistic traditions were also adopted, though not exclusively, in the court of Serfoji II, the Maratha Raja of Tanjore (b. 1777; r. 1798–1832), who was restored as the heir to the kingdom of Tanjore, which had been under British control since 1773. Serfoji II was provided with British protection and education and developed a strong taste for European knowledge, print cultures, and visual conventions and encouraged painting by Indian artists trained in European styles.[22] Similarly, the Travancore ruler, Maharaja Swati Tirunal, invited Alagiri Naidu of Madura to the Travancore court in the 1830s for his skills in Western-style portraiture.[23] In their willingness to encourage the new styles of painting, these South Indian royals struck out a different path from their contemporary in Mysore, whose deliberate abstinence from these new influences was akin to that of Mahrana Fateh Singh of Mewar, who in the nineteenth century declared that all things old would be embraced and new ones rejected.[24]

The production of Mysore palace art in the late nineteenth century and the twentieth revealed new resolutions of the relationship between the aesthetic and the political. It is perhaps a sign of the success of Krishnaraja Wodeyar III's attempt to reestablish his links with the dynasty that had been eclipsed in the eighteenth century that contemporary art historians fail to acknowledge the extent to which Mysore royal traditions were continuously "invented" throughout this period. This invention must be distinguished from the early twentieth-century return to tradition that was fostered by the Bengal school.[25] In the early nineteenth century, the turn to tradition, whether partially as in Tanjore or more completely in Mysore, was a medium for addressing royal anxieties about legitimacy vis-à-vis the colonial masters. In early nineteenth-century Mysore, such artistic production also attempted to bind semifeudal elites in new forms of subservience.

A profusion of portraits executed in styles ranging from the naturalistic (as in the album of portraits commissioned by the Maharaja of artists, writers, and officials of his court) to the flatter "folk"-style representations of Krishnaraja Wodeyar III yielded place, by the end of the nineteenth century, to academic renderings in oil of royal personages.[26] Mural painting followed a similar trajectory. Together, these productions reveal obsessive and even sterile representations of the Mysore royalty. But my interest is not as much in affirming the art-historical account of the period's aesthetic achievements or in reducing the visual to a mere illustration of the evolving idioms of political power in nineteenth- and twentieth-century Mysore as in proposing a reading of Mysore's political history based on these productions.

Through an analysis of popular print culture of the late nineteenth and early twentieth centuries, Christopher Pinney has argued that it could be used to construct an alternative history of popular nationalism; for instance, the widespread circulation and popularity of Bhagat Singh's image suggests that revolutionary nationalism and sacrifice enjoyed a firmer hold on the national imagination than did Gandhian nonviolence.[27] He sets off the popular prints against official textual histories as an index of the limits to the powers of the official nationalist semiotic. It is not possible to draw a strict parallel between the mass production and circulation of prints in the twentieth century and the more restricted circulation of images in the nineteenth. Indeed, the Mysore productions remained largely official, though they marked a sharp move away from the kind of work that was preferred in and around the regions of direct Company rule, such as Madras. With no necessary correspondence between the realms of the politicoeconomic and the sociocultural in Mysore or between the substantive and formal practices of power, there is a need for a sharper focus on the disjunctures, discontinuities, and inversions, not just the "continuities" alone, of this densely semiotic world.

Portraying the Royal Visage

In what was no doubt the first widely reproduced portrait drawn of Krishnaraja Wodeyar III, the five-year-old prince was portrayed as a round-faced child, vulnerable and unself-conscious despite his large turban and the attention that has been thrust upon him. Arthur Wellesley reported that the young king was "remarkably decorous, considering the untoward circumstances which had preceded his elevation."[28]

About a year later, a more stylized portrait of this child king recovered his poise and royalty, portraying him as a scion who "endeavours in public to preserve a dignified gravity of countenance."[29] There are nevertheless clear influences of the use of naturalistic conventions in the latter portrait.[30] Thereafter, the portraits of the king trace a curious trajectory, attaining an even greater degree of stylization throughout his long and uncertain tenure on the throne of Mysore.

In his active encouragement of the painting of innumerable portraits of himself in formal indoor and outdoor settings, Krishnaraja Wodeyar III was more like Nizam Ali Asaf Jah II of Hyderabad or Serfoji II of Tanjore.[31] In Tanjore portraiture, Peterson notes "the heightened individualization of the subject, and a naturalistic portrayal of the face and figure," similar to

KRISHNA RAJA

Curtur, or Sovereign of Mysore

Figure 9. One of the earliest portraits, possibly by Thomas Hickey, of the five-year-old
Krishnaraja Wodeyar III, installed as Mysore's child king. Krishna Raja, Curtur, or
Sovereign of Mysore, engraved by C. Picart. From Buchanan, A Journey from Madras
through the Countries of Mysore, Canara, and Malabar, vol. 1, frontispiece. Robert J.
Del Bontà Collection, E980. Photograph by Robert J. Del Bontà.

those found in representations of the Mysore king.[32] Krishnaraja Wodeyar III was always portrayed in the three-quarters view, looking back at the viewer, usually facing left, whether seated on a chair, in formal or informal poses, hunting, riding, or participating in the *vasanthotsava* (a spring festival). Douglas Barrett has traced the first use of the three-quarters view in Deccani painting instead of the preferred royal profile to the late sixteenth-century portrait of Burhan Nizam Shah II, but even in eighteenth-century southern India, three-quarters views were usually associated with the more relaxed rendering of ordinary figures and not with members of the royalty.[33] Peterson notes a similar turn away from the stylized portraits of the eighteenth century to the "frontal stance or the ¾ view of European portraiture."[34] She characterizes the new value that was given to frontality in royal portraiture as a compromise between the divine and the human figure.[35]

Figure 10. A new frontality is achieved in this portrait of a noble couple (possibly Krishnaraja Wodeyar III and one of his wives) worshipping Shiva-Parvathi: they face the viewer rather than the idol. Noble at Prayer, date and artist unknown; watercolor and polished gold leaf; 40 x 50 cm. Courtesy of Karnataka Chitrakala Parishath, Bangalore. Photograph by Muni Mohan, 2008.

Krishnaraja Wodeyar III was always portrayed in his princely regalia, replete with the Mysore turban, enhanced by devices such as a flower in his hand or by comparison to his epic counterpart, the god Krishna. Molly Aitken says, "Portraits were painted to be seen in a political context" and in no way represented the artists' personal vision of the king.[36] Yet retaining the human imperfections of the man-king rendered him into someone more recognizable than an icon: the visage of Krishnaraja Wodeyar III began to bear the marks of age over several decades as his characteristic handlebar moustache turned gray in several paintings.[37] In the Mysore productions, the unswerving adherence to the three-quarters-view portrait was an attempt to achieve visual stability, recognition, and an illusion of permanence even in times of great political uncertainty.

Such portraits were by no means the only known modes of representing the nobility. A three-quarters-length portrait of Dewan Purnaiya, done in oils by Thomas Hickey as early as 1801, portrayed an aristocratic Mysorean counterpart of his British masters. Purnaiya here communicates the strength of character that the British expected of the richly attired Dewan;[38] Justice holding her scales proclaims the virtues of colonial rule. Purnaiya was not to disappoint his new masters, and the British regime had reason to admire his financial acumen, even as it ignored the unhappy conditions under which extortions occurred.[39] Purnaiya looks off the frame in a classic form of indifference to the beholder, upholding the fiction of denying the theatricality of the subject.

No such portrait of Krishnaraja Wodeyar III exists, not even the softly modeled and shaded oil painting by the artist Manji, done in 1847, in which the king is shown in his daily wear with a towel thrown carelessly over his shoulder.[40] The king always engages the eye of his beholder, even in those portraits that are clearly experimenting with forms of hybrid naturalism. These shades of illusionism were abandoned as the more stylized forms of portraiture took firmer hold, portraying the king in his durbars, among "courtiers," and among his women. Overall, the portraits of Krishnaraja Wodeyar III achieved a curious hybridity, simultaneously striving to be on a par with the hieratic image in its direct mode of address while allowing human vulnerabilities to be clearly depicted.[41]

Nigel Chancellor identifies an 1805 painting by Thomas Hickey of three women—two of them wives of Krishnaraja Wodeyar III—as part of the British attempt to promote smallpox vaccination.[42] Although it is difficult to agree with such a programmatic use of royal portraiture, especially before a time of mass viewership or circulation, the painting does suggest

Figure 11. Krishnaraja Wodeyar III, *date and artist unknown; watercolor on paper with gold leaf; 18 x 22 cm. Courtesy of Karnataka Chitrakala Parishath, Bangalore. Photograph by Muni Mohan, 2008.*

Figure 12. A visibly aging king is depicted with a towel thrown over his shoulder though bearing other formal markers of royalty. Manji, Krishnaraja Wodeyar III, *1846; oil on thin cloth or coated paper; 38 x 48 cm. Courtesy of Karnataka Chitrakala Parishath, Bangalore. Photograph by Muni Mohan, 2008.*

that oil portraiture conventions were quite well known in the Mysore court, though European painters were kept out of the Mysore court.[43] The Maharaja often entertained his European guests by unveiling his collection of paintings, which, "with the exception of a few paintings executed by a European painter who was for some time in the late Maharaja's employ, does not contain any trace of the influence which European art has exercised over most of the native courts of India."[44] In his later years, however, he made gifts of European paintings of Arthur Wellesley to the British, a curious example of cementing his loyalty to the colonial power.

By the late nineteenth century, when Chamarajendra Wodeyar X assumed the throne, the stylized oil portrait had become more firmly entrenched, and thereafter the academic portrait in oils was the preferred style for dozens of portraits of the royal family. What did such a sharp shift signify about the new roles and functions of the Mysore palace as opposed to the ideals of kingship that had informed the actions of Krishnaraja Wodeyar III?

The patronage of Brahmans, temples, and mathas through land grants was reduced after the king was divested of his power in 1832. An even more serious diminution of the palace establishment followed the king's death in 1868. In a major stocktaking of the palace establishment, Major Elliot produced, according to his brief, an exhaustive audit of palace assets, em-

Figure 13. Krishnaraja Wodeyar III with his newly adopted son, Chamarajendra Wodeyar X, at prayer before an assortment of indexed gods and goddesses, crowned by Chamundesvari. Krishnaraja Wodeyar III Worships the Goddess Chamundeshvari, *1859, artist unknown; lithograph; 18.5 x 29.5 cm. San Diego Museum of Art, Edwin Binney 3rd Collection.*

ployees, and claimants. Among the concerns of the British administration was the large number of relatives and retainers who were on the palace payroll, accounting for a good fifth of the city's population, many of whom were in a position to claim hereditary rights. The phalanx of legal and illegal wives of Krishnaraja Wodeyar III, along with his *bungaroos,* or royal concubines, totaled twenty, of whom six women were still alive, which led to the British insistence on monogamy (at least in the public, licit domain) among succeeding monarchs.[45] Recognizing that the "system of illegitimate marriages is of very old origin," Elliot strongly urged that "they [legitimate and illegitimate descendents] should be induced to betake themselves to habits of economy and forethought, and to put a restraint upon the indiscriminate marriages which have unfortunately hitherto been too much encouraged in the palaces."[46] No direct reference was made here to the dense network of marital alliances through which the Maharaja "incorporated" parts of the southern Mysore kingdom, forms of filiation that held little meaning in the new political order.

The reconstruction of the Mysore monarchy was amply achieved in the figure of Chamarajendra Wodeyar X, whose education in the styles and leisure activities of the aristocratic British gentleman was closely supervised by G. B. Malleson. Modern education itself became the new resource used by members of the Ursu caste to find a footing in the late nineteenth-century political order. At the same time, representations of the royal family revealed new sensibilities and bore striking parallels to British portrayals of their monarchy. Simon Schama says that by the middle of the nineteenth century, the domestic was increasingly the framing device in royal British portraiture, resulting in "a calculated combination of the ritual and the prosaic."[47] In Mysore, too, a turn toward the depiction of the Mysore dynasty as a royal family resulted in the domestication of royalty, as seen in a set of images from the late nineteenth century. The luxuriant plurality of wives and concubines of Krishnaraja Wodeyar II had made way for a more companionate monogamous marriage in the time of Chamarajendra Wodeyar. In a striking photograph of the period, Chamarajendra Wodeyar is seated on a chair, surrounded by his five children.[48] Despite the absence of his wife, this is photographic testimony to the monogamy into which he had been tutored (he had only one official wife) and is a celebration of new ties of affect with his children. The concern with tracing an unbroken royal ancestry that had preoccupied his father was replaced by a new focus on heirs.

Figure 14. A new domestic setting for the Wodeyar royal family: a richly embellished paint-
ing in two panels, replete with eulogies to the Mysore rulers, frames a relaxed photographic
portrait of Chamarajendra Wodeyar X with his five children, c. 1888. Photograph with
opaque watercolors and gold leaf on paper; 57 x 48 cm. From Arivar, Glimpses from the
Mysore Royal Art Collection, *exhibition catalog (Bengaluru: Taj West End, 2008).*

The shift in the third decade of the nineteenth century toward realism and the domestic and familial setting within which the effect was achieved were therefore quite important. In 1885, Chamarajendra Wodeyar invited the up-and-coming Indian artist Ravi Varma and his brother Raja Varma to Mysore, and two family portraits were executed of the one-year-old heir apparent, Krishnaraja Wodeyar IV. In one he is seen crawling toward a rattle, and in his frank engagement of the viewer, bears a startling resemblance to the playful child god Krishna, though in a corporealized style that Ravi Varma would later use to portray the gods. Although the prince is dressed in diaphanous garments, he is richly jeweled and placed on luxurious velvet. Another oil portrait of the same time shows Krishnaraja Wodeyar IV seated in a pram, flanked by his two older sisters. The relaxed portrait of royal domesticity achieved with such success in the photograph of Chamarajendra Wodeyar and his children was now dramatized in the Ravi Varma portraits of the royal household. The artist strove for and achieved a resemblance to the subjects in different ways from the creators of the Mysore-style paintings of Krishnaraja Wodeyar III, in which Chamarajendra Wodeyar, the "heir apparent," was portrayed as a miniaturized adult (see Figure 13). The shift from dynasty to family, which now included the *yuvaraja* (brother) and sisters of the new Maharaja, would achieve a new texture for the Mysore royalty. By the end of the first decade of the twentieth century, there was a prodigious supply of oil portraits of the family, ranging from those of the regent Vani Vilas Sannidhana (1895–1902), to the sisters of Krishnaraja Wodeyar IV.

More important, the royal marriage no longer signified the strengthening of ties with local branches of the Ursu clan, but rather indicated the emergence of a new pan-Indian royal order. The realization that the Mysore royalty did not rank as highly as the Rajput chiefs led to a search for matrimonial alliances with Rajput royals, and in 1900 a bride was found from the little Kathiawari kingdom of Vana.[49] The marriage linked Mysore's royal family to the emerging colonial order of filiations and rank. The portrait of this marriage, commissioned by the regent Vani Vilas Sannidhana and executed by Ravi Varma from a photograph, was printed at Varma's Art Litho Press to herald a new phase in the portability of images of the royal family.

The naturalized settings in which Ravi Varma placed his subjects were a sign of the growing distance from earlier symbols and conventions. One would be hard pressed to find a rendering of either Chamarajendra

Figure 15. A portrait of Krishnaraja Wodeyar IV as a child that strongly alludes to the child god Krishna. Ravi Varma, Krishnaraja Wodeyar IV as Child, *1885; oil on canvas; 91.4 x 76.2 cm. Mysore Palace, Mysore. Photograph by Janaki Nair, 2008.*

Figure 16. A formal portrait of the royal children outdoors. Ravi Varma, Krishnaraja Wodeyar IV with Siblings, *1885; oil on canvas; 101.6 x 152.4 cm. Mysore Palace, Mysore. Photograph by Janaki Nair, 2008.*

Wodeyar or Krishnaraja Wodeyar IV in the Mysore style, which was by this time more strictly reserved by Mysore artists for the portrayal of gods and goddesses. By the beginning of the twentieth century, a fresh challenge was posed to the Mysore-style paintings when Ravi Varma single-handedly transformed the way in which not just the royals but the gods were portrayed and corporealized.[50] After making his first two contributions to the Mysore palace in 1885, Ravi Varma, who had already achieved his fame in executing a series of fourteen Puranic oil paintings for the Gaekwad of Baroda, sought and received a commission from the Mysore palace to execute nine Puranic paintings.

Ravi Varma arrived in Mysore in 1904 to flesh out the gods on a recognizably human plane.[51] This marked a major turning point in the productions of the palace artists, who were urged to master academic-style oil painting almost a century after the palace had been exposed to its devices and conventions. The grandson of artist Thippanna, K. Keshavaiah, first attempted to produce an oil painting of the new Maharaja in 1903.[52] In 1906 he was personally urged by the new king to learn the techniques of the modern master, Ravi Varma; this training would make him one of the most accomplished oil painters of the Mysore palace in the early twentieth century.[53]

"The World Is Being Seen"

The larger portraits of Krishnaraja Wodeyar III were displayed at the palace itself, though several small books published by the palace litho press carried pictures as frontispieces. S. K. Ramachandra Rao suggests that what did circulate through the homes of the wealthier residents of Mysore were large numbers of religious paintings turned out by the court artists,[54] though clearly smaller representations of the king must have been intended for circulation among members of the Ursu clan. Elsewhere in Mysore, images of the king were inserted in murals on the walls of the temples, for instance, at the Narasimhaswamy temple at Sibi, Tumkur, built at the turn of the nineteenth century, where he is seen in posthumous dialogue with Haider Ali and Tipu Sultan.[55] Most striking is his insertion into the portrait gallery on the eastern walls of Dariya Daulat, where he is placed alongside several regional powers of the late eighteenth century. It is likely that this entire wall was repainted during his reign, because the styles of execution are quite similar to some of those seen in the Mysore manuscripts.

Yet even the most prodigious efforts of the palace artists could not quite match the techniques of mass reproduction and the challenges and opportunities presented by the print medium, particularly as it made images of the royals as portable as those of the gods. Technological changes in the latter part of the nineteenth century aided new modes of representation, and photography was put to a range of new administrative and anthropological uses even as artists acquired new skills to color or refine photographs.[56] Mark Zebrowski suggests that an already sterile artistic oeuvre of the eighteenth century and the early nineteenth was dealt a death blow in Hyderabad when the Nawab Mir Mahbub Ali Khan turned to the well-known Lala Deen Dayal, who moved to the city as official photographer in 1884.[57] Sujith Parayil has noted a similar shift to a focus on photography in Travancore, resulting in the freer circulation and use of images of the Travancore royals.[58]

The Mysore palace was slower to take to the attractions of photography, with a sharp shift occurring only in the early twentieth century, reshaping the skills of the palace painters and extending the circulation of portraits throughout the Mysore kingdom. In the time before color photographs, palace artists played an important role in making over black-and-white prints and bringing them to life.[59] Formal photographic portraits were augmented with color tints, though in Mysore there was no attempt at producing the bizarre dream worlds of photographers seen at smaller courts such as Indore, which are discussed by Pinney, or the "magical realist" styles of Shivaji II, which emerged alongside gilded Tanjore-style portraits of Serfoji II and his son.[60]

In Mysore, photographs became part of a largely formal oeuvre, with the government budget earmarking funds each year for the circulation of monochrome portraits of the Maharaja Krishnaraja Wodeyar IV. In just one year, 1915, it was reported that three types of portraits of the king were ordered, six thousand brown (sepia?) for free distribution to all primary educational institutions in the state, two thousand colored portraits for high schools and colleges, and two hundred copies of the portrait on satin obtained from England, of which one hundred were sent to select large public meeting halls and the rest kept for sale.[61] Requests were pouring in from diverse government offices and other government institutions such as the observatory, the Garden Department, and municipality offices.[62] Palace artists such as Keshavaiah were trained in tinting photographs from 1911 and perfected the skill under a visiting Russian artist in 1912.[63] Meanwhile, the appetite of officials and royal family members for painted portraits of themselves remained undiminished: Keshavaiah kept a stock of canvases of blank faces adorned with the rich Mysore *peta* (turban) to meet the needs of his aristocratic clients.[64]

What had been entirely transformed between the time of Krishnaraja Wodeyar III and that of his namesake in the twentieth century was not merely the technologies of mechanical reproduction but the style of kingship itself. The nineteenth-century monarch rarely moved out of Mysore except to trace the sacred geography of Melkote, Nanjangud, Srirangapatna, or the hunting grounds of Kittur near Mysore.[65] Making the king more familiar with, and therefore within, the territory of Mysore state was the achievement of Chamrajendra Wodeyar's travels through the length and breadth of Mysore, where "darshans" were arranged among those for whom the Wodeyar dynasty could have been only a fading memory during the decades of "palace exile" of Krishnaraja Wodeyar III. From his discovery of India outside the palace walls, Chamarajendra Wodeyar returned full of ideas and initiatives, ranging from the establishment of technical institutes and zoos to the introduction of horse racing and the practice of holding industrial exhibitions.[66]

In the twentieth century, such perambulations around the region became less important as a means of tying king to subjects, as Krishnaraja Wodeyar IV achieved an even wider public presence, whether by consenting to address the Congress Exhibition in Madras in 1903 or visiting Europe in 1936.[67] The circulation of his portraits served the purpose of ensuring that the king was made into a popular and beloved figure, providing a new semiotic cohesion to the territory whose boundaries had not changed since 1799, a cohesion that had earlier been attempted through the many mural portraits of Krishnaraja Wodeyar III. Twentieth-century Mysore, however, was quite unlike Travancore, where images of the king circulated more freely as the "sovereign emblem of the trade state," leading to legal disputes over the "right" to his image.[68]

Historicizing Mysore Modern

Were the artists of the Mysore palace of the nineteenth century insulated not just from European painters but from the style of Europe itself, and was Company-style painting avoided in favor of indigenous practices? It would be difficult to assert such strict abstinence on the part of the early

Mysore artists because there were exuberant experiments with perspective and new narrative forms in their work even in the nineteenth century,
and lavish use of recognizable architectural features and technological innovations in paintings of the colonial period.[69] Even when paintings conformed to older pictorial conventions, as in the *Bhagavata Purana* manuscript, the styles of borders used to separate panels were strikingly similar
to those at Dariya Daulat, with repetitions of Islamic wall patterns, foliate
bands, brown pillars, and arches taken from Tipu's palaces at Bangalore
and Srirangapatna.[70] After the 1830s, a series of attempts was made to use
the idiom of religious maps to pictorially record important pilgrimage
spots.[71]

　　Portable religious maps, says Susan Gole, were often the memoirs of
pilgrimages, because "the devout pilgrim would visit all the eighty-four
sites made holy in the Krishna legend, and then take home a map to show
where he had been."[72] For the more sedentary Krishnaraja Wodeyar III, the
experience of these sites was mediated. A set of fixed maps is in the small
chitramantapa (picture gallery) of the Prasanna Venkatramanaswamy temple adjoining the Jaganmohan palace in Krishnavilasa Agrahara.[73] Built in
the late 1820s and early 1830s for Subbaraya Dasa, a Vaishnavite Brahman
from the Maharashtra region, the temple was grateful acknowledgment
of his important role in curing those afflicted by the cholera epidemic of
1828.[74] Krishnaraja Wodeyar III, who supported several pilgrimages by
Subbaraya Dasa and his retinue to the major temples of the Karnataka
region and beyond, satisfied himself with this sacred geography on the
walls of the tiny chitramantapa above the temple itself. The maps allowed
Subbaraya Dasa's royal visitor to go on a vicarious pilgrimage through the
sacred sites of the larger political unit of which his kingdom was a part.[75]
The images on the walls were not subordinated to the deity, as were the
murals of the Sweta Varahaswami temple (built in 1809) or the Prasanna
Krishnaswamy temple (built in 1825) of the palace compound. In the chitramantapa, maps of Mysore's sacred sites, such as Melukote, Nanjangud,
and Srirangapatna, were placed alongside maps of pilgrimage sites from
further afield, such as Hampi, Tirupati, Pandarpur, Kasi, and Srirangam.
These maps included topographical features such as rivers, tanks, walls, or
forts and combined a bird's-eye view of the territory with front elevations
of temples in a creative mixture of perspectives.[76]

　　"Company-style" paintings that appeared from the fourth decade of the

Figure 17. A sacred map of Srirangapatna showing the principal temples, four lines of fortification, and palaces, as well as Jumma Masjid. Detail from a mural in Chitramantapa at Prasanna Venkatramanaswami Temple, Mysore. Photograph by Clare Arni, 1994.

nineteenth century appear to have become the preferred style for recording historical events in Mysore. The company style is defined by Mildred
Archer as that "which objectively observes the Indian scene in all its aspects, including natural history and human society."[77] In Mysore, such productions were few, coinciding with the time when Krishnaraja Wodeyar III
accepted his new destiny under British rule. One such remarkable painting celebrates the establishment of an English school in Mysore in 1833.
The school was supported by the king throughout his life, even after it was
transferred to the Wesleyan Mission to run in 1840. A new school building was commissioned in 1866, and the event, reported in many newspapers, was memorialized in a painting.[78] Executed by Thippanna, the chief
chitragara (artist) and superintendent of the court artists, *Opening of the
English School in Mysore* records a significant moment of transformation
in an old educational order and a new eagerness on the part of the king to
conform to colonial expectations.[79]

Portrayed in his recognizable three-quarters profile on a chair, the king
is slightly elevated above the British officials, including Commissioner
Lewin Bowring and Ashtagram Superintendent Major Elliot. The artist
strove to achieve an equal meeting of minds and political statuses. Though
an attempt was made to remain true to the architectural features of the
colonial-style building, the pictorial space was a stage, framed by the suggestion of movement on three sides. Every effort was made to enhance the
pomp and grandeur of the king in these paintings, enlarging or diminish-
ing colonial masters or Indian and foreign durbarees depending on their
relative importance rather than their distance from the viewer. There was
not too obsessive a reliance on verisimilitude, with many decorative elements included on the margins and even within the picture.

Two other paintings record Krishnaraja Wodeyar III at the European
durbar (c. 1835) and the zenana durbar (c. 1850).[80] Venkatasubbu's depiction of Chamarajendra Wodeyar's adoption (1865) and coronation
(1868) forsake the Mysore style altogether and record all pictorial details
of the formal investiture of the child king, a moment of triumph for the
beleaguered Wodeyar dynasty. In the adoption picture, Chamarajendra
Wodeyar is displayed to the court as the heir apparent, propped on the
bent knee of his aging father. In several pictures, which combine old and
new symbolic conventions, Chamarajendra Wodeyar is depicted as a miniaturized adult.

Attention was also paid to the Wodeyar genealogical tree at this time

Figure 18. Thippanna, Opening of the English School at Mysore, *c. 1866; ink and watercolor on paper, 46.5 x 57 cm. Jayachamarajendra Art Gallery, Mysore. Photograph by Clare Arni, 2008.*

of diminished political autonomy, as insistently in writing as in pictorial representation. Among the earliest examples is in the chitramantapa at the Prasanna Venkatramanaswamy temple.[81] The upper sections of four painted panels, which were purportedly taken from the Mysore palace, bear painted portraits of twelve Mysore Wodeyars from Raja Wodeyar (1578–1617) to Khasa Chamaraja Wodeyar VIII (the father of Krishnaraja Wodeyar III, 1776–1796), with their reigns designated in *pattas* (denoting a reign of twelve years), years, and months.[82]

In the best known of these pictorial genealogies, created by Thippanna in 1856, all twenty-two kings of the Wodeyar family are shown, from the time of Yadu Raya in 1399 to the time of Krishnaraja Wodeyar III.[83] This seamless and well-integrated santanambuja consists of a total of thirty-five portraits (since it also includes portraits of yuvarajas, or brothers of the king), with nearly half of the kings facing left and the other half facing right, all in three-quarters view. The throne, the most important visual symbol of Mysore kingship, was resurrected from the stores of Srirangapatna in 1799 and substantially refurbished in 1812.[84] All political disturbances and challenges to Wodeyar authority were effaced in the painting by placing every king on the throne and under the royal canopy, with no reference to the power of the *dalavais* (hereditary commanders of military forces), usurpers such as Haider Ali and Tipu Sultan, or the British victors.[85] Similar genealogies were produced even in the 1870s.

A series of murals at the Jaganmohan palace, completed in the 1860s, represented Wodeyar rule as a period of continuous power that had been denied in the realm of the economic or political. By the late nineteenth century, these midcentury anxieties would be transformed into an institutionalized separation of symbolic and actual power, of which the murals of the Mysore palace were the fullest expression. The preoccupation with tracing common antecedents gradually yielded place to the announcement of legitimate descendents, shaping both the visual and the historiographical traditions.

Pageants, Processions, and the Illusion of Permanence

It was in the Amba Vilas of the old palace within the Mysore fort that Krishnaraja Wodeyar III "received his European guests and transacted the ordinary business of the day."[86] On the walls of this room were the portraits of officers connected with the Mysore administration, "which His Highness was accustomed to uncover and point out to his European visitors."[87] A large portrait of Arthur Wellesley painted soon after the siege of Seringapatam was treasured by the king and was among the rare *khillats* (royal honors or gifts) he sent to Queen Victoria in 1861.[88]

Murals were commissioned in several places: at the *janmamantapa* (a structure commemorating a birthplace) at Chamarajanagar (which Krishnaraja Wodeyar III had built in 1774 to commemorate the birth of his father) at a chitramantapa in the Mallikarjuna temple near Talkad, as well as in the Prasanna Venkatramanaswamy temple at Mysore.[89] However, the richest representations are on the second floor, or the Rang Mahal, of the Jaganmohan palace. Sometime in the early 1860s, Krishnaraja Wodeyar III

Figure 19. Venkatasubbu, Chandra Vamsha Kamala Vriksha, *1871; ink and opaque watercolors on paper board, 74 x 99 cm. A "lotus genealogy"* (santanambuja) *of twenty-two Mysore Wodeyars, the most recent being Chamarajendra Wodeyar X (at the apex). The regnant kings were distinguished from other relatives by their placement under the royal umbrella of the golden throne. Courtesy of Karnataka Chitrakala Parishath, Bangalore. Photograph by Muni Mohan, 2008.*

moved his court of painting to the new but modest Jaganmohan Palace, where he entertained his visitors.[90] The Rang Mahal, on the topmost floor of the palace, consists of an outer and an inner hall, the latter flanked by two narrow antechambers to the north and south. The palace was built around 1861, but it is clear that the paintings were done around 1865.[91] The principal artist appears to have been Sundarayya.[92] The outer hall is profusely decorated with delicate foliage interspersed with animals, mythical and real. This bestiary clearly testifies to the virtuosity of the Mysore artists, who made no attempt here to narrate events or produce historical memory but merely wanted to decorate in a manner that would display their imaginations and skills.

The inner hall is quite distinct from the outer in terms of theme and style. Here the Mysore king's displaced political power is recovered within the realm of the symbolic in very interesting ways. Among the privileges of the palace establishment of Krishnaraja Wodeyar III that were drastically trimmed down when he surrendered power to the British in 1831 was the Dasara durbar. Although he made a plea for at least 100,000 C.P. for the celebrations, he was finally allotted only Rs 25,000 for a modest celebration.[93] The Dasara was revived as a public event only in the 1880s.

The central hall celebrates the Dasara pictorially as an announcement of the king's renewed power following the British acceptance of his right to adoption.[94] The Jambusavari procession of the Vijayadashami festival, on the last day of Dasara, dominates the upper walls of the central hall of the Rang Mahal. The walls contain other bands of decorations: below the main Jambusavari procession on the eastern wall are symmetrical portraits of heavily decorated women; in addition there are the sacred cows and horses of the state. The lower section of the middle part of the wall has scenes of Krishnaraja Wodeyar III on his hunts around Mysore.

Piercing the western wall is the large santanambuja, which is focused on Krishnaraja Wodeyar III, around whom the Mysore dynasty springs into being. The santanambuja here is even more inclusive than Thippanna's, incorporating on its right the Puranic rulers such as Vasudeva and Krishna, with historical ancestors on the left. The god Krishna and Krishnaraja Wodeyar III are portrayed somewhat differently than their respective ancestors or descendents, but the iconographic parallels between the Puranic hero and his nineteenth-century namesake are a repetitive feature of this hall.

Flanking both sides of the santanambuja are portraits of Indian and foreign rulers, though the artists felt no obligation to represent only the king's contemporaries. To the left are the portraits of fifty Muhammedan kings ranging from the "Rustom son of Sohrab" and the Badshah of Iran to regional heroes such as Haidar Ali and Tipu Sultan and the Nawabs of Arcot, Hyderabad, and Bengal. The fifty portraits of Hindu kings to the right include contemporaries from Kerala and Tanjavur to rulers of smaller *samstanams* such as Gadwal and Kodagu in addition to several officials of the court.[95]

In addition to bearing the thirty portraits of the officials of the Mysore court, this wall serves as a biographical dictionary of many contemporaries of Krishnaraja Wodeyar III and is praised in the report of the Archaeological Department as "valuable from the historic as well as the artistic point of view." But the portraits are most significant in terms of the idea of power that is achieved by such an arrangement. Rather like the sacred geographies of the chitramantapa at the Prasanna Venkatramanaswamy temple in Mysore, which allowed a sedentary king to vicariously travel through India, these portraits summon a whole universe of rulers to the presence of Krishnaraja

Figure 20. Portraits of Muslim rulers mythical, historical, and contemporary. Detail of mural on west wall of Rang Mahal. Jayachamarajendra Art Gallery, Mysore. Photograph by Clare Arni, 2006.

Wodeyar III because they are all, from both left and right, made to face the lotus genealogy over which he presides. On this wall are portraits of the Mysore kingdom's officers, a new visual unity of bureaucratic office that interrupts the genealogical unities proclaimed in this space.

A *vamsa vriksha* (genealogical tree) adorns the eastern wall of the northern antechamber, showing the king seated on his throne and surrounded by the names of his descendents. The tree stems from a moon-mouthed pot to signify the lunar dynasty from which the Wodeyar dynasty sprang. The *vamsavatarana vaibhava* (the wealth of the family, i.e., ancestors and descendents) in the background extols the glories of the dynasty.

Wrapped around the northern, eastern, and southern walls, the Jambusavari procession foregrounds Krishnaraja Wodeyar III in his state carriage, once more in his familiar three-quarters pose. The elephant-drawn carriage is several times larger than the animals, and the king is not alone; seated in his carriage on a lower plane is his newly adopted heir, Chamarajendra Wodeyar X, depicted with the gravity of an adult.

Many of the other bands on the walls of the Rang Mahal are devoted to portraying the leisurely pursuits of Krishnaraja Wodeyar III; even when his own portrait does not appear, as in several portrayals of chess strategies, it is his love of the game that is depicted. He is shown, for instance, participating in the *vasanthotsava* on the eastern wall of the southern antechamber or in several hunting poses in a central panel on the eastern wall.

If the western wall of Dariya Daulat at Srirangapatna was dominated by scenes of preparing for and winning a war, the equally staged scenes of a procession are portrayed in the Rang Mahal at Mysore. The calendrical ritual is preferred as a symbol of continuity and permanence rather than the singular, glorious triumph of battle. A central five-sectioned panel on the eastern wall portrays Krishnaraja Wodeyar III as a hunter. Here, too, the historical record is forsaken for the assertion of a style of kingship, for what is the hunt if not a stylized form of war? Thus, whether the king shoots a tiger at Kittur or at Chattanahallli, his quaintly dated bow and arrow visually connect him to epic heroes and legendary battles.[96]

Through the invocation of tropes from the life of the epic hero Krishna, the king's royal body is turned into a sacred one in an interesting shuttling between god and king.[97] Vasudeva and Krishna are incorporated in his santanambuja, and the epic hero is also in the *vasanthotsava* scenes on the eastern wall of the northern room, cavorting with his *gopis* (milkmaids).[98]

Figure 21. *Krishnaraja Wodeyar III with his son in the Jambusavari on Vijayadashami (the tenth day of Dasara). Detail of mural on east wall of Rang Mahal. Jayachamarajendra Art Gallery, Mysore. Photograph by Clare Arni, 2006.*

Figure 22. Krishnaraja Wodeyar III celebrating the vasanthotsava by squirting color on the women in the palace. In the upper part of this mural (not visible here), Krishnaraja Wodeyar III is shown witnessing the festivities. Detail of mural in southern antechamber, Jayachamarajendra Art Gallery, Mysore. Photograph by Robert J. Del Bontà, 1990.

Figure 23. Krishnaraja Wodeyar III on his hunts in the forests of Mysore (clockwise from upper right): Kittur, Kottagala, Chamarajanagara, and Chattanahalli, with a central panel named Bangadi Shikari. Detail of mural on east wall of Rang Mahal. Jayachamarajendra Art Gallery, Mysore. Photograph by Clare Arni, 2006.

What is striking about the arrangement of these texts of power around the Rang Mahal are the stylistic resemblances to the murals of the Dariya Daulat, with which there are more than superficial continuities. In the rows of people of Mysore who are shown witnessing the procession and are framed architecturally, there are echoes of the eastern wall at Srirangapatna. The bands that separate these panels use the same limited palette as at Srirangapatna, mixing decidedly Persianate floral designs with Hindu decorations. The final, and perhaps the most flattering, indication of the extensive borrowings from the Dariya Daulat is the incorporation of the *babri* motif (stylized tiger stripes) in a band that divides two panels.

Yet the distinctions between the two sets of art practices are even more significant than their similarities. In their very mimicry, the Rang Mahal murals reveal a moment of transformed power relations and lay claim to a very different kind of legitimacy and power. At Dariya Daulat the mural is placed on the outer walls, entirely of a piece with the architecture in its grandeur. In the Jaganmohan palace the murals are interiorized and relegated to its topmost floor. If the Mysore triumph over the new British aspirants to power on the subcontinent dominates the walls of Dariya Daulat, the colonial masters are massively absent in the Jaganmohan Palace murals, which focus obsessively on contemporary and past Indian monarchs.[99]

Here, on full display, are the preoccupations of a "monarch" only too conscious of the precariousness of his claims to the throne, despite the "heir apparent" who is announced to the world by riding alongside Krishnaraja Wodeyar III. Here the threatened monarch obsessively emphasizes a royal and unbroken lineage. Contrary to the turbulence of political uncertainties in the eighteenth century, it is the very stability of "indirect rule" and the guaranteed boundedness of the Mysore territory that is on full display. Mysore was no longer a territory to be won or extended by war and instead relied entirely on the capricious policy of the British, yet no important "hat-wearer" is represented on these walls. By their very absence in these representations, the British have more than established their power because they, rather than the people of Mysore, are the ones addressed by this painting.

Yet there are inescapable ironies in these representations as well. Where Tipu Sultan was represented in Dariya Daulat at all, it was as a committed soldier, ever ready to march to war. Krishnaraja Wodeyar III was under no such compulsion, and in many relaxed portrayals he is shown as a man devoted to leisure. He is either among his forebears and descendents or among the women of his court. In this aestheticization of the very excesses that he was accused of when his kingdom was taken from him, the king appears to enjoy a new security of tenure, engulfing the viewer in his megalomania. Flanked, moreover, by the officials of his court, Krishnaraja Wodeyar III signals his willingness to be subordinated to a bureaucracy, a full flowering of which would occur in the period after 1881.

The absence of "perspective" that the British found so troubling in the murals of Srirangapatna was of no consequence in cultural productions such as these, which despite, or perhaps because of, their proliferation signaled that they were an unreliable index of power. The sheer brilliance of the rendering in these rooms and the themes that so obsessed the king are ironic testimony to the idea of kingship that the Maharaja might have cherished earlier, though "divine right" had decisively been replaced by a "contractual constitutionalism" when the god-king was made into a man-king.[100] By the end of the nineteenth century, there were more than ample signs that the only way in which the Mysore family could retain its hold on the kingdom was by strictly conforming to the role of a limited monarchy. The period of Chamarajendra Wodeyar's rule was singularly free of any need to establish a cultural practice that resisted the colonial modern. As early as the last quarter of the nineteenth century, it was clear that royalty could survive in India only in the highly institutionalized form that subordinated the cultural to the economic and political modernities ushered in by colonialism.

Announcing a New Monarchy

In the twentieth century, the iron frame of the Mysore bureaucracy had reduced the Maharaja of Mysore to a token presence, at a distance from the real seat of power in all senses of the term. Ideals of kingship had come a long way from the patronage of Brahmans, temples, and mathas, all of which had been institutionalized by governmental regulation, the first finding a firm foothold within the bureaucracy itself and the latter two anchored in the Muzrai Department. The constitutional if improving monarch shook free of the tropes that surrounded his namesake, the epic hero Krishna, and was more firmly associated with liberal governmental schemes and programs such as the building of boulevards, dams, and textile mills.

What purpose, then, might another set of murals, of the Dasara procession, have served in the already overdecorated Mysore palace in the twentieth century? The walls of the marriage pavilion on the ground floor of the palace, rebuilt in 1912, are covered with a series of twenty-six large-scale murals executed between 1934 and 1945 by palace artists such as Y. Nagaraju, Y. Subrahmanya Raju, K. Keshavaiah, S. N. Swamy, S. Shankara Raju, and S. R. Iyengar. The large oil paintings done on board and mounted on the walls feature the birthday and Dasara processions of Krishnaraja Wodeyar IV passing through the city of Mysore. Modeled on photographs, the paintings reflect the topography of Mysore accurately, though the privileged groups of participants and witnesses who are meticulously identified appear more stiffly posed. The artists have retained the cast shadows of horses, men, and elephants in a glorious tribute to the triumph of photographic realism. Both spectacle and spectator are thus honored on these walls because, unlike the murals at the Jaganmohan palace, where the anonymity of the spectator is amply asserted, panel after panel on the vast walls of the marriage pavilion at the Mysore palace decenter the king and his entourage, or at least render them equal to the bureaucrats, soldiers, members of the Mysore family, or British officials. The actual spectator or tourist enters the vast space of the marriage pavilion and journeys through Mysore city and its landmarks against the tide of the still procession on its walls, only to eventually reach the Maharaja and his entourage: he is distinguished from the spectators in the picture only by his caparisoned elephant and white horse (in the Dasara and birthday panels, respectively).

The complete subordination of the royal palace to the apparatuses of the state had by now been achieved, because the pageant was a representation of what the Dasara had become, a spectacle that was rapidly being emptied of its sacral contents. The king became a figure toward whom love and affection, even loyalty, might be shown, though he was largely drained of any "incorporating" role. Indeed, he and his royal family are distinguished from the detailed portraits of officials and spectators through attention less to their distinctive features than to their richly caparisoned mounts in the murals, whether horse or elephant.

There is another important change that is seen in the murals at Mysore. Although the Dariya Daulat murals at Srirangapatna relied entirely on pictorial devices to construct history and contemporary politics, with no use of text to identify the figures, not even in its parade of kings, the murals at the Jaganmohan palace left nothing to chance.[101] Not just the figures,

Figure 24. Krishnaraja Wodeyar IV, Kantirava Narasimharaja Wodeyar, and Jayachamarajendra Wodeyar on a caparisoned elephant, flanked by officials of the Mysore darbar and the administration, who are portrayed in greater detail. K. Keshavaiah, Dasara Procession, 1941; oil on board. Panel from the marriage pavilion, Mysore Palace, Mysore. Photograph by Janaki Nair.

such as kings, Nawabs, and durbarees, but state horses and cows, the specific parades and festivals, and a variety of chess moves are identified in Kannada. The concern with identity is taken to a new level in the paintings at Amba Vilas, where it is even more precise, and the fidelity to the "original" is flourished as proof of the painter's virtuosity. The spectator or tourist is aided throughout with elaborate keys to the paintings, much as are the photographs from which they are drawn. Although the contemporary viewers of the Srirangapatna mural needed no aid to help them reconstruct that historical event, both the Mysore murals at Jaganmohan Palace and those in Amba Vilas rely as much on textual confirmation as on the portrayal itself.[102]

Only one mural disturbs the ocular triumph of photographic realism. In his rendering of Ayudha Puja, which forms part of the Dasara panels (done in 1938), Y. Subrahmanya Raju sets the stage with mythical beings, be they *rishis* (sages) at prayer, an aging king (from the epics), the queen and her attendants, or the courtiers. A mounted goddess, Durga, to whom weapons are offered in worship, has acquired a certain tactility so that she appears to be no more of an icon separated from her supplicants than any other figure. To her right is a monkey brigade, and winged *gandharvas* (heavenly musicians) shower flower petals on her from above. This, too, is given the depth of field of the other panels, evoking as much admiration as awe, as do the paintings of the gods by Ravi Varma.

To the spectator or tourist at the Mysore palace, the panels form a small part of all that is truly awesome because the armory on display, the richly carved doors and ceilings, the chandeliers and stained glass, and the throne captivate the visitors. The representations of Krishnaraja Wodeyar IV invoke neither a Puranic genealogy nor the reflected glories of his contemporaries; there is no attempt to avoid acknowledging the power and prestige of the colonial Mysore bureaucracy, of which the Mysore palace is but an ornament. Yet the Mysore palace and its murals achieve, more successfully than the murals of the Jaganmohan palace, the depth of historical distance for which the nineteenth-century king had long yearned, not because of its artistic achievements alone but because of the opulence of its setting.

A Mysore Public

Nothing better underlines the fate of the elusive quest of Krishnaraja Wodeyar III for British recognition of a Mysore dynasty grounded in antiquity than the historic neglect of the paintings at Jaganmohan Palace.[103] By the turn of the century, modes of spectation and indeed taste had been so thoroughly reconstituted that the palace began to be increasingly associated with events such as the marriage of Krishnaraja Wodeyar IV in 1900. In 1915 the palace was turned into a picture gallery, and by 1924 James Cousins had persuaded the yuvaraja to start an Indian art gallery, for which acquisitions were quickly begun. In the first catalogue, he provided a potted and somewhat bizarre "history" of Indian art that attempted to show why Mysore was well poised to be the center of an Indian "renaissance." To Cousins, "The nineteenth century was a period of progressive degradation in Indian art particularly painting," saved by the "sudden" reappearance of the "true inheritors" of an Indian art tradition in the Bengal school.[104] Through the inclusion of several original-sized reproductions of paintings from Ajanta and Sittanavasal, samples of Bengal modern art, and works of K. Venkatappa he attempted to assist the visitor in constructing a continuous visual history. A handful of nineteenth-century Mysore works, largely portraits, were included in this collection, which was dominated by representatives of the Bengal school.

On the in situ artistic wealth of the palace, that is, the murals on the top floor of the building, Cousins remained studiously silent. The silence would continue, with the exception of an exhaustive inventory by the Archaeological Department in 1938, in nearly all tourist guides and gazetteers.[105] The art gallery was thus privileged in the public eye as a large though eccentric collection of paintings and objets d'art that lacked any curatorial perspective, over the original designs of the palace itself.

As we know, by the time Cousins began his promotion of an Indian renaissance style, the battle over modern taste had already been won by the academic realism of Ravi Varma in the main Mysore palace. With the transfer of the nine Puranic paintings to the Jayachamarajendra Art Gallery, as it is now called, the collection began to exert a new and powerful spell on the Mysore public. Up to the present day, neither the portraits done in the Mysore "traditional" style nor the upper rooms attract the attention of most visitors. The official postcards, bowing to popular demand, largely feature the Ravi Varma paintings and thereby extend the circulation of those images. The murals on the top floor and the large numbers of nineteenth-century Mysore-style paintings have been excluded from this form of circulation and denied the chance of renewing public taste.

Figure 25. The shift from tracing ancestors to mapping descendants: Krishnaraja Wodeyar III looks down from an oil portrait in the background on three generations of his descendants, Chamaraja Wodeyar X, Krishnaraja Wodeyar IV, Yuvaraja Narasimharaja Wodeyar, and Jayachamarajendra Wodeyar. Y. Nagaraju, Mysore Royal Family, *1926; oil on board; 152.4 x 289.6 cm. Mysore Palace, Mysore. Photograph by Janaki Nair.*

It was in any case a form of realism that attained for the Wodeyar family an unbroken and unchallenged genealogy that all their strivings of the nineteenth century had not achieved. Yet if oil paintings based on photographs became part of the artistic commonsense, the photographic style could be mimicked by the painting with interesting effects for the portrayal of stability, legitimacy, and permanence. A remarkable oil painting by the European-trained artist Y. Nagaraju, which was done in 1926, is a confident assertion of Wodeyar dynastic continuity, in which the troubled "reign" of Krishnaraja Wodeyar III is an anchoring memory for the three generations that follow. It posthumously brings together Chamarajendra Wodeyar, once more in his more relaxed paternal mode, with his two sons, Krishnaraja Wodeyar and Kantirava Narasimharaja Wodeyar, as well as the young prince, Jayachamarajendra Wodeyar.

There is a reminder of the man who enabled this little tableau in the form of a framed picture on the wall, content that his tortuous negotiations with the British had yielded fruit in the undisturbed continuity of his line over what he saw as his patrimony. Indeed, as Etienne Balibar reminds us about modern nationalized families, a concern about common *descendents* rather than common *antecedents* dominates this portrait, as the artist seamlessly blended genealogy into a visual chronotope, condensing the layeredness of time through the use of realism's devices.[106]

Conclusion

Only by separating the artistic productions of a princely state under colonial rule from the political and economic conditions under which the state was established does it become possible for art historians to celebrate Mysore's aesthetic achievements. I have argued here that the large and manifold artistic productions of the 150-year period of princely Mysore's existence can be seen as the direct expression of neither political power nor its absence. Instead it should be read as a relatively autonomous sphere for the practice of a new power, shifting and aligning in consonance with the demands that were made by the paramount colonial power on the one hand and, on the other, in response to developing popular tastes and modes of spectation that were being nurtured in other spheres of life. Far from being a homogenous period in which one identifiable form of princely power was exercised, there were several identifiable stages through which the practice of power in Mysore actually passed.

CHAPTER 3

Srirangapatna: Capital City to a Topography of Conquest

T HE DECLINE OF TIPU SULTAN'S SRIRANGAPATNA brought forth the following lament from the poet John Leyden:

How quickly fled our Sultan's state!
How soon his pomp has passed away!
How swiftly sped Seringa's fate
From wealth and power to dire decay![1]

How quickly indeed had Srirangapatna, the capital of the Mysore rulers for nearly two hundred years, become a squalid, "melancholy" backwater by the end of the nineteenth century. The remains of the fort at Srirangapatna, the capital of the Mysore region until 1799, are in stark contrast to the well-kept fort walls that enclose the palace complex at Mysore city. The current state of these two forts could be a useful starting point for the ways in which these two spaces have been reinscribed in the nineteenth and twentieth centuries: the former, a ruined but still powerful reminder of a bygone military power, "girt by the Cavery's holy stream / By circling walls in triple row," the latter a nineteenth-century creation that fulfilled no military purpose but served to mark Mysore as a royal city.[2] Srirangapatna's relatively quiet existence as a space of monuments, tombs, and temples is strikingly different from that of the bustling though graciously laid out and richly embellished city of Mysore.

How reliable as an index of power are princely monumental and artistic legacies? Srirangapatna and Mysore pose the question sharply, because the current bleakness of the former and the very profusion and ostentation of the latter speak of the very different ways in which the practice of power transformed these spaces in the nineteenth and twentieth centuries. Tipu's dominions had been studded with forts, which were the more important monumental legacies of his time compared to the modest palaces at Srirangapatna and Bangalore. In contrast, once he was relieved of the labors of expanding or defending the borders of his province, fort-building was hardly a priority of the restored Mysore monarch; yet the fort of Mysore city was reconstructed and remodeled as a central node of a resignified royal power in a process that continued well into the twentieth century.

The new symbolic realms that were produced at both Srirangapatna and Mysore, one entombing a formidable power and the other refurbishing a depleted royalty, had long-term ideological effects among subject populations. Monumental legacies of different princely regimes and their preservation or destruction were claims to authority and legitimacy that were continuously being fashioned in response to changing political contexts and sometimes conflicting notions of power, while simultaneously shaping the tastes and loyalties of an emerging modern public. The destinies of the two cities of Srirangapatna and Mysore, separated by no more than fifteen miles, were intertwined through the nineteenth and twentieth centuries because they bore the burdens, respectively, of memorializing Tipu's defeat and proclaiming Wodeyar authority, with enduring consequences for their contemporary status as historical sites. In this chapter and the next I trace the trajectories of these sites through the nineteenth and twentieth centuries.

The Sultan Is Dead! Long Live the King!

In his 1930s reassessment of the legacy of Haidar Ali and Tipu Sultan for the history of Mysore, the biographer Mahmud Khan Mahmud Banglori reminded the reader: "Tipu Sultan is supposed to be revengeful, but history is witness to how Kitchener took out the bones of Mehdi Sudani from his grave and set them afire. Bani Abbas destroyed the graves of Ummayids. But there is not a single example of such madness in the history of Sultanat-i-Khudadad."[3] This is an unusual comparison of the relative levels of civility of victors in war, but sacralizing and desecrating graves and mausoleums were both tactics of power that were practiced by a wide range of regimes. Perhaps Banglori was contesting the long-held pride of the British in the civility they had shown their slain foe, Tipu Sultan. In their reinstatement of the Wodeyars, moreover, it became clear that there was no decapitation of kingship or princely power, either in colonial political theory or in practice; there was only the resignification and reinstatement of a monarchical government as a dependent under overarching colonial rule.

The British victors allowed the dead hero to be buried alongside his father at Srirangapatna in 1799 while casting the shadow of death more powerfully over the city by draining it of all life. What, then, does one make of the victors who memorialized the capital of an enemy, Srirangapatna, as a space wracked by death? What lessons about power and authority may be read from the simultaneous creation of the new capital, Mysore, in the image of a remembered sovereignty, and how does the arrangement and interpretation of these artifacts or monuments continue to animate contemporary historical accounts and memories? Assessments of Tipu Sultan's reign, for instance, have been largely divided between those who echo the vilifications of his British counterparts and those who claim him as a national modern hero.[4] This ambiguity has persisted well into the present day, with several calls being made in the name of Kannada linguistic or Hindu nationalism to exclude him from institutionalized memories, as in the subdued bicentenary commemoration at Srirangapatna in 1999 or in the textbook controversies of 2005.[5]

No such controversy or critical assessment surrounds the memory of the Wodeyars in the nineteenth and twentieth centuries: even long after the princely state ceased to exist, this memory has translated into genuine warmth and affection for the Mysore royal family.[6] In important ways, the ambiguous responses to the legacy of Tipu Sultan and the cherished memories of the Wodeyars were rooted in the crucial days between May 4, 1799, and June of that same year. The defeat and death of Tipu Sultan at the hands of British forces were followed by the reinvention of Wodeyar rule in Mysore, which came to represent a unique moment in modern subcontinental history, because in no other place that came under British control did a Hindu dynasty, and one whose memory had been dimmed in the intervening forty years, take the place of a Muslim one.[7] No other moment exemplifies the extent to which the princes of India were a creation of British policy than the 1799 creation of the kingdom of Mysore.[8]

The Haidar–Tipu period has been subordinated in the annals of the Mysore royal family (*Mysore Samsthanada Prabhugalu: Srimanmaharajara Vamshavali*), which were commissioned by Krishnaraja Wodeyar III (1864); revised by his successor, Chamrajendra Wodeyar (as *Vamsaratnakara*); and finally published in two volumes in 1916 and 1922. The book provides a strictly genealogical account of the history of Mysore, presenting a roll call of Wodeyar kings from the mythical ancestors of Yadu Raya to Krishnaraja Wodeyar III. Yet the power of the Mysore Wodeyars had already been seriously challenged in the time of "Dalavai Rule" under Dalavai Devarajaiah and Sarvadhikari Nanjarajaiah (1734–59), even before Haidar Ali's seizure of power.[9] Indeed, as Banglori reminds us, "only through usurpation can a new dynasty be created [even in modern times]."[10] Instead of terminating this fading memory of the Wodeyars, the British victors in 1799 revived their fortunes and retrieved them from relative obscurity to resume the throne of Mysore at the erstwhile capital, a more precipitous loss of power than under Tipu Sultan. Thereafter, the narration of an unbroken Wodeyar lineage became possible, and the rise of the Mysore dynasty, "like a phoenix," from the ashes of 1799 was taken as a sign of its remarkable durability.

Yet the claim of continuity was established only after a significant spatial break was staged and fostered in the days following the successful siege of Srirangapatna. On June 30, 1799, more than a month after the defeat and death of Tipu Sultan, the five-year-old Krishnaraja Wodeyar III was "sworn in" as the Raja of Mysore. The British felt compelled to distance themselves from the legacy of the defeated Muslim "usurper" by installing the young Raja not at Srirangapatna, where Raja Wodeyar had first staked his claim to a dynasty in 1610, but at Mysore, the place forsaken by that first dynast, which in the Haidar-Tipu period had dimmed in significance.[11] "It would be cruel as well as improper" to crown the prince at Srirangapatna, Arthur Wellesley said, "because if we do, we must fix him in Tippu's Palace, along with Tippu's women."[12] The young king was led to a throne placed beneath a makeshift *pandal* (a large tent) by Lieutenant General Harris and Meer Allum, representing the Hyderabad Nizam.[13] The fabled ivory *musnad* (throne) that the young scion ascended had been recovered from where it had been abandoned in Srirangapatna, thus creating a symbolic link with the time before 1796 when the Wodeyars had been stripped of even their notional powers by Tipu Sultan. The choice of Mysore, ill suited as a royal capital because it lacked even a single decent habitation where the throne could be placed, heralded a long process of inventing a new monarchy subordinated to British colonial purposes.

The test of "antiquity" was the basis on which Governor-General Wellesley decided between Tipu's descendents and the forgotten Wodeyar dynasty as the power to be installed in a reterritorialized Mysore. The symbolic transfer of power placed a revived dynasty, now rendered "ancient" compared with the Mahommedan usurpers, on the throne at Old Mysore while the British retained their hold on the more important seat of power. Srirangapatna was occupied by East India Company forces under the leadership of Arthur Wellesley and the new Resident, Barry Close.[14]

In this chapter I trace the transformation of Srirangapatna, a city of considerable antiquity, from a vibrant capital city in the eighteenth century into a topography of conquest in the nineteenth century through the systematic reinscription of the site from the perspective of the British victors of the historic siege of May 4, 1799. Mysore state, as the beneficiary of colonial rule, willingly participated in such a reinscription. Nor has this legacy been entirely reversed in the postcolonial period. As a result, although today the spotlight is certainly on Tipu, he is still seen from the standpoint of the victors.

Srirangapatna and the Specific Memory of Defeat

As I noted earlier, the sacred maps in the chitramantapa at the Prasanna Venkatramanaswamy temple (c. 1836) include a map of the island of Srirangapatna in all its topographical detail, combining within the pictorial space both an aerial perspective and building elevations (see Figure 17). True, the map accords central space to the two main temples of Sri Ranganatha (the core of which was built circa A.D. 894) and Narsimhaswamy (built in the mid-eighteenth century); the third important temple, to Gangadharaswamy, is not shown as part of this Srivaishnavite sacred landscape. Most compelling are four (not three) layers of fortification that enclose, in addition to the two temples, the Jumme Masjid of Tipu Sultan (built in 1787); the Mysore Wodeyars' palace (a simple two-storied building with a *kalyani,* or pond, in front of it); and the Lal Bagh palace. Outside the fort walls lie the Gumbaz, the cenotaph to Colonel Baillie, and the town of Ganjam. The Dariya Daulat is conspicuous by its absence, but the major coordinates of the island are otherwise remarkably accurate.

This representation is unusual because it omits neither the memorials of the British nor the precolonial monuments that mark the multiple pasts of the island capital. It is equally unusual because it recovers quite another optic of the island from the ones that were assiduously cultivated throughout the nineteenth century. Srirangapatna was sacralized in quite a different way by the British victors, as the site on which the most important battle for control of the Indian subcontinent had been won. "The Fort of Seringapatam, the Gift of God, 28th Sikhyada H, 1213": so read the inscription in Persian below the representation of the storming and breach of the fort displayed on the British medal struck in memory of May 4, 1799; the reverse showed the British lion mauling the Mysore tiger, this time under a banner inscribed in Arabic "assud ulla il ghaulib" (the conquering lion of god), symbolizing a victorious crusade.[15] By the end of the nineteenth century, Srirangapatna would become a necessary place of pilgrimage for many British travelers who wished to retrace the historic siege of the fort once thought to be impregnable. In some senses, the whiff of grapeshot and the thunder of cannons were not diminished by the intervening decades because the territory was haunted by those memories.

There was an eagerness to the way in which the Mysore government participated in such memorializing, on the one hand by adding to the list of memorials of the victors and on the other by dismantling the few remains of Tipu's fort palace. By this time, Srirangapatna was in any case unrecognizable in terms of the way it had been described by many visitors from the end of the eighteenth century.

Figure 26. N.W. View of Seringapatam, *colored aquatint with etching by John William Edy after Robert Hyde Colebrooke. From Robert Hyde Colebrooke,* Twelve Views of Places in the Kingdom of Mysore. *Drawn on the spot by Colebrooke; engraved by J. W. Edy. Robert J. Del Bontà Collection, E1172. Photograph by Robert J. Del Bontà.*

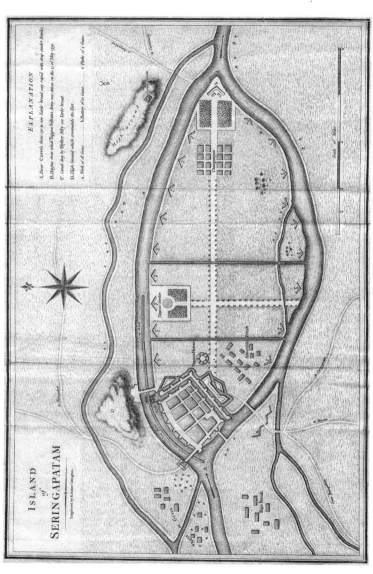

Figure 27. A first attempt at "mapping" the embattled island of Srirangapatna in 1792, after the end of the Third Mysore War. The map, intended for military purposes, reconstructs the main structures on the island (Tipu's residence, the fort, and Shahar Ganjam); the river Cauvery (A); the heights from which Tipu's army was driven in 1791 (B); the canal dug by Haider Ali (C); and the high ground from which an attack on the island could be launched (D). Courtesy of the Clare Arni Collection.

The Shahar Ganjam, which occupied the area between the fort and the Lalbagh, was "an extensive suburb or town . . . full of wealthy industrious inhabitants" and made the insulated capital of Tipu "the richest, most convenient and beautiful spot possessed in the present age by any native prince in India," to use words from Major Dirom's description of Srirangapatna in 1792.[16] Writing soon after the British triumph in 1799, Governor-General Wellesley noted that "Seringapatam" was the concentrated site of many important institutions in Tipu's Mysore: "His capital was not only the object of his pride, but the center of his power; it was the strongest fortification, the principal granary of his army, his only arsenal, and the repository of his treasure and the prison of the legitimate claimant of his throne as well as of the families of all his great chieftains."[17] The very name Srirangapatna came to denote the awesome might of the Mysore kingdom among the other powers of late eighteenth-century southern India.[18]

The loot and plunder of the capital by the victors in the aftermath of the defeat was followed by the depletion of its administrative and symbolic functions, which ensured the swift decline of the preeminent city of the Mysore region into a miasmic backwater. In the words of Arthur Wellesley, in charge of the Mysore command after the victory, to his brother, the Earl of Mornington, Richard Wellesley:

> Nothing . . . can have exceeded what was done on the night of the 4th [of May 1799]. Scarcely a house in the town was left unplundered, and I understand that in the camp, jewels of the greatest value, bars of gold etc, have been offered for sale by our soldiers, sepoys and followers. I came in to take the command on the morning of the 5th and by the greatest exertion, by hanging, flogging, etc, in the course of that day I restored order among the troops, and I hope to have gained the confidence of the people.[19]

The total value of the loot, which consisted of coins, jewels, richly worked cloth, furniture, carpets, and so on, amounted to about £1,600,000 and was distributed in steep grades to the subalterns and colonels alike.[20] Wellesley was only too aware of the hostility of the local population to the new British occupants, and he intervened to prevent the auctioning of Tipu's extensive wardrobe, which, if bought as relics by the "discontented Moormen of this place," he anticipated, would be disgraceful and unpleasant.[21] He was not mistaken: just seven years later, the standard of

Tipu's army would be flown atop the Vellore Fort in ill-fated defiance of the new colonial masters.[22]

The political importance of Srirangapatna in the Mysore imagination was not lost on Arthur Wellesley, who, as Kate Brittlebank demonstrates, became the "white raja" of Srirangapatna through his six-year association with the island capital.[23] Unlike the restored Raja, Wellesley occupied the Dariya Daulat itself, supervising the repair of the place, having received instructions from his brother, Governor-General Wellesley, to "commence the repair or improvement of the fortifications and to proceed in clearing the place, and making it strictly a military station," measures that were of "essential importance" to the security of the victory.[24] British troops were stationed in Srirangapatna until it was abandoned in favor of the more salubrious environs of Bangalore in 1809.[25] Four years before this, a new Residency had been constructed at Mysore, and the requisite arrangements were made for the "permanent establishment of all the public departments of the Raja's Government" there in order to consolidate governmental functions, which until then had been divided between the two cities.[26] By the end of the first decade of the nineteenth century, Srirangapatna was largely abandoned by both the British civil and military administrations, leaving only a small regiment stationed there.

The brief British occupation did little to offset the decline of the erstwhile capital. Little wonder that Francis Buchanan said in 1801: "The town of Seringapatam is very poor. The streets are narrower and more confused than in any place that I have seen since leaving Bengal."[27] The effects of conquest on the city were almost instantaneous, with the population dropping from at least 150,000 to about 32,000 within a year after the defeat.[28] The city was practically deserted in 1837, and a small population of 7,000 was left in Commissioner Lewin Bowring's time, rising to a mere 12,560 in 1891.[29] The island of Srirangapatna belonged to the British and was rented to the Raja of Mysore (in return for company use of the Bangalore fort) for a sum of Rs 50,000: by 1868, its modest income of Rs 25,155 meant that the Mysore palace sustained heavy losses in retaining this piece of real estate.[30] Bowring suggested in 1871 that the island be traded for Bangalore, over which the Raja had sovereignty, because Srirangapatna had no political, religious, or other value to the British. On the other hand, he said that "Seringapatam . . . would be specially important to the Raja as being the seat of his ancestors, and invested with a sacred character, so that a mere money payment may not represent its value accurately."[31] "Dreariness and desolation are now the characteristics of the place," the *Mysore Gazetteer* of 1869 declared, adding, "It would be hard to find a spot on which the tide of history had wrought so great a change in so short a time (only 70 years) as to have converted the proud capital of an empire and the seat of a sumptuous court into a straggling and pestilential village."[32] In 1881, under the Instrument of Transfer to Chamarajendra Wodeyar, British sovereignty over the island ceased and it was joined to the territories of the Maharaja.[33]

Silencing the Past

The steady depletion of the city was accompanied by attempts at recasting its topography through demolition and building. It is interesting to note that at this time the British interest in Mysore's historic monuments was quite fickle. Of the principal monuments that dated from Tipu's time, there were some that had survived the last siege. The palace of the Mysore Wodeyars was partly destroyed in 1800 and the materials used in the construction of another palace at Mysore.[34] By 1869, all that remained were "a few mud walls and a sunken granary."[35] Within the fort was the principal palace (or Lal Mahal) of Tipu Sultan. In the words of Francis Buchanan, who was unsparing in his criticism of what he found at Srirangapatna:

> The palace of the Sultan at Seringapatam is a very large building, surrounded by a massy and lofty wall of stone and mud, and outwardly is of a very mean appearance. There were in it, however, some handsome apartments, which have been converted into barracks, but the troops are very ill lodged from the want of ventilation common in all native buildings. The private apartments of Tippoo formed a square, in one side of which were the rooms that he himself used. The other three sides of the square were occupied by warehouses, in which he had deposited a vast variety of goods, for he acted not only as a prince but as a merchant.[36]

Lord Valentia's description of the audience hall at the Lal Mahal was more appreciative; it was a very handsome room, about seventy feet wide in front and forty feet deep:

> The walls are painted red with a gilt trellis work running over it, formed by the tiger's scratch (babri), the favourite ornament of Tipu. Sentences from the Koran in letters of gold on a red ground,

each about a foot high, run around the room as a cornice. Each pillar is a single piece of wood, painted red and highly varnished. They have bases of black marble. The shape is fantastic, bulging much towards the base and again narrowing.[37]

Such decoration was distinctly different from the lavish use of figures at Dariya Daulat and may reflect the new ideal of (more sternly Islamic) kingship to which Tipu aspired.

The structure, though ruined, was rebuilt and used as "barracks, store rooms and manufactories for a period of 30 years" until they came into the possession of the Maharaja.[38] When the acting Superintendent of Ashtagram sought possession of the gun carriage in 1841 for a sandal store, the Maharaja was unwilling to surrender what was important "both as private property and on account of their former celebrity,"[39] because "it was connected to the Palace of the Late Tippoo Sultan." In any case, he had given up Tipu's palace in Bangalore in exchange.[40]

Commissioner Mark Cubbon seized the opportunity to exert his authority over the Maharaja because the real battle was over the control of public buildings in Srirangapatna and Mysore, and he decided to prevent further demolition.[41] In September 1841, Captain Montgomery reported that "the fine wooden pillars which supported the terraced roofs of a large part of Tippoo's zenana have been removed and replaced with mere sticks" and that the modern buildings "were completely destroyed, with doors, windows and window frames wrenched out for disposal."[42] Cubbon ordered the sale of the materials for public purposes, now justifiably suggesting that all the buildings be pulled down because they were "beyond profitable repair." He also suggested that all public buildings on the island be brought under the control of the Commissioner in the interests of preservation.[43] Without any delay, the palace was taken over and the buildings torn down.[44] By 1869, only a fragment remained of what had been converted into a sandalwood *koti* (warehouse).[45]

At the extreme east end of the island was the Lal Bagh palace, which Buchanan said "possesses a considerable degree of elegance, and is the handsomest native building that I have ever seen."[46] Robert Home had said in 1792 that the cypress garden of Lal Bagh "abounded with fruit trees, flowers and vegetables of every kind. But the axe of the enemy soon despoiled it of its beauties, and those trees which once administered to the pleasures of the master were compelled to furnish materials for the reduction of his capital."[47] Mark Wilks added that "the intermediate time between the 7th and 16th (of February 1792) [had] been industriously employed in the formation of materials for the siege, by the reluctant, but indispensable ruin of the extensive and beautiful garden of the Lall Baugh."[48] According to another eyewitness account of the damage done to the eastern end of the island by the company troops:

> The greatest part of this [formerly large and handsome town] was destroyed before the approach of the Confederate Armies, in order to make room for batteries to defend the island, one portion of it only being suffered to remain, of about half a mile square, for the accommodation of the merchants and the convenience of the troops. This is called the pettah [emporium or market town] of Shahir Ganjam.[49]

Home spoke of what remained of Shahar Ganjam in 1792: "This pettah of modern structure built in the centre of the island, is about half a mile square. The streets, regularly crossing each other, are all wide, shaded on each side by trees, and full of good houses and a strong wall surrounds it."[50]

The Lal Bagh palace was occupied by the first British Resident, Barry Close, before the Residency was constructed in Mysore in 1805. In that year, the Governor-General himself prohibited its demolition, and it was then transferred to local authorities.[51] Such respect for the residence of Tipu did not last, and it is a sign of the confidence with which the British now ruled India that Governor Lushington of Madras wrote on February 28, 1829, to the superintendent of the gun factory at Srirangapatna ordering the palace to be pulled down carefully "in such a manner as to render available materials for a small church" in the Nilgiris. Nearly all the wooden materials used in building St. Stephan's Church at Ootacamund, which was readied for worship by 1830, including several teak pillars and the main door of the palace, were taken from Srirangapatna, while some salvaged timber was used to build the church's mission school.[52]

The only extant palace of Tipu Sultan is thus the Dariya Daulat, set on the banks of the Cauvery between the fort and the Shahar Ganjam. As we have seen, its preservation was driven largely by growing British concerns about memorializing the victory that "raised the reputation of the British arms in India . . . seldom approached in any part of the world."[53]

It is sobering to think that had Arthur Wellesley not achieved the honor of defeating Napoleon at Waterloo and become the duke of Wellington, Dariya Daulat may well have gone the way of Tipu's other palaces. The

Palace in Daryud Daulat Baugh-, Seringapatam

Figure 28. Dariya Daulat, c. 1900, before the protective screens were installed. Postcard. Courtesy of the Clare Arni Collection.

murals were refurbished during Wellesley's occupation of the palace. It was once more in his memory that Lord Dalhousie issued the famous minute of 1854 calling for the palace's renovation after a long period of neglect. A sum of £5,000 was spent on this renovation.[54] An "illuminated copy of the minute in which he [Dalhousie] recorded these orders" was thereafter hung among the many artifacts on display to remind visitors that, although the physical structure and its decorations may have been authorized by Tipu Sultan, it was his "successor" who was being commemorated. Dariya Daulat had been preserved because it "most immediately and most vividly brings before us of this day the memory of that great man, with the early period of whose glorious career the East India Company must ever be proud to connect the history of its rule."[55] Thereafter, the memories of the two famous occupants were intertwined and museumized as a "form of practical memory" even by the Indian state.[56] Dariya Daulat was fully repainted in 1886–87, for Rs 11,417; further improvements were made before the viceroy's visit in 1920.[57]

Who would remind the paean writers of the time that not only had the two Wellesley brothers, Arthur and Henry, been included as part of the first Mysore Commission by their Governor-General brother, Richard, the Earl of Mornington, but that Arthur Wellesley had taken a smaller part in the storming of Srirangapatna and was inferior in rank to General Baird, whom he superseded?[58] Moreover, Srirangapatna was also the place where "the great Duke of Wellington lost his force, and lost himself and lost heart and sustained his one defeat."[59] Given the task of reclaiming Sultanpet Tope in April 1799, Wellesley's regiment was severely attacked and retreated in disorder, with twelve of his men captured. Colonel Wellesley's honor was recouped only the next day, when he went out and recovered the site.[60] These events were not allowed to color the post-Waterloo recuperation of the great soldier's early training ground. By the third decade of the twentieth century, the site of Tipu's new town, Sultanpet, was a neglected spot, remembered if at all only as a step toward an eventual British triumph.

The fort of Srirangapatna retained its strategic importance for a while, but a proposal in 1801 to demolish the fort was opposed by Arthur Wellesley as too hasty a political move because the fort was still considered the "seat of power" by the inhabitants. Even when the city was abandoned as a military station a few years later, the fortifications were retained, though as an aide-mémoire. Writing in the latter half of the nineteenth century, Malleson spelled out the reasons for retaining the fort in its unrepaired state:

[Because] the breach has remained unrepaired, the position of the besieging army can still easily be traced, and the traveler, viewing the difficulties so daringly conquered, can understand, as by a touch of the magician's wand, how it was that the great soldier, who made his first successful debut as a stormer at the head of the supports at Seringapatam, was able subsequently to make of the materials similar to those he then commanded, an army which beat the soldiers of Napolean, and of which he could proudly affirm, that with it "he could go anywhere and do anything." If that result was the goal of the great military career of the Duke of Wellington, the real starting point was Seringapatam.[61]

Moreover, as Lewin Bowring pointed out, "As the breach that was made is still visible and the walls are for the most part intact, a lively and accurate idea may be formed of the state of things when the memorable assault took place."[62] As early as 1815, several of the muskets and bayonets from the siege of Srirangapatna were used in decorating the guardrail of St. George's Church cemetery in Madras, in a lasting if displaced memorial to that victory.[63]

Still, suitable alterations had to be made to prevent too active an effect on the imagination: if the island was indeed sold to the Maharaja in exchange for the Bangalore fort, Bowring said, "it would be necessary to stipulate against the fortress being further strengthened" because it still posed a threat to British power if seized by a rebel force. He thus recommended that the British break down the curtains of walls at intervals of one hundred yards.[64] He may have remembered that as early as 1804 a group of *paleyagaras* (warrior chieftains) had attempted to take the fort.[65] In 1806, fearing a Vellore-style mutiny, Wellesley had the inner fortification razed to the ground and a row of tamarind trees planted there instead. This did not prevent an unanticipated mutiny in 1809, when Colonel Bell, commandant of the garrison, took forcible possession of the treasury following the decision of the governor of Madras, George Barlow, to get all officers to sign a test of allegiance. Bell's rebellion was joined by two battalions of British Native Infantry who marched under the command of

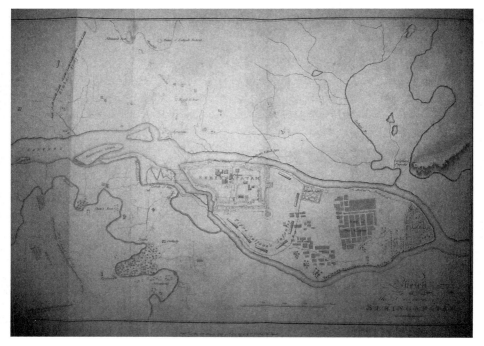

Figure 29. Srirangapatna, early 1800s: a fuller, more accurate topography of the conquered island capital. Courtesy of the Clare Arni Collection.

Colonel Macintosh from Chitradurga, emboldening Bell to threaten to blow up all the bridges over the Cauvery. The protest ended only when, on learning that officers all over the country had accepted the new test, all the mutineers were taken prisoner under the orders of the British Resident, Arthur Cole.[66]

The structures of Srirangapatna that were associated with Haidar and Tipu and their historic reigns were thus refashioned in a number of different ways: by demolition (the fate of two of the three palaces), by absorption into a narrative of victory that was staged elsewhere (as in the reflected glory of Waterloo that lit up Dariya Daulat), or by the reinscription of the topography of the island as a memorial to the heroic dead.

Sacralizing the Dead

Long after the British retreat from the island capital, the site was inscribed only by those who wished to memorialize the dead of 1799. Sibbalds' Redoubt marked the place at the foot of Karighat Hill approaching Srirangapatna where a small regiment had fallen in 1792 to the defenders of the capital. Similarly, the obelisk to the memory of the officers of the Seventy-Seventh and Twelfth regiments who had died in the siege was planted southeast of the fort but was largely neglected.[67] Bowring lamented in 1871 that "little attention was paid to the monuments of the brave men who fell on our side, nor are any of them remarkable." On the other hand, the mausoleum, or Gumbaz, had been preserved, he remarked, even though it contained the remains of "our implacable foe": it was, further, "a proof of the toleration of the British government that the Mussalmans of Seringapatam were permitted to place within Tippu's tomb a tablet which records in glowing and fanatical verses the death of the zealot."[68]

In many ways, granting a symbolic presence to the British dead of the Mysore wars was a way of visually compensating for the quiet grace of the monument on the island that was allowed to stand as a memorial to the "permanence" of the British victory. The Gumbaz was built in 1784 by Tipu, and until 1799 it contained the graves of Haidar Ali and his favored consort, Fakrunissa Seydani Begum. Tipu was buried at the same site with the full military honors that were accorded him by the triumphant British following their victory of May 4, 1799. The mausoleum was set within an elegant garden, a simple square structure surmounted by a dome, with a minaret at each of its edges. Most striking in this relatively unostentatious

Moslem erected over the remains of Tippoo Seringapatam.

Figure 30. Tourist images of the much-visited Gumbaz or mausoleum of Haider Ali and Tipu Sultan at Srirangaptna; the structure is here called a "moslem." Postcard, c. 1900. Courtesy of the Clare Arni Collection.

structure were the pillars of black polished hornblende on the corridor that surrounded the beautiful "house of sleep" of both the Mysore rulers. The ivory-inlaid doors of the Gumbaz were refurbished during Dalhousie's visit to Srirangapatna in 1854.[69]

The Gumbaz and its surroundings also provided the setting for playing out a politics of equivalence. The 1780 "Baillie disaster" of the Battle for Polilur was memorialized in the guidebooks as a heroic and little-understood moment, for "there is nothing finer or more terrible than Baillie's resistance to the overwhelming army which surrounded him" at the time.[70] His death in captivity in 1792 was an ignominy that was finally undone in 1816, when his nephew, Lieutenant Colonel John Baillie, Resident of the Lucknow court, commissioned a memorial. In a posthumous reclamation of honor, his memorial was placed directly before the

Gumbaz.[71] Similarly, the whitewashed obelisk of Colonel Grimstone of the Thirty-Fourth Regiment, who had been in charge of the jail in 1799, was a curious construction, surrounded by a wall where the inscription was at such an elevation that it could be read only by climbing a few steps. "Tradition has it," said Edmund Bull, "that having used undue severities in the execution of his duties, the worthy colonel died suddenly and the wall was erected to prevent his grave from being defiled."[72]

Along with the garrison cemetery, established in 1800 and containing graves of Europeans who died as late as 1867, the tombs large and small even eclipsed the island's ongoing association with the funerary rites of Hindus and its hoary Vaishnavite tradition.[73] By the 1870s, Srirangapatna had become a place for British "pilgrims" to visit, particularly soldiers who were stationed in Bangalore, for whom the likes of G. B. Malleson wrote their potted histories. In Malleson's view, Srirangapatna was a synecdoche for Indian history: "Its history presents a nearly accurate type of the history of Hindustan. Originally Hindu, threatened then by the Mohammedans, then by the Marathas, converted then into the Mohammedan capital of southern India, the strong fortress finally succumbed to the power which had subdued all three."[74] The introduction of the railway in the late nineteenth century increased the population and encouraged more British visitors. In 1907, Reverend E. W. Thompson lent his talents to the production of a short history of the siege, which was republished in 1923 with a guide to the visitor that began as follows:

> The visitor to Seringapatam whether arriving by road or rail, can scarcely do better than proceed direct to the Breach at the North West angle of the fort. Thence let him walk along the Northern rampart following in the track of the column that was opposed by the Sultaun himself. On the way, the Temple, the Delhi Gateway, the so called Dungeons and the Water Gate should be visited. A fine bird's eye view of the Fort and the surrounding country may be had by climbing the minaret of the grand Mosque. The heat of the day may be passed most pleasantly in the Darya Daulat Palace where breakfast and tea can be served. The tomb of Haidar Ali and Tippu Sultan may be visited in the cool of the afternoon, while those who have a taste for the pleasure of melancholy cannot find a better time for viewing Scott's Bungalow, and the Garrison cemetery than when the shades of evening are about to fall.[75]

Sally Port where Tippoo fell Seringapatam.

Figure 31. Officers posing in front of the sally port at Srirangapatna symbolically stage its "reconquest." Postcard, c. 1900, showing the place where Tipu Sultan was killed in 1799. Courtesy of the Clare Arni Collection.

Until 1903, the fort walls at the northwest edge of the island and the breach were left in their original battered condition.[76] In that year Lord Curzon suggested that the Government of Mysore put up a parapet across the breach and set up an obelisk in memory of the British assault and the British officers who died in the siege. A grateful Mysore government had no difficulty in honoring this request: as Dewan M. Kantaraj Urs would later comment: "The restoration of Mysore to His Highness the Maharaja Sri Krishna Raja Wodeyar III in 1799 is an event of great significance in Mysore history redounding greatly to the credit of the British nation. . . . As a centenary memorial of this great event the Government of Mysore raised in 1899 a monument on the south western angle of the fort in Seringapatam."[77] It is likely that the earlier memorial gave way to the obelisk of polished stone.[78] Set up in 1907, the slabs of the obelisk were inscribed with the names of British officers who fell and the Indian and British units that fought in the siege, even though "there is nothing ornate about the memorial."[79]

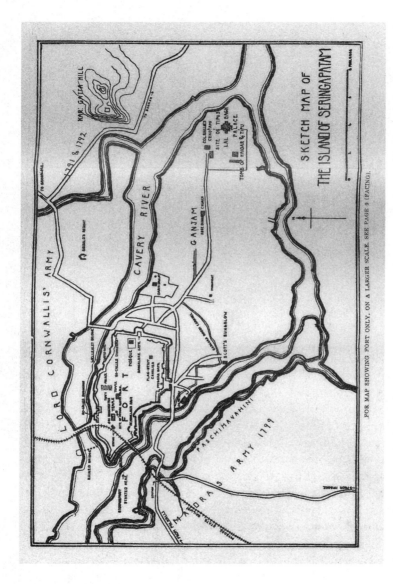

Figure 32. *The positions taken by British troops on May 4, 1799, are clearly marked for the benefit of twentieth-century tourists on this map of Srirangapatna.* E. W. Thompson, Last Siege of Seringapatam, 1923; reprinted in Asian Educational Services, 1990.

The reduction of this fortified island capital to a topography of conquest may be judged by the detailed entries and descriptions of the monuments of Srirangapatna. Its long history as a sacred Hindu site and its
strong claim of being the coveted seat of political power for centuries
were overshadowed by more recent events. Nearly half of the sites listed
by the Archeological Department in 1936 were those associated with the
encounter between the British and Tipu Sultan. For instance, the southeast fort wall was marked as the spot where Cornwallis's troops assaulted
Srirangapatna in 1791, leading Tipu to reinforce that bastion. The site
marked "Kaul Bazaar" memorialized not the prosperity of the new town
established by Tipu called Shahar Ganjam, "full of wealthy inhabitants,"
but the signing of the humiliating Treaty of Srirangapatna in 1792.[80] The
list included "Inman's dungeon," a large structure with a battery on its
top and a low vaulted cellar, which was similar to Baillie's dungeon and
so was named after the person who discovered the site in 1895 rather than
its more famous occupant of early 1800s, the dreaded Maratha peasant
guerilla Dhondia Wagh.[81]

Other alterations, even when they were public works, marked the gratitude of the restored Mysore dynasty to their British masters, as when Dewan
Purnaiya proposed "to construct a bridge on the north of Seringapatam
to be called the Wellesley Bridge, the expense to be entirely defrayed
by the Raja's government."[82] The curious granite pillar north of the
Srirangapatna French Rocks Road a short distance from Srirangapatna
was similarly a sign of Purnaiya's gratitude to Resident Josiah Webbe, who
had supported the former's claim to a proportion of the Mysore revenues.[83] Although the Mysore government in 1914 "traced" the place where
Krishnaraja Wodeyar III was born to construct a memorial and surrounding garden that were completed in July 1915, Srirangapatna's chief attraction to the tourist (to be distinguished here from the Hindu pilgrim) was
as a site of defeated power.[84]

The liberties taken in visually "re-creating" this historic fort capital and
its eventual capture resulted in an altered topography. Of Ker Porter's representation of Seringapatam it was said in the 1930s:

Detail is crowded in and the Breach, Mosque and inner Sally Port
gateway, though far apart in reality are crowded together, while
incidents which happened at widely separated points are to be seen

Figure 33. Aerial view of Srirangapatna showing the obelisk erected at the point where the fort was breached in 1799. Photograph by Clare Arni, 1998.

in close association. Even the Lal Bagh, a garden about three miles distant, finds a place in the picture! All these details, however, are intended only to provide the scenic background for a picture in which national heroes are usually depicted.[85]

Srirangapatna was singled out by *Indian Engineering* in 1926 as one of the most important war memorials in India, to which "frequent excursions are made from Bangalore by the men stationed there."[86] War memorials at Srirangapatna thus served not only to honor old soldiers but to inspire new recruits and provide historical instruction. It was perhaps in this spirit that Edmund Bull reminded readers in his 1927 guide *Romantic Seringapatam* of "the magnitude of such achievements as the storming and the taking of Seringapatam," adding that "the objects of interest memorialized in the fortress today are of a personal rather than a political character."[87] Constance Parsons declared of the island of Srirangapatna that its "main objects of interest are prisons and tombs," but even such a "melancholy place" was not without its uses in reminding visitors of an extraordinary late eighteenth-century encounter.[88] "In the Fort," Colonel Browning wrote with flourish, "a few houses remain where once there was a great capital, and the ancient temple of Vishnu looks down, as if in mockery, on the ruins of the Palace of the Muhammadan Sultan."[89] By this time, the island's neglected sanitary conditions had led to a steady population decline, with the population dropping to 7,372 in 1911; following a serious outbreak of malaria in 1919, all *karanjis* (large tanks) and wells were sealed, forcing the *dharmadarsis* (managers or superintendents of religious institutions) of Srirangapatna to employ "Srivaishnava Brahmin watermen to fetch water from the river."[90]

Crucial to the vicarious pleasures of revisiting the site of the East India Company's great battle with Tipu Sultan was the spot where he had fallen. E. W. Thompson spent a good part of the prefatory notes to his book in correcting a "popular error," because the steps traced by innumerable tourists over the ruins of the island fortress took them to the water gate on the north face of the fort, where a tablet had been installed by the Mysore government to the northeast of the Gangadhara temple.[91] Thompson's reconstruction of the death showed that it occurred at a gate that had been demolished in Wellesley's time, at least one hundred yards east of the spot where the Mysore government had mistakenly placed the marker. It was later taken up in a Mysore Archeological Department request for "a suitable monument," though this was not erected until many decades after Indian independence.[92]

The Kannada poem translated by John Leyden attributes the defeat of Tipu Sultan to his fall from the grace of the presiding deity of Srirangapatna: "Ah! As soon as Crishna's favour fled, /Our Prince, our kingdom pass'd away." The British victory, too, was placed at the lotus feet of the lord of Srirangapatna, who, along with the deities at Srirangam and Sivasamudram, formed a sacred Vaishnavite geography of the south: "The Anglian race, unknown to fly/revering Runga's sacred name/Their red war banner wav'd on high."[93] By this rendering, the town of Srirangapatna, which was built around the temple of Sriranganatha from the early twelfth century and expanded by Thimmana Hebbar in 1454 "using materials from 101 Jain temples at Kalsvadi, five miles to the south," retrieved its status as a site of Hindu pilgrimage only under the watchful eye of the British.[94] Thus, if Tipu is claimed to have "dismantled" the Narasimhaswamy and the Gangadhareswara temples in Srirangapatna, causing the image of Narasimha to be removed to the Sriranganatha temple, Krishnaraja Wodeyar III is credited with its restoration in 1828.[95]

How was the geography of the town as a site of Hindu pilgrimage transformed in the period of Tipu's rule? The evidence is clearly contradictory, and both the patronage of temples and the likely reduction of the *gopuras* (towers over the gates of the temples) may have been for strategic reasons: Parsons alludes to the fact that both the Narasimhaswamy and the Gangadhareswara temples had lost their *gopuras* because they overlooked the palace and might have "offered landmarks to an enemy," while the Ranganathaswamy temple posed no such threat.[96] The fate of the Varahaswami idol in the early nineteenth century shrouds the easy depiction of Tipu's excesses in some mystery. The precarious legal status of the island of Srirangapatna for most of the nineteenth century ensured that the island was much more strongly marked as a site for remembering the British conquest.

There was one icon, however, that had an afterlife of a different kind, because it followed the Mysore royal family from Srirangapatna to the new capital of Mysore. Its move signified in important ways the altered landscapes and changing destinies of the two cities as well as the desperate claims to power by the newly revived dynasty. This is an important reminder of the seriousness with which the symbolic reinscription of the space of the two cities was taken by the victors and their principal beneficiaries. An early optimism about the success of "indirect rule" gave way after the Nagar rebellion of 1831, and direct British rule of the Mysore state inaugurated an anxious period when both the power and the authority of Krishnaraja Wodeyar III were seriously threatened. The latter part of the nineteenth century, then, constituted something of a trough presaging the exuberant building of a royal capital at Mysore city.

Conclusion

Although Mysore city was subordinated to Srirangapatna in terms of both antiquity and religio-political importance from the early seventeenth century, its fall was precipitous through most of the nineteenth century, when Tipu's capital itself was drained of life. However, its fate was dramatically altered by the early decades of the twentieth century. Meanwhile, the unmaking of the capital city, Srirangapatna, and its remaking into a memorial of death and suffering right up until the twentieth century, was amply aided by the new Wodeyar regime. No wonder that every room in the new guest mansion at Mysore (Lalit Mahal Palace) was hung with engravings of the British history painters' records of the defeat and death of Tipu Sultan.[97]

Writing on the fundamental opposition between memory and history, Pierre Nora characterizes the former as "affective and magical, perhaps even out of focus, compared to the prosaic, analytical realms of history."[98] He continues, "History's goal and ambition is not to exalt but to annihilate what has in reality taken place."[99] Yet Tipu remained in the realm of the imagination, of which a new sacred memory was produced. It would, of course, preserve some sites, some materials crucial to its work—monuments, postcards, medallions—but an environment of memory would be an impossibility in such a secularized historical discourse. *Lavani* (ballad) singers such as Vishakanta Rao were well known for their "renderings" of his life and exploits.[100] Mohammad Iqbal, the celebrated Urdu poet and philosopher, was among those who made a pilgrimage from Lahore to Srirangapatna to spend time at the Gumbaz in 1929. He returned to Lahore and wrote a paean in his *Javid-Namah* (The Book of Eternity):

I have lighted a different fire in the heart.
I have brought a tale from the Deccan.
. . . .

There I heard from his holy grave;
If one cannot live a manly life in this world
Then to sacrifice life, like a man, is life![101]

It was not long before the new nation-state annexed Tipu to a roll call of national heroes. The recovery of Srirangapatna as a historic capital, because the "reigns of Haidar Ali and Tipu represent a glorious epoch in the History of Karnataka," occurred in the fiftieth year of Indian independence (1997), when the Archaeological Survey of India crafted the monuments built by Tipu—the Dariya Daulat Bagh, the Gumbaz, the fort, the Jumma Masjid, the place of Tipu's death, and the dungeons—into a new and proud history of the state.[102] This overall intention has not been achieved through suppressing the importance of the British conquest, and indeed, as I have said earlier, the museum display at Dariya Daulat accords a certain equivalence to the heritages of Tipu and Wellesley. The pictures of Tipu's dramatic defeat and death and of the mourning by his family over his body, along with the poignant pencil portraits of his sons, banished from Srirangapatna to the Vellore fort and thence to Calcutta, vie with the murals, the swords, the flintlocks and matchlocks in constructing an image of a heroic military leader. Despite its popularity as a sacred site and for its monuments, in its subordination to the brilliance of neighboring Mysore, Srirangapatna bears the enduring mark of the defeat of 1799.

CHAPTER 4

The Museumized Cityscape of Mysore

Throughout the nineteenth century, Mysore only fitfully took on the mantle of a royal city in a stark reflection of the uncertainties of princely rule under paramount British power. In June 1799, Lieutenant Colonel Kirkpatrick had recommended Mysore as the preferable capital to Bangalore because the latter "would be nearly at one extremity of the Mysoor State and very close to the Nizam's frontier." By the 1830s, these military compulsions were no longer relevant.[1] A further, and equally unique, diminution of Mysore city's importance occurred in 1836, when the British, who had already moved their army to Bangalore, made it the princely state's administrative capital.

It was only in the early twentieth century that Mysore, though somewhat unfairly referred to in 1870 by Comissioner Lewin Bowring as a "petty village," was transformed from being a "place of no antiquity" into a royal city of splendid monuments.[2] By this time, not only had the split between the administrative and ceremonial capitals been sealed and institutionalized but the Wodeyars' historic association with Srirangapatna had been broken and its place taken by Bangalore. This chapter traces some important nineteenth-century moments in the struggle between the paramount power and the Maharaja of Mysore, whose spatial claims to Mysore city were as gravely undermined as his quest for the return of his kingdom to direct rule. Until the 1880s, the consequences of severely circumscribed princely authority threatened to turn Mysore into a barren historic site. Mysore did, however, emerge as a royal city in the first few decades of the twentieth century, and it successfully acquired *a depth of historical distance.* Increasingly turned into a museumized cityscape studded with ornamental buildings to which an overall schema of city planning was sometimes subordinated, the royal city and its annual pageants together produced powerful resonances among the population of the princely state, becoming fitting supplements to the image of modern Mysore.

The Movable Icon of Varahaswami

In 1809, an idol of Sweta Varahaswami from Srirangapatna was removed to a newly constructed temple in the Mysore fort. Chikkadevaraja Wodeyar is said to have procured the image of Sweta Varahaswami in the 1670s from Srimushna (in present-day South Arcot) and set up the image in the newly constructed temple at Srirangapatnam. "But as the temple was demolished by Tipu," says C. Hayavadana Rao, the idol was removed to Mysore and set up there by Dewan Purnaiya, who "had this temple built with the materials from a Hoysala building in Shimoga District."[3]

The renewal of ties with the old and forgotten capital of Mysore occurred in ways that eclipsed the records and legends that surround the more dramatic arrival of the idol in Srirangapatna. Chikkadevaraja's military triumphs in the late seventeenth century had culminated in the theft of this interesting trophy from Srimushna. In 1675, as the copper-plate grant recording Chikkadevaraja's conquests to the east, west, and north of the Mysore region has it, "The ancient image of Varaha at Srimushna, which had been removed during the Yavana invasion, he brought to Srirangapatna and set up."[4]

The *Srimanmaharajara Vamsavali* reports the "seizure" of the image from Srimushna.[5] The Tanjore king Shahji II (A.D. 1684–1711), son of Ekoji, boasted that Mysore had only one important Vaishnavite shrine, while the Thanjavur country enjoyed an embarrassment of riches (Vaishnavite shrines such as Srirangam, Srimushna, Kumbakonam, and Mannargudi and Saivite shrines at Madhyarjana, Madurai, and Rameshwara). On hearing of this boast, Chikkadevaraja sent emissaries with bribes; they negotiated with the *archakas* (temple priests) at Srimushna and, in the dead of night, stole the stone image of Sweta Varahaswami (or Bhuvarahaswami) and brought it to Srirangapatna, "where it was installed on the right hand side of the palace in a fine temple, and worshipped along with new stone idols of Ambujavali and Ubhayanachiyar."[6] The temple itself appears to have been in existence since 1499.[7]

The choice of wartime trophies, Richard Davis reminds us, must be understood in the context of how "Hindu rulers of the medieval period appropriated and relocated select religious images . . . with attention to their mythical identities as part of a political discourse."[8] The lives of the Varaha image reveal that the shifting of religious icons for political reasons was far from confined to the medieval period. That image became an important symbol of the negotiations between Vaishnavism and Saivism made by the Wodeyar dynasty when the capital was first moved from Mysore to Srirangapatna in the early seventeenth century and then returned to Mysore at the turn of the nineteenth.[9] Allegiance to Vaishnavism, with which the island of Srirangapatna had been historically associated since the late ninth century, became a strategic necessity when Raja Wodeyar occupied the place in 1610, largely as a way of asserting himself as a legitimate claimant to that seat of power.[10]

Actual conversion took much longer. The 1675 inscription referred to earlier was composed by none other than Tirumalarya, the prominent poet of Chikkadevaraja's reign, who encouraged this conversion. The *Srimanmaharajara Vamshavali* reports that under the influence of the "Brahmin Pradhan Tirumala Iyengar" (Tirumalarya), the Ursu clan exclusively adopted the Vaishnava faith and attempted to repudiate all links with Saivism, which was associated with Sudras.[11] Thirteen upper-caste Ursu families took a pledge of allegiance to Vishnu and adopted the five *acharas* (types of conduct or behaviors) and related practices of Kshatriyas: "[Although we had] taken birth among the loftiest of kshatriyas, devotees of the Lotus Feet of the Lord, without understanding this faith, and out of ignorance abandoning our caste traditions, and in violation of the four *varnashrama acharas* [observance of caste customs], [we] became adherents of the religion of the Sudras, Saivism, [and] gave and took women in violation of caste norms."[12] Before long, the thirteen families pleaded that they be allowed to resume, alongside their new sectarian allegiance, the worship of their *kula devatas* (clan or family deities), whose neglect after their conversion had caused new hardships.[13]

The traveling Varaha idol was therefore tied to histories of self-definition and claims on power and space that continued well into the nineteenth and twentieth centuries. The Mysore annals claim that the temple at Srirangapatna was destroyed by Tipu Sultan, though the idol continued to be worshipped in a *mantapa* (structure) at the Ranganathaswamy temple.[14] The Mysore Archaeological Department reports similarly include the Varahaswami temple in Srirangapatna among three temples in the Mysore region that had been demolished. Another nineteenth-century source, Devachandra's *Rajavali Kathasara*, reports, with no reference to any previous destruction, that the Sweta Varahaswami temple was built for the idol at Mysore by Dewan Purnaiya in 1809, a decade after the capital traveled to that city.[15]

The Varahaswami temple anchored the Wodeyars in their new capital while becoming the site of yet another history: that of the Sri Vaishnava Brahmatantra Parakala Matha. Destined to become the "official" matha of the Wodeyar family, particularly after the nineteenth century, the Parakala matha's history affirms the conversion of the Ursu community to Srivaishnavism with none of the ambiguity of the Palace annals.[16] The Srivaishnava matha shuttled between Srirangapatna and Tirupathi from the early eighteenth century to the early nineteenth as the fortunes of the Wodeyars waned and waxed.[17] In 1799, the matha head then "advised Purnaiah, Dewan, to build the temple of Sri Sweta Varaha at Mysore to serve as the nucleus of the future Mysore State."[18] This hagiography makes no mention of the destruction of the original temple at Srirangapatna, recording only the strengthened power of the matha, located at the Varahaswami temple, until new premises adjoining the Jaganmohan Palace were built at the turn of the twentieth century.[19]

Indigenous and Colonial Models of Power and Authority

The shift of the Varahaswami temple signaled a continuous effort to forge a new order of legitimacy through the construction of temples within the Mysore fort space throughout the nineteenth and twentieth centuries. The fort itself was rebuilt with the stones dismantled from Nazarabad, in a deliberate reversal of Tipu's plans. A great deal of imaginative effort was required to reconstruct what had been dismantled by Tipu Sultan. As Wilks recounted:

> The town and fort of Mysoor, the ancient residence of the rajas, and the capital from which the whole country derived its name was an offensive memorial of the deposed family, and [Tipu] determined that the existence and if possible the remembrance of such a place should be extinguished. The fort was leveled with the ground and the materials were employed in the erection of another fortress on a neighbouring height which he named Nezerbar; and it is a curious example of that vicissitude in human affairs, which history so often preaches in vain that the very same stones were re-conveyed to rebuild the same old fort of Mysoor in 1799.[20]

Wilks saw no irony in reporting the British determination to rebuild the pre-Tipu structure, and he offered no explanation for the continued existence of all the temples in the Mysore fort area during Tipu's reign. Following the British re-creation of the Mysore fort, however, a continuous reinscription of the fort space was undertaken in order to avow, or even disavow, competing religiosities, a process that continued into the 1950s. The addition of the Prasanna Krishnaswami temple in 1825 and the restoration of the Trineshwaraswami temple were two important changes to the fort complex.[21]

The palace, too, as C. Hayavadana Rao reported it in the 1930s, "corresponds in respect of principal chambers, with the old Palace at Seringapatam"; he strongly suggested that the models for the Srirangapatna palace were taken from the historic Vijayanagar capital Hampi in a claim to both continuity and antiquity.[22] According to Aya Ikegame, the space of the fort was transformed throughout the nineteenth and twentieth centuries to conform to the twin demands of city improvement and the king's traditional role as a protector of dharma.[23] Because the colonial strategy after 1831 was to render the Raja a private individual deprived of any political roles and functions, the palace and its administration functioned as a separate "state," at least until 1868. Ikegame suggests that within these constraints, the space within the Mysore fort came to signify new meanings of kingship even under the colonial regime. These ideals were largely realized, though only well into the twentieth century on the eve of Indian independence.

Ikegame provides a new and useful optic for discerning the meaning and making of princely India, distinguishing between the little kingdoms such as Pudukkottai, Ramnad, or Sivagangai and substantial princely states such as Mysore. She emphasizes, moreover, the importance of renewed or reinvented rituals in forging new links between ruler and ruled.[24] However, the steadily accumulating value of a new visual aesthetic, often overtaking the sacred as the logic of ordering space, remains unexplored in her account. In the two sections that follow, I extend Ikegame's reading of the spatial practices within the Mysore fort and city in the nineteenth and twentieth centuries.

In the early decades of the nineteenth century, Mysore bore no resemblance to the descriptions of its flourishing court culture at the time of Kantirava Narasaraja Wodeyar I or Chikkadevaraja Wodeyar.[25] In 1803 Lord Valentia described it as consisting of "one street about a mile long" and the Raja's palace as "small and neat but not finished" while adding that there was a great deal of empty space in the fort.[26] The fort continued in existence long after it had outlived its military purpose to become a walled royal enclosure within which the young king settled many of his relatives in close proximity to the palace.

After 1831, there was even doubt about "whether after resigning the Government the Raja shall be required to remove his residence from the country of Mysoor," as the "Mysore Family" of Tipu had been required to do.[27] Though no such eviction eventually occurred, the Mysore palace remained an undistinguished structure even in 1869. "As with most native courts," the *Mysore District Gazetteer* noted, "there is no attempt at isolation, and except in front where there is an open space, the palace is pressed close on all sides by the dwellings of the poor inhabitants."[28] Indeed, the quadrangular fort, 450 yards on three sides and slightly longer on the south side, had mean and ill-planned defenses, while the sloping glacis around the fort was similarly "covered with houses" except on the east side.[29] Many years later, Bowring wrote, "There are few good houses in the town, the majority being of wattle and mud, while the Raja's Palace within the fort, can scarcely be considered worthy of the name. It is surrounded on all sides by houses, many of them of a mean description, and although there are some fine temples hard by, with summits gaily decorated with gold, and it is itself a somewhat lofty building, it evidences little architectural taste or skill," being more commodious than elegant.[30]

The idea of maintaining some distance between monarch and subject was partially realized after the death of Krishnaraja Wodeyar III in 1868, when improvements of the fort were started in 1872–73 and the dense warrens of private buildings were removed to make way for a visually isolated and imposing palace structure.[31] Until then, the space within the fort was still one over which the Maharaja exerted some authority, though Krishnaraja Wodeyar III felt that a failure to claim public space might only further diminish his authority. He hoped to prevent further insults to his honor in public by privatizing parts of the city, as when he proposed to enclose the racecourse for his personal use.[32]

The struggle over the Old Residency (Government House) brings out the question of the king's honor most sharply. In 1832, the building was surrendered by the Maharaja to the British authorities. Beginning in 1841, the Maharaja began making a plea for the return of the Residency to his control, which was done in July 1841. Just as in the case of Srirangapatna, the brief tussle that ensued between Mark Cubbon and the Maharaja of Mysore made it clear that both sides were amply aware of the importance of retaining visibility, and therefore authority, in the space of Mysore city. Soon after this building was handed over to the Maharaja, Cubbon insisted that it was "the only tolerable habitation for Europeans in that place . . . [where] the inmates . . . were not subject to almost constant fever." He wanted it reclaimed without delay to house the offices of the Superintendent of Ashtagram.[33] A petulant Maharaja offered alternate sites, claiming that he had made the Residency into a "private pleasure house" for health reasons.[34] He further requested permission to enclose a portion of the racecourse and the entrance to the Karanji tank to enhance the privacy of his palace. Cubbon's sharp reaction reduced the Maharaja's claim to special status when he said that the king could acquire land on the same terms as any other subject of Mysore by paying due compensation to the displaced *ryots* (peasants).

The Maharaja replied that "he had never heard of any distinction between the Public property of the Princely State and the private or personal property of the Sovereign of that state."[35] Being forced to use money to acquire private property would be seen as a distinct loss of the Maharaja's princely authority, which had already been seriously challenged on at least one visit to Srirangapatna. Cubbon read more sinister designs behind these plaintive protests. Cubbon said that "the Residency must be preferably kept permanently in the hands of the actual rulers of the country, an edifice heretofore respected as the seat of British authority."[36] He was convinced that the Maharaja's real object was to dispossess the Superintendent and occupy the building in anticipation of a return of his country and full powers.[37] Left with no alternative but to comply with the orders of the Governor-General, the Maharaja returned the Old Residency to the British authorities in August 1841.[38]

The relationship between the spheres of the public and the private as they pertained to the Mysore king were never satisfactorily settled in his lifetime. At the time of his death, Mysore was still a city largely sustained by the palace. In 1836, there were 6,224 persons employed at the palace, but by 1868 these numbers had swelled to 9,687, excluding 619 relatives, who were employed for annual pay of Rs 689,424.[39] These people accounted for a fifth of the city's population.[40] Moreover, according to Major C. Elliot, the Superintendent of Ashtagram, who was placed in charge of palace duties, a parallel state with twenty-five departments was being run within the fort. In the massive rationalization exercise that he undertook, the number of employees was brought down to 3,196 persons, excluding 625 members of the Maharaja's clan. The administrative apparatuses were reduced to three

major (or *cutcherry*) departments and eight smaller ones. The establishment of the late Maharaja, whose annual costs had amounted to about
Rs 1,600,000, was pruned to just Rs 825,000.[41] The cap put on the civil list,
though periodically revised, remained sufficiently large to afford the palace household a degree of comfort and dignity verging on opulence. By
1868, there were just two other large "pleasure bungalows" in the city, exag-
geratedly called the Jaganmohan Palace and the Lokranjan Mahal, though
many major and minor homes belonged to the royal family.[42] Three chief
festival and ceremonial occasions of the palace were continued with suitable alterations: the birthday of the Maharaja, the *shradhum* (oblations for
the dead in Hinduism) for the late Maharaja, and the Dasara durbar.

All vestiges of autonomy were drained away from the adopted heir of
Krishnaraja Wodeyar III, whose life was a long and continuous education
in the many aspects of being a modern monarch, akin to an English aristocrat. Viceroy Lytton offered some early advice to the new child prince in
a letter of 1876:

> It is my wish, that during the remaining years of your minority,
> Your Highness should visit as frequently as possible . . . all parts
> of the province of Mysore in order that . . . you may make your-
> self personally acquainted with those portions of its territory and
> population which you may hereafter be called upon to govern.[43]

Unlike his sedentary father, Chamarajendra Wodeyar participated enthusiastically in the "discovery" of Mysore, and indeed India, finding to his
surprise a deep-seated respect for the throne throughout Mysore.[44] In 1867
a proposal was made to move the young prince to Bangalore for his education, but it was given up, leaving the Wodeyar family with its precarious hold on the city of Mysore.[45] Additional properties were nevertheless
acquired in Bangalore in 1873, and in 1874 in Ooty, where the young heir
was schooled in the manners, habits, and tastes appropriate to an English
squire; as he wrote to a friend in 1875 from Ooty, "We are reading, walking,
running and everyday cricket playing [*sic*]," in addition to learning riding,
polo, and hunting.[46]

The prince undertook tours to other loyal Indian states and was exposed to the "benefits" of British rule in other parts of India. This experience fostered a lasting fascination with pageantry, as well as with the

ideal of the "improving monarch." The Dasara festival was revived as a public event, with British approval, after a gap of fifty years. In addition, Chamarajendra Wodeyar chose to recreate the wonders that he had seen on his northern tour in the late 1880s. The idea of an industrial school was taken from his visit to Jaipur, a zoo was started on the lines of what he had seen at the Ayodhya Nawabs' bungalow in Calcutta, and in 1888 an exhibition of industrial crafts and arts of the state was inaugurated to coincide with the revived Dasara pageant.[47] Even the newly established Representative Assembly was at first conceived as a display of gratitude to the Maharaja rather than a serious place for debate and discussion. All of these elements were enduring signs of the march of progress in Mysore.[48]

By the end of the century, Mysore had expanded a great deal, with extensions to the southwest and improvements to the older parts, making the city unrecognizable in terms of what it had been two decades before.[49] Chamarajendra Wodeyar participated willingly in the production of spectacle: under the watchful eye of the Mysore bureaucracy, some moves were made to endow the city with a style of architecture that was functional and yet perceived as royal. *Indian Engineering* poured out its customary scorn on the "unpleasant architectural effect" of efforts at "improving the appearance of the city."[50] The Lansdowne Bazaar Building was faulted for its poor plastering and the Maharaja's College for its "huge pillars and narrow openings," while Jubilee Institute was mocked for its "promiscuous jumbling of semi circular arches, Ionic and Corinthian columns with imitations of Hindu Architecture" and the Marimallappa's school for "its awkward arrangement of pillars in the central hall."[51] Such comments refused to value the hybrid styles achieved through the fusion of the Western, imperial, and Indian religious architectural forms.[52] The Oriental Research Institute and the Maharaja's College, for instance, used sturdy European classical features, such as pillars and pediments; even when they were embellished with bas reliefs on narrative themes drawn from the puranas (epics), these decorative features remained subordinated to the structure itself.[53]

In time, even European architects and landscape designers, or Anglo-Indian and Indian architects with similar training, were more than willing to oblige those Indian princes whose growing appetite for new structures was matched by deep pockets. They also devised styles that appealed to the new public that thronged Mysore during the annual public events.

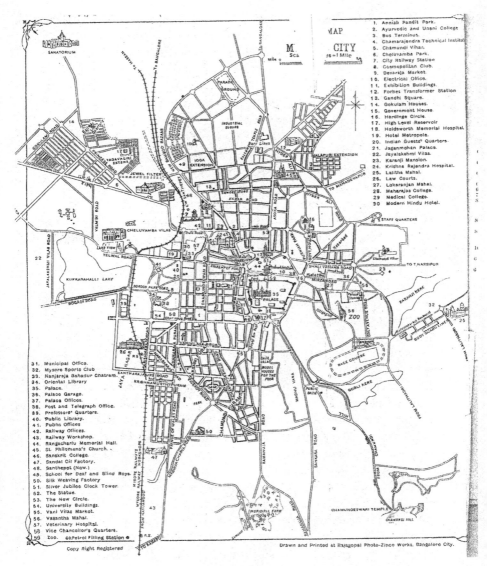

Figure 34. Tourist map of Mysore, c. 1930. Courtesy of the Clare Arni Collection.

Inventing a Royal Capital

The transition of the Wodeyar ruler from the slighter image of the improving monarch to one who publicly aligned himself with being part of a new spectacle, while engaging with the points and thrusts of politics on a low-key register, occurred in the twentieth century with Krishnaraja Wodeyar IV. If the return of Mysore to the "direct rule" of the Wodeyars in 1881 was conditional on good governance, that is, nurturing spaces of loyalty to colonial rule, the Mysore administration was careful to develop equally new roles and uses for the royalty. Thus the Representative Assembly convened in 1881 by the first Dewan of Mysore after rendition renewed the links between ruler and ruled but in a setting that announced the decisive break between splendid power and depleted authority.

A new division of labor was achieved between the cities of Mysore and Bangalore, royal and administrative capitals, respectively, in the first few decades of the twentieth century. As a former schoolmate of Krishnaraja Wodeyar IV, M. Mirza Ismail—first Huzur secretary, then private secretary, and finally Dewan—knew only too well, a decisive break between the Mysore administration and the king had been achieved and spatialized, with Mysore city remaining the home of the royal family. The splendor of the palace and the royal city was to be sustained to nourish and sustain the love, loyalty, and awe of the masses, values that could not be generated by good governance alone. "Even the pomp and circumstance associated with [the Wodeyars]," Mirza wrote, "has its real and abiding value in this curious world. Volumes might be written on the advantages of benevolent personal rule, but I will only remark that authority does well to clothe itself in dignity, even in splendour."[54] He may not have been exaggerating when he said, "It would be hard to find anywhere in the world a spectacle more brilliant than [Krishnaraja Wodeyar IV's] Dasara Durbar. But the magnificent display was intended for the enjoyment and benefit of the people. *They met no desire of his own.*"[55]

According to Aya Ikegame, new twentieth-century concerns for public health and hygiene profoundly altered the shape of the palace complex, though it also reflected a respect for the older obligations of kingly dharma in a confined and highly stylized setting.[56] To extend and reorder the thematic developed by Ikegame in understanding the Mysore palace and fort complex as an example of the successful blending of sacred and civic conceptions of power, we would have to look beyond the fort walls at changes that were wrought in the city of Mysore. The new and relatively unanticipated role played by the Mysore rulers as a *supplement* to the progressive image of the Mysore administration must therefore be understood. Ikegame rightly demonstrates the separation of the palace from the state as it occurred particularly after 1831.[57] But the return of the king to the public sphere, this time in a supplementary role that substantially altered nineteenth-century conceptions of the king as a private individual, cannot be ignored. Although the conception of the king as a representation of the "divine" was far from absent, the new figure of the "man king" was one around which a new public was mobilized, not least through the conscious deliberations of the bureaucracy.[58] The systematized pageantry of the Dasara durbars and the reorganization of the space of Mysore as a space to amuse, display, and instruct, in short, an "exhibitionary complex," formed a crucial feature of the twentieth-century palace culture.

In his discussion of the common founding moment of two contradictory forms that addressed the question of order and reorganized modes of spectation or the spectacular in the modern period, namely, the (Foucauldian) carceral archipelago and the exhibitionary complex, respectively, Tony Bennett says:

> The exhibitionary complex was also a response to the problem of order, but one which worked differently in seeking to transform that problem into one of culture—a question of winning hearts and minds as well as the disciplining and training of bodies. As such, its constituent institutions reversed the orientations of the disciplinary apparatuses in seeking to render the forces and principles of order visible to the populace—transformed, here into a people, a citizenry—rather than vice versa. They sought not to map the social body in order to know the populace by rendering it visible to power. Instead, through the provision of object lessons in power—the power to command and arrange things and bodies for public display—they sought to allow the people, and en masse rather than individually, to know rather than be known, to become the subject rather than the objects of knowledge.[59]

Bennett's argument is that the exhibitionary complex—the museums, panoramas, spectacles, and exhibitions usually established with the involvement of the state—"provided new instruments for the moral and cultural regulation of the working classes."[60] I am extending Bennett's use of the term to the production of Mysore city itself as a museumized cityscape that produced another set of effects appropriate to the historical conditions of its possibility: it associated the Mysore Wodeyars with a long and antiquated claim to the space of the city of Mysore. The very success of this twentieth-century invention effaced the tenuous claims to legitimacy of the nineteenth century. These efforts exerted an enduring influence on the people of Mysore, shaping ties of loyalty and devotion among the members of an emerging Mysore public. The increasing confidence with which the royal family annexed public property and persuaded the state to underwrite its aesthetic ambitions was thus amply matched by the gratitude of its subjects.

Pamela Price's discussion of the new political idioms that were forged by Baskar Setupati of Ramnad, a *zamindari* (large landholding) in Tamil Nadu, is attentive to this realm of political practice. By the end of the nineteenth century, she suggests, "a public sphere had emerged with groups who sought control over the state. The ritual innovations of Baskara Setupati in 1894 were orientated towards public opinion. The protection of royal authority in the Ramnad zamindari had become dependent on influence in this new type of political domain."[61] A similar process is discernible in the symbols and styles of authority developed in the Mysore palace that were increasingly addressed to an emerging modern public.[62]

In 1902, Krishnaraja Wodeyar IV inherited the kingdom and the confidence that arose from his willingness to participate in the affairs of the state from behind the able shoulders of the bureaucracy. He also actively participated in matters of building design and city aesthetics. One of his earliest steps after attaining his majority and taking over the reins of the palace was the replacement of the statue of his father, Chamarajendra Wodeyar, installed by the visiting Viceroy Curzon in 1902, with "a better likeness." The existing equestrian statue, executed by Onslow Ford, though a fine work of art, "never commended itself to his Highnesses' family and friends as a faithful likeness or to the people of Mysore generally as a suitable presentment of their late revered ruler."[63] The Maharaja's father was no remote presence in the lives of his subjects, as we have seen, and "numerous spectators" were said to have been disappointed by the absence of a true likeness.[64] Robert Colton was therefore asked in 1904 to "study local conditions" and "avoid errors of detail" to produce a bronze statue "in accordance with Mysore ideas and sentiments."[65]

In the new insistence on verisimilitude we may detect an effort to create a more intimate and enduring mark of Wodeyar kingship on the city's
landscape than was achieved by the ritualized journey of the king during
the Dasara. No longer the object of veneration, this "realist" representation of the king only confirmed that the royalty had turned into a familiar,
familial, and therefore beloved institution. Installed in front of the northern gate of the palace, in Curzon Park, which was built in 1902 to replace a
mass of houses, swamps, and a moat, the Maharaja's statue epitomized his
popularity "with both Europeans and natives," who saw him as "devoted to
his family" and "conscientious in attending to business," as B. L. Rice, the
director of the Archaeological Survey, would recall.[66]

There were other important signs in the early years of the twentieth
century that a new relationship was being forged between the Mysore
royalty and the subjects of a royal city that now extended well beyond
the fort walls. I shall discuss four of these aspects in turn: the altered relationship between figure and ground of the Mysore palace; the simultaneous expansion of the abodes of the royal family in various quarters of the
city, with important implications for the relative rights of royalty and the
public; changes and alterations to the palace complex itself throughout
the first five decades of the twentieth century as the royalty responded
to the demands, from the state as much as from the public, for a sumptuous spectacle; and finally, a new pedagogical relationship to the Mysore
public, via an art gallery and industrial exhibition, that complemented
the striving for a "Mysore Modern" that had already been undertaken on
the economic front.

A Place Apart: Isolating the Mysore Palace

Throughout the nineteenth century, British authorities and commentators
remarked on the Mysore palace's undistinguished presence, pressed on all
sides by poorer types of housing occupied by the relatives and employees of the palace. An initial attempt to clear the space east of the palace,
"thickly surrounded by a number of private dwelling houses," commenced
in 1872–73, when the palace establishment was cut down and the claims
of the various legitimate and illegitimate heirs of Krishnaraja Wodeyar III
were drastically curbed. Some of the properties east of the palace were acquired and a nagarkhana (store of large drums) block constructed in their

place. Portions of the palace considered unsafe were pulled down and rebuilt, houses crowding the west side were cleared, and a system of underground drainage was gradually introduced.[67] The Rendition of 1881, when authority was returned to the Maharaja from the British Commissioner, occurred at a public durbar held at the *sejje* (extended front porch) of the palace; it was a far grander, more public, and secularized event than either the coronation durbar of 1868 or Chamarajendra's wedding in 1878.[68]

The clearing of the fort and the area around the palace was aided in part by the fire of 1897, which burned down a considerable portion of the largely wooden palace.[69] The new Maharaja, Krishnaraja Wodeyar IV, was anxious for a new palace to be built as "an architectural beauty," and plans were furnished by Henry Irwin, a Madras government architectural consultant who had designed the viceregal palace at Simla.[70] A large Palace Division was started for the purpose of construction. The elevation of the new palace was in an Indo-Saracenic style, but many of the decorations and carvings were in styles drawn from Mysore history, particularly the Chalukyan style.[71] Built largely of stone quarried from the nearby Chamundi Hills and the region of Srirangapatna, the structure was fifteen years in the making (1897–1912). The new palace, first inaugurated and occupied in 1907, won high praise from the otherwise critical writers of *Indian Engineering,* who described it as "one of the grandest buildings in India."[72] Still, there were continuous additions and alterations to the main palace and the complex itself.

The palace, however, was still not as clearly separated from its earlier moorings within the fort as the administration believed desirable.[73] The Trust Board set up under Mysore City Improvement Regulation III of 1903 removed 7,497 houses in old city areas, providing extensions with broad roads for the displaced. By 1909, some efforts were being made to clear the fort space: as was reported in the *Madras Mail:*

> The bazaars and small houses principally occupied by retainers of the palace, with which the interior of the fort was crowded, have all been swept away; the ditch has been filled up and converted into a wide road, named after the Gaekwar of Baroda, shrubberies and gardens have been planted around the walls, and in the open space outside the east gate [sic; along the northern fort wall] a fine park, named after Lord Curzon, has been laid out.[74]

Figure 35. Mysore palace, nearing completion, showing the smaller sejje *(porch), c. 1912. Aya Ikegame Private Collection.*

Figure 36. Mysore palace after the reconstruction and expansion of the sejje *(porch), c. 1932. Aya Ikegame Private Collection.*

Opportunities for the total isolation of the palace from the surrounding buildings once more arose in 1915–16, and Mirza Ismail recounts this bureaucratic triumph in detail:

> A difficult decision had to be made by the Maharaja as to whether the numerous houses, most of them belonging to his own relations, within the Mysore fort enclave, were to be allowed to remain or to be acquired and demolished. The fate of the house in which his own mother was born and brought up was involved. The total area of the Fort is barely 100 acres, [256,520 square yards] and houses big and small were huddled together forming an untidy mass, in close proximity to the Palace. The acquisition of these properties meant an expenditure of some Rs 1.3 million to 1.5 million, by no means a small sum in those days. I was however, in favour of this, while many were opposed to it. The Maharaja asked the Dewan, his maternal uncle, Sir Kantaraj Urs, who owned one of the houses, and R. H. Campbell, his Private Secretary, to advise him jointly on the matter. They decided in favour of status quo. Economy in the case of the Dewan, sentiment in that of Kantharaj Urs, and conservatism and peace in that of Campbell were doubtless the considerations that influenced them.
>
> Just about this time, Mr. [Patrick] Geddes, who had made a name for himself as a town planner, appeared on the scene. I consulted him, expecting that he would suggest the clearing of the area, but he, more than anyone else, was emphatically against such a proposal. He used some very poetic language . . . in giving his reasons—how wonderful it was to see the Ruler living in the midst of his people, his Palace towering above their dwellings and sheltering them and so on. He was most eloquent in describing the beauty of the existing state of things. This was another and a serious obstacle in my way. But His Highness decided at last in favour of acquisition.[75]

Mirza's persistence bore fruit, and a sum of Rs 1,159,800 was spent on one round of acquisition in 1915. By 1916, orders had been issued by Dewan Visvesvaraya "for the removal of certain buildings immediately at a cost of Rs 75,000." He said further, "All the open spaces near and in front of the Palace may be tidied up and suitably laid out by the Superintendent,

Government Gardens [G. H. Krumbiegal], and then handed over to the Palace for maintenance."[76] Another "26 unsightly houses" were marked for acquisition, leading five house owners to voluntarily sell their houses to the Mysore City Improvement Trust Board, with a few properties left standing.[77]

By the end of the 1920s, the Mysore palace, which had for so long been visually crowded by housing, was splendidly isolated and set within a vast clear space, ruled by the laws of symmetry and visual balance more than by the tenets of the classical *shilpasastras* (classical treatises on the making of the arts). It radically altered the relationship between figure and ground, increasingly isolating the structure to enhance its "sculptural" qualities. In 1930 the *Mysore Gazetteer* reported on the replacement of the untidy houses within the fort with parks and lawns: "A comprehensive design for the final layout of the entire palace and the surroundings of the Palace and the whole interior of the fort has been prepared. When this layout is complete, the Palace will be a building of great beauty and splendour."[78]

Mirza's dreams of a beautiful city space were realized by the efforts of Gustav Hermann Krumbiegal, a trained landscape gardener. Appointed in 1908 to the post of superintendent of government gardens and museums, Krumbiegal enjoyed a long and influential career in city aesthetic design before attaining the rank of chief economic botanist to the Mysore government.[79] Krumbiegal began by noting that the principal parks of Mysore were the Gordon and Curzon parks, though the latter could be firmly placed in neither the ornamental nor the landscape category. Because the reconstructed palace had no garden, Krumbiegal saw the need for considerable alteration of the surroundings to create a natural approach to the palace.[80] Entrusted with the task of designing the garden in the Mysore fort, at first between the north gate and the Palace, Krumbiegal set the palace against a vast expanse of meticulously laid out flowerbeds and lawns, but as a sight that should be on full view through the gates that pierced the massive fort walls, even necessitating the creation of an eastern gateway for the fort to lead the eye through the ornamental gardens to the domes of the palace. In 1918 he shared his vision of what Mysore should become, in which he turned the various aspects of the topography and the now completely dysfunctional fortification into design elements:

> We must aim to give each feature at Mysore its own individual charm and avoid repetitions and similarities. . . . Now the scenery outside the walls had its own dignified effect in its simplicity at

outline, and the massiveness or grandeur of its component parts i.e. the Fort wall, the solid blocks of sunk lawns of the ditch, the fine and straight avenue and the large Doddakere Tank.[81]

What Krumbiegal envisaged and realized in his designs for Mysore city was a radical transformation of the conventions of visual perception. In its nineteenth-century setting, the Mysore palace had been placed in the midst of the city, jostled by housing, and as a structure was matched by the towers of the temples as landmarks, a solid mass of buildings between and within which the voids or empty spaces were marked or spelled out. Krumbiegal's vision inverted this logic and, through the clearance of all but the temples that stood on the fort premises, achieved a new solidity for the palace. More important, there was an increased legibility to both the environs and the apartments of the palace, which was defined as the private space of the royal family, set apart from even members of the clan. A new visual order was achieved, replacing the more direct tactile, vocal, and visual elements with a distant and isolated solid. The fort walls were surrounded by the velvety moss-covered glacis, and the sculptural solid of the palace was to be glimpsed through the fort gates, dazzling onlookers with its decorative excesses and sumptuous domes.[82] "The ground enclosed by the fort walls, not occupied by the palace, the palace square and the temples, is now a garden," a 1930 guide to Mysore said, adding that "acres of emerald turf and beds of glowing flowers cover the once plague stricken areas."[83] It was this figure–ground relationship, the mansion set in sweeping grounds, that was repeated in the homes of the royal family that were scattered across the Mysore cityscape to produce a museumized landscape, replete with boulevards and attractive nodes.

From the turn of the century, the family of the Maharaja was gradually settled on a series of sites around the city, which in some cases required realignment of roads, walls, and other existing features, including the displacement of entire villages. The question of the rights of the Maharaja and his family to the space of the city, not just that of the fort complex, had to be resolved. The emergence of the Maharaja's family from the palace and fort complex and their claims as the royal family to the public space of the city, once more raised the question of the family's private rights versus the public's access and rights to the city. The construction of the mansion of the third *maharajakumari* (sister of the Maharaja) and the vast grounds on which it was set clearly illustrate some of the ways in which a new relationship between private and public was achieved.

Figure 37. Mysore palace as it is today. Photograph by Janaki Nair, 2007.

Redefining the Public and Private in Royal City Space

Krumbiegal's visions for Mysore as an aestheticized space were more than amply aided by the assertive aristocratic tastes of Krishnaraja Wodeyar IV and Mirza Ismail, both of whom worked to produce a new authority for the Mysore royalty. This meant extending the vision well beyond the fort walls to claim city space for the members of the royal family and the upper-caste Ursu families. The redefinition of the public space of the city as one to which the family could legitimately lay claim and offer aesthetic solutions was inaugurated in the first decade of the twentieth century. Mirza often expressed his impatience with and disapproval of the ways of the Mysore Public Works Department (PWD), even dismissing some of its constructions as a "standing disgrace."[84] The Maharaja was more systematic in submitting notes on a wide range of aesthetic issues, from minute changes of decorations within the palace to larger questions relating to the acquisition of properties, particularly to the members of the Ursu clan.

The mansion for the first maharajakumari, Jayalakshammani (sister of Krishnaraja Wodeyar IV), who was married to Kantharaj Urs, was completed by 1907. Jayalakshmi Vilas Mansion stood on a ridge at the western edge of the city, separated from the town by Kukkerhalli Kere, a sheet of water. It consisted of three different buildings joined together as one massive structure.[85] Its outer pediments used ionic and corinthian columns with entablatures, and doric arches connected the building to its wings. The interiors were decorated in "pure Hindu style," and a shrine to Bhuvaneswari at the back of the building had a dome with a finial.[86]

The construction of the mansion for the second maharajakumari (Krishnajammani) was begun in 1902 to the east of the city, bordering Karanji Lake.[87] Completed in 1914, the Karanji mansion was spread over thirty-eight acres and built in an Indo-Saracenic "Rennaissance" style.[88] The question of building an appropriate mansion for the third maharajakumari, Cheluvajammani, had arisen during the regency of Vani Vilas Sannidana.[89] In 1907, the Maharaja expressed the desire to make a "suitable residence" for his third sister to the west of Vontikoppal Hill.[90] This required not only the acquisition of the parade ground and the relocation of the Sillahdars (mounted and armed troops) to a suitable site elsewhere but also the displacement of Vontikoppal village altogether. "It is important from the sanitary point of view," said the Maharaja's private secretary, E. Machonochie, to Dewan Madhava Rao, "that the villagers should be induced to move to some unobjectionable site, in the neighborhood and not come crowding into the quarters occupied by their friends and relations in the city."[91] The request was quickly complied with, leading the villagers to petition the Mysore authorities against the acquisition. Though the Maharaja asked that fresh sites be provided for the new village, he emphasized the necessity of maintaining a firm upper hand.[92]

The clash between the claims of the villagers of the new Vontikoppal village and those of "Sirdar" Lakshmi Kantharaj Urs, the husband of Cheluvajammani, was between the aesthetic desires of the royal family and public rights of access. The villagers enjoyed a direct cart track from the village to Belagola Road that they wanted to retain, but their rights to Vontikoppal Road were strongly contested by the sirdar, who demanded that it be sold to him because it divided his property.[93] He wrote, "The road is used by the carts at all times, both day and night and it would be impossible to keep order and prevent people from trespassing on the mansion grounds, unless I build compound walls on both sides, which will look hideous to the mansion. . . . How did the carts come from Yedatore prior to this road was opened [sic]?"[94] At first the municipality refused to oblige the sirdar.[95] But in less than a year it was compelled to sell the road to the sirdar for a sum of Rs 3,000.[96] Similarly, a proposal to straighten the road in front of the mansion for the convenience of traffic was vetoed by the Maharaja in order to retain the visual coherence and dignity of the mansion.[97] Finally, in lieu of the old parade ground (26 acres), which was included in the grounds of the mansion and was used by the sirdar as stables, the government was made to acquire 172 acres in Woddarpalya for a new parade ground.[98]

Not all acquisitions went unchallenged, and an important case called into question the status of the royal family's acquisitions. In October 1912, lands from Paduvarhalli village were acquired for the third maharajakumari's mansion. A case was filed by Murti Rao, a landowner, questioning "whether the purpose for which the lands were acquired was a public one."[99] The palace acknowledged that the displaced people were finding it difficult to procure suitable sites, but because they had assumed such a threatening attitude, the Maharaja would not help them. Instead it was argued that "not only is the acquisition strictly legal but the purpose of the acquisition which is to provide a suitable compound for the residence of a member of the Ruling Family, may fairly be regarded as a 'public' purpose and the Government need not feel any delicacy on his Highness' behalf, in appearing as a defendant in the suit."[100]

The suit was decided in the state's favor in the district court, on the grounds that "in Mysore, suits do not lie against the government."[101] But the plaintiff found support in the Mysore chief court, which refused to affirm the lower court's decision and even asked whether the court was "entitled to decide that the purpose in Government notifications is not a 'public purpose.'"[102] This emboldened Murti Rao, who refused to accept the freshly negotiated compensation of Rs 200 per acre. Lakshmi Kantharaj Urs, meanwhile, sought Mirza Ismail's influence with the municipal authorities to prevent Murti Rao from building on the land himself.[103] Despite Mirza's refusal to interfere with the workings of the municipality, Lakshmi Kantharaj Urs pressed on with his plans for "a decent garden laid out as inexpensively as possible" and designed by Krumbiegal.[104] Extensive additions were made to the grounds of Cheluvamba Vilas even as late as 1927 under Krumbiegal's advice.[105]

The emergence of the royal family from the space of the fort and the palace into other parts of Mysore defined city space in very specific ways, sometimes by defying municipal law. The classical lines of many buildings of the late nineteenth century, with columns and pediments, though orna-

Figure 38. Cheluvamba Vilas Mansion (mansion for the third maharajakumari). Photograph courtesy of the Central Food Technology Research Institute, Mysore.

mented with Hindu motifs, yielded place to a richly ornamental Mysore "baroque," replete with Rajputana domes. According to David Cannadine, the Indo-Saracenic style of building palaces across the country, from Baroda to Mysore, was exuberant in its asymmetries and its aura of instant antiquity.[106] Questions relating to the aesthetics of public architecture arose repeatedly during discussions over changes to the entrance of the Jaganmohan palace, the several mansions that were being built for the yuvaraja, and the plans that were made from 1916 for a new guest mansion where European visitors to the palace could be lodged or entertained.[107]

In approaching the Bombay architect E. W. Fritchley, the palace authorities implicitly expressed their appreciation of his company's previous involvement with the bedroom and office blocks of the main palace.[108] Fritchley had expressed his interest in Mysore buildings as early as 1910, proposing interventions that would make the third rajkumari's mansion and the new palace offices "a work of art."[109] Fritchley was clear that the new palace, as the guest house was now referred to, should not be in the same class as a government house but "something worthy of [Krishnaraja] Wodeyar's leading position in India."[110] The several designs that Frtichley presented were in the modern Tudor style, the Gothic style, the classic style, the Indian style, and the Baronial style, of which the last was at first preferred by Krishnaraja Wodeyar. Shortly thereafter, the Maharaja expressed his keenness to adopt the design of the Kapurthala palace for the mansion in Mysore and asked Fritchley to prepare drawings based on the photograph of the place, which the architect successfully evaded.[111]

What was finally built, as Mirza Ismail pointed out to end the wrangles about the architect's commission and charges for unused drawings, was a classical structure based on palace architect Lakshminarasappa's elevation and worked on by Fritchley.[112] The arrangement of the building into three different blocks and the garden plans both interior and exterior were extensively reworked by Krumbiegal, although the interior decorations were Fritchley's. The high costs of construction, moreover, first made the palace administration confine construction to just one central block costing Rs 1.5 million, though two other blocks were also added by 1932. Fritchley's own description of his design was classic Renaissance, with "domes in a pictorial style, as a palace for residence and out in a countryside away from congested business streets."[113] Fritchley's plans were reworked considerably to reduce expenses and not create a slavish imitation of a European style.[114]

The new guest mansion was thus an attempt to produce a new and frankly European-style building after decades of experiments with Indo-classical styles that had recklessly taken features from various epochs. Not all aspects of the aesthetics of a splendidly isolated sculptural edifice were achieved. Krumbiegal and Mirza envisaged the palace as a magnificent terminal point for Narasimharaja Boulevard, which swept away from Chamundi Hills. But this was not to be: as Mirza pointed out to Krumbiegal, the Maharaja's sanction for the construction of several houses along the new road to the mansion in continuation of Narasimharaja Boulevard "puts an end to our idea of giving a fine approach road to the Mansion through an extensive park."[115]

If the palace asserted a new historical presence, it was as a duty to the Mysore public and to the state. The reconstituted royal sought less help from tropes of the epic hero Krishna than from those of his predecessor, more willingly lending his name to the signs of a modern economy: Krishnaraja Boulevard, Krishnarajasagar Dam, and the Krishnaraja textile mills. Reciprocity, meanwhile, took on a new meaning that defined the relation between palace and state, the latter taking on the responsibility of financing the invention of the royal capital. The palace, and the Maharaja in particular, meanwhile forged a new relationship to the subjects of Mysore, who were increasingly constituted as a modern public.

Mysore Palace: From Private Residence to Public Display

The responsibilities of the state in upholding the pomp and splendor of the palace were most evident in the prolonged building and rebuilding of the Mysore palace and structures on the fort grounds that occurred from the time of the fire in 1897 well into the 1930s. The constant transformations of the palace complex were signs that the Mysore public was gaining a more credible contour as the palace increasingly became the site around which the public life of Mysore city revolved, particularly during the Dasara celebrations. Arrangements were periodically made, as when the Karohatti was converted into a chattram in 1918, for the "use of villagers that throng into the capital during Dasara and Birthday festivities."[116]

To briefly recount the important moments in the rebuilding of the palace: during the fire of 1897, which raged for three days, more than 30,000 square feet of the 149,382-square-foot palace burned down, including the sejje and the three stories rising above it, the Sanskrit library and music rooms, the verandah on the western side, the Balakhana on the southern side, and the Amba Vilas, which adjoined the Balakhana. Of these, the Amba Vilas was an entirely new durbar hall, principally used for durbars and state functions.[117]

The new three-story structure, finally completed in 1912, measured 244.5 by 156.5 feet and was topped with towers and a central gilded cupola of six stories, 143 feet tall. It consisted of the sejje, a marriage pavilion with a glass ceiling supported by iron pillars to the south, and an armory and library to the north. Two staircases led to the first-floor durbar hall, measuring 150 feet by 45 feet. To the northwest side of this were the drawing and music rooms, and on the south was the Amba Vilas durbar hall, with a stained-glass roof supported by iron pillars. Three other types of ceilings were used: plaster ceilings with stucco, carved teakwood, and lightly embossed metal sheets.

Both the external features and the internal embellishments of the palace combined a concern for safety and used materials such as stone, brick, and iron. Far exceeding the estimate of Rs 2.5 million and in the end costing Rs 4.4 million, the palace was built on the plans provided by Irwin, while the interiors were decorated using indigenous mythological and allegorical themes, of which the Ravi Varma commission formed a part.[118] Unlike the new palace at Pudukkotai, which was built at about the same time, no fully formed vision of the Mysore palace and its relation to the surroundings was in place at the time of its original design, and indeed, what exists today evolved through an unusually protracted process of building and rebuilding.[119]

Irwin's designs passed the acerbic tests of *Indian Engineering* despite being somewhat florid, though the publication had earlier condemned the palace for having tried to manage the construction through its newly established department called the Palace Division instead of leaving the matter to "competent contractors in Madras and Bombay."[120]

For the occupants of the palace, practical matters relating to private space became far more urgent. The palace was handed over to the royal family in 1907, when the *gruha pravesham* (housewarming) was conducted, but the first Dasara durbar could be held in its new setting only in 1910.[121] In that year it was realized that "no suitable provision was made for living rooms or offices" because the emphasis had been on "accommodation . . . for ceremonial purposes only," such as that provided by the *sejje* and the marriage pavilion. The provision of four rooms for living and office space were said to be "mere apologies," and at least "one block of suitable living apartments" was urgently required.[122] The new bedroom block was completed by 1916–17, whereas the new office block was completed only in the early 1920s.[123]

By the late 1920s, Mysore had become a place to which crowds from both within and outside the city would throng during the Dasara season. The principal attraction was the Dasara procession, enhanced by the pleasures of the Dasara exhibition. Equally important were the temples in the fort complex, which, as Ikegame suggests, were by 1927–28 being seen as important aesthetic features for which the state government had responsibility for maintenance and repair.[124] At this time, the temples in the fort complex included the Trineshwaraswami temple (the oldest structure in the area), the Sweta Varahaswami temple (1809), the Prasanna Krishnaswamy temple (1825), and the Lakshmiramana temple (dating from the fifteenth century).

Burton Stein describes the royal court's transformation into a temple-space at festive times in South India.[125] We may get a sense of how much the practice of kingship had changed from the models on which it had been based, for although the royal cosmos was produced by alternating religious and temporal codes, secular compulsions were beginning to dominate. Given the numbers pressing into Mysore each year for the Dasara, fresh plans were made for the expansion of the durbar hall. How was this addition to the palace to be financed and carried out as a "government work"? Justifications for the proposed expenditure, this time by the government, rested on two principal points: the responsibility of the king to be available for comfortable viewing by the public and the financial viability of the expansions. If the original design was first faulted for having stressed only the ceremonial functions at the expense of private ones, ceremonial functions once more came to the foreground:

> When the Palace was originally designed, the external architectural effect seem [sic] to have dominated every other consideration.... The portico with its very massive pillars in front and the Durbar Hall itself with similar huge pillars rendered it quite impossible for any state function being held in a befitting manner. The low roof of the Hall added to the discomfort and suffocation of those assembled in it. The design was so bad that it was impossible either for those that were in the Durbar Hall itself or *for the public assembled in the quadrangles and the* maidan *[empty ground] in front of the Palace to have a view of the throne and of His Highness* during such occasions. The state functions lost much of their grandeur and significance under the circumstances. It was therefore a compelling necessity that these obstructions which precluded a clear view of the throne from all points should be removed.... The portico was accordingly dismantled and as a temporary measure the Hall was extended by about 60 feet eliminating as far as possible, all obstacles to the view of the public, as well as of persons in the hall itself.[126]

A temporary durbar hall was built entirely at palace expense.[127] The proposed new durbar hall, measuring 245 feet and intended to extend by 60 feet on both sides of the temporary structure, required the demolition of the existing Bidadi block and the construction of a new one, in addition to a Nagarkhana opposite the new palace frontage. The total cost of the new buildings was Rs 1.8 million, to which the palace promised to contribute Rs 300,000 for the Bidadi block: the rest, it was argued, "being entirely for public functions," had to come out of public funds. The suggestion was made that the government seek a loan to include the costs of building the new durbar hall (Rs 1.5 million), in keeping with principles adopted for public building in Delhi.

The proposal to expand the sejje came at a time when the palace was increasingly willing to accommodate the expanding number of spectators.

Figure 39. Krishnaraja Wodeyar IV and Kantirava Narasimharaja Wodeyar at a durbar
(royal assembly) in the richly embellished durbar hall, mid-1930s. Postcard. Courtesy of the
Clare Arni Collection.

Aya Ikegame therefore concludes that "the fort thus gradually transformed
its function into that of a stand for viewing the rituals and ceremonies of a
theatre state."[128] I would emphasize, however, following Pamela Price, the
formation of a new Mysore public that was addressed through the displays
associated with the Dasara, which was designed to evoke awe and reverence, to incorporate newly "governmentalized" categories of the Mysore
public, to amuse, and most important, to instruct. The durbar was thus
redefined as a space for the distribution of honors, though in largely unexpected ways. It assumed a duplex character, serving religious or secular
needs as the occasion demanded, in response to new developments and
pressures that had altered the composition of the public. In 1936, the question of admitting Adi Karnatakas to the birthday and Dasara durbars came
up.[129] A committee formed to go into the question was largely in favor of
admission: only Srikanteswara Iyer was absolutely opposed to the proposal, which would "cut at the root of Sanathana Dharma" and violate the
"express provision prohibiting such entry into dwelling houses [palaces]
of Sanathanists." Other submissions hovered in between.[130] The Maharaja

aesthetic of palace ground design. By 1928, the decision that the state must maintain the temples for aesthetic reasons had been strengthened. Although the addition of the Gayathri temple was first proposed at the site of the Kille Kacheri offices in 1929, it was intended as "a *structure similar to and symmetrical with* the Trineshwaraswami Temple" that was to be built in order to "complete the proper layout of the Fort."[142] The temple, which replaced the Kille Kacheri stores, was completed in 1949 and, with the Bhuvaneswari temple (completed in 1953), achieved the absolute symmetry of the fort complex for which Krumbiegal had so long striven.[143] The inversion of the figure–ground relationship and the new coordinates to which the temples and palace complex conformed, with the temples facing toward the Palace rather than the more auspicious east, were now complete and symmetry maintained.[144]

Work on the new east gate, for instance, which had been planned at least since 1918, was conceived according to the demands of perspectival vision. The palace proposal to place the statue of Krishnaraja Wodeyar IV in a circle, probably to match the statue of Chamarajendra Wodeyar before the north gate, was strongly disapproved by Krumbiegal on the grounds that it would mar the line of vision; he stressed the need for open "sun gardens."[145] The new east gate, later called the Jaya Marthanda Gate, was optically aligned to provide the best view of the palace and the grounds. The fort walls adjoining the east gate were also realigned to provide continuity. When a design of the "pure Moghul style" was suggested, it was firmly rejected as out of keeping with the overall style of palace architecture.[146] The awkward alignment of the fort wall to the road itself, which was found to mar "the effect of this important frontage of the Palace," was resolved by a new road realignment.[147] Most important, the gate design dispensed with the sacred principles of fort building that required each entrance to be flanked by Kote Anjaneyaswami and Vinayaka temples, features of all the other three existing gates.[148]

The New Aesthetics of Exhibition

New aesthetic tastes that involved an appreciation of symmetry and rolling lawns, new economies that burgeoned out of the annual pageants at the palace, and a new and admiring public secured by ensuring a friendly press—by the mid-1930s it appeared as if the Mysore royalty was well served in its pursuit of praise from the colonial regime and Mysore public. In

August 1927, on the occasion of the silver jubilee of Krishnaraja Wodeyar IV, the sirdars, palace officers, Ursu gentlemen, and palace *vidwans* (scholars), officials, and servants chose to express their love and gratitude to the Maharaja in a curious way, by rebuilding the clock tower of Mysore city to a height of ninety-two feet and installing a clock and bell specially imported from France.[149] The clock tower had long been a feature of Victorian cities and after the 1860s began to be erected in many cities of India, a formal proclamation of the imperial order with its emphasis on the economic use of time.[150] If bell ringing marked the amount of time that lapsed between one ritual and the next in medieval Europe, says Richard Sennett, "the quantification of time . . . was the time shown on clock faces; in this sense secular time meant *visible* time without ritual."[151] Together with the other monuments of a cityscape that lent an aura of historicity, the clock tower became a feature of the Mysore cityscape, spatializing manmade, secular time that questioned an earlier indifference to divided time. It also made for a legible and imageable city. This was done by placing the square tower, topped by a domed canopy, on a base in the middle of a well-tended garden, isolating the tower from surrounding structures.

By this time, Mysore beyond the fort and palace complex had also been spatially transformed through the efforts of the Mysore City Improve-

Figure 40. Silver Jubilee Clock Tower rebuilt in honor of Krishnaraja Wodeyar IV's golden jubilee (1902–27). Postcard. Courtesy of the Clare Arni Collection.

ment Trust Board and consisted of many well-developed areas, such as Lakshmipuram for the Ursus and Jalapuri for the untouchable castes, as well as roads, squares, and circles that conformed to the principles of modern city planning.[152] Beginning as early as 1903, when the Trust Board was set up, these new suburbs were built as much to relieve congestion as to "visualize and fix once again the social stratification articulated by class, caste and religion."[153] Clock time and grid space, those features of modern city planning that combined the economic uses of time with the functionalist uses of space, took their place within a city aesthetic that had, through the strategy of locating members of the royal family in mansions at elevated points of the city and through embellishing these residences richly, acquired the profile of a royal city.

Throughout the early decades of the nineteenth century, the royal family was also becoming increasingly alert to the demands and changing tastes of a touring public and to the affective ties of the population. The argument that the responsibility for the construction of the palace, royal buildings in Mysore, and their maintenance rested on the state paralleled the claim that the palace was a private domain. The steady transformation of the Jaganmohan palace, which in the nineteenth century had been a spacious bungalow belonging to the palace for the entertainment of European visitors, into a public art gallery is a revealing instance of negotiations made by the palace authorities to create an exhibitionary space that would awe, educate, and entertain the public. A parallel development was the annual Dasara Exhibition, organized to display the products and schemes of Mysore made modern. It achieved a new semiotic coherence to Mysore as a territory of production and consumption, endowed with resources and new capabilities.

The royal family first began to use the Jaganmohan palace, to the west of the fort complex, after the fire of 1897: from that year it became the site of the Mysore Dasara celebrations despite its unsuitable construction.[154] The compulsions of adding grandeur to what was a large and spacious, if somewhat plain, bungalow led to the construction of a vimana on the palace in 1898 to "break the flat surface of the topmost terrace."[155] In 1900, the marriage of Krishnaraja Wodeyar IV was celebrated by extending the plain porch of the Jaganmohan palace with a highly decorated but temporary marriage pavilion.[156] By 1913, a large number of public events, including the annual birthday and Dasara durbars, the marriages of the third maharajakumari and the yuvaraja (younger brother of the Maharaja), and the reception of more than one viceroy, had been held in this pavilion. Until then, the maintenance of the marriage pavilion had been the responsibility of the state, while that of the main structure had remained with the palace.[157] The palace, however, made the argument that the marriage pavilion was the state's responsibility because it was used primarily for state functions, such as the annual meeting of the Representative Assembly at Mysore.[158]

By 1913 there was no alternative to turning the pavilion into a permanent structure.[159] By 1915, Jaganmohan Palace had been turned into an art gallery, and less than ten years later, James Cousins set up "the first permanent compendious gallery of Modern Indian painting in South India" at the palace.[160] Thereafter, the Jaganmohan Chitrasala became a place for a new and expanding band of domestic tourists. The number of visitors was so encouraging that tickets were introduced in 1927, and from 1933 catalogues of the paintings were regularly produced and sold to the public. The Chitrasala continued to be "a popular resort" well into the 1940s, with the number of visitors nearly doubling, from 26,053 in 1943 to 45,974 in 1945–46.[161]

The palace's transition from a place where the Maharaja entertained his European guests in the nineteenth century, surrounded by the images of displaced royal glory, to one that entertained and educated, signified a decisive shift to making the city an exhibitionary complex. A private collection of objects to which there had previously been restricted aristocratic access was now open to a paying public. This collection of objects was also set within a new taxonomy of progress.[162] Indeed, the Jaganmohan palace was denuded, rather as Dariya Daulat had been, of its original meaning as a space that announced political legitimacy to become a site that fostered new modes of spectation, progressively ignoring the Rang Mahal on the upper floor to focus on the art objects below.

If the principal aim of the gallery was to shape the artistic and historical sensibilities of the Mysore public, the Dasara Industrial and Agricultural Exhibition, which became an annual event (with some breaks during the twentieth century), had a different pedagogical goal, familiarizing the public with the natural resources and products of Mysore but also actively instructing the people in the ways of being modern, whether in matters of hygiene or nutrition.[163] Mysore had sent some of its largely primary products, such as cereals, spices, and gums, along with a few other manufactures, such as dyes and drugs, to the Paris Exhibition of 1878.[164] The first exhibition of industrial products in Mysore was held in 1888 to coincide with the Dasara festivities. In 1905, inspired by the Indian Industrial and Agricultural Exhibition of the Indian National Congress to be held at Benares, plans were made to hold a similar exhibition to coincide with the visit of the Prince and Princess of Wales in January and February 1906.[165] Despite stern discouragement from the Resident, the Mysore government went ahead with its plans, envisaging "lasting benefits to the country and its people from a healthy stimulus of its agricultural and industrial pursuits, by the dissemination of useful information."[166]

Before long, the exhibition had become an annual affair, with a firm commitment to the education of Mysore's *ryots* (peasants) and artisans through examples of progress and improvement from elsewhere.[167] Advertisers and exhibitors from other parts of India were soon attracted to this annual event, and the large number of awards attracted large numbers. Encouraged by the response, which in 1907 included sixteen thousand paying visitors and five thousand free ones, from "Patels, Shambogues, Sheikdars and Inspectors" to "owners of cattle" and ordinary rural producers, the government was strongly urged to make the exhibition an annual event to exploit the pedagogic value of repetition.[168] As many as 13,911 exhibits were brought to Mysore from fifty-eight different Indian locations. Not only was a permanent site chosen for the exhibition, but a series of lectures on a variety of subjects was added for the instruction of visitors.[169]

The exhibition received even greater encouragement under Dewan Visvesvaraya, who went further, suggesting district-level exhibitions and a permanent museum of Mysore products instead of the ten-day Dasara event. Interest flagged for a while after his retirement, when suggestions were made that the exhibition be held only once every three years; as Dewan Kantaraj Urs wrote to Mirza Ismail, "More and more difficulty is experienced every year in making it really useful and instructive."[170] The exhibition petered out but was revived with great panache by Dewan Mirza Ismail in 1927. After this, it was made into a large, well-organized, annual event that drew exhibitors, consumers, producers, and spectators, making the Mysore Dasara Exhibition a fitting and grand supplement to the ceremony and pomp that attended the Dasara festivities, drawing on and adding to the crowds. There were many ways in which the Mysore public was being instructed not only in the methods of production but in new forms of consumption as well, as the splendid *Dasara Handbook,* put together specially for the event, clearly revealed. By the 1930s, the Mysore Dasara exhibition was not merely putting buyers in touch with sellers but promoting Mysore's products.[171] Thus "Mysore's Wembley," as it began to be called, was increasingly made self-supporting from stall rent, gate fees, and advertisement revenue and was, by the war period, touted as "the most useful and well organised exhibition in India."[172]

The Image of the City

Clock time, grid space: those monotonous aspects of city development took on a different meaning in Mysore, enhancing the legibility and image-ability of a city that was fashioned from a remembered idea of sovereignty. That this "historical city" was far from exempt from all the troubles that plagued most Indian cities—the squalor of its poorer parts, the shabby pro-vision of basic services, and the unsanitary state of its markets—becomes far clearer from the municipal records. M. A. Sreenivasan, who became the president of the Mysore Municipal Council and the chairman of the Mysore City Improvement Trust Board in the 1930s, records his frustration at having worked with a reluctantly modern population.[173] His memoirs are interesting precisely because he demonstrates an intimate link between the squalid neighborhoods and the public face of the royal city (which housed many of the mace bearers who made the pageant of the Mysore palace possible).[174] His contribution to refining the production of a royal, histori-cal city lay in renaming the streets: "In consultation with the Professor of Indian history and the Director of Archaeology, I thought of more uplift-ing names like Ashoka, Harsha, Shalivahana and Akbar, for the important roads like Dodpet . . . Paigambar (the Prophet) Park instead of Slaughter house park . . . Valmiki for Kurubarahatti, and so on."[175]

It was a sign of the extent to which the Maharaja's role within princely Mysore had been loosened from its sacral moorings that annual rituals at the palace became increasingly sensitive to the political vagaries of the new public. In the turbulent days leading up to the Mysore Chalo move-ment in late 1947, when Jayachamarajendra Wodeyar was asked to join the Indian union, the annual birthday procession was canceled. In place of the customary state procession in the evening, "a procession was ar-ranged . . . of Sri Chamundeswari on the Chamundi hill, and all the deities of the temples in the fort in the quadrangle of the palace."[176] The fiction of princely power could no longer be sustained, for even the love and loyalty of the people of Mysore could not have guaranteed the king undisturbed passage through the city.

By this time, in any case, Mysore city's relationship to the former capital of Srirangapatna had more or less ended as it became increasingly tied to the administrative capital of Bangalore, where the shift from sovereign to governmental power was signaled in more prosaic building styles. Indeed, a self-conscious deployment of a Mysore monarchical style of architecture occurred in the postindependence years with the building of Vidhana Soudha, ironically at the very moment when Mysore state formally ended its 160-year existence.[177] As a result, it was still Mysore and Srirangapatna that attracted and held the attention of tourists.

Conclusion

Today the road to Mysore cleaves Srirangapatna, leaving the fort to its west and the rest of the island to its east, a historical space dismembered by the instruments of modernity. Tourists are allowed only a short time at the fort site before they are taken on to be dazzled by the royal city, with its amusements and spectacles, and then are transported at dusk to be overawed by the power of modern technology at Brindavan Gardens, "the Versailles of Mysore." It is a tour that quickly leaves the landscape of conquest and death behind to emerge in a space whose streets are full of "history," where one may receive a lively sense of the legendary lifestyles of the Mysore Wodeyars.

Yet to reduce the history of Mysore city to the successful production of this royal image or to judge present-day Srirangapatna's feebler claims to being a cityscape at all, would be to miss the ways in which these twin cities bear the marks of a practice of power. As Michel Rolph Trouillot reminds us, "Power itself is never so transparent that its analysis becomes superfluous. The ultimate mark of power may be its invisibility."[178] I have revealed the success with which Tipu Sultan's legacy has been reinscribed and subordinated to a renovated history of Mysore. The renovated walls of the Mysore fort bear no marks of the struggle between contending conceptions of power and authority or of time. The stones of the dismantled Mysore fort were brought back from Nazarabad to encircle and corral a king who was gradually reduced in power and subordinated to a bureaucracy. By the twentieth century, the immaculately tended fort had been refashioned to serve largely aesthetic ideals and visions while retaining its status as a sanctified enclave.

CHAPTER 5

K. Venkatappa and the Fashioning
of a Mysore Modern in Art

O N JUNE 1, 1916, K. Venkatappa, who had left Mysore in 1909 for Calcutta with a scholarship from the Maharaja of Mysore, returned after seven years at the Government School of Art in Calcutta, where he had been among Abanindranath Tagore's privileged band of pupils.[1] The Mysore palace was impressed with the phenomenal progress shown by this young painter.[2] At Calcutta he had enjoyed the tutelage of Abanindranath and earned a modest reputation as a member of the increasingly acclaimed Bengal school of art, which had pioneered a new "nationalist" aesthetic.[3] Could Venkatappa's return be seen as something of a retreat from the privileges and risks of the emerging art world of Bengal to the relatively safer spheres of princely patronage and select audiences at the Mysore palace?

Not quite. The complexity of Venkatappa's negotiations—of the palace culture that he had briefly left; of the emerging modern art world of critics, buyers, exhibitors, and promoters; and of the Kannada national consciousness that was in the making—defies definition as "reluctant modernity" or even as an anti- or nonmodern subjectivity. For twenty-four years, that is, until 1940, when he was rudely dislodged from his privileged position, Venkatappa built a career that combined assiduous devotion and loyalty to the Maharaja, who was at once his patron and his public at the palace, with a cautious cultivation of a new art public. He simultaneously strove to distinguish himself from the milieu of other palace artists to which he had been born. Both in his choice of genres and subjects after his return to Mysore and in his relationship to the field of agents who constituted the new world of artistic production, Venkatappa carefully deployed his educational capital while simultaneously staging a break, denying too easy identification with Abanindranath and his pupils. Far from being a retailer of the new nationalist aesthetic, as was repeatedly claimed by art critics and historians alike, and rather than going forth "like an apostle" "to transmit the light of the Master," as did most of Abanindranath's other pupils, Venkatappa staked out a lonely path for himself, celebrating his estrangement from the emerging world of modern art.[4]

An "Anti-economic Economy"

We have seen the kinds of transactions relating to questions of legitimacy and authority as they were defined in a range of representational practices in mural and portrait painting or in redefining architectural space. Venkatappa represents a new moment in the twentieth century when the art critic, the art collector, the artistic reproduction, the student, and linguistic state formation replaced the royal patron as crucial elements in his eventual consecration as Mysore's modern artist. The insistence with which Venkatappa declared his reluctance to embrace the imperatives of the evolving field of artistic production was itself a form of participation in it, characterized by Pierre Bourdieu as "anti-economic economy."[5] Among the many lessons that Venkatappa had learned while at Calcutta, and more specifically from his admission to the charmed circle at Jorasanko, the Tagore household, was the extraordinary importance of a "specific capital" that was denied to those whose destinies were dictated by caste or hereditary callings. It was perhaps as a way of compensating for his inheritance that Venkatappa carefully cultivated abstinence, of the sexual and the material kind, and developed a style of work that was eccentric and unpredictable.[6] Venkatappa's career disrupts the narratives of how the twin demands of nationalism and modernity were negotiated by his contemporaries, providing an unusual optic with which to discern links between art forms and social formations in periodizing the modern.[7]

For many who have written about him, Venkatappa's personal dispositions—his memorable eccentricities, his excessive litigiousness, and his obsessive austerity—were the unmistakable signs of artistic genius.[8] Yet the emerging art world and its bourgeois public required art critics, galleries, exhibitions, and art journals alike, which were as crucial to the legitimation of an artist as the work of art itself. We cannot, therefore, make sense of Venkatappa's uniqueness without considering his position within the emerging structure of opportunities and rewards.

Venkatappa's staged indifference to the material world was not altogether unique. After all, the Bengali artists shared his calculated "interest in disinterestedness," in keeping with the emerging nationalist aesthetic's critical distance from the more mercenary and imitative trends within Indian art at the time.[9] Abanindranath's scornful reference to the "evil spirit [that] smells of trader's greed," who "sells himself at a fixed price and sometimes at a high value," all in the service of "wealthy people," was somewhat disingenuous.[10] Abanindranath's distaste was possible not because the Bengal school kept itself sternly aloof from the lures of the market but because many, though not all, of its artists were already endowed with sufficient economic and social capital to risk failure. To the extent that the cultural milieu of the Bengal school was coterminous with that of the Bengali *bhadralok,* an emergent Bengali middle class, it was one with which Venkatappa, by virtue of his caste, class, and regional or provincial origins, was unequipped to fully integrate.

Making an Artist of an Artisan

Venkatappa was born in 1886 to a Chitragara family, traditional workers in gold leaf whose ancestors had long served under the Vijayanagar kings. In the early nineteenth century, Venkatappa's forefathers had arrived in Srirangapatna from Chitradurga to seek refuge in the court of Krishnaraja Wodeyar III and participated in the revival of the Mysore style of painting in the early nineteenth century.[11] Of Venkatappa's father, Durgada Krishnappa, himself an employee of the Mysore palace, we know very little except that he shared the same caste and social background as most of Venkatappa's contemporaries employed in the palace—K. Keshavaiah, S. Shankarappa, Y. Nagaraju, Basavaiah, and M. Rama Narasaiah.[12] Caste continued to be considered the ideal preserver of a "traditional artistic culture," and later writers even suggested that "traditional artists alone deserved to be encouraged" in the propagation of artistic ideals.[13]

Both Venkatappa and his father were witnesses to the arrival of Raja Ravi Varma and his brother at the Mysore palace in 1904, and Venkatappa's only oil portrait of a woman probably dates from that period.[14] Ravi Varma's formidable reputation and his own noble origins, no doubt, went a long way in ensuring that this painter was treated with far more privilege than any of the Mysore palace painters of the time.[15]

Venkatappa, unlike Keshavaiah, did not master the new medium, leaving the cloistered world of the palace painter for the privileged but alienating world of the Calcutta Art School, which offered quite different instruction from what he had received at the Mysore Industrial Institute. By 1909,

Figure 41. An early miniature portrait by K. Venkatappa (1886/87–1965), A Young South Indian Woman, *late nineteenth century; opaque watercolor and gold on paper, 7.3 x 5.0 cm. San Diego Museum of Art, Edwin Binney 3rd Collection.*

the entire range of elements so crucial to a modern art establishment—critics, publishers, exhibitors, and middle-class patrons—was harmoniously at work in promoting the work of Abanindranath and his pupils.[16] The severe attacks on the Bengal school that were launched in the assembly or the press were a sign of its growing influence rather than its marginal status: indeed, it was said that "much of the power and vitality of the Tagore school is a gift from the opposition camp."[17]

Venkatappa had little by way of preparation for this new world: traditional painters, though frequently encouraged to upgrade their skills, were strictly subordinated to the production regime at the palace. Of the three major art schools that had been established by this time, the one at Madras alone actively encouraged students from hereditarily artisan castes to seek training in European academic norms. Venkatappa had passed all the examinations offered by the school for external candidates; K. Keshavaiah had attended the Madras school on a scholarship from the palace before returning as supernumerary painter in 1902.[18] In contrast, both the Bombay and the Calcutta art schools were decidedly elitist by the 1890s. In Calcutta this elitism was most marked, says Partha Mitter, with "the majority of boys belonging to the bhadralok castes," even if, like Surendranath Ganguly, they came from desperately poor backgrounds.[19] Exemplifying the hierarchy between the traditional artist and the gentleman painter were the salaries paid to Lala Iswari Prasad (of Lucknow) and Abanindranath Tagore, respectively, at the Calcutta art school: Rs 75 and Rs 300.[20] The caste heritage clearly had its uses even in Calcutta, with Venkatappa and Iswari Prasad assigned to producing indigenous pigments.[21]

The Calcutta art school did provide some new opportunities: Venkatappa was among the five artists chosen to illustrate the much circulated text of Sister Nivedita and Ananda Coomaraswamy's *The Myths of the Hindus and Buddhists;* with Nandalal Bose, he provided the illustrations to Abanindranath's pioneering article "Indian Iconography"; his works were regularly included at the annual exhibitions of the Indian Society of Oriental Art in Calcutta, which also frequently arranged sales.[22] The inclusion of his works at the India Society of London in 1910 earned him handsome praise from the art critic William Rothenstein, words that have ever since been cited as enduring evidence of Venkatappa's early genius.[23]

Relentless promotion of the Bengal school was done in the pages of *Modern Review* from its inception in 1907; yet one searches in vain for reproductions of the Mysore artist's work, even at a time when he was unquestionably close to Abanindranath. At least one later critic deplored this systematic exclusion. N. Vyasa Ram complained: "Most people know about the Bengal art only through the pictures appearing from time to time in the *Modern Review.* Unfortunately, however, ... personal considerations in these matters are likely to exercise greater influence in the matter of selection than merit."[24] Nothing seems to have come of S. V. Ramaswamy Mudaliar's suggestion to O. C. Gangoly, writing on living Indian artists in 1923, that Venkatappa be included as the "only one in south India."[25] A sign of Venkatappa's own discontent about the bewildering social milieu of which he was part was his search for alternative accommodation as a guest of Gaganendranath Tagore in Darjeeling in 1914. He was appalled that

Figure 42. An example of Venkatappa's productions during his Calcutta sojourn. K. Venkatappa, Buddha and His Disciples, c. 1913; watercolor, 12.75 x 27.75 cm. Venkatappa Art Gallery, Bangalore. Photograph by M. N. Muralidhar.

"flesh, fish and vegetables are cooked and served by the same Brahmans in the same kitchen."[26]

At any rate, Venkatappa had a fierce sense of loyalty to his patron, the Maharaja of Mysore, which he cited when turning down an attractive offer from Percy Brown of a government post as "Art Adviser."[27] He returned to Mysore in 1916 when his scholarship had ceased, and there sought the Mysore palace's support for a visit to England to learn bronze casting, though the war put an end to these plans.[28] Drawn instead to the world of music at the palace school headed by Veena Seshanna, he received personal instruction in the veena.[29] In many ways, the period at the palace music school served as a useful interim arrangement by which Venkatappa avoided immediate absorption as a palace artist while staking a claim to royal patronage on somewhat different terms.

Redefining the Palace as Patron

As a scholarship student returning to the palace of his patron, Venkatappa could hope for none of the privileges of a Ravi Varma. Yet he did use the newly gained cultural capital to his advantage, marking himself off from the Palace artists in more ways than one. Venkatappa refused to take up a government job until the war was over, claiming that his "education was not quite complete," although he firmly turned down the suggestion that he return to the Calcutta school even with a scholarship, saying that he had learned all that it could offer.[30] Venkatappa attempted to turn his metropolitan experiences as well as his newly acquired asceticism to his advantage. Yet his need for a working relationship with the palace establishment set obvious limits to a radical redefinition of princely patronage, as his encounters with the private secretary to the Maharaja, Mirza Ismail, soon revealed.

Mirza believed that Venkatappa's immersion in music had rendered useless the fine arts training that had been "acquired at an enormous [palace] expense and trouble."[31] Mirza set Venkatappa to work on a set of three landscapes for which the artist was to provide written explanations "so that spectators may easily understand"; he also assigned Venkatappa the design of a seal for Mysore University.[32] Mirza saw little reason to distinguish Venkatappa from other palace artists, who were frequently asked to paint portraits of various personages, and he asked Venkatappa to paint some portraits of the Maharaja in 1918.[33]

Venkatappa resisted identification as just another palace artist until the prestigious commission to decorate the walls of the Amba Vilas durbar hall set him firmly apart. Like the other palace artists, Venkatappa broke with the tradition of his forebears; the Mysore-style painting was abandoned and saw a brief revival only in the work of Y. Subrahmanya Raju. At the same time, Venkatappa's Calcutta training had taught him to reject the large-scale oil paintings in the new academic realist oeuvre of Ravi Varma, which was enthusiastically adapted by the other Palace painters. At Calcutta, Venkatappa's work conformed to the evolving Bengal style, although his use of flat areas of brilliant pure color were reminiscent of the miniature tradition, and his somewhat stiff, archaic figures were distinct from the dreamy, vapory, creations favored by the other Bengal school artists. Back in Mysore, he struck out in unexpected directions, drawing on his academic training, reviving the dated technique of painting miniature portraits on ivory, developing a distinct style of landscape painting, and going beyond prevailing palace art conventions in proposing the medium of plaster of paris for a series of bas reliefs at Amba Vilas.

The contrast between the career of Venkatappa and that of his contemporary K. Keshavaiah is instructive. Keshavaiah's ancestors had come from Turuvekere near Tumkur, probably during the time of Tipu Sultan. His grandfather Gurikar Tippanna had been the most celebrated artist of Krishnaraja Wodeyar's court, of which Venkatappa's grandfather too had been a part.[34] Tippanna's only son, Chennakeshavayya, began his career as an artist and retired from the palace establishment as an accountant. In 1897, Keshavaiah was sent by the Mysore palace to train at the Madras School of Arts for three years.[35] In 1901 he was appointed to the post of palace artist for Rs 10 a month, though he was soon able to combine palace work with teaching at the Chamaraja Technical Institute in Mysore.[36] Keshavaiah worked entirely in oils, though he was not averse to an occasional production in the traditional style.

The job of palace artist was unenviable, quite distinct from the leisurely contemplative life of a gentleman artist so evocatively depicted in Nandalal Bose's drawing of the group at Jorasanko.[37] Apart from keeping up with his heavy teaching schedule, Keshavaiah was expected to produce several paintings for the palace on a variety of subjects, for which he was reimbursed enough to meet the costs of his materials.[38] His assignments ranged from restoring old paintings, painting the Mysore coats of arms on carriages, and refurbishing *chiks* (blinds) to making enlargements of photographs and painting landscapes to order. Painters were not automatically entitled to palace honors, and Keshavaiah fought in vain to have his name added to the Durbar Honors list of the Mysore palace or at least to be named to a permanent well-paid post.[39] As late as 1943, Keshavaiah earned Rs 35 per month, marginally more than his fellow palace artists, who earned between Rs 20 and Rs 35.[40] Gifts or presents from the Maharaja himself were rarer, though artists were urged to await princely "rewards" rather than charge for their time and labor.[41]

Similarly, Lakshman Krishna, also of the Chitragara caste, came to Mysore from Belgaum when the construction of the new Mysore palace was begun in the late nineteenth century. Although he was not formally trained, he acquired the skills of clay modeling and designing and earned Rs 2 a day for his labors.[42] He was made a molder and painter in 1909 and designated head painter in 1916.[43] That year he was assigned to head the group that would repaint the murals at Dariya Daulat, a task that took nearly three years.[44] In 1917 he applied to the Palace Maramath Department for higher pay and asked that "the present designation of my office be changed and a more dignified name" be granted.[45] Though his salary did improve over the years, neither his designation nor the assigned work was altered.

Palace artists were frequently ordered to paint portraits of various royal personages from photographs for distribution to institutions all over the state. Keshavaiah executed four of the murals for the Kalyana Mantapa depicting the Dasara and birthday processions between the 1920s and the 1940s.[46] There was little by way of artistic freedom to relieve the sheer hard labor of the palace artist, who was frequently reminded of his lowly status in the palace hierarchy, as when palace artist Abdul Azeez was asked to varnish the paintings of Ravi Varma in 1907. When both he and Keshavaiah were assigned to paint a series of pictures of gods and goddesses, they were merely expected to follow the advice of assorted palace officials.[47]

Venkatappa did everything to avert this destiny, recasting and even mystifying the labors of artistic creation. Throughout his life, he made a self-conscious attempt to assume the position of a distracted, even mad, genius, indifferent to the mundane world of praise and profit. He therefore refused the costs of his materials while accepting a present of Rs 50 from the Maharaja for his landscapes.[48] Venkatappa spurned a job in the government arranged by the Inspector General of education in 1918, resisting all attempts to draw him onto the payroll of the palace.[49] He found it unthinkable to even consider completing the panels of the Dasara procession begun by Abdul Azeez, for which, he claimed, he was tempted with offers of "30 to 35 thousand rupees"![50]

Crucial to Venkatappa's self-definition was the manner in which he distinguished the artist from the artisan; the latter was a category that Venkatappa struggled to get away from.[51] He was painfully aware of the limited liberties of a palace artist, from whom he distinguished himself in 1935 as "an independent man."[52] One way of announcing the difference was to cultivate a stern asceticism to distance himself equally from the palace-controlled artist and producers for the new bourgeois art market.

Fashioning a Self-image

Venkatappa's acceptance of celibacy as an ideal, his strict code of self-reliance, and his principled austerity were the logical, if somewhat extreme, outcomes of his translation of the mystical, spiritualized aesthetics propagated by the Bengal school into a principle that governed the more intimate spheres of everyday life. He was gently mocked for his desire to lead a pure life while at Calcutta; would "Appa" return from his visit to the Himalayas, the legendary abode of the sanyasi (ascetic), Abanindranath wondered in 1913.[53] He did, bringing with him new and enduring principles for living yielded by his contemplation of the mountains.

It is a sign of Venkatappa's emerging sense of self that he maintained a diary, largely in English, from as early as 1913, with few breaks, until 1958. It may be that when he inscribed the words "Self Help is the best help" on May 6, 1913, he formalized what was to become an obsessive austerity in his private life, taking the vow of *aparigraha* (refusal to possess wealth in excess of one's needs), in a curious blend of modern artistic subjectivity and religious asceticism.[54] His adoption of a vow of *brahmacharya* (celibacy) similarly revealed a yearning for the mystical aura of one who conserved his psychic and sexual energies for artistic production. His spiritualized persona and his strict code of living became, as Ravikumar Kasi has pointed out, inseparable from Venkatappa the artist.[55]

Had Venkatappa confined himself to the world of the palace, he could well have maintained the "purity of his life," though in anonymity.[56] That the artist is known to us at all today is because of his relationships with his publics—whether critics, buyers, students, publishers, or exhibitors and, most important, the emerging moral and intellectual leadership of the Kannada nation—relationships that were admittedly unorthodox and far more complex than the mythologies have tended to suggest. If Rabindranath Tagore, who visited Mysore in 1922, expressed surprise that

Venkatappa had not yet become a sanyasi, it was with good reason;[57] the artist did not entirely reject the emerging world of modem art, nor did he neglect the more material aspects of life. As he himself indignantly pointed out to James Cousins in 1928, "I was not rich but never lived the life of penury as you have baselessly stated in the Madras catalogue."[58] He steered himself through this period by forging very specific relationships to many people and institutions, thereby making it possible to cautiously expand his publics beyond the sphere of the palace without sacrificing the limited securities of that domain.

The Making of an Artist's Publics

Critics

In India as elsewhere, the emergence of an aesthetic regime brought the art critic into existence alongside the modem artist, the former legitimating the work of art through praise or denunciation. Ananda Coomaraswamy, who described critics as those who made up for what the artist lacked, also called the critic the "servant of artists."[59] Abanindranath Tagore alone, it was claimed, had the rare ability to combine the roles of artist and critic.[60] There was early recognition in *Modern Review* that the defeat of "Ravi Varmaism" was enabled only by "intelligent connoisseurs who have learnt the art of judicious appreciation."[61] Ravi Varma's raw appeal could be countered only by disabusing the ignorant person of the "childish notion" that a "work of art, if it is a really good one, is bound to appeal to him however deficient he may be in his knowledge of Art."[62] At the same time, the critic had to be distinguished from the charlatan, for too many "disappointed drawing masters, photographers, poster designers, jute brokers, members of the Indian Civil Service and many England-returned gentlemen of erudition" crowded the scene.[63] The naïve ideology of the untutored person, who disparaged the Bengal school artists for "painting fingers bigger than hands and nails bigger than fingers and eyes half shut just like those of confirmed opium eaters,"[64] could be countered only by a Stella Kramrisch, an Ananda Coomaraswamy, or a William Rothenstein. Indeed, the Bengal school artists appear to have leaned more heavily on contemporary interpreters than had artists such as Ravi Varma.[65]

The value of the critic in producing an educated public was further enhanced by his ability to secure patrons for the struggling artist, especially as royal patronage became unreliable.[66] Venkatappa realized that stepping out of the face-to-face culture of the Mysore palace brought its own share of risks that called for reliance on the critic. There were others who shared his background, such as Kundanlal Mistri of Baroda or Y. Nagaraju of Mysore, who, after testing the waters of the modern art world, even visiting Europe, returned to the comforting security of the palace.[67] Venkatappa, though denied his trip to the West, grasped the opportunities of the art world with both hands while keeping a foot firmly in the palace establishment. When William Rothenstein purportedly said in 1910 that he "would place Mr Venkatappa at the head of that [revivalist, i.e., Bengal] school, and was even inclined to go further and place him at the head of any living school," this praise was cherished for decades by Venkatappa's contemporaries and biographers as an enduring sign of his "international reputation." The comment was seen as more authoritative than that of a Bengali critic who found the artist "lacking in heart."[68]

Venkatappa's career after his return to Mysore was transformed by contact with James Cousins and G. Venkatachalam. More a promoter than a critic, Cousins came to occupy an important position not only in the palace establishments of Travancore and Mysore but also among collectors and cultural nationalists of southern India. He arrived in India in 1915 as a journalist and joined the world of Annie Besant at Adyar.[69] Any deficiency in art criticism was more than amply made up by the enthusiastic appreciation of the Bengal school he expressed in the pages of *New India,* although his early knowledge of this work was confined to reproductions in the *Modern Review.*[70] Cousins's vapid prose, replete with general platitudes about the Indian Renaissance and the Bengal school, thrived in the Adyar environment, where reiteration of the new spiritualized aesthetic and flattering, if unspecific, remarks on the works of artists themselves were more than adequate.[71]

Venkatappa met Cousins in September 1923 through S. V. Ramaswamy Mudaliar, a businessman and collector who had commissioned an ivory miniature portrait from the artist.[72] Cousins talked about Venkatappa on his lecture circuit and invited him to do a portrait of Chand Bibi in watercolor. When he set up "the first permanent compendious gallery of Modern Indian painting in South India" at the Jaganmohan palace in 1924, Cousins persuaded the yuvaraja of Mysore to buy two of Venkatappa's paintings—*Mahasivarathri* and *Veeneya Huchchu (Mad after Veena).*[73] Of *Mahasivarathri* Cousins later wrote: "This picture was admired for its own merits and bought by His Highness before *he knew anything of the artist who painted it.*"[74] The artist thus withdrew from the anonymity of palace production to an exalted status in the 1920s and 1930s as Cousins and G. Venkatachalam publicized his art widely in India and elsewhere, recommended his work to exhibitors, and arranged the sales of pictures, including those that had been returned unsold.[75] They amply made up for the neglect of Venkatappa's work by the *Modern Review.*

Venkatappa had done *Mad after Veena* in 1921 in response to a query from his guru Abanindranath, who had heard that Venkatappa had more or less abandoned art in favor of music. Abanindranath ironically evoked the metaphor of marriage when he said to the celibate artist: "The art of painting is your first wife; do not neglect her for the new bride, music. All arts are sisters; if you do not care for all of them, you will place yourself between the quarrelling muses."[76] The artist portrayed himself as a mad genius, gaunt and unshaven on his knees before the veena, which dominates the picture as a whole, and the winged goddess of music. Behind him to the right are the scattered objects of his earlier concern: high on a pedestal but shrouded in cloth is the bust of his guru Abanindranath. The muses of painting and drawing are lashed to a post, mute and helpless, as rats gnaw at abandoned paints and brushes.

Abanindranath disapproved of this literal portrait even though he considered it technically very good and was brutally frank when he said: "You may be mad after *vina* or painting but that is not sufficient to put it into a picture. . . . Your picture must contain something which is of permanent interest for only then it can appeal to many."[77] He had not accounted for emerging tastes. Burjor N. Treasurywalla, a tireless collector and one of Venkatappa's earliest buyers, made an offer for the painting in 1922, which Venkatappa rejected because it was too little.[78] A visitor to the Madras art exhibition in 1923 similarly was discouraged by the price.[79] Cousins finally arranged for the yuvaraja to donate it to the Jaganmohan Chitrasala in Mysore.[80] Cousins chose this painting in keeping with his commitment to the new spiritualized aesthetic, for he sought to direct the work of Indian artists to the tastes of his Western audiences, "who preferred," he claimed, "religious pictures, pictures of symbolic and imaginative kind, pictures giving intimate glimpses of human life in India" to "natural scenery."[81] Yet asserting Venkatappa's status as a legitimate practitioner of the new Indian aesthetic was an important part of the critic's work, which was consistently done by Venkatachalam, Cousins, and Ramaswamy Mudaliar in the 1920s.[82] So highly did Cousins rate his importance as a critic that he was deeply offended when the Madras Exhibition of 1928 awarded Venkatappa a gold medal for just one painting, while he himself was given only "a certificate of merit."[83]

Figure 43. *A literal rendering of Venkatappa's penchant for music and his neglect of art in this painting made him very popular among a wide range of Kannada litterateurs. K. Venkatappa,* Mad after Veena, *1921–22; watercolor. Jayachamarajendra Art Gallery. Photograph by Clare Arni, 2006.*

The legitimizing authority of the critic came to good use in the long run: William Rothenstein's comment was produced before the magistrate's court in 1925 as evidence of Venkatappa's international reputation; expressions of Cousins's praise also made their way into the courtroom in 1937.[84] By the mid-1920s, Venkatappa was also claimed by the small yet growing band of Kannada litterateurs, a circuit that had little to do with the world of Cousins and Venkatachalam. Aspiring essayists and novelists, such as Shivarama Karanth and K. V. Puttappa (Kuvempu); poets such as V. Sitaramaiah; and Kannada newspapers and journals such as *Prabuddha Karnataka, Vishwakarnataka,* and *Tai Nadu* placed descriptions and reproductions of Venkatappa's works in circulation, thereby winning him many admirers and converts, who became important in the development of his authority as the first Mysore modern artist. There were writers, such as N. Vyasa Ram, who saw in Venkatappa's art "only an improvement on the indigenous style of Mysore," though Ram was thankful that the artist had "not fallen into the pitfalls of the average Bengal artist in the matter of light and shade and physical proportions."[85] Venkatappa's growing reputation among the Kannada litterateurs permitted him to challenge Cousins the critic.[86] The depiction of the artist as a mad genius appealed to a wide range of Kannada litterateurs, such as Shivarama Karanth, R. R. Diwakar, Kuvempu, V. Sitaramaiah, D. V. Gundappa, and B. M. Srikantaiah.[87] In 1924 the *Karnataka Handbook,* published on the occasion of the session of the Indian National Congress held in Bangalore, proclaimed Venkatappa the true pioneer of modernist art in Karnataka, citing a motley set of examples from his work, such as *Mahasivarathri, Ardhanariswara,* and his ivory miniatures.[88]

Venkatappa, who began doing landscapes in 1926, with astonishing success, reversed the order of "progress" that had been charted by Cousins, who described an early Ooty landscape as "an example of western style painting in which the artist had attained high ability before turning to his own Indian art."[89] Venkatappa objected to Cousins's claim that he had turned to music out of frustration at not being recognized as a painter. By 1938, there were further signs that Venkatappa no longer needed endorsement of the kind offered by Cousins. The latter's entry in the revised Chitrasala Catalogue was wrong, he said, because "my technic *[sic]* is not a copied one or one in which both Moghul and Rajput schools are combined as you have erroneously mentioned, but a genuine one suited to my taste and genius."[90] He now traced a genealogy that made no reference to his years at the Calcutta school. Yet Venkatappa's relationships to his

Figure 44. A turn to the landscapes of Ooty made Venkatappa the toast of the Kannada literary scene. Venkatappa Art Gallery, Bangalore. K. Venkatappa, Reflection Ooty Lake, 1926; watercolor, 18.5 x 25.75 cm. Photograph by M. N. Muralidhar.

patrons, whether royal or bourgeois, were equally troubled given the ease with which he believed he had been wronged and above all poorly valued.

Collectors

Venkatappa's refusal to sell his work after 1926, when he decided to start a painting school and studio in Bangalore, has overshadowed the artist's earlier anxieties about the question of a just price for his work. Far from being indifferent to the value of his work, Venkatappa emerges from his diaries and correspondence as obsessively concerned about the prices commanded by his art, especially work from his early career. Not even his frequent assertions that such concern was more about proper recognition of his artistic genius detract from his ability to strike a hard bargain.

In part, Venkatappa's indignation at receiving just Rs 400 from the Rani of Cooch Behar for his ivory portrait of her late husband stemmed from the high expectations he had of royal patrons; even Venkatachalam had led him to believe that he would be paid several thousands.[91] Cousins's assurance that Venkatappa could expect a generous donation toward his studio or school failed to persuade the artist to part with the second portrait.[92] Instead he demanded a rather steep price, calculated against the number of landscapes that he could execute in the same time.[93] Similarly, he returned the sum of Rs 150 given by S. V. Ramaswamy Madaliar for his ivory portrait in 1924.[94] And though there were eager and determined buyers for his Ooty landscapes in 1926, especially *Elk Hill Walk* and *Dawn*, which were on display in Bangalore, Venkatappa refused to part with them for what he considered "very poor" prices.[95]

What does one make of an artist who preferred to keep many of his works unsold and refused commissions that offered too little by way of compensation? What was that critical threshold that signified recognition, so that, while responding to disappointing offers on grounds that they disrespected his artistic genius, he could still bargain for marginally higher prices? He also used the courtroom as a stage to defend, perhaps even build up, his reputation as an artist, rather than material gain. The same man who repeatedly sought the help of astrologers in the early 1920s changed rather dramatically after he was first approached to do work at the Mysore palace.[96]

In Venkatappa's dealings with a Bombay collector, Burjor N. Treasuryvalla, we may discern his negotiations of the contradictory promises of the art market. Treasuryvalla was a zealous collector of modern Indian art, seeking out new artists and persuading more established ones to part with their work for little or no payment. Treasuryvalla was a collector in the classic nineteenth-century mold, choosing to hoard his treasures, only reluctantly showing them to guests, and never permitting his possessions to leave his house for exhibitions.[97] He began a long and patient correspondence with Venkatappa in May 1920, when he first expressed his keenness to "enrich the small collection of work by Bengal school artists."[98] After wooing Venkatappa for more than four years, Treasuryvalla acquired three of his paintings and commissioned several others that were not delivered. Describing Venkatappa's *Mrugathrushna* as "a veritable masterpiece," Treasuryvalla declared: "There is hardly any other painter amongst the disciples of Tagore except Nandalal who could have produced a work of such extreme beauty."[99] But such lavish praise did not make up for what Venkatappa considered meager payment of Rs 100. Three years later, Treasuryvalla paid only a marginally higher amount of Rs 130 for Venkatappa's *Buddha* picture after much haggling.

While commissioning a series of paintings, Treasuryvalla took extraordinary liberties with the artist, specifying not only the sizes but also the themes, the kind and quality of the colors, and demanding a "generous use of gold" in pictures with themes of "Hindu mythology."[100] He requested a set of *raginis* (melodic structures personified as women in illustrations) featuring women with "beautiful gold sarees with broad gold bands at the edges," executed, of course, in "permanent colours."[101] Yet Venkatappa refused to honor his many requests and instead sent Treasuryvalla his unsold pictures.

Venkatappa demanded, and received, as much as Rs 800 from Treasuryvalla for the last painting that he sold to him in 1924 *(Sita and Mareecha)*, shortly after he was approached by the palace authorities to decorate the Amba Vilas durbar hall.[102] This spoke of a newfound confidence, of an artist unwilling to take mere praise in lieu of hard cash and recognized the importance of drawing the line between executing a commission and slavishly accommodating the desires of his patrons. Treasuryvalla's demands were those of a patron not unlike the Maharaja, brazenly dictating every aspect of the artistic production, reducing the artist's role to a display of draftmanship and skillful use of color. Venkatappa had also learned that it did not always pay to accommodate the desires of the buyer, having obliged the Rani of Cooch Behar by narrowing her husband's nose to acceptable proportions, without reward.[103]

In what way could the artist declare his autonomy while earning a fair value for his work? The commission to decorate parts of the Mysore palace, for which he was approached as early as 1924, was finalized just when Venkatappa was beginning a series of landscapes at Ooty, which proved an instant success among a range of cultural nationalists, and it may well have been this encouragement that hardened his resolve to set up his "painting school and studio" at Bangalore.[104]

Palace Patrons

The commission from the palace released Venkatappa from the tedium of making a living without reducing him to the level of palace artist. Even the choice of genres reflected a new division of labor: the plaster of paris bas reliefs, largely illustrating mythological themes, were immovable and meant for the restricted pleasure of the patron. The small and pleasing landscapes in watercolor had broader appeal and, like the ivory miniatures of the Maharaja and experimental charcoal portraits, were available for wider circulation and appreciation. That he was not averse to showing off his skills as an academic portrait painter was obvious in these diverse media.

Figure 45. A portrait
of the royal patron on
an unusual medium.
Venkatappa Art Gallery,
Bangalore. K. Venkatappa,
Krishnaraja Wodeyar IV,
1939; ivory miniature,
13.0 x 8.5 cm. Photograph
by M. N. Muralidhar.

Figure 46. A return to a
naturalistic rendering of
the body. K. Venkatappa,
Physical Development:
Sardar Gopalraj Urs, 1923;
charcoal on paper, 67 x 50 cm.
Venkatappa Art Gallery,
Bangalore. Photograph by
M. N. Muralidhar.

The series of low bas reliefs in plaster of paris was proposed as a way of "harmonizing" the new parts of the palace with the existing "crude and gaudy" upper portions of the palace that were already in place.[105] The subjects that Venkatappa first proposed for the walls of the durbar hall ranged from illustrations of mythological themes, such as *Shakuntala's departure from Kanva's ashram* and *Draupadi swayamvara* (Draupadi choosing her groom) to "love scenes." He declared his loyalty to the king by proposing an episode from the Puranic history of the Yadavas, from "which the Mysore Royal Family descends," namely, Srikrishna's *upadesha* (advice) from the Bhagavad Gita.[106] These suggestions were readily accepted by the Maharaja, and the artist, in turn, agreed to accept whatever the royal patron offered. The contrast with the world of Treasuryvalla could not have been starker. Shaking free of the bourgeois public after 1926, Venkatappa refused to sell any more paintings, indignantly spurning Treasuryvalla's last bid to freely procure a tempera rendering of Shivarathri in exchange for lending his collection of works by the artist to a Bombay exhibition.[107]

The privileges Venkatappa enjoyed between 1926 and 1940 were certainly not given to any palace artist. For the first of the reliefs, *Departure of Shakuntala*, completed in late 1928 and approved by the Maharaja himself, he received a princely sum of Rs 5,000.[108] His work alone was singled out for mention as a "masterpiece" in the palace administration report on the artists' annual productions.[109] By 1931 he was allowed the use of a set of rooms above the palace dispensary as a separate studio.

The clearest expression of privilege was the extraordinarily long time Venkatappa took over each bas relief: the second bas relief of Siddhartha was completed only in 1934, a good five years after the first, and the third, the *Dance of Siva*, was completed in 1939. In those fourteen years, Venkatappa only briefly turned his attention away from the bas reliefs when he did a series of landscapes at Kodaikanal in 1934.

Meanwhile, the Mysore studio became a place of pilgrimage, especially for Kannada litterateurs such as D. V. Gundappa, Kuvempu, V. Sitaramaiah, and R. R. Diwakar, who were treated to private showings of the artworks by lamplight in select groups. The cultivation of this new public could well have been Venkatappa's way of coming to terms with the dwindling importance of the palace. Even so, the abrupt termination of his commission a few weeks after the death of Maharaja Krishnaraja Wodeyar IV in August 1940 was an unexpected shock.

Figure 47. An exaggerated emphasis on the muscularity of the boy hunter. K. Venkatappa, Eklavya Learning Archery, *1925; bas relief, 145 x 78 cm. Venkatappa Art Gallery, Bangalore. Photograph by M. N. Muralidhar.*

Figure 48. K. Venkatappa, Shakuntala's Departure, *1928; bas relief, 145 x 78 cm. Venkatappa Art Gallery, Bangalore. Photograph by M. N. Muralidhar.*

Figure 49. A second round of landscapes of Kodaikanal brought Venkatappa wider popularity within Mysore. K. Venkatappa, Coaker's Walk and Strabilanthus, 1934; watercolor, 36.0 x 25.5 cm. Venkatappa Art Gallery, Bangalore. Photograph by M. N. Muralidhar.

What the new Maharaja (Jayachamarajendra Wodeyar, 1940–47) might have found so objectionable is only a matter of speculation. By taking nearly fourteen years to complete a handful of bas reliefs, Venkatappa compared poorly with the pace of either a Ravi Varma or a humbler palace artist such as Keshavaiah, and the artistic aura that he had so carefully built up did little to compensate.[110] Venkatappa's bitter exchange with James Cousins in 1938 must have cost him dearly, for the latter was a cherished adviser to the palace, and the Chitrasala in particular.[111] Venkatappa seems to have sounded his own death knell in his artless letter of condolence to the new king: "It is no exaggeration if I say that his late Highness was a fountain of patronage to all sorts of aesthetics, and that evil days, I fear, seem to have fallen upon aesthetic subjects from the days of his death."[112]

The Maharaja wasted no time in dispensing with the services of Venkatappa: on September 23, 1940, the artist received news that the new Maharaja did not want any more panels and he had to vacate the palace dispensary after Dasara.[113] The palace remained cool to Venkatappa's entreaties that he be allowed to complete his commitments to the late Maharaja, and on September 25, 1940, the only complete panel, the "Dance of Siva," was removed to Amba Vilas.[114] Venkatappa moved residence to Bangalore, where he remained until his death.

In 1943, when it became clear that the palace was unyielding on the question of fair compensation, Venkatappa filed a suit in the magistrate's court against the Mysore palace for breach of contract and claimed compensation of Rs 40,000.[115] The suit was dismissed by the district magistrate, a decision that was upheld by the High Court in 1946 on grounds that the palace was not a legal entity and the sovereign was "not liable to be sued in his own courts without his consent."[116]

The courtroom had long been the stage on which Venkatappa had striven to establish his artistic genius. The case against the Maharaja was no exception; Venkatappa hoped to recoup his honor rather than make good the loss of a patron. Few of the nationalist papers reported more than the legal details of the argument, adding some sarcastic comments about the new Maharaja.[117] The artist had long shunned publicity by discouraging the reproduction of his works in the popular magazines and the press and withdrawing from the exhibition circuit when he resolved to establish a studio.[118] But reproductions of works of art went a long way in building an artist's public: Venkatappa's distrust was yet another way of drawing a line between himself and the likes of Ravi Varma or even the Bengal school.

Exhibitors and Art Publishers

If Ravi Varma's national popularity was enhanced by the mass-produced oleographs that invaded every home, the work of the Bengal school was no less actively retailed by the exhibitions and excellent reproductions of the Indian Society of Oriental Art.[119] More important, as Abanindranath himself admitted, "Our pictures are in every household today because of Ramananda Babu. . . . By his perseverance and financial investments in superior colour and half tone prints he had created a demand where none existed before."[120] Chatterjee's *Picture Albums,* though privately dismissed by Havell as "Chatterjee's trash," placed a range of high-quality reproductions of works by the Bengal school in national and international circulation. Reducing the "tyranny of the Ravi Varma oleograph," as Cousins put it, was enabled solely by the *Modern Review,* which redefined taste even in

South India, where Ravi Varma had not yet relinquished his hold over a pious public.[121]

Neither Cousins nor the fine arts associations in Bangalore to which Venkatachalam and art dealer Fred Harvey belonged compared with institutions like the Indian Society, although, beginning in 1924, exhibitions were frequently held and Cousins and Venkatachalam toured the country with slides of various artists.[122] Though Venkatappa's distrust of reproduction bordered on paranoia, he was not entirely averse to high-quality reproductions: in 1911–13 he did the series on the Ramayana for *Myths of the Hindus and Buddhists*.[123] At other times, he sent gifts of photographs of his work to friends and well-wishers and even offered R. R. Diwakar photographs in lieu of works for exhibition in Dharwar.[124]

If the "national" art publishers cold-shouldered the artist, there were far more eager takers in Mysore and other Kannada-speaking regions of the south, especially after the mid-1920s, when Venkatappa's works were increasingly sought by a range of struggling poets, writers, and journalists. *Prabuddha Karnataka* published a long article about Venkatappa with reproductions of his works in 1926.[125] Two years later, it introduced readers to the now famous *Mad after Veena*, accompanied by a detailed biographical sketch.[126] By this time, both *Viswakarnataka* and *Tai Nadu* were carrying regular reports on the artist's plans for a school, extending the aura of the brilliant and talented artist.

Venkatappa remained ever alert to the irreducibility of pictorial work, which was neither mere illustration nor "secondary to the printed work."[127] Upset by the reproduction of *Mad after Veena* in Shivarama Karanth's book *Bharatiya Chitra Kala*, he refused to accept the complimentary copy.[128] Venkatappa pointed to the irreparable harm done by poor reproduction, privileging the "linguistic account" over the "pictorial" one, for that only encouraged some Western critics to continue maligning Indian work.[129]

Venkatappa kept a stern eye open for any reproductions that appeared without his permission, demanding apologies (in the third person) from those who had reproduced his work in journals and even threatening some with lawsuits.[130] *Rangabhumi*, the journal of the Amateur Dramatic Association of Bangalore that published his *Mahasivarathri*, was severely rebuked for "grossly misrepresenting the work of the 'world renowned' artist," for which Editor B. Sreenivas duly apologized.[131] Faced with the threat of litigation, it was safer to admit defeat, as A. R. Krishna Sastri did when he readily admitted that Venkatappa's picture was "murdered" in

Prabuddha Karnataka, though he said "that was the best we could do in this country."[132] Only a long and tedious exchange of letters, blocks, and proofs allowed V. Sitaramaiah to use Venkatappa's works as illustrations in his book of poetry.[133]

As Walter Benjamin has noted, "That which withers in the age of mechanical reproduction is the aura of the work of art," a withering that was fiercely resisted by Venkatappa.[134] Coming to terms with an ever-expanding scale of art viewers, whether in galleries or exhibitions or even in reproductions, meant taking risks, for which he was clearly unprepared. He saw no particular value in popularizing his work, in marked contrast to Nandalal and his enthusiastic, even programmatic, embrace of reproduction as a vehicle for the circulation of new artistic ideals.[135] Venkatappa made impossible demands of those who wished to publish his work, not always related to the quality of the reproduction. Approached by the assistant editor of the *Hindu* in 1926 for a photograph of his landscape *Elk Hill Walk* for publication, Venkatappa declared that the "cheap paper" used was unworthy of his work.

Venkatappa's exasperation with inattentive reproduction came to a head when two photographs of the palace bas reliefs appeared in *Udbodhan,* the Bengali monthly of the Sri Ramakrishna Mission. In its 1935 (Ashwin 1342) Puja Special Number, the journal carried reproductions of Venkatappa's *Renunciation of Buddha* and *Rama Gifting the Signet Ring to Hanuman.*[136] The Rama picture, which had inadvertently been reproduced in the reverse, angered Venkatappa enough to seek palace help on the grounds that the mistake damaged not only the artist but "the fair name of our progressive model state which is well known for its civilisation and Fine Arts."[137] Not just aesthetic principles had been violated, he claimed, but religious sensibilities, for the reproduction showed Rama "giving the ring with the left hand and wearing the sacred thread on the right."[138] The explanatory note may well have compounded Venkatappa's indignation, because greater importance was given to Abanindranath Tagore.[139] The mission was quick to carry a written apology in the 1342 Magh issue, and it reprinted the blocks the right way up in its Jaistha issue.[140] This did not prevent Venkatappa, an adept at court procedures, from filing a suit for libel and claiming damages of Re 1.[141]

Venkatappa may have filed the suit in a fit of pique, for the photographs of the bas reliefs had been taken by Swami Nikhilananda, who had promised to reproduce them in "selected artistic periodicals in America."[142] To discover them published in a Bengali religious journal instead must have been a blow to Venkatappa's aspirations, and the suit seeking Re 1 was an attempt to recoup his honor. It was no more than a pyrrhic victory when the court found in his favor: one of the two witnesses who appeared on his behalf to testify on the maintainability of the suit for libel, Shahid Suhrawardy, frankly admitted that Venkatappa's work did not appeal to him.[143] Percy Brown, the second witness, was more appreciative, but the judge, who Venkatappa noted was hostile to his counsel, spoke at length on the pettiness of the complaint, awarding Re 1 in damages but only half the costs.[144] Yet it is a sign of how much Venkatappa depended on such verdicts as proof of his fame that he reported his victory to Abanindranath as similar to Whistler's famous one-shilling suit against Ruskin.[145]

Students

Throughout his life, Venkatappa described himself as "a student of fine art" and was acknowledged as an exemplary student, "quiet and gentle-manly" and "a credit to the state he represents."[146] Yet his diaries and records reveal a remarkable indifference to reflection on art practices and even to dialogue with other artists.[147] Even when he consulted his guru Abanindranath in 1937, it was only to clarify the *sastraic* (scriptural) injunction about how many hands were permitted in representations of Shiva.[148]

In striking contrast to Abanindranath's other pupils, who fanned out across the country to head various institutions of art, Venkatappa studiously avoided being attached to any institution.[149] He refused to be tempted by the possibility of a job at the Andhra Jatheeya Kalasala at Machilipatnam in 1920 (a job later accepted by Promode Kumar Chatterjee), and turned down C. R. Reddy's 1928 invitation to join the Andhra University Faculty of Arts and Music and "make a name that will live for centuries."[150] The only students who were lucky enough to receive instruction from him were Anand Mohan Sastry and Ram Mohan Sastry, who were recommended by Srinivas Rao of the Machilipatnam school in 1926.[151] Venkatappa was an exacting teacher and so grudging in his appreciation of the students that when he received news that the two had been taken onto the staff of the Machillipatnam school he dismissed it as reflecting an "increase of incompetent persons as teachers, lecturers and writers on Indian art throughout India."[152]

In view of Venkatappa's reputation, it need not surprise us that his resolve to start a free school of art in Bangalore remained unrealized. He
asked several people, including Mahdi Hasan of Osmania University, to
send him worthy students but made conditions too difficult for potential students; he refused M. V. Sitaramaiah because he was already married and a group of others because they were "older than 14 years," and
he dismissed Narayan Sangam, a student of Nandalal from the Bombay
Presidency who had been sent by Abanindranath, as a mere "beggar."[153]
He had no more than the minimum contact with the other artists associated with the palace.[154]

Venkatappa's long-cherished desire that his works should, above all, instruct rather than serve merely as decoration or cater to private pleasures
remained unrealized until 1941, when his own Bangalore studio turned
into a private gallery through which groups of critics, writers, scientists,
and nationalists were conducted by the artist himself. When the royal patron had all but vanished and the bourgeois buyer was spurned, what else
could fulfill his aspirations except the agencies of the nation-state?

Palace to Museum: Consecration by the Kannada Nation

Venkatappa negotiated a shift away from the durbar hall and the palace to
the museum and gallery, retreating from the patronage of the Maharaja
to the (posthumous) patronage of the nation-state. How do we explain
the apparent paradox by which an artist was consecrated by the very agencies that he so conspicuously denounced? Venkatappa so shunned publicity and even dialogue with other artists of his time that one wonders at
the source of his authority over the field of modern artistic production
in Karnataka. The issue is more puzzling given the slightness of his output, even in his most creative years between 1910 and 1940. After this he
did no new work, occupying himself instead with "reorienting his works"
until his death in 1965.[155] Yet so completely did he dominate the aesthetic
universe of the new Kannada nation that a premier state gallery has been
named after him.

Shivarama Karanth recalls that Venkatappa simply shut his studio
when a visitor explained that his landscapes were just like photographs
(see Figure 44 and Figure 49).[156] In a recent work that takes a hard, even
unsympathetic, look at the mythologies that have obscured the artist,

Ravikumar Kasi asks how "it was that an artist like Venkatappa could re-main so determinedly indifferent to the groundswell of nationalism, unlike the numerous writers, poets, scholars and journalists who were inspired to participate in defining the contours of the new nation-state" and its cultural responsibilities.[157] Perhaps it is wiser to reframe the ques-tion to ask instead how it was that, despite his marked indifference to the world of political events and even to the aesthetic challenges of new na-tionalist art, Venkatappa could have enjoyed preeminence?

Ananda Coomaraswamy had denounced the artist who longed to be hung in a gallery or museum, the space that was correctly dedicated to the care of ancient or unique works "in imminent danger of destruction."[158] Venkatappa rejected the relative anonymity of the palace walls for a wider public of art-loving people without ever quite relinquishing his distrust of the dangerously untutored public eye. As early as 1926, he resolved to bequeath his art legacy to an imagined community of art lovers. Even his limited contact with the incipient moral intellectual leadership of the Kannada nation had revealed to him the contours of this new mission. A remark by R. R. Diwakar is revealing: "People here [Dharwar] do not know the essence of true Indian art and your work will be an eye opener to them as it was to me."[159] Kuvempu similarly counted himself among those who had been transformed by Venkatappa's landscapes, which drew the highest praise from Kannada litterateurs. The artist was acclaimed by the scientist Homi Bhabha, who, while at the Indian Institute of Science in Bangalore in the 1940s, described Venkatappa as "the only one in India in which [sic] modern painting has given us pleasure as great as that of the greatest art of the past."[160]

Like the other artists attached to the palace at Mysore, Venkatappa had decisively broken with the Mysore school of painting that was his legacy. In his Calcutta years, Venkatappa had adhered to the evolving Bengal school style in his choice of subjects (largely figurative illustrations of Hindu legends), media (tempera and watercolors), and style (the minia-ture tradition of the Rajput and Moghul oeuvres). After the early 1920s, when he also did a few plaster busts, he worked primarily in three genres that sharply diverged from all his years of careful nationalist grooming. He chose a rather dated medium—ivory miniatures—for portraits of famous personages, and he executed a series of meticulous landscapes and a series of bas reliefs in plaster of paris, all of which appeared to hark back to his academic training rather than his Bengal years. Venkatappa's landscapes of Ooty and Kodaikanal, painted in 1926 and 1934, respectively, were such a success among a wide range of Kannada litterateurs that he appears to have fulfilled their collective yearning for a *yugapurush*, a man of the age who would rescue tradition in redefining the modern without being slavishly regimented by it.

Only from the 1950s do we find overt references to Venkatappa's gradual equation of the public with the "national public." Regretting his inability to participate in the Dasara Exhibition in Mysore in 1950, the artist claimed that his paintings were "specially created" and "zealously preserved" for installation in a gallery for the benefit of students and the nation.[161] To the governor of Madras, Krishna Kumar Singhji, who solicited work from Venkatappa for display in the newly opened Madras Gallery in 1951, he wrote that he was protecting his works from the art-knowing millionaires of Ahmedabad and Bombay in "order to give them over to the Indian nation," by which he claimed he was honoring a promise that he had made to Gandhi.[162]

Venkatappa was sought out not only by provincial art schools and exhibitors as far afield as Machilipatnam, Rajahmundry, and Dharwar but also by those who saw him as an exponent of a specifically Karnataka idiom of nationalist art. Inviting Venkatappa in 1927 to exhibit his work at a conference of teachers from the Bombay Presidency at Dharwar, R. R. Diwakar, editor of the Kannada weekly *Karmaveer,* also urged the artist to elaborate on the "theory and philosophy of Indian art" and inquired whether "there are any distinguishing features in Karnataka art."[163]

The Congress exhibition, with its awards and certificates of merit, was an important location for otherwise busy congressmen to nurture new aesthetic sensibilities. It was probably at the Congress exhibition in Madras in 1928 that nationalists of the Madras Presidency had an opportunity to see Venkatappa's Ooty landscapes, for which C. Rajagopalachari hailed him the "Turner of India."[164] Although there was no specific visual reference in his work to the geography of the Kannada nation or its people, his works held Kannada intellectuals in thralldom. Kuvempu, only just emerging as one of Karnataka's modern writers and poets, was moved to write poetry dedicated to *"varnashilpi"* ("sculptor of color") Venkatappa. Equally smitten were those who were rising in the firmament of Karnataka politics, such as Kengal Hanumanthaiya and S. Nijalingappa. The latter encountered Venkatappa's works while a student of Central College and was later entranced by his landscapes. For this range of cultural and political nationalists, Venkatappa's Karnataka origins and his relationship to the Mysore palace established his credentials as a national-modern artist rather than as a pioneer of a vernacular idiom.

Conclusion

On October 5, 1940, Venkatappa left Mysore for Bangalore, where he had purchased some property for his studio and school in 1928.[165] In 1974, the Karnataka (erstwhile Mysore) government acknowledged his pioneering role as Mysore's modern artist by giving the only state-run art museum in Mysore and indeed in India his name. The move from Mysore represented a sharp shift away from the courtly culture of the Mysore palace of which he had so long been a part but which was now clearly threatened with extinction. Abandoning the leisurely world of Mysore for the administrative capital was also a shift in loyalties, not so much from the royal patron to the bourgeois art market as to the new arbiters of state power and, indeed, taste. Ironically, the very court verdict that had so forcefully asserted the unassailable power of the Maharaja succeeded in convincing Venkatappa that the world of royal patrons and palace artists had come to an end. Soon after his appeal against the palace was dismissed in 1946, he received an offer of Rs 5,000 from the Maharaja, along with the freedom to do as he wished with the remaining panels, but Venkatappa no longer wished to be beholden to the capricious princely culture of old Mysore, or indeed that of any other princely state; even V. V. Srinivasa Iyengar's offer to arrange for him to join Travancore State was turned down.[166]

Venkatappa's actions a few days after the dismissal of his High Court appeal reveal a man who had finally come to terms with the new field of forces. On the night of October 28, 1946, Venkatappa read in *Tainadu* that his appeal had been dismissed. On November 20 of that year, Venkatappa did something he had resisted all his life: he mounted all the certificates of merit and medals awarded to him since 1910. "Though framing them and showing them to visitors was against my will and taste all these 36 years," he confessed in his diary, "yet the inner urge to bring them to light was great, so I took them out of the trunk in which they were locked ever since they were received."[167] Between November 23 and 25, he displayed these as well as his works in chronological order for several officials and former

officials of the Mysore state.[168] It could not have been entirely a coinci-
dence that the artist was asked in November 1946, shortly after the case
ended, to head the Karnataka Academy of Fine Arts as president, a post
for which he recommended K. Keshavaiah instead because the Kannada
nation had already laid claim to Venkatappa as a modern Indian artist.[169]

Venkatappa donated the ivory miniature portrait of Bhup Bahadur
from the early 1920s to the Madras Gallery in 1954.[170] In that same year,
his bas reliefs were sought out by Kamaladevi Chattopadhyay, then president of the All India Handicrafts Board, for permanent display in Delhi.[171]
Kamaladevi's reference to the bas reliefs as frescoes considerably irked the
artist, but it is more than likely that the board's offer of Rs 25,000 fell a
little too short of the Rs 40,000 he demanded.[172] Venkatappa refused to
part with his work, and the bas reliefs, wrenched from their proper place
on durbar walls, retained their allure in the gallery space of the more eager
Karnataka nation when the state's Modern Art Gallery was set up in 1974
in his memory.

CHAPTER 6

The Illicit in the Modern:
Banning the *Devadasi*

THE COLONIAL AUTHORITIES were reluctant modernizers, conceding little to the demands of the nascent Indian bourgeoisie and even retarding the possibility of transformation of the Indian economy.[1] On the other hand, preserving the domain of the private for the continued reign of Indian patriarchy, that is, the active retention of an undemocratic domain, was a preferred mode by which the circle of collaborators was enlarged in some regions of India. The household, and specifically conjugality, it is argued, increasingly became the only space in which autonomy and self-rule could be preserved, the domain in which the loss of economic and political control could be compensated.[2] Within this domain, the prehistory of political nationalism was enacted and nationalist sovereignty was first secured.[3] Was the sphere of the family, as Tanika Sarkar and Partha Chatterjee seem to suggest, preserved from state interference in all parts of India?

Such a schematic distinction has been challenged by recent feminist scholarship. Doubts about whether the "nationalist resolution" of the women's question was pertinent beyond the regions where it has been noted have been raised by studies of non-Brahman politics in western India and its willingness to shape a distinct relationship to the colonial state in order to limit Brahmanism itself; matrilineal communities such as that of the Nairs, who pressed for active legislative interventions in family forms and rights to property in the late nineteenth and early twentieth centuries; and new resolutions between the social and the political that women themselves sought in the third decade of the twentieth century.[4] The patterns that have been detected for Bengal or North India may be less useful in making sense of the intersections of state intervention, community demands, and women's agency in states such as Mysore, where the bureaucracy displayed a duplex character, simultaneously functioning as the moral-intellectual leadership of the Mysore nation and as the autocratic power that made decisions, even those relating to the personal domains of sexuality and family life, in the name of a public good. How was the law invoked in the Mysore bureaucracy's attempts to transform the social fabric on the one hand (i.e., intervene to modify community practices) and make the population more governable on the other (i.e., make the uniformity of the governed subject the main goal of its legislative efforts)? What were the productive effects of such administrative or legal intervention in realms that had produced bitter contests in British India? Two specific instances of this paradox are discussed in this chapter and the next.

Mysore's Social Reforms

Social movements lacked intellectual force and were organizationally weak in Mysore, unlike those parts of colonial India under direct rule, where male cultural nationalists in the nineteenth century and first-wave Indian feminism beginning in the 1910s foregrounded the women's question, though in very different ways.[5] Civil social institutions relating to the reform of religion or the family were more vigorous in the neighboring Madras Presidency, although new associational spaces that transformed the meaning of caste were visible in early twentieth-century Mysore. Members of the Mysore Brahmo Samaj, for example, were reluctant to support a widow's remarrying in Bangalore, and other associations such as the Bangalore Literary Union, the Ranade Society, and the Widow Remarriage Association confined their energies to holding occasional talks and speeches.[6] Mysore's weak civil social institutions called for early governmental intervention: the Mysore Civic and Social Progress Association, set up in 1915, was a step in this direction.

In sharp contrast were the state's efforts at passing and implementing regulations and laws intended to recast family life and to develop private sources of normative behavior that were delinked from religion. On the one hand, such initiatives indicated an interest in extending the scope of state legality at the expense of a host of nonstate law-ways; on the other, their uneven success was an indication of the very limits of the reform imagination and the incomplete reach of governmentality. Transforming the family, recasting sexuality, and reshaping ties of affect, both for the sake of administrative convenience and to reform social practices that had become an increasing embarrassment, involved redrawing the boundaries between forms of licit and illicit sexual activity.

For both colonial authorities and national elites, the realms of family (reproductive) and nonfamily (nonreproductive) female sexuality were inseparably linked as sites of reform or transformation. In southern India at least, and Mysore in particular, an abolitionist drive undergirded by moral concerns was launched by the bureaucracy against the *devadasi,* or temple dancing women, at the turn of the century. By the third decade of the twentieth century, a different kind of split marked Indian concerns about the maintenance of the family order and the boundaries between licit and illicit sexuality, particularly concerning the sexual health of the Indian population.[7] This chapter discusses one moment in this modernizing process and its definitions of domestic and nondomestic sexuality, especially as it was aligned with women's rights to property within and beyond the family. What were the legal administrative measures surrounding the gradual disempowerment of the devadasis attached to *muzrai* temples (supported by state grants for religious or charitable purposes)? And in what ways did Mysore state later anchor the rights of women to property within the space of the newly defined reproductive family?

By no means were the goals of such reforms democratic, much less antipatriarchal. Modernity, as well as the traditions it supplanted or incorporated, continued to be the bearer of patriarchal ideologies. If the measures undertaken by the colonial government did little to level gender relations, neither did the initiatives of the princely state. Furthermore, with the idealization of the middle-class woman as the subject of reform, class and caste inequities were rarely addressed and were even positively affirmed.[8]

Bringing Light and Air to the Temple Institution

In 1929 Muthulakshmi Reddi, the first Indian woman legislator and an indefatigable campaigner against the devadasi system, moved a bill to end the dedication of women to temples in the Madras Presidency. In her statement of objects and reasons for the bill, Reddi complained of the inadequacy of Sections 372 and 373 of the Indian Penal Code in preventing such dedication and insisted that "a legislative enactment is therefore necessary in dealing with the practice of dedication per se."[9] Deploring the fact that the agitation of "high minded Hindus" for devadasi abolition since 1869 had not yielded legislation, she praised the princely state of Mysore for setting a good example by passing a government order for complete abolition as early as 1909.[10] Because Mysore was also a Hindu state, this was a clear indication, she said, that "Hindu religion does not sanction immorality in either man or woman."[11]

The abolition of a practice which "in the name of service to God has condemned a certain class of women to a life of either a concubine or prostitute" became law in Madras only in 1947, decades after what was achieved by mere administrative fiat in Mysore state.[12] The Mysore government's attempts at rewriting Indian tradition provoked neither alarm that religion was in danger nor accusations of ignorance of the *sastras*, or preceptual texts.

In fact, the Mysore government's order of 1909 represented only the final stage in a process of producing a new moral order that had begun in the early 1890s. That was when the first steps were taken to align notions of dharma—righteousness, or law with suasive power, protected by the Maharaja—with an emerging colonial judicature by a bureaucracy pledged to developing and expanding forms of justice that were no longer embedded in or derived from cultural forms characteristic of the precolonial order. It was equally an attempt to align the Mysore royal family, and not only the Mysore population, with new norms of conjugality, monogamy, and licit sexuality.

Although the rhetoric surrounding the decision to resume direct rule in Mysore was saturated with the idiom of improvement, the primary British concern was the state's subsidy payments. As we have seen, one of the serious charges made against the Maharaja was about the free and easy manner in which he had granted inams "not in reward of public services, but to favourites and companions."[13] The fact that these inam grants were of lands that lay in the fertile wetlands along the Cauveri and Hemavathi rivers and among rich garden lands outside Bangalore only aggravated the situation.[14]

Yet East India Company officials did not overlook the fact that precolonial monarchical authority had been established and legitimized through such grants. The temple, for example, was a key institution in the formation of social communities, a site where both symbolic and material resources were redistributed, rendering "public, stable and culturally appropriate exchanges at the level of politics and economics."[15] The assumption of direct rule in 1831, then, was prompted as much by an anxiety about the resurgence of monarchical forms of power that could become the locus of challenges to colonial power as by the continued payment of the Mysore subsidy.

After the rendition of 1881, administrative power rested more or less wholly in the bureaucracy headed by the Dewan (chief minister) and his council of ministers.[16] The responsibilities of the newly independent administration under Dewan Rangacharlu were enormous, not the least of which was the payment of an enhanced subsidy of Rs 3.5 million (though the enhancement was deferred for a period of five years, and then a further ten years) and the repayment of loans contracted during the devastating famine of 1876. Of utmost urgency was a land revenue code on the lines of the Bombay code, which had come into force only in 1888, after which all land in Mysore was surveyed and settled by 1899.[17]

Land revenue settlements in Mysore occurred alongside the scrutiny of inams by the Inam Department. The term *inam* itself, as Burton Stein has pointed out, had both contracted and expanded in the period of British rule in the new order instituted by Thomas Munro in the early nineteenth century. An Arabic word meaning gift, usually of landed income, it was "an honour or a mark of distinction from a ruling authority."[18] Although it had previously referred to one type of alienation of land revenue, the term was extended to refer to "all extant alienations of land revenue," while it was simultaneously emptied of its moral content and came to mean a "contingent, utilitarian and service-oriented alienation" that could be resumed by the state.[19]

The word *muzrai,* derived from the Persian word *mujra,* meaning deductions or allowances, referred to grants for religious and charitable purposes.[20] Throughout the period of direct British rule, the administration of the Muzrai Department presented a thorny problem, because interference in the use of the economic and cultural resources of the temple could lead to conflicts over legitimacy and authority, as well as political conflicts between religious elites. Nevertheless, the colonial state, despite intermittent avowals to the contrary, penetrated, reorganized, and secularized the meaning and content of temple rituals, revenues, and finances and reinscribed the social status of the temple within colonial society.[21] As a consequence, the decision was made to appoint six high-caste *dharmakarthas* (managers or superintendents of religious institutions) to superintend temple rituals, offerings, and so on, as was done in Madras, to exempt the government from "performing acts which were connected with idolatrous buildings and practices."[22] In Mysore, where direct rule was temporary, it was considered undesirable to transfer the management of religious institutions to private committees: feuds had erupted in the two places where such committees had been formed, so the management of these temples stayed with government officers.[23] In an effort to control the "misappropriation" of revenue, a regular audit of the accounts of each institution was prepared and compared to the *tasdik pattis* (lists of sanctioned temple expenditures).[24] The state also reserved the right to replace managements that were inefficient and resume lands when more efficient managements could not be found.[25]

Persistent demands made in the Mysore Representative Assembly after 1883 for reforms in temple management led the Mysore government to appoint a special officer as muzrai superintendent.[26] The new officer, A. Srinivasacharlu, briskly went about the business of introducing new budgets and sanctions, appointing *dharmadarsis* (temple managers), and revising and regulating the tasdik pattis.[27] All of this was intended to restore the original objects of grants made to temples, secure better officials as heads of temples and mathas (monastic institutions), and, in short, "to impart to the worship and rituals therein more impressiveness and solemnity by a stricter conformity with the spirit of the Hindu religion as expounded by accepted authorities."[28]

The muzrai superintendent's brief was to bring "light and air" to the mysterious womb of the temple in both a literal and a metaphorical sense, expose the misdeeds of the custodians of temple rituals and revenues, and "clean up" both the temple surroundings and the rituals and practices. An opportunity to effect a serious and irrevocable change in the political economy of the temple presented itself soon after he assumed charge. The muzrai superintendent was presented with a bill of Rs 12/5/4 as payment to a woman called Ramamani who had performed *tafe* (dancing) services at the car festival of Bhoganandeswara Temple at Nandidurg, Chikkaballapur. He agreed to pay only reluctantly, saying that such tafe services were an unnecessary waste of money that could be better spent on "improving sanitation."[29] Promising to issue a circular outlining the legitimate services of devadasis in temples, Superintendent Srinivasacharlu categorically asserted that they did not include dancing.

The official's decision may have been prompted in part by the growing clamor in the neighboring Madras Presidency of the anti-*nautch* (literally, anti-dance) campaign conducted largely by educated upper-caste Hindus.[30] Mysore appears to have escaped any such vociferous campaign. Throughout the late nineteenth century, as R. R. Diwakar shows, "cities and town like Bangalore, Mysore, Mulbagal, Kudoor, T. Narsipur" had quite a few communities of dancers attached to temples supported by "rich merchants, landlords, and connoisseurs of dance." Indeed it was "the excessive influence exerted by them on their patrons" that led to the gradual growth of the anti-nautch movement.[31] In 1891, however, the newspaper *Vrittanta Chintamani* pointed out that the abolition drive was prompted by fears of female empowerment within the new colonial dispensation. Thus it noted that some dancing girls of Madras were very rich, lived in large houses, kept carriages, and paid large amounts of municipal taxes: this entitled them to vote in municipal committees. The paper suggested that these rights be withdrawn to reduce the embarrassment faced by respectable gentlemen who had to beg these "low women" for their votes.[32] To some extent, upper-caste discomfort with these cultural traditions was an indication of the success of missionary critiques of "bad" Hindu practices and the work of the Leagues for Social Purity and Temperance in various parts of the country.[33]

The Mysore official issued the promised circular only in 1898 during the revision of the tasdik pattis of the Nanjangud and Melkote temples (which were among the largest of the temple institutions in Mysore).[34] He directed that tafe women not be admitted to any kind of service in the two temples, and although they could be paid while they were alive, their posts should not be filled after their deaths.[35] Even in 1898, there appears to have been no sustained discussion of what constituted the "legitimate services" of devadasis: the muzrai superintendent was obviously secure in his belief that the "immorality" of devadasis was too self-evident to warrant discussion. The unilateral decision of the government to reform temple traditions by divesting devadasis of their roles, however, soon required detailed elaboration as the implications gradually unfolded to both those disempowered by the decision and those who stood to benefit from it. The very antiquity of these services was called into question and the sources of their authority questioned.

Correcting an Anomalous Customary Law

The textual antiquity of the tradition of temple dancing is somewhat uncertain, but tracing the genealogy of the temple dancer was crucial to her abolition. There are no known direct references to dancing in the temple in the oldest books of dance theory, the *Natyashastra* and the *Abhinaya Darpana;* according to Gayathri Spivak, the first mention of it was in the eleventh-century collection of stories the *Kathasaritsagara*.[36] Yet as a *nitya-sumangali,* an ever-auspicious woman, the devadasi was to deal with the "dangerous divine," a role that was only later overshadowed by her artistic performances in the temples and in the court.[37]

Inscriptional evidence from medieval Karnataka is more revealing. Before the eleventh century, there is only mention of the word *sule* (meaning prostitute) in inscriptions. In the eleventh century, a time when the temple as an institution was expanding, the word *patra* (role of singer or dancer) was gradually attached to them.[38] The word *devadasi* itself is conspicuous by its absence in this period, although it was then current in the inscriptions of neighboring regions as well as in the *vachana* (a Kannada poetic form dating from the twelfth century) literature of the Virashaivas.[39] By the twelfth century, when the temple adopted more complex rituals, specific duties were assigned to temple women; indeed, the temple complex came increasingly to resemble the king's court, and the devadasi's relationship to the deity approximated the courtesan's relationship to the king.[40] The sacred prostitute gradually became the custodian of the arts of singing and dancing.

For her services to the temple, the devadasi enjoyed grants made either to her personally or to the temple. These included grants of lands, some of which were made by upper-caste women themselves.[41] By the late nineteenth century, the devadasi tradition was a decidedly matrilineal one. Under a male guru, the young dedicated girl underwent rigorous training in *nritya* (dance) and *gita* (song) which entitled her access to a structure of cash payments through the temple or personal land grants from the sexual alliances she developed with upper-caste patrons.[42] Her strict professionalism, says Amrit Srinivasan, "made her an adjunct to conservative domestic society, not its ravager," an assertion borne out by the number of female donors of grants to temples for the services of devadasis.[43]

Successive Mysore censuses since 1891 had entered two communities such as *natuvas* (male members of a community of dancing masters or musicians) and *kaikolas* (members of a hereditary group of performers) in the category "dancers and singers," acknowledging those, traditionally males, who served as the musical accompanists of female temple dancers. One temple in Mulbagal alone had fourteen *nartakis* (female dancers) in the late nineteenth century, and women such as Baikur Venkatalakshmi, Tirumakudlu Sundaramma, Chandravadavamma, Puttadevamma, Mugalu Tripurasundaramma, and Jetti Thayamma of Mysore were among the famous dance practitioners of the early twentieth century.[44] Yet the census report noted that the kaikolas were concentrated in the Mysore district, the smaller number of natuvas largely in Kolar District, indicating that self-perceptions among these communities were already changing, as members of these communities from other districts of Mysore were inserting themselves into other categories.[45]

Even in 1901, a considerable number of females had been adopted into the natuva community; nearly 64 percent of those reporting themselves in the census as natuvas and kaikolas were females, although their absolute numbers had precipitously dropped during the decade, from 7,442 to 2,163.[46] The decrease of 5,279, or 71 percent of the population under this heading, was due to the fact most referred to themselves as *banajigas* (members of a merchant class or caste). In 1901, however, before the reform effort of the Mysore administration had begun leading to the decline of this community, the census reported: "At the present day [the devadasis] are a distinct caste having laws of their own and their own constitutional *settis* (village headmen) and *yajamans* (community headmen) whom they obey."[47] A less drastic decline in numbers (to 1,745) was reported in the 1911 census, although the geographical distribution was somewhat altered: most members of the community were concentrated in the Bangalore and Kolar districts. Mysore, the seat of princely power, had by this time ceased to provide the necessary patronage to these performers, forcing them to reclassify themselves or seek employment elsewhere.[48]

Despite the well-known fact that adoption of girls from a range of castes was common among those classified as professional dancing girls, colonial administrators and law officials alike attempted to consolidate singers and dancers into one identifiable caste, with ambiguous outcomes. Kunal Parkar has shown that although customs based on caste could be claimed as the basis for upholding certain rights of dancing girls, the emphasis on the nondomestic sexuality of temple dancing girls kept these customs distinct from the legally sanctioned ties that linked marriage, chastity, and property.[49] The unchastity charge in particular, which became crucial in late-nineteenth-century denials of widows' rights to property, was also crucial in denying devadasis' rights in temples.

By the time Ananthakrishna Iyer wrote his voluminous *Mysore Tribes and Castes* in the early 1930s, a censorious attitude toward the devadasis was already a part of the middle-class optic. The natuvas merited a separate chapter in his work, although they were not a caste, and in his anxiety to make them, rather than the devadasis, the key figures in this community of performers, Iyer was forced into further contradictions. The word *natuvan,* he emphasized, "is an occupational term, meaning a dancing master which is applied to males of a dancing girl group to train girls in dancing."[50] What, then, were the women of this community called? Although a photograph marked *Natuva Dancing Woman* accompanies the text, devadasis are referred to throughout his account as a separate category of "Professional (performing) Women" and as one of the ten endogamous groups constituting the community of performers. In order to explain the "disproportionately high number of females (64 per cent) amongst the natuvas enumerated in the 1901 census," Iyer acknowledged "the greater care bestowed on female than on male children" and also the continued recruitment of girls from various castes who were adopted by professional women dancers, initiated into *aksharabhyasa* (literacy) and to a life of dancing and singing.[51]

By Iyer's own admission, devadasi women and natuva men belonged to the same occupational category: some devadasi women became professional dancers, while others formed domestic relationships with natuvas. Even those women who did not become devadasis enjoyed a considerably higher status than other categories of women under Hindu law in that they were allowed to adopt daughters. In the case of devadasis, moreover, "the children belong to the mothers, and the girls born or affiliated inherit her property, the male members being only entitled to maintenance."[52]

We must not exaggerate the power enjoyed by devadasis, who, despite their relative autonomy, nevertheless remained dependent on that triad of men within the political economy of the temple: the priest, the guru (teacher), and the patron.[53] Yet, because their sexual services were embedded within the wider cultural sphere of symbolic and material exchanges in the temple, devadasis enjoyed a position quite distinct from those of proletarianized sex workers, and even *basavis.* Once more, we turn to Iyer. Basavis, Iyer says, were women drawn from a range of lower castes, distinct in most cases from those that dedicated girls to the life of devadasis. Thus the Bedars, Dombars, Holeyas, Madigas, Kilakkyatas, and Voddas often dedicated their girls as basavis at the local temples. Sonless parents often chose to dedicate a daughter, who thereafter functioned as an "honorary son," continuing to live in her father's house, inheriting his property, and performing his funeral rites.[54] She usually developed a relationship with one man of the same or a higher caste who paid her father back for the expenses he had incurred. Her children were legitimate and were entitled to a share in their grandfather's properties. Basavis enjoyed enviable property rights and, like their devadasi and Nair counterparts, inhabited the very heart of Hindu laws of inheritance rather than remaining islands of exception within Hindu law.

The legal rights of devadasis, as Kunal Parkar and Kay Jordan have clearly shown, were at first acknowledged, if somewhat reluctantly, by the colonial judicature.[55] In *Chalakonda Alasani v. Chalakonda Ratnachalam* (1864), Jordan says a disapproving Madras High Court admitted the rights to property and inheritance of a mother and her two dancer daughters:

> It must not be forgotten that such prostitution is strictly in accordance with Hindu law and customs; and these women compose a distinct caste, numerous and not seldom possessed of wealth; they do not adopt their profession from choice but it is their's [sic] by the accident of birth, and it is . . . in accordance and not at variance with Hindu law. Our courts are therefore bound to administer to them that law, uninfluenced by any fastidiousness founded upon Western views of morality.[56]

Similarly, the Madras and Bombay high courts admitted the rights of dancing girls to adopt one or more daughters and the right of daughters to inherit in preference to sons.[57] The introduction of the Indian Penal Code (1860) and Criminal Procedure Code (1861), which prohibited the prostitution of minors, led to a slew of challenges to these rights in the courts of Bombay and Madras. Judges such as Justice West of the Bombay High Court were quick to introduce a conception of community legal consciousness over custom as the source of authority for the law in order to disallow dancing girls' rights.[58] Spheres of female economic power were recast as aberrations morally, if not legally, inconsistent with the body of Hindu law. Thus by the late nineteenth century, the existence of women with property rights was posed as a "problem" because "the right of the daughter to inherit property [was] in violation of the ordinary canons of Hindu Law." Though the issue was never satisfactorily settled by civil courts, the revenue authorities frequently registered the *pattas* (deeds to property) of a deceased *raiyat* (peasant) in the name of his basavi daughter, a right that even male inheritors in the Hindu line (as defined by the colonial authorities) admitted was hers by custom.[59]

Although the dedication as basavis of girls under age eighteen was made an offense under Section 372 of the Indian Penal Code, Muthulakshmi Reddi noted that temple authorities, parents, and the general public honestly felt that it had religious sanction, "and the law is not absolutely against it."[60] The basavis' duties within the temple, however, were only nominal, and in Iyer's words, "They did not prostitute themselves promiscuously for hire," as did devadasis.[61] Their links with the temple institution were therefore far more tenuous than those of the devadasis, whose performances were central to temple rituals and earned them respect well into the last decade of the nineteenth century. To categorize a wide range of practices as prostitution, as Parkar has shown, was to open the door to the criminalization of the profession, as occurred in late colonial rule.

Resuming the Devadasi's Right to Property

The 1898 order of the Mysore muzrai superintendent only deepened the crisis for devadasis resulting from the disappearing patronage of local political elites after the establishment of British rule in Mysore. If competing claims over temple resources had been made throughout the nineteenth century, the new order served to multiply them. In 1898 Vydya Srikantaiah of Gauribidanur sought the permission of the government to resume tafe service inams (presumably granted by his forebears) on the grounds that the tafe women were not rendering service in accord with the sastras.[62] The Kolar Deputy Commissioner, however, found that these women were rendering daily tafe services as required of them and were in possession of title deeds as well.[63]

The muzrai superintendent, however, was quite determined to put an end to the practices of dancing in temples and temple processions. In this he was amply aided by public opinion, which was opposed to the continued indulgence of the Maharaja in practices that were an embarrassment to the moralities of the middle class. Thus Karnataka Prakasika despaired of seeking government assistance for social reform, reporting that "a nautch party" had been held at a wedding attended by both the Dewan and the Maharaja in 1896.[64] On a far more disapproving note, Vrittanta Patrike reported in 1896 that the royal family had spent Rs 16,000 on dancing girls for a royal wedding; worse yet was the respect accorded to these women, who were paraded through the city of Mysore with the bride and groom in "howdahs."[65]

Srinivasacharlu's successor was more zealous, issuing strict orders disallowing such "detestable creatures" from accompanying the Maharaja's procession on his tour of the Sivaganga and Melkote temples in 1900, despite the admission of the palace controller that the duties of "dancing girls," though not defined anywhere, certainly included tafe services.[66] The content and nature of royal ceremonies were defined by the bureaucracy. Assured that his actions would meet the approval of the British Resident in Mysore, Srinivasacharlu said he "intended to do away with dancing girls who sometimes accompanied the *Isthakabal* party [welcoming group] of the Maharaja at major temples" at Melkote and Sivaganga, for example, and accordingly issued orders to all Deputy Commissioners responsible for the local arrangements during such visits.[67] Every effort was made to see that women were prevented from dancing in the temples. The administration prided itself on granting no exceptions to the new rule, even when petitions were presented by women such as the dancer of T'Narsipur or Meenakshi of Tirumakudlu in 1905, both of whom claimed that they had vowed to dance at the Girija Kalyana at Nanjangud to be cured of their maladies.[68]

Instead of mere official disapproval, a lasting solution was sought to the embarrassment of seeing devadasis continue their role in temple rituals. How better could the practice be banned than by cutting the source of the devadasis' livelihood, that is, suspending the payments and resources that sustained the devadasis and their arts? The muzrai official recognized this when he ordered that positions that fell vacant in muzrai temples after the death of a devadasi should not be filled. Over a period of time, this would lead to a decline in the employment of devadasis in temples, and temple rituals themselves would therefore undergo change by adapting to their absence. Not only did this represent a far greater incursion into the traditional duties and rights of devadasis, it ensured that the change would be irreversible.

The first spirited challenge to the new situation came from the twelve devadasis who worked for the Srikanteswara temple at Nanjangud, a prominent temple complex that had long enjoyed princely patronage. In two emotional petitions that cited the authority of the *Veda Bharata Shastra* agamashastra (scriptures relating to temple practices and rituals) and *sampradaya* (a system of religious practice), the women reminded the sovereign of his duty to protect hereditary occupations such as theirs.[69] Unlike the Brahmans, they said, who had *chattrams* (resting places for pilgrims or travelers) and mathas to take care of their needs, the devadasis had only their artistic skills with which to render service to God and earn their livelihoods. Like the priests, they should be allowed to serve God by serving king, guru, and priest, who were akin to God, and thereby give and receive fulfillment.[70]

Between the tremulous signatures of the devadasi women affixed to a handwritten Kannada petition and the typed government orders in English lay a chasm that separated prevailing notions of dharma, protected by the king, from the modalities of modernity set in motion by his bureaucracy. The first petition of Kittasani, Nanjasani, Kalyanisani, and six other women emphasized the sovereign's duty to protect customary practices and scriptural duties without recognizing that the Maharaja himself was powerless to intervene on their behalf. Their appeal received no more than cursory attention from palace officials who dispatched it to the government on January 16, 1905, as a matter unconcerned with the palace. In a recognition of the shifting relations of power, the devadasis' next petition was addressed to the superintendent as well, requesting reinstatement of their rights in accord with family traditions but now expressing a willingness to adapt to the changed circumstances. Their skills in music and dancing, they said, should not be allowed to languish and die for want of state patronage; the devadasis therefore offered to perform at state gatherings if necessary.[71]

The Mysore officials sought reference to the sastras as the indisputable word on the duties of devadasis.[72] We have already noted the ambiguities of the sastraic record compared to the epigraphic record, so in 1906 the Dewan's request for clarification about "how far the sastras enjoin the service of dancing girls in temples" was itself an invitation to legitimize a particular, rather than universal, sastraic tradition. The *agamiks* (scholars well versed in agamasastras) entrusted with the task masterfully demonstrated, through citation of a group of texts dealing with temple rituals—*Shaiva, Pancharatra, Vykhanasagamasastras*—that devadasis did indeed have specific services to render in the temple.[73] From the moment they woke up, bathed, put on fresh clothes, and adorned themselves with flowers, they spent the day participating in temple rituals that included waking up the deity with song and dance rituals, lighting the lamps in the evenings, and performing prescribed musical and dance oblations at set times. In addition, the agamiks said, the scriptures required them to perform a series of special rituals on specific days throughout the year. In turn, devadasis were entitled to a share of the offerings as a temple honor and to payments from temple revenues. Indeed, the nonperformance of these duties by the devadasis was deemed so grievous a violation of the temple code that the priests were required to perform rituals of atonement *(prayaschitta)*.[74] They concluded their commentary, submitted to the government on July 24, 1906, with the suggestion that although this was what the sastras said, the government should do whatever was appropriate.

The valorization of textual authority by the Mysore officials produced this ambiguous response, and the agamiks were then called on to provide a definitive statement and were among the many who determined the structure of temple tradition. There was little in their testimony, moreover, that could be deployed by government officials seeking legitimation of the decision to do away with the devadasis and their role in temples. Attention was then trained on the "personal purity and rectitude of conduct and celibacy which were considered essential in the case of female servants of god."[75] The sastraic authorities were once more summoned to adjudicate on the question of whether strict *brahmacharya* (celibacy) was expected of devadasis.

In the second memo of August 16, 1907, the agamiks complied with the expectations of the authorities by reiterating the need for strict *brahmacharya* among devadasis "even though they may have tied the *tali* [necklace that is a sign of marriage]"—in other words, even though they were married to the deity. They raised the specter of a world turned upside down, which it was the duty of the government authorities to set right: "Due to *kala vaishamya* [the corruptions of the time] all *varnashrama acharas* [observance of caste norms] have come to confusion. If you, as upholder of the dharma, make them follow sastraic injunctions, it will be good for the country, king and people."[76] The evocation of a powerful dystopia had long served as the format for voicing upper-caste male anxieties, particularly about the sexual appetites of women.[77] The Mysore administration was now confident that the decision to discontinue the services of devadasis could be turned to their advantage if the devadasis could be shown to have violated sacred traditions, with the Mysore administration emerging as protectors of true dharma and restorers of purity.

The original object of the institution of the devadasi system could be set aside because the state of immorality in which these people were now found amply justified the government action in removing them from the sacred institutions such as temples.[78] The new measures, which had been applied only to the two large temples, were now extended to all muzrai institutions in Mysore: devadasis who held land directly, and possessed deeds to prove that, were confirmed as the owners of that property in perpetuity on the payment of quit rent. The government could not resume land even when lands were held by the temples, not the women, because such donations could be resumed only if services were not performed. Because devadasis could not be dispossessed for nonperformance of their duties, the government advocate made the ingenious suggestion that the Inam Department could certainly enforce the new rule against "women who [had] not preserved their chastity and celibacy." By making celibacy, not just the performance of dance rituals, a condition of their continued enjoyment of temple grants, the state adroitly contained the crisis produced by its own illegality in ending "local law-ways."

It is also striking that the Mysore administration was constrained in its actions by two contradictory sets of rules: the sastraic injunctions and concepts of dharma that were theologically derived, on the one hand, and by the drive toward defining a legality delinked from religion, on the other. The officials' resolution of the contradictory pulls was not the repudiation of either one but a judicious application of each side of the argument to convince different constituencies. This staved off possible orthodox accusations about ignorance of the sastras, and therefore alienation from the people they sought to govern, while simultaneously satisfying the urges of those who cast themselves as modernizers, redefining and recasting traditions that were an impediment to the transformed political and economic uses of the temple complex.

The second councilor, K. P. Puttanna Chetty, commended the government for its "high moral courage" in excluding devadasis from their temple services. Yet it was not just women who had been found lacking in the morality appropriate to temple offices: the venality of male *archakas* (officiating priests of temples), "men of little learning and not of high moral character," was legendary. However, there is no further reference to this lapsed tradition in the final government order of 1909, which abolished the employment of devadasis in muzrai institutions.[79] Women alone ("notoriously of loose morals") bore the responsibility for the degeneration of high ideals and were therefore held responsible for their descent into oblivion.

The absorption of the artistic dance traditions of devadasis into a "national culture" forged by upper-caste nationalists after suitable reforms has been documented elsewhere and does not concern me here. What is striking about this moment in Mysore history is the speed with which new traditions were forged: thus, in 1908 the new muzrai superintendent, while conceding that Srinivasacharlu had been mistaken in his belief that tafe services were not scripturally ordained, argued against the reversal of his predecessor's 1892 decision by observing that over the past fifteen years, people had "become accustomed to the idea of doing without."[80]

The determination of the bureaucracy to put an end to the temple services of devadasis did not end with the passage of the government order. The government still had to deal with petitions from devadasis who resented the abrupt termination of their services in temples or the transfer of their remuneration to other people.[81] In 1919, in response to the concerns of a member of the Legislative Council who urged stern actions to restore "the decency and purity of public worship," the muzrai secretary called on the Deputy Commissioners of every district to report on the implementation of the order. Their responses clearly showed that they were fulfilling the wishes of the government quite efficiently. In most cases, inam lands and temple perquisites given to tafe women had been resumed after the deaths of incumbents.[82] The district collectors of Kadur, Mysore, and Chitaldurg reported that there were no devadasi inams in their districts. The Shimoga district collector said that although one inam had been resumed, four other holders had been categorically informed that the perquisites they enjoyed were only for their lifetimes. Other district collectors, of Hassan, Tumkur, and Bangalore, reported brisk action against the inam holders; in Kolar District alone, as many as thirty-three temples still enjoyed tafe-service inams.

Because the active rendering of service was no longer the criterion for enjoying the tafe-service inams, devadasis such as Muniamma, who had served both the Sri Gopala Swami and the Sri Chandrasekhara Swami temples of Srinivaspur, Kolar District, for fifty years, suddenly found their claims to personal inam grants challenged by non-tafe members of the temple family.[83] In the case of Muniamma, the government ruled that the lands belonged to her family and not to her personally despite the appellant's claims that she had paid the land revenue from 1900 and enjoyed the land absolutely and exclusively. Other temple officials, who clearly stood to benefit from the resumption of tafe-service inams, lost no time in divesting the female descendants of devadasis of such land. Thus the 5.5 acres of dry land and the 1.16 acres of wetland of devadasi Seshi of the

Sri Someshwaradevaru temple of Nambihalli in Srinivaspur taluk, which were legally made over to Venkatalakshmamma in 1873 and enjoyed by the latter's female descendants, were resumed in 1929 as a *devadaya*, a land grant for service to the temple.[84]

Though these realms of relative autonomy were eroded in the colonial period, there were systematic ways in which the system rewarded primarily lower-caste women who served higher-caste men. Priyadarshini Vijaisri's account of the wide range of practices that came to be known as "sacred prostitution" in Andhra Pradesh and Karnataka shows that the question of caste hierarchy was inseparable from the purported freedoms of dedicated women.[85]

Defining Domestic or Licit Domains of Female Sexuality

Throughout the nineteenth century, the cumulative effects of the implementation, then repeal, of the Contagious Diseases Acts in British cantonments in India, the intermittent use of lock hospitals to regulate urban prostitution, and the gradual growth of Leagues of Social Purity and Temperance consisting of missionaries as well as Indian anti-nautch campaigners produced something of a backlash. Indigenous male elites increasingly felt themselves reduced to the level of clients when they had once been patrons, and they portrayed the surveillance measures of the British authorities, who were unable to distinguish family women from others, as a violation of community honor. Once more the resistance to colonial intrusion into the private domain was articulated as resistance to colonialism itself: at its annual meeting the 1888 Congress therefore passed a resolution seeking to abolish British laws regulating prostitution on the grounds that the honor of respectable Indian women was at stake.[86]

Yet by the end of the nineteenth century new kinds of morality were taking shape: Pamela Price has shown that a nautch party organized at a private gathering in 1894 embarrassed the Raja of Ramnad into issuing an elaborate letter to the press distancing himself from such activities.[87] The Mysore king, in contrast, remained subordinate to the emerging bureaucracy, which took the decision to outlaw the practice. Through the suppression of the polyvalent roles of the devadasis, the Mysore authorities had begun drawing the lines between respectable and disrespectable female sexuality in ways largely consonant with dominant nationalist discourse, especially in the period of Gandhian nationalism.[88]

Chastity in "thought, word and deed" was seen as critical for the development of the moral force of a *satyagrahi* (volunteer for nonviolent action). Although Muthulakshmi Reddi campaigned to enfranchise devadasi inams and delink them from service to the temple altogether, she shared the puritanism of her male counterparts and encouraged devadasi women to marry and domesticate themselves.[89] A vigorous and eloquent campaigner against the devadasi tradition who invited the wrath of conservative upper castes in the 1920s and 1930s was the reformed devadasi Moovalur Ramamritham Ammaiyar. Her clear-eyed accounts of the degradation of women like her were deployed as part of a wider critique of Brahmanic society.

Another sign of the shift from a defense of certain forms of sexuality in the name of "tradition" to a more active dissociation from such traditions was the fate of the reprint of *Radhika Santwanam,* a book-length poem written by an eighteenth-century courtesan of the Thanjavur court, Muddupalani.[90] It subverted traditional erotic genres by focusing on women's sexual pleasures. In 1910, Bangalore Nagarathnamma, herself a renowned learned musician, courtesan, and a Gayaka (a member of one of the endogamous groups from which devadasis were drawn), entranced by the sophistication and literary merit of Muddupalani's subversive work, published a fresh edition of the book. Responding to the outrage of some reformers who declared the poem obscene and vulgar, the colonial authorities seized all copies of the book in 1911 under Section 392 of the Indian Penal Code. It was clear that, on the critical question of subordination of female sexuality, the interests of empire and nation were not necessarily in opposition.

The gradual erosion of the material support for the artistic abilities of the devadasi resulted in her decline as a professional dancer, producing in its place a proletarianized sex worker. Now a threat rather than an adjunct to the patriarchal household, the devadasi became indistinguishable from her urban counterparts and from the basavis in the rural areas. Beginning in the 1930s, the expanding markets for prostitutes in cities such as Bombay found ready recruits among the devadasis and basavis of Mysore.[91] Bangalore Nagaratnamma's own survival as a skilled musician and the patronage she continued to receive were exceptional rather than the rule.[92] Not only had the Mysore government invented a split between respectable and disrespectable sexuality; it had realigned access to property along such axes as well. Once the critical relation between new patriarchal definitions of female sexuality and women's rights to property was redefined, it became possible, especially in the 1930s, to legislate against immorality, on the one hand (evidenced by the passage of the Suppression of Immoral Traffic in Women and Girls Act of 1937), and for the rights of women to property, on the other. As the devadasis were symbolically and materially deprived of their resources, and consequently unable to practice their artistic skills, they were reduced to the status of proletarianized sex workers. As R. R. Diwakar would recall, "The art fell on evil days from 1910 to 1930 when there was much prejudice against these professional women."[93] When the extension of Hindu women's rights to property did take place, with the relatively uncontested passage of the act amending women's rights under Hindu law in 1933, it was middle-class, upper-caste women, whose sexuality was restricted to the domain of domestic monogamous life, who stood to gain. Having declared women's rights to property under Hindu law an anomaly when those rights were linked to nonpatriarchal forms of marriage and family, the state could now bestow rights on women within the framework of the patriarchal household.

What new codes of morality did the new nationalist patriarchy propose for men themselves? Here the Gandhian ideal of celibacy was far less pervasive, and, not surprisingly, one of the persistent demands of first-wave feminism was that men put an end to their moral double standard.[94] Even the ideal of companionate marriage pursued with such vigor in colonial India was not one that necessarily entailed the strict monogamy of men. Although there was certainly a contraction of legitimate spheres of male sexual fulfillment, the growth of prostitution in an illicit subterranean sphere, suppressed from public view, ensured that the "natural" promiscuity of men would continue to have a mode of expression. Writing in 1930, Ananthakrishna Iyer speculated on the origins of the devadasi system thus: "The founders of this institution made this an outlet for safeguarding family women for the good of the country."[95] This understanding resonated in the arguments made by opponents of proposed strictures on the practice of prostitution during debates on the Suppression of Immoral Traffic Act in the 1930s.[96]

Among the fantasies of male nationalists for a companionate marriage was the wife who would consent to the "natural" promiscuity of men, provided it did not disrupt domestic arrangements. In his brief sketch of Bangalore Nagaratnamma included in a collection of writings on the luminaries of Mysore, D. V. Gundappa (DVG) spoke at length of the virtues of one of her patrons, a Mysore High Court judge, Narahari Rao.[97] Narahari Rao attended Nagaratnamma's performances daily and resolved to become her patron. DVG reconstructs a dialogue between Narahari Rao and his wife that bears detailed quotation:

> When Narahari Rao desired to become a patron of Nagaratnamma, he first sought the permission of his lawful wife (Dharmapatni). He called his wife and said:
>
> > NARAHARI RAO: Listen, I want to ask you something. I need your permission.
> >
> > WIFE [who remains unnamed]: Will anyone believe that you need my permission [for anything]? Tell me what you want me to do.
> >
> > N: It's not that way. This is a special situation. I have become enamoured of Nagaratnamma's music for several days now. She sings very well. I wish to be able to listen to her music now and then. If you have any objections, tell me now and I shall let go of this interest.
> >
> > W: It is my will that your desires be fulfilled.
> >
> > N: I will ensure that you are not inconvenienced by this.
> >
> > W: How can it be an inconvenience to me? You have done your duty by the family. Our children have grown and are standing on their own feet. Our daughters are married. Our sons are educated. Now it is our duty to keep you happy.
>
> Thus this noble woman (mahathayi) gave her permission. Only then did Narahari Rao go ahead with his plans.[98]

We do not know whether such a conversation did take place, but it is interesting that DVG reports this exchange approvingly just before he speaks of the embarrassment caused by Narahari Rao's patronage of Nagaratnamma to the government of Mysore, whose employee he was. When the Dewan learned of the daily visits of Narahari Rao to Nagaratnamma's quarters in the official government carriage, he requested that Narahari Rao not sully the government image by visiting Nagaratnamma with the mace bearer and official vehicle. Narahari Rao was suitably chastened and readily stopped his use of the government vehicle, though he continued his patronage of Nagaratnamma. He moved his "pleasure court" to the southwestern part of Bangalore, which was suitably named Mount Joy.[99]

Conclusion

The Mysore bureaucracy pursued an agenda of social reform with a zeal that was unmatched in British India. In many ways, therefore, it anticipated by several decades and even thwarted the emergence of a nationalist moral-ethical leadership until the 1920s and 1930s. In the incident recorded by DVG, the split that was achieved between the spheres of the public and the private need not surprise us: what is striking is that the moral objection to Narahari Rao's actions came from the government rather than his wife. The granting of patronage to a devadasi, hitherto a public expression of power by zamindars, notables, and chieftains in precolonial India, given in return for religious honor and sexual services, had to be privatized in modernizing Mysore. Only as long as their patronage of public women such as Nagaratnamma remained a private matter could public men, judges such as Narahari Rao, uphold and dispense a new order of justice delinked from princely forms of power and authority. Meanwhile, the modernity of the middle-class woman was expressed in the form of her consent to a type of patronage that recalled an older extended sexual order. Her "modernity" consisted in permitting the continuation of a reformed patriarchy; promiscuity was a privilege of the modern male as long as he remained attentive to his duties as a father.

CHAPTER 7

The Licit in the Modern:
Protecting the Child Wife

I N 1893, THE GOVERNMENT OF MYSORE rejected the will of the majority of representatives of the Mysore Assembly, who opposed a regulation to prevent infant marriage, declaring that "the regulation is in some quarters regarded as an undue interference with the liberty of the subject, but [general sentiment] demands the abolition under the authority of law of certain usages which are as much opposed to the spirit of the Hindu Sastras as to the best interests of society."[1] Forty years later, Dewan Mirza Ismail spoke on behalf of a "general sentiment" that expressed the opposite view. Overriding the majority opinion in the Representative Assembly that favored extension of the Indian Child Marriage Restraint Act of 1929 to Mysore, he said: "The balance of considerations seems to be in favour of leaving things alone. . . . To be real and lasting, reform must proceed from within. It cannot be imposed from without."[2] In the space of a few decades the Mysore government had moved from a position of confident interference in "social questions" to a position that was firmly tempered by caution, perhaps even a self-critical assessment of the previous regulation's successes. What in the intervening period accounted for this dramatic shift in the state's attitude toward marriage reform?

What did remain stable across this period was the autonomy of the Dewan, who placed himself above representative institutions as arbiter of public opinion. This becomes clear when we consider in detail Mysore's Infant Marriage Regulation of 1894 against the totality of legislative initiatives of the princely state, which were aimed at extending the generalized legal form throughout Mysore society without effecting the social transformations adequate to such a vision.

Subaltern Encounters with the Will of the State

When the "state's emissary" (law) touched the lives of Chambar Ganga and Chavalanu ("alias Chavaluga") of Arikere Village of Mulbagal Taluk of Bangalore District in November 1895, it confronted the two men with a new will, the will of the state, determined to penetrate and reorganize one of the few domains in their wretched lives over which they believed they retained control.[3] What had these Madigas, whose abject poverty and ritually impure status permitted them no more than a precarious existence on the very margins of the village, done to attract the attention of the puni-tive machinery of the state? The arrival of the police *daffedar* (head peon, in charge of ten or more people) of Yaldur Police Station on the morning of November 24 was portentous, for he brought with him the threat of criminal prosecution if the two men proceeded with plans to marry Muni, the daughter of Chambar Ganga, to Ganga, the son of Chavaluga.[4] What might have been an innocuous and licit affair now took on the dimensions of a criminal, illicit act, a turn of events for which the Madiga men were not adequately prepared.

From the beginning of 1895, any persons involved in the celebration of the marriage of a Hindu girl aged less than eight years invited simple imprisonment of up to six months and/or a fine, following the passage of the 1894 Regulation to Prevent Infant Marriages among Hindus.[5] Ganga and Chavaluga had only a small inkling that the celebration of the mar-riage was in "open defiance of all lawful authority."[6] The celebration of a marriage among the marginalized Madigas could not have evoked much interest in the village, except among the elders of the caste and invited oth-ers; certainly the lower echelons of the government machinery were rarely involved in such marriages. Indeed, the Government of Mysore, function-ing from the administrative capital of Bangalore, could have been no more than a dim presence in the lives of the Madigas. Although their traditional caste calling as leather workers could have placed them in the category of village artisans, there was little to disguise the fact that their place in the village occupational order was as agricultural labor, engaged to work on the fields of the upper-caste landlords. Their lowly status kept them at a remove from the machinations of the village elite.

Yet the new order had already announced itself in the village when, on November 22, 1895, Patel Muniya Gowda (the village headman, who be-longed to a dominant agrarian caste) summoned the two men to inquire about the age of the prospective bride. Although Chambar Ganga said that she was about eight years old, the patel called for the Register of Births and Deaths and established that the girl was no more than seven years, two months, and twenty-eight days old at the time. Thus a singularly unremarkable event in the life of a Madiga family, the birth of a girl child, which heralded no more than fresh responsibilities and burdens in their quotidian existence, threatened to take on new and ominous portents. Ironically, this happened just at the moment when the bride's father believed he had relieved himself of some of the burdens of rearing a female child. A young Madiga girl had to be protected until her marriage not only from the prying eyes of her own caste men but from the upper-caste men who enjoyed privileged sexual access to lower-caste women, and sometimes even marriage offered little protection against upper-caste lust.

Chambar Ganga underestimated the lengths to which the local officials were willing to go to test the new legal powers bestowed by the state. When the village patel, convinced that his duty was to deter Chambar Ganga from performing the marriage and, in the presence of other village officials such as Shanbogue (accountant) Ramappa, Muddappa (patel), and other upper-caste villagers, informed him that such a marriage contravened the provisions of the new law, the Madiga replied, "What have we to do with your rules? You may do as you like, we will perform the marriage according to our customs."[7] Angered, no doubt, that a mere Madiga should repudiate his new authority, the patel reported the case to the daffedar and to the taluk magistrate. The daffedar visited the Madiga quarters on November 24, 1895, in order to reinforce the seriousness of the government's intention to uphold the new law over and above any customary practices.

During the period of colonial rule, the dominant agrarian elite in Mysore, particularly the village headmen, were invested with enhanced powers. For the most part, these headmen belonged to the Vokkaliga and Lingayat castes. In multicaste villages such as Arikere, the power of the patel, a hereditary village post, was derived from his economic dominance in the village, from his caste status, and from his appointment to a state office. Functioning along with the shanbogue, or village accountant, who was usually Brahman, the upper castes constituted a formidable phalanx of power in the village.[8] Between them, the patel and shanbogue helped in the collection of revenue and kept village accounts, the registers of landholdings, and all other records relating to land revenue.[9]

The official registration of Muni's birth signified a new period of rule by records that touched the private lives of all colonial subjects. The pragmatics of colonial rule necessitated the synchronicity and regular periodicity of the censuses, for example, for which the ground was prepared in a range of local registers using uniform categories.[10] Yet the Madigas of Arikere were probably tied to the landowning castes in a variety of other ways through structured caste and economic hierarchies that subordinated them. Dispute settlement, for example, was an essential aspect of the village headman's duties in the *panchayat* (court of arbitration). Therefore, economic and political authority could and did translate into juridical authority.[11] However, as Bernard Cohn points out, "a panchayat in which dominant caste men participate usually does not take cognizance of matters internal to other castes—marriage, succession when property is not involved, caste rules regarding commensality and pollution, disputes over caste property."[12] The jurisdiction of village judicial institutions, as opposed to intracaste councils, was therefore clearly defined, and the former largely worked in ways that supported the decisions of the latter. Presumably, then, if the Madigas satisfactorily established that the celebration was consistent with local law-ways, the marriage would be upheld. In response to the state's emissary, then, both Chambar Ganga and Chavaluga declared that the girl had completed eight years of life by their reckoning. More important, they pointed out that although "*kudike* [a form of widow remarriage] was lawful and allowed in their caste," they had no knowledge of any other rule.[13] Because they had already made expensive preparations for the wedding, they decided to go ahead with it.

The insistence by the two men that kudike was allowed within their caste was central to the discourse on child marriage. A number of other lower-caste men and women who were faced with prosecution made a similar argument. In September 1896, Haladasaya and Soma, two Kuruba (shepherd-caste) men of Chickbasur, Kadur Taluk, argued that the local law-ways of the Kurubas allowed not only widow remarriage but also adult marriage.[14] Muniga and Sanjiva, two Agasa (washerman-caste) men who were warned by the officiating priest in 1896 that child marriage was now liable to criminal prosecution, replied that this "was allowable in the caste."[15]

Chambar Ganga and Chavaluga pleaded that the new law did not apply to them. Their assessment was partially correct, for in the Dewan's decision to introduce a regulation that several people considered undue interference in the freedom of individuals, he had cited the figures obtained from the Census of 1891 as proof that child marriage was an "evil" largely because an unconscionable number of girls under age nine were widows.

Thus, he said, though there had been only an 18 percent gain in Mysore's population between 1881 and 1891, there had been a 50 percent increase in the number of marriages of girls under the age of nine: 3,560 widows were also under age nine.[16]

The existence of child widows had troubled upper-caste reformers in other parts of India from at least the middle of the nineteenth century. The inauspicious and sexually repressed existence of the upper-caste widow only exacerbated the problems posed by child marriage. Campaigns for a law that would permit the remarriage of upper-caste women had yielded fruit in 1856 when the Widow Remarriage Act XV was passed. At this time, the colonial state had thrown its weight against the practice of female infanticide in parts of western and northern India by imposing severely punitive regulations against offending communities.[17] Interest in widow remarriage was aroused when the Law Commission of India, while attempting to codify penal laws in 1837, discovered a causal link between the prohibition against widow remarriage and infanticide: the shame and secrecy surrounding an unwanted pregnancy forced a widow to kill her newborn.[18] By any yardstick this was a criminal offense, and the colonial state recognized that permitting a widow to remarry would confine her sexuality and was preferable to a system that encouraged criminality.[19]

The Mysore administrators and their colonial counterparts elsewhere were well aware that strictures against widow remarriage were most closely observed by the upper castes. A wide range of castes and communities permitted widow remarriage: in response to Malabari's 1886 "Notes on Infant Marriage" urging that the age of twelve be used as the age of consent for girls, several colonial officials used census data to prove that at least two-thirds of the Indian population practiced widow remarriage.[20] In Mysore, the strictures against widow remarriage were rarely observed, except among the Brahmans and the Komatis (Vyshyas). In some cases, widow remarriage was encouraged; child marriage, on the other hand, was fairly common except among newly Hinduized tribes and animist communities.[21] Large communities such as the Kurubas practiced adult marriage, and no social opprobrium attached to women who remained unmarried.[22]

The two Madiga men of Arikere held onto their customary practices against the determined effort of the state to reform local law-ways. They were doomed to certain punishment. Adding crushing injury to insult was the size of the fine levied against them by the district magistrate in April 1896: for agricultural laborers who earned little by way of cash, the three rupees that each man had to pay could only have been an unwelcome burden. Because the fine had to be paid in the lean premonsoon season of April, when they commanded even fewer resources, it was even more burdensome. They may have been forced to choose between two equally ignominious options: seeking a loan from the local moneylender, which could drive them further into debt, or serving seven days in prison.[23]

Even when the Mysore authorities had successfully prosecuted them, the arguments made by the two men were cause for more than a little discomfort among the interpreters of the new regulation: if the Muslims had been exempted from the application of the regulation because they did not prevent the remarriage of widows, asked one official, was it fair to prosecute the Madigas, who followed similar rules?[24] By what logic did the Mysore government transform the local law-ways of some social groups while withholding the use of its power against others? What could a "rule of law" that discriminated among religious groups and, within religious groups, between castes, claim as the basis of its legality?

The Making of the Infant Marriage Regulation

The debates leading to the passage of the regulation were infused with exactly such concerns for the preservation of "caste laws," although they were voiced by members of those upper castes that feared changes. As early as 1891, some members of the Mysore Representative Assembly raised the question of applying to Mysore the amendment to Section 375 of the Indian Penal Code that raised the age of consent for girls from ten years, in accordance with the 1860 code, to twelve.[25] Non-Brahman members of the assembly were sharply rebuked for attempting to legally define what was appropriate for other communities in a mixed-caste assembly.[26] In 1893, when the subject was still being discussed, Anantha Shetti, a Vyshya (trading caste) advocate from Chitradurga, said that the passage of any regulation aimed at restricting child marriage would effectively prevent Vyshyas from observing their caste rules.[27]

Another significant group raised objections to the proposed regulation, though on entirely different grounds. Muslim members of the assembly, Hafizullah Khan and Gaus Sheriff Sab, objected that "since Muslims permitted widow remarriage, it should not be applicable to them."[28] But the Madigas or Holeyas could not claim the exceptional status of Muslims.

At first the administration remained unconvinced that the provisions of the amended code needed to be extended to Mysore. Because the criminal law amendment dealt with the age at which consumption took place, the Dewan was convinced that such extension was unnecessary in a state where, even if girls were married before the age of twelve, consummation rarely occurred before that age.[29] He was more attracted to the idea of a regulation that would prevent the marriage of old men to young girls. The debate in the assembly had centered around three kinds of questions: whether it was appropriate for the state to interfere in religious matters, whether any such legislation would violate the authority not only of the sastras but of parents and guardians, and whether it would go against collectively decided caste norms. Some Brahmans reacted ferociously in the name of caste rights to the proposal that there be no more than thirty years' difference between a groom and a bride, arguing that such restrictions would effectively prohibit Brahman men from acquiring wives to perform certain religious ceremonies (e.g., *agnihotra,* offering oblations to fire).[30]

Contrary to those who claimed that child marriage was an unmitigated evil, those who protested against extension of the regulation to Mysore argued that there were several advantages to the early marriage of girls: it led to greater accommodation within marriage and greater obedience on the part of the wife, and it prevented immorality among "strong and healthy men above 40" who were prevented from marrying. The sexual desire of the child bride was not admitted as even a possibility. As Tanika Sarkar points out, colonial, revivalist, and medical-reformer strands of opinion "agreed on a definition of consent that pegged [it] to a purely physical capability, divorced entirely from sexual, emotional or mental compatibility. Consent was put into a biological category, a stage when the female body was ready to accept sexual penetration without serious harm."[31]

There was no great enthusiasm for the proposed legislation. Only the newspaper *Vrittanta Chintamani* gave unwavering support to the introduction of the Age of Consent Amendment to Mysore, which it did by darkly hinting at the brutal details of the Phulmani case.[32] In 1890 Phulmani, the ten-year-old wife of thirty-five-year-old Hari Mohan Maiti, had died of injuries she sustained during sexual intercourse.[33] The uproar in the Indian and English press led to a highly publicized trial in Calcutta in which Maiti was tried and sentenced to twelve months' hard labor for manslaughter. This sentence, however, provoked an outcry from the orthodox community and the revivalist nationalists.

In Mysore, the *Karnataka Prakasika* at first welcomed the British Indian amendment as no violation of the sastras: child marriage, it argued, should be seen as a violation only of the health of the child wife.[34] A short while later, this paper, too, was swept up in the growing tide of protest, led by Bal Gangadhar Tilak, among others, against the interference of the state in domestic affairs.[35] Yet another famous case of the 1880s involving a child wife showed that the colonial state did not hesitate to enter the protected domain of the family when cases were filed against women's claims to independence, as in the restitution of conjugal rights. Rakhmabai was an educated woman who had been married at the age of nine to an older, consumptive husband, Dadaji Bhikaji. Although her marriage was not consummated, Rakhmabai found the atmosphere in her marital home uncongenial to any intellectual advancement and was living in her parental home when she was sued for restitution of conjugal rights.[36] As Sudhir Chandra and Uma Chakravarti have noted, the primary impetus for the pursuit of conjugal rights with such vigor was Rakhmabai's family property.[37] Rakhmabai herself said "that money and property considerations are at the bottom of the persecution with which he and his advisers follow me."[38] Rakhmabai was found guilty by the colonial judicature, charged and sentenced, and finally relieved of the legal suit only by paying off Bhikaji.[39]

The Rakhmabai case presented the orthodox and the revivalist nationalists with an example of the dangerous ways in which educated women could plot against uneducated husbands. Women such as Pandita Ramabai, however, bitterly lamented the eagerness with which the colonial government responded to nationalist pressure, hinting at a compact between British and Indian patriarchies in making and retaining the distinction between the private and the public.[40]

Dewan Seshadri Iyer, probably aware of the scale of protests unleashed by the passage of the amendment in British India, decided to disarm his opposition by seeking the sanction of the religious authorities of the state, and he procured the support of the heads of the leading mathas in Mysore, who unanimously declared that child marriage and the marriage of young girls to old men were opposed by the sastras.[41] The Dewan claimed that the religious heads themselves despaired of their loss of authority in the conduct of family affairs. With such protection, the Dewan proceeded to outline a regulation that far exceeded the British Indian amendment in its scope and applicability. The proposed bill prohibited the marriage of girls under age eight altogether and that of girls under age sixteen to men over fifty.[42]

The logic behind the decision to make age eight the legally marriageable age for girls was not quite obvious: if anything, its arbitrariness spoke of the state's ability to impose a despotic legal order rather than protect the rights of women or girl children within families. This becomes clearer when we look at the operation of the act. Because the Mysore regulation made child marriage itself, rather than consumption, punishable, the decision on age eight as the age of marriage would provoke the least resistance among upper-caste constituents. Prepuberty marriages, though not sexual consummation, were prescribed for a number of upper castes according to the sastras, and colonial medical sociology had placed the onset of puberty for girls in tropical climates between the ages of ten and twelve years. Although the bill appeared to be quite radical in its prohibition of child marriage, then, it was excessively cautious in defining the limits of female childhood, appearing instead to be absorbed with an extension of the legal form itself.[43]

Having staved off possible orthodox opposition through a legitimate reading of the sastras, the Dewan was equally prepared to face other possible objections with arguments that were more in keeping with the modes of governmentality he espoused: the indisputable statistical evidence of the association between child marriage and widowhood. In his social history of caste in modern India, Nicholas Dirks has suggested that in the late nineteenth century the colonial state devised modes of governance based on the census and the anthropological surveys to constitute an "ethnographic state."[44] The state's systematic effort to obtain and collate information on aspects of Indian society and economy succeeded in objectifying and quantifying Indian social experience, enabling individual caste groups and even governments to chart their progress on various measurable scales.[45]

The census came in handy in the discussion on infant marriage. The Mysore Census of 1891 had drawn attention to the existence of child marriage and one of its most pernicious consequences, early widowhood.[46] As many as 11,157 girls were declared to have married between the ages of one and four, against 512 boys. The situation worsened for the next category, in which there were 180,997 wives for 8,173 husbands. The figures gradually equalized only by about the age of twenty. Even more striking was the high proportion of child widows under age nine (3,554) compared with boys who had lost their wives (220). There were 20,000 under-age widows compared with 100 wifeless boys. In an aggregate sense, because widowhood was pervasive among all age groups, this meant that "every fifth Hindu female was a widow." Further, only the non-upper-caste Hindus had a high proportion of women who had married a second time, compared with a high proportion of men in all castes who had married more than once.[47]

But there were some social groups, such as the Brahman orthodoxy, that remained unmoved by the evidence in the sastras as advanced by the religious heads, refused to be embarrassed by the statistical proof of social degeneration, and were unperturbed by the anguished cries and whispers of child brides and widows.[48] Opponents of the regulation were quick to point out that the support of large sections of the assembly could not be taken as universal consent. In an expression of their dissent, they submitted a petition signed by 164 members of the assembly that protested against the extension of the government's authority to the domestic domain in a way that undermined the authority of parents or matha heads in matters of marriage.[49] Outnumbering those members of the Representative Assembly who favored legislation (fifty-three), they suggested that fines were preferable to imprisonment as a mode of punishment.[50]

The government officials were quick to point out that their decisions were not going to be decided by the debate in the assembly, choosing to go ahead with a measure to restrict infant marriage. As a small concession to their orthodox opponents, they reduced the age below which it was illegal for girls to be married to men over fifty: it was reduced from sixteen to fourteen years.[51] The regulation still left large sections of Mysore society untouched: it was applicable only to Hindus, insisted on a procedure by which the government had to sanction prosecution in every case, and affirmed that no offense could be tried by any court inferior to that of a magistrate.

No doubt the government used the authority of the *mathadhipathis* (heads of monastic institutions) to wear down the opposition mounted by upper-caste Mysore elites, but its actions were aimed, just as in the case of the devadasi reform, at producing new sources of authority delinked from religion that would determine family forms and affective ties. Its reliance on the records and statistics on the effects of child marriage on the Mysore population would form the basis for its intervention in the intimate spheres of family that disregarded elite opinion. Whether these interventions produced the desired transformations in family structures and marriage patterns would depend on the extent to which the new sources of authority became acceptable among the different sections of the population.

The regulation that made "criminals" of Chambar Ganga and Chavaluga, however, did not challenge the validity of the marriage itself. The question of whether a regulation restricting child marriage should in fact make such marriages null and void was one that had long marked the debates on the legislation. In his intervention during the debate on the Age of Consent Amendment in the Madras Presidency, Sir T. Madhava Rao had suggested that levying a fine on those who performed the marriage was far preferable to derecognizing the marriage: "The effect of this will be to leave the existing order of things as little disturbed as possible and yet diminish the number of marriages before the age limit, and thereby diminish the number of virgin widowhoods which will be an important gain."[52] The Mysore Infant Marriage Prevention Regulation pursued the same logic, recognizing the advantage of attacking the agencies responsible for such alliances rather than inviting explosive reactions by declaring the marriages illegal. Yet in declaring the performance of such marriages illegal, an unprecedented contradiction was produced, as pointed out by an advocate of Mysore during the debate on the proposed regulation: "This regulation, by punishing the promoters of an Infant Marriage without declaring that marriage as illegal would for the first time make an act right in civil law but wrong in criminal law."[53] Also, once the provisions of the act were better known among the rural population, the strictures placed in the way of child marriage could be treated as a mere inconvenience rather than as a serious deterrent. When goldsmith Naranappa arranged the marriage of his daughter Munilakshmamma, aged just over five and a half years to Subbarayappa, aged thirty-five, he was repeatedly warned by Patel Kempareddy of Karyapalli in Kolar District that this was against the law.[54] Naranappa first agreed to drop the alliance, then continued with preparations for the marriage, saying that he had already taken a large loan from the groom for the expenses and that they would "meet the consequences." Subbarayappa and Naranappa, who were fined fifteen rupees each, and the groom's father, who was fined five rupees, were probably able to count these fines as an unavoidable addition to marriage expenses.[55]

Imposing a New Legal Regime

Despite its difficulties, the passage of the Infant Marriage Prevention Regulation may be seen as part of the Mysore state's effort to encompass and absorb those aspects of civil and social life that lay outside its reach and produce a population out of the disparate communities and their nonstate law-ways—governmentality, in short. Did the Mysore government possess the technologies adequate to such a task? Even the dissemination of law was no simple task. The *Vrittanta Patrike* urged the dissemination of the new regulation, which few knew was in force.[56] For several years after its passage, people facing prosecution were able to plead "ignorance of the law." Thus Sesha Iyengar, of Halthore Village in Belur Taluk, who arranged the marriage of his eighteen-month-old granddaughter Thirumalamma to Raghunathachar, aged eighteen years, pleaded not only that he was an old man who wished to see his granddaughter settled before he died but that it was customary in his (Brahman) community to marry girls "aged two and above" and that he was unaware of any change in that law, though this did not save the old man from prosecution.[57]

The provisions of the new regulation were announced in villages through the use of tom-toms.[58] The more efficient mode of communication was rumor: a single prosecution in a district could have a multiplier effect, serving as a warning to even far-flung villages that dire consequences awaited those who pleaded ignorance of the law. Although officials of Chikabasur in Kadur Taluk realized that the two Kurubas, Haldasaya and Soma, were acting in accordance with their caste customs when they got their children married, they prosecuted the two men and their wives, saying, "The provisions of the regulation have been clearly infringed and it is necessary to show the villagers how such marriages are viewed by the government."[59] The sentence, simple imprisonment ranging from ten days to two weeks, was particularly harsh because the two fathers were of advanced years.

Even the officials responsible for the governance of sexuality in the village were not exempt from the new dispensation. In Somasethahalli, Gauribidanur Taluk, not only were Ranga, a thirty-year-old groom, and Muniswami, the father of his three-year-old bride, Rangi, liable for prosecution but Patel Narse Gauda and the officiating priest, Venkatramanbhatta, were prosecuted as abettors.[60] It appeared that village headmen were unusually efficient in warning lower-caste men against infringing the law.[61] However, they were willing to look the other way when men of their own caste were involved, and some patels celebrated child marriages within their own families.[62]

In the sixteen-year period between 1896–97 and 1910–11, when most prosecutions took place, the total number of cases was 202, of which 175 resulted in the prosecution of 475 persons.[63] There was clearly more at stake in the Government of Mysore's passage of the Infant Marriage Regulation than the pursuit of an ideal of a model state, as Gustafson suggests.[64] Compared with the lackadaisical implementation of the amended criminal code in British India, Mysore's determination to prosecute was quite impressive. In British India the concessions made to the revivalist nationalists were patent when, just five days after the Age of Consent Amendment was passed in 1891, Governor-General Lansdowne issued a circular to all local governments urging them to apply the act only with "the utmost care and discrimination," adding that "prosecutions plagued by doubts should be postponed." Not surprisingly, there were very few prosecutions under the act in the early years after it was passed, and they dwindled to nothing shortly thereafter, when even inquiring into the operation of the act had become a wasteful bureaucratic exercise.[65] Similarly, in 1932 the Calcutta High Court set aside convictions made after the Sarda Act was passed, leading to a large number of complaints in the press about the leniency of the act's application.[66]

Protests on a similar scale were not heard in Mysore after the 1894 regulation came into force. The Mysore government trod fearlessly on ground that the Government of India did not enter. Only Baroda and Mysore had introduced infant marriage prevention regulations in 1894 and 1904, respectively, and they implemented them with vigor.[67] *Suryodaya Prakasika* published details of a marriage in 1904 between a fifty-four-and-a-half-year-old school headmaster, Srinivasachar, of Devanahalli, who had married the daughter of his Sanskrit teacher Anantha Thirthachar, a girl of just eight years and nine months, in flagrant contravention of Section 4 of the 1894 regulation, which forbade men over fifty from marrying girls under fourteen. The Dewan, N. Krishnamurthi, lost no time in urging an official enquiry into this violation, which was more grievous because the offender was a teacher, and a government official to boot. The Mysore law, wrote the secretary to the General and Revenue Departments, "is an exceptional one and our officials ought to set an example to the public by their scrupulous obedience to it." He therefore recommended that both officers be removed from service.[68]

Mysore subjects could not as easily be prosecuted in British India, and many took advantage of that fact.[69] In 1899, a fifty-two-year-old judge of the Mysore court was accused of having evaded Mysore's marriage law by celebrating his fourth marriage to a girl who was under fourteen in the Madras Presidency.[70] Venkatachar said that he had been on the lookout for a bride after the death of his third wife in 1895; that he had been "offered" the girl bride by her father, who said she was at least fourteen; and that although Venkatachar had not examined the horoscope, "the girl's physique" confirmed that her father was telling the truth. Clearly dissatisfied with his response, the registrar of the Chief Court requested proof of the age of the wife at the time of marriage, which Venkatachar failed to provide, but he escaped prosecution. Without this piece of evidence to prove that he had violated the law, the Mysore government could not, despite its best intentions, establish a case against one of its own officials.

New Knowledge of the Legal Subject

The power of a law such as the Mysore regulation against infant marriage critically relied on detailed knowledge of aspects of the family structure and marriage relations: violation could be proved only if the age of the girl could be proved. In his discussion on the "nation-form" Etienne Balibar notes the significance of the shift from systems of alliance that were subordinated to the control of church and family to those that were supervised by the modern state: "Today, it is the state which draws up and keeps the archive of filiations and alliances."[71] Was such an absolute rupture with older modes of retaining the memory of filiations and alliances possible under conditions of colonial rule? There was no such reliable system of records that government officials, especially district magistrates, could use to establish criminality. Thus, although Chambar Ganga's daughter's age was easily established by the government records, Venkatachar's wife's age could not, though the two dates of birth were separated by only a few years, which speaks volumes about the unevenness with which government machinery impinged on literate versus illiterate and on upper-caste versus lower-caste families. A large number of cases liable for prosecution had to be dropped for want of accurate information about the age of the girl child, especially when the age of the bride fell short of the stipulated minimum by just a few months or even a year.

Because the new rule by records had not yet become universal, other forms of corroboratory evidence were admitted in the process of affixing guilt. The *jatakam* (horoscope) drawn up at the time when a child was born, especially among upper-caste families, was admitted as an acceptable document for cases filed under the Infant Marriage Regulation.[72] By the turn of the century, other kinds of written evidence, though personal, were also admitted as corroboratory evidence. The pleader Nittur Gundappa, who filed a case against his own son-in-law, Shammanna, on June 27, 1895, for marrying his five-year-old granddaughter Lakshmi to the son of the shanbogue of Mudugonahalli, who was twenty-two, was amply prepared to convince the government. Nittur Gundappa's granddaughter had been born on October 5, 1889, as recorded in the jatakam and corroborated by an entry in his private diary. The diary's status as an acceptable document testified to the government's willingness to trust the written word as opposed to the mere word of witnesses, especially when that record was not intended as proof in a criminal case. Oral proof was crucial, though often internally inconsistent and insufficiently precise unless buttressed by documentary evidence.[73]

When prosecuting officials were distrustful of peasant notions of time, it usually worked to the advantage of the accused. Mysore officials were well aware that the new time discipline of the day measured in hours and minutes was difficult enough to achieve in capitalist workplaces such as factories, mines, and plantations, despite whistles, gongs, and fines.[74] The peasant was still immured in a more expansive workday and in a time reckoned by calendrical seasons. Urging the inspector general of police to drop the case against the Vokkaliga (agriculturist-caste) parents of seven-year-old Chenni, who had married her to Mudli, aged twenty-five, at Bennakanakere, the Deputy Commissioner of Tumkur wrote: "As they belong to the ignorant class of Vokkaligas, their notions as regards time must be very vague and cannot be fully relied on."[75] Not even the traditional intellectuals of the Mysore countryside, the Brahman priests, were expected to be fully conversant with the time of the official Christian era. The disjuncture between the popular rural methods of remembering events and life cycles and the official record produced a situation in which the exact age of a bride according to the Register of Births could not be known to all. In a case in which five Brahmans of Abbani (Kolar District), including the priest, were named as defendants, only the grandfather of the bride was finally convicted because it was thought that the others could not have known the exact age of the bride.[76]

With a government machinery intent on establishing the age of a bride or the date of a marriage from reliable documents, the fabrication of documents was not uncommon. The parents of three-year-old Rangi, of Somasethihalli Village, mentioned earlier, declared that her marriage to thirty-year-old Ranga had occurred before the enforcement of the Infant Marriage Regulation in 1895. Thirty-one witnesses were summoned and examined, of whom eleven disclaimed all knowledge of the marriage. Of the remaining twenty, fourteen said the marriage took place in February 1895, a month after the regulation began to be enforced, and the others said it had occurred in August 1895. The accused, amply aided by the patel and the Vokkaliga caste head, produced a *lagna patrika* (wedding invitation) as evidence that the marriage had taken place in February. A minor bit of sleuthing on the part of the Mysore officials revealed that "shuda navami of the month Magha of the year Jaya to which 4 February 1895 corresponded" was "inauspicious" and concluded that falsification of documents was prima facie evidence supporting prosecution.[77] Thus prosecution under the regulation, when it did not rest upon the infallibility of the governmental record, could and did rely on the administrator's knowledge of the very customs and law-ways that the regulation sought to replace.

The Dispersal of Penal Responsibility

The charge of criminality attached not only to the fathers, and sometimes both parents, of the bride and groom but to guardians, priests, and others who aided and abetted the crime. In cases in which the groom was over eighteen, he, too, was liable to prosecution. In all cases, however, the child wife was irreducibly the victim, placed at the center of a legal-juridical discourse that often made criminals of her parents, husband, and other members of her natal and marital families and yet permitted her no more than a name and an age. On some occasions she was subjected to medical examination to establish her age, but her own voice remained muted and muffled throughout the period when the governance of her sexuality passed uneasily between the state and the system of alliances of which she was a part.

By no means were all women thus produced as objects of reformist discourse: the arrangement and performance of marriages was, after all, one of the few occasions when the wife, mother, and grandmother played an important role, sometimes emerging as the key agents in cementing an alliance. Pierre Bourdieu's distinction between "practical" and "official" kin is crucial in understanding this gender difference: practical kin, largely women, arranged the marriage, but official kin, largely men, celebrated it.[78] Mysore officials were only too attentive to the colonial sociology of caste, assuming for the most part that lower-caste women were more likely to be active agents in marriage transactions than were their upper-caste counterparts. Tippi, a Bedar (hunting-caste) woman who in 1895 arranged the marriage of her seven-year-old daughter Rangi to Dama, aged twenty-six, was sentenced along with Dama to pay a fine of Re 1 or face simple imprisonment.[79] Indeed, the infant marriage regulation sometimes became a weapon for men anxious to chastise women who arranged alliances all too independently.[80] The new regulation had its uses in settling private scores, even at the risk of questioning the preferred alliances of South

Indian kinship systems.[81] Although some women were not prosecuted for want of evidence, several others paid fines and even went to jail for their active roles. If the bride's father was considered the chief offender in the cases of higher-caste child marriages, officials did not hesitate to send both sets of parents to jail in a number of cases involving lower castes.[82] Even in 1917, when the number of cases prosecuted had sharply dropped, the Panchala parents of an underage bride and her groom at Srirangapatna were convicted.[83]

The same social order that permitted the existence of enclaves of female power linked to nondomestic sexuality forced most other women to conform to a reformed patriarchal morality. Like the primary guardians of child brides or grooms married to child brides, some women paid a heavy price for their actions and were rarely exempted from the full force of the regulation. Bharamavva of Davangere Taluk, who arranged the marriage of her son to an underage bride, was asked to pay Rs 7 as a fine in 1902 or face twenty days' jail.[84] Her husband, Bharamayya, on the other hand, was absolved of all responsibility for having arranged the match. No concessions were shown to women of lower castes, such as Gollar Papakka of Yemarahalli, on the question of fines.[85]

Even when a child bride was reduced to no more than a powerless cipher, a victim of caste law-ways, the enhanced status of women in other stages of the life cycle, as older wives, mothers and grandmothers, and heads of households, was readily acknowledged. The conviction of Chennamma, a Kuruba woman who was nearly sixty years old, was therefore a foregone conclusion: she was the sole officiating guardian of her son Chenna, aged about fifteen years, whom she decided to marry to a six-year-old granddaughter by her elder son.[86] Only in the rarest of cases were women actually excluded from prosecution for acting under the "influence of males."[87] Only on the rarest of occasions were women seen as exercising no power within the family. If there was one area in which the government fiercely adhered to a gender-neutral definition of agency, it was in its pursuit of female family members who shared responsibility for the crime of child marriage.

The Increased Visibility of the Legal Form

Despite the skepticism of several contemporary writers and present-day historians, the working of the infant marriage regulation was indicative of the determination of the Mysore bureaucracy to question, and even

TABLE 1

Number of unmarried children ten years old or younger per 10,000, Mysore State

YEAR	MALES	FEMALES
1891	9,989	9,740
1901	9,996	9,904
1911	9,999	9,959

Source: Census of India, 1911, vol. 25, Mysore, Part I, Report, 96.

realign, caste traditions on the question of marriage. Successive censuses showed there was a marked decline in the proportion of males and females who married under the age of ten (see Table 1). Ascribing these "satisfactory" figures to the operation of the marriage regulation, the Mysore census commissioner, V. R. Thyagaraja Aiyar, pointed out that although Baroda, another princely state, had convicted far higher numbers of people under a comparable act (23,388 in the period from 1904 to 1910 alone), Mysore had more favorably transformed marriage habits. This may have had to do with a far higher incidence of child marriage in Baroda from the outset, a fact that Aiyar quietly chose not to emphasize. If anything, the Baroda comparison clearly showed that punitive measures alone could not accomplish social transformations of any substantial kind. Nevertheless, if in British India submitting annual reports on prosecutions under the Age of Consent Amendment had turned into an empty bureaucratic exercise, the declining number of cases prosecuted under the Mysore regulation, especially between 1921–22 and 1927–28, was a sign of how effective the Mysore legislation had been.

By no means was female sexuality pried away from the instrumentalities of caste and kin alliances in which it had been embedded and returned to the woman in a newly emergent "analytics of sex."[88] If anything, other moves of the Mysore government were clearly aimed at producing more thoroughly patriarchal family forms. In a detailed report commissioned by the Mysore Economic Conference in 1913, V. S. Sambasiva Iyer noted that one of the reasons for the poor supply of labor from the Malnad region was the prevalence of imposition of a *thera,* or bride price, which stifled population growth and encouraged illegitimate sexuality. The heavy price demanded for brides in the area, he argued, prevented a large number of poor men from marrying, thereby resulting in a large number of unmarried "grown up girls" who were nevertheless "entangled in criminal cases, being charged with infanticide or abortion."[89] He therefore recommended the active discouragement of this practice as a means of augmenting population growth in the area. Upper-caste "modernizers" thus showed no hesitation in relying on the instrumentality of the state to regulate social practices that hampered the progress of Mysore's "imagined economy."

The state's insistence on regulating the difference in age between older grooms and their young wives was part of an effort to ensure that hierarchies of gender were not so heavily weighed against women. The praise that Mysore earned from several women's groups and the Indian press was for attempting to produce liberal changes, though through largely illiberal means.[90] Even *Karnataka Prakasika,* which had first welcomed and then warned against the introduction of such invasive regulations in the early 1890s, was convinced by the end of the decade of the need for state intervention and repeatedly suggested that child marriages be declared null and void.[91]

To those who had long applauded Mysore for taking exemplary action against a range of intractable "social evils," it came as a great surprise that Mysore refused to introduce a bill comparable to the British Indian Child Marriage Restraint Act of 1929. The act, known as the Sarda Act after the author of the bill, raised the age of consent to fourteen for females and eighteen for males after a bitter and protracted debate within and beyond the Indian legislature. In the 1890s, women had played a relatively small part in the debates.[92] However, the Women's Indian Association, the All India Women's Conference, and the National Council of Women in India all put considerable energy and resources into urging the passage of the bill, even demanding that the Sarda Bill's modest proposals on the age of consent be raised to sixteen for women and twenty-one for men.[93] Indeed, Mrinalini Sinha suggests that this was a moment when the Indian women's movement strove to produce a new unity for women, supervening the rules of community to which they had until then been subordinated. Although this "novel political universality" was too fragile to override either the new or the old communal divisions that were respectively mobilizing "untouchables" and Muslims at this time, it signaled a brief unity of the political and social in the women's movement. However, Sinha rightly suggests, "The true contribution of the Sarda Act was not so much legal as political and ideological: it served to redefine the sphere of social reform work."[94]

A similar bill was introduced in Mysore by K. P. Puttanna Chetty, former president of the Bangalore municipality and a respected member of the assembly. The principles of the bill were passed by 98 votes to 87. This time, however, Dewan Mirza Ismail reversed the use to which "general sentiment'" had been put by his predecessor to justify interference with "the liberty of the subject."[95] He announced that "public opinion" had it that "more harm than good was likely to accrue if such a penal measure was enacted as law."[96]

Little was produced by way of evidence in support of such a suggestion. If anything, public sentiment on the issue, even in relatively conservative circles, appeared to be decisively in favor of legislating change that would raise the age of consent and, as a consequence, the age of marriage. At a public debate in Sanskrit that was organized in Bangalore on March 24, 1931, between Veerakesari Seetharama Sastry and Dharmadeva Vidyavachaspati, both the debaters made extensive use of quotations from scripture to oppose and support the proposed legislation, with the audience voting decidedly in favor of change.[97] Yet even census statistics, which had been prominently deployed in 1893 to buttress the cause of government intervention, were not summoned to augment Mirza's argument, not even to suggest that the 1893 legislation had sufficiently realized its objectives.

The Representative Assembly had no legislative powers and was established in 1881 to bring members face to face with the administration once a year. At that time it was considered the best way of preventing troubles in the state, such as the Nagar rebellion.[98] By 1932, we may note, the Representative Assembly had been considerably expanded and even included two nominated women members. Was Mysore state in the 1930s weakened in its resolve to usher in a limited form of modernization? Had the field of political forces changed in a way that limited its powers in making the legal form, delinked from any theological roots, part of the "common sense" of Mysore civil society? Could the hesitation on Mirza's part have sprung from an acute awareness that, as a Muslim, he could hardly throw his weight behind an issue that had divided Hindus in all parts of the country? It is tempting to conclude that Mysore in the 1930s was merely enacting, after a lag, the defense of the private domain that had been staged elsewhere in the late nineteenth century.[99] Even the visible, though weak, women's movement was divided, with a section of it emphatically declaring the household (and, by consequence, marriage) an autonomous sphere into which state laws could not enter.[100]

Such a conclusion can be sustained only if the government's reluctance to raise the age of marriage is seen in isolation from the totality of its legislative agenda. As I have already discussed in the introduction, the Hindu Law Women's Rights Bill became law in 1933, bestowing on women new rights to property, adoption, and maintenance a full four years before a comparable British Indian act was passed. Also, the Mysore bill was unhampered by the kind of acrimony that characterized a similar bill's passage in the rest of India.

Although it opened up property-owning households to the possible interventions of the state apparatus, regulating the traffic in women (and thereby the circulation of women to sustain the institution of the modernized reproductive family form) through a penal law prohibiting certain forms of marriage was considered far less important. In this forty-year period between 1894 and 1932, Mysore state had aimed at developing a discourse of legality to work alongside, if not replace, local law-ways, changing them in some ways without causing a thoroughgoing social transformation. Instead, Hindu law, first defined in a way that deprived some segments of Indian women of their rights to property in the name of sexual propriety, now rewarded the domesticated sexuality of wives, sisters, and widows with rights to property as a "concession." Permissive laws rather than penal sanctions were more appropriate to the requirements of property-owing households.

When penal sanctions were introduced to regulate sexuality in the 1930s, they operated against a wholly different segment of women, namely, proletarianized sex workers. On this proposed legislation the Mysore Ladies Conference displayed a far from surprising unanimity. The Suppression of Immoral Traffic in Women and Girls Act of 1937 forcefully reasserted the notion that women were property. The "traffic" in domestic women was restricted to marriage relations, which had been sufficiently reformed, but the traffic in proletarian sex workers had to be regulated and suppressed from public view, though not eliminated.[101] The apparent contradictions in Mysore's legal initiatives may be better understood within a framework that recognizes the relatively modest ambitions of Mysore state and its bureaucracy in overseeing a modernization of patriarchy without endangering its roots.

Between 1894 and 1932, the government adamantly refused to make any amendments to the 1894 regulation, allowing neither those that sought to restrict its scope nor those that would extend it. To a plea from a member of the Representative Assembly that Vyshyas be exempted from the regulation, the government replied that concessions had already been made in that the minimum age of marriage for men had not been specified.[102] In 1905, 1906, every year from 1909 to 1914, 1922, 1927, and 1928, motions were introduced in the Representative Assembly to raise the age of marriage for girls and boys, but even discussion was disallowed. When in 1922 two members of the Assembly asked for penalties to be introduced against those marriages in which the bride was at least six years younger than her groom, the government found the principle of the legislation unacceptable, always arguing against proposed changes by saying that "people themselves are alive to the advantages of a late marriage and perform marriages at a fairly advanced age."[103]

It was only with some reluctance that the government finally allowed a Mysore bill to be presented.[104] The bill was distinct from its British counterpart in two important respects, which its introducer, N. V. Narayana Murthi, explained were intended to make it more widely "acceptable."[105] The bill retained the ages for men and women at fourteen and eighteen in accord with the Sarda Act but permitted parents who wished to celebrate the marriage of their underage daughters in their lifetime to do so with the approval of the district magistrate on their guarantee that consummation would not take place until she was fourteen. Second, the period after the marriage when complaints could be filed was reduced from twelve months to six.[106]

Of the thirty members who took part in the discussion of the bill, the twelve who expressed their opposition to the measure deployed the same arguments used forty years before: the change was an unnecessary infringement of personal liberties, a violation of sastraic injunctions, and unnecessary in a state where the majority of castes practiced postpuberty marriages. The opposition came for the most part from predictable quarters: orthodox Brahman members such as Belur Srinivasa Iyengar and Muslim members such as Ibrahim Khan. Among the more surprising opponents were K. T. Bhashyam Iyengar and Kamalamma Dasappa.

Bhashyam Iyengar was the advocate who had first proposed that Hindu women's rights to property be improved. In 1928 he called for a legislative measure to end gender disqualifications in the Hindu laws of inheritance, in response to which the government appointed the Hindu Law Women's Rights Committee.[107] By the 1930s, Bhashyam objected to government interference in "social and religious matters," which he said was not only unwelcome but unnecessary in a situation in whish "post puberty marriages were fast increasing," although he advanced no support for this assertion.[108] When D. S. Mallappa, a supporter of the bill, reminded Bhashyam that at the Mysore Youth Conference that year he had himself admitted that early marriages had produced deleterious effects, Bhashyam weighed in against government interference in marriage reform.[109]

Even more surprising than Bhashyam's opposition was that of Kamalamma Dasappa, one of two women who had been nominated to the assembly in 1930. She spoke against not only her own previous positions but the dominant mood in the Indian women's movement.[110] In 1931, the official organ of the Women's Indian Association welcomed the introduction in Mysore of the bill, which they claimed had been drafted "in response to the Mysore Ladies Conference."[111] The Mysore Ladies Conference had passed a resolution calling for the age of marriage to be fixed at sixteen and twenty-one for women and men, respectively.[112] However, Dasappa claimed that the women at two meetings in Davangere and Bangalore had opposed government interference in household affairs.[113] Emphasizing the need for education rather than legislation, she claimed, like Bhashyam, that observable changes in marriage customs were well under way. Unlike her male counterparts, including Bhashyam, who framed their opposition in terms of the sastras, Dasappa relied only on logical argument. Sakamma, the other woman member of the assembly, herself married at the age of thirteen to a rich coffee planter and widowed three years later, called upon the Mysore government to extend the Sarda Bill to the state.[114] In 1932, she pointed out that upper-caste women had of late been marrying at eighteen and nineteen, not earlier: "If the proposed measure is passed it would enable the parents to perform such marriages courageously."[115] The clearly divergent opinions of the two women were quickly seized on as proof that women, in whose name the abolition of child marriage was being sought, were themselves not agreed on the virtue of such legislation.[116] In fact, this is further proof of how the "dangerous" demand of Harijans for separate electorates politically ended the rare unanimity with which women's associations had rallied around the reformed age of marriage.

In her women's journal *Saraswathi,* which she started in 1917, R. Kalyanamma, herself a Brahman child widow, commented on the opposition to the Sarda Bill:

> In opposition to the Sarda bill, people raised a hue and cry about sastras . . . promoters of the Pauranic way are meeting in small Sanatana Dharma assemblies and do anti-national work. . . . In this day and age, when the whole world is changing, we cannot cite sastras which were composed at some time by someone for some purpose. Sastras that are opposed to the changes are like snowflakes trying to challenge the sun.[117]

Kalyanamma was no admirer of the Mysore Ladies Conference, whose annual meetings, she said, were occasions for ineffective "disorderly grandeur" and whose sole purpose was to elect the wives of administrators to the All India Women's Conference.[118] Still, she recognized the necessity of running campaigns for legislative change.[119]

Ignoring the sizable segment of women whom journalists like Kalyanamma may have represented, the government, which had long opposed any changes to the 1894 regulation, chose to cast its decisive vote behind the opponents of the bill. This was not a decision in favor of some unadulterated "tradition," much less a decisive stand against social reform through legislation. It was instead a recognition that the molecular changes first inaugurated in the early 1890s were adequate, and further transformations would warrant social changes on a scale that the government was unprepared to undertake.

What had changed by the 1930s was not the Mysore government's interest in "the women's question": it is clear by now that that had never been its central concern. It was rather a question of deploying its limited resources in ways that would enhance the efficiency of the state apparatuses. The number of cases filed before courts on the question of women's rights within families was indication enough that the domain of legality had expanded to the extent possible under the constraints of colonial rule, that the limits to the representation of human relations as legal relations had already been reached.[120] This was a partial realization of the "nationalized" family identified by Balibar in the case of the French nation-state: "As lineal kinship, solidarity between generations and the economic functions of the extended family dissolve, what takes their place is neither a natural micro-society nor a purely 'individualistic' contractual relation but a nationalization of the family."[121]

Conclusion

On May 9, 1937, a group of people came together in Bangalore's Banappa Park to condemn the proposed marriage of a sixty-five-year-old widower, Kalappa, to a young girl of seventeen who remained unnamed.[122] The audience, five hundred strong, which included several Congress sympathizers, was urged to pass an assortment of resolutions saying that "no man above 50 years should be permitted to marry a woman less than 25 or 35 years, that widows should be allowed to remarry and that free scope should be given to the public to make speeches and pass resolutions." This was followed by a decision to start an organization, the Jana Jagruthi Sangha, or the Mass Awakener's Union (MAU), presumably to be devoted to these rather mixed aims, and the office holders, who were immediately elected, included a significant number of young leftists such as N. D. Shankar, S. Ramaswamy, K. Sreenivasa Murthy, and C. B. Monnaiah. Several members of the newly formed MAU later staged a protest at the wedding hall, for which they were arrested and held until the ceremony was over, but not before they were interviewed by several advocates and journalists with nationalist sympathies.

What did the figure of the woman represent in the emerging left-wing critique of Mysore society? Had this event been followed by sustained debate on such questions, it would have been easier to admit that this was merely a delayed discussion of issues that had gripped nineteenth-century reformers elsewhere. But it was not, and the figure of the woman as well as the objectionable marriage of Kalappa dropped completely from sight; the women's question as it emerged briefly at the time of the constitution of the MAU disappeared from the agenda, never to reappear. At the center of the discourse on protection, however, the child bride remained muffled and silent.

The MAU's swift transfer of its political energies to the more fruitful spheres of labor organization was strategically wise. By the 1930s, the women's question as it had been framed throughout the nineteenth century to stand for questions relating to the imagined new collectivity of the nation no longer carried the same charge. In part, this was a result of the growing visibility of the women's movement, which had transformed the agenda of social reform by speaking more directly of women's rights while enabling segments of Indian women to sculpt entirely new subjectivities. But in equal part, by the 1930s, the agents of modernization recognized that a reformed nationalist patriarchy was already in place, requiring no further initiatives on the part of the state, or even those of its opponents, except when a threat to patriarchy itself arose. The historical significance of the modernizing project of Mysore state lay primarily in its modest pursuit of a legal order, but not one directed at constructing autonomous rights-bearing subjects, within and beyond the family, an impossibility under conditions of colonial rule.

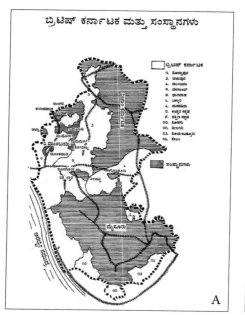

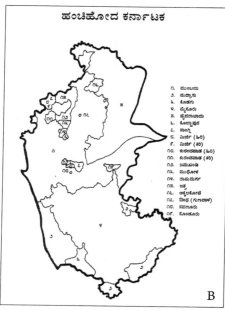

Figure 50. Real and imagined Karnatakas: (A) British Karnataka and smaller kingdoms; (B) the nineteen separate administrations under which Kannadigas lived (note the outline of contemporary Karnataka); (C) the unified Karnataka of 1956; (D) the Karnataka that the leaders wanted; (E) Karnataka today. From H. S. G. Rao, Karnataka Ekikarana Itihasa, 402–6.

CHAPTER 8

Giving the State a Nation:
Revisiting Karnataka's Reunification

I N 1956, MYSORE'S INDEPENDENT EXISTENCE ended as it became part of an expanded new state. It would be easy to trace the political rumblings fifty years later—separatist movements in Kodagu, similar expressions of discontent in Uttara Karnataka, and the state's own acknowledgment of its failures in that region—to the unfulfilled goals or viability of linguistic states.[1] Indeed, these rumblings appear to confirm the early misgivings of many Mysoreans about the embrace of their fellow language speakers to the north.[2] Added to this has been the widespread dissatisfaction with the role of the state in nurturing and developing the community of Kannada speakers.[3] Indeed, the love of language expressed by a range of Kannada protagonists in various ways have dismayed the early campaigners for unification. One of the more energetic campaigners, Patil Puttappa, described the predicament thus: though Mysoreans had achieved political integration, "the emotional unification has not occurred. Today's youth do not have an imagination, nor do they know the history of what happened earlier."[4] Kannada *nationalism,* in its broader and more inclusive sense, followed rather than preceded the establishment of the *state* of Mysore or Karnataka, with unexpected consequences. Of what, then, did unification consist?

Territorializing Caste or Language?

Nationalist accounts of karnataka ekikarana (Karnataka Unification) have adopted the familiar mode of all nationalist histories: the "idea of Karnataka" has existed from the time of the earliest dynasties in the southern and northern Karnataka regions, but its historical "unity" was broken in the thirteenth century with the sack of Dwarasamudra by Malik Kafur. A striving for linguistic unity is traced back to the time of the Vijayanagar kings: the rule of the Bahmani sultans marked a break in the cultural continuity of the region.[5] The classical heritage of Islam was thus kept away from the cultural history of Karnataka or, more properly, Kannada.[6] Unification narratives, however, acknowledge that although Kannada suffered blows from at least the fourteenth century, the territorial disintegration and dismemberment of the Kannada people occurred with the defeat of Tipu Sultan and the start of British rule in 1799.

The demand for a unified linguistic state gathered political force only in the third decade of the twentieth century, following the Congress's acceptance of the principle of linguistic state formation. The creation of Pradesh Congress Committees for states that did not yet exist, such as Karnataka, was an acknowledgment of the yearnings of substantial proportions of Kannada speakers who lived in the British-ruled provinces of Bombay, Madras, and Coorg (Kodagu) and in the princely state of Hyderabad. Therefore, in nationalist narratives, a long-held desire for a unified Karnataka was fulfilled in 1956, and the cartographic wounds inflicted by British rule for strategic or administrative convenience began to heal.[7]

The corrective to the nationalist version of karnataka ekikarana takes as its starting point the well-known opposition of some political leaders and intellectuals in Mysore to the idea of submerging the princely state within a larger political and administrative unity.[8] A unified Karnataka would bring large numbers of Lingayats from the northern Karnataka regions and forever alter the demographic composition that gave Vokkaligas the edge in Mysore state politics. This interpretation was of course amply aided by the States Reorganisation Commission (SRC) Report itself, which singled out Mysore as the state haunted by bitter acrimony between the two castes. The territorialization of caste within the broader discussion of language politics could be resolved, according to the SRC, only within an administrative unity in which "no community may be dominant."[9] State reorganization was thus seen as the panacea to the divisive politics of caste rivalry and to the dangerous possibility of two states formed on communal rather than linguistic grounds.

This raises the question of what was reterritorialized when Mysore, later renamed Karnataka, came into being—language or caste? The self-evident rivalries of dominant castes dog all analyses of Karnataka politics up to the present day, despite the fact that there is much that they fail to explain.[10] In some ways, the historiography of this moment thus looms like a specter over all subsequent developments. A return to this founding moment of modern Karnataka may therefore be imperative to generate new approaches to an understanding of its contemporary history.

The Shifting Grounds of Unification

In 1944, D. V. Gundappa (DVG) addressed the Karnataka Sangha Rajoth-sava at Bangalore's central college with a program for building up the language:

> There are important tasks that must be undertaken for the welfare of Kannada. 1. [Both] the population of Kannadigas and the Kannada country must be expanded. . . . 2. Secondly, the governments of Kannada speaking regions must adopt Kannada as their own [i.e. make it official]. . . . 3. Thirdly, wherever possible, Kannada regions must be united to form a state. To begin with the areas which are under British rule must be brought together and united under one government. . . . 4. Fourthly, arrangements must be made for an institution of higher learning for the Kannada people.[11]

By the time that the SRC was established in 1955, DVG had become a staunch opponent of unification. Among the large number of people who were opposed to the idea of linguistic unification while supporting the idea of two states, Karnataka and Mysore, were former Dewans such as M. Visvesvaraya and M. Mirza Ismail, scholars such as M. P. L. Sastry, congressmen such as A. G. Ramachandra Rao and T. Channaiah (who had also earlier supported unification), and caste associations (in addition to the Vokkaligara Sangha) such as that of the Kurubas. This assortment of cultural "royalists," nondominant castes, technocrat-administrators who had built Mysore's formidable reputation as a model state, and others, cloud the clarity provided by a singular focus on communal difference in historical accounts of unification.

Equally heterogeneous were the votaries of unification within and outside the Mysore legislature: socialists such as Gopala Gowda and well-known writer-poets of Mysore such as Kuvempu (both Vokkaligas), literary figures such as Aa Na Kru (A. N. Krishna Rao), critics of unification turned supporters such as the writer Shivarama Karanth, and representatives of parties such as the Praja Socialist Party (notably J. Mohamed Imam, then the leader of the opposition), who also disturb the strictly "communal" categories.[12] Gopala Gowda spoke of the confusion thrown up in discussions of unification between 1953 and 1955: he was distrusted by both sides of the debate, for betraying both Mysore and his caste, on the one hand, and for betraying the unification movement, on the other. It was anomalous indeed, he declared, when an opposition leader (J. Mohamed Imam, Praja Socialist Party, leader of the opposition in the House) spoke like the chief minister and ministers (such as T. Channaiah and A. G. Ramachandra Rao) spoke on behalf of the opposition![13]

Neither the nationalist nor the communal modes of conceptualizing the moment seem adequate in explaining developments in Mysore in the early 1950s. The historiographical focus on caste and secular power has thrust the form taken by the debate on a possible Karnataka into the shadows. The rethinking on unification that occurred between 1949 and 1955 may provide important clues to the conceptions of democracy and development that were being fashioned. The crystallization of the linguistic nation after the state occurred when the stage had already been prepared by another political logic, the logic of state-led "development." Did the language question as it was posed by its northern Karnataka votaries have the potential for a form of democracy resisted by the political order (in Mysore) that had grown accustomed to the building blocs of communities? Conversely, did developmental discourse play a crucial role in marking the passage from the limited literary love of language and country as it was expressed in the demand for karnataka ekikarana and an expanded political mobilization? In other words, what were the stakes on both sides of the debate as they shaped the practice of democracy in Karnataka?

I would like to return to the contentious official debates on the wisdom of karnataka ekikarana for the crucial insights they provide on the *imagined economy* of Karnataka state.[14] The substantive official debates in the Mysore Legislative Assembly and Council between 1953 and 1955 occurred in three successive stages: on the Andhra State Bill in December 1953–January 1954; the (Seshadri) Fact Finding Committee Report in March–April 1955; and the SRC Report in November–December 1955. This series of debates focused above all on the question of development. The term was used primarily in two senses, to refer to the historical achievements of the "model" Mysore state and to discuss the potentialities for expansion offered by the acquisition of new territories. Development was used in arguments by both the protagonists of and the opponents to the idea of an expanded Mysore state.

Was development merely the smokescreen for real anxieties about the likely political dominance of Lingayats? Or was development the only possible "script" for the garrulous outpourings of legislators, a discourse incited by the very space of its enunciation? What, on the other hand, were the attractions of its inclusiveness? The many unabashed discussions of caste and its links to political power in both the assembly and the council reveal that there was no hesitation at all in naming "enlightened self interest" for what it was.[15] However, once Congress and other politicians were reconciled to the inevitability of linguistic states, the development discourse became the principal means of reorganizing the political order and developing a notion of hegemony outside the framework of representative politics. The attempt to turn a potential political threat into an opportunity via the discourse of development focused strongly on the economy, particularly the process of accumulation without risking radical social change.[16] Mysore Chief Minister Kengal Hanumanthaiya's support for the recommendations of the SRC in 1955 was thus no mere rhetorical appeal to his dissident party members to accept Karnataka as a fait accompli but an effort to imagine a new economy and forge new political goals through development and planning, namely, "a modality of political power constituted outside the immediate political process itself."[17]

Bjorn Hettne's suggestion that disenchantment with unification was linked to the "Vokkaligisation" of the Mysore Congress is clearly an insufficient explanation of the specific form taken by both the opposition and the chief minister in their attempts to debate unification.[18] My purpose here is to discuss the discernable shift within lawmaking bodies away from history and its affective sentiments about love of the Karnataka country to geography and the economic value of the landscape as a "natural resource." The refashioned leadership spoke of *another Kannada nation* using the "modernist idiom of secular nationalism, scientific technology and economic development."[19] No doubt the reliance on development and its enabling material conditions did succeed in displacing the question of caste, at least in this territorialized form. The nearly total absence of a popular nationalism in the Karnataka region meant that when "the people" did conceptualize the nation, they laid claim to language as a precious cultural object, a form of self-definition against outsiders within the state and not as a vehicle of democracy.

My argument is set out in four sections. The first sets the demand for the state of Karnataka against the general backdrop of southern Indian participation in the national movement, with the demand for linguistic states gaining visibility at the moment of independence. There was neither a historical nor a proposed homogeneity to the geographical south, and indeed there were some significant distinctions between states that highlight the specificities of the Karnataka case. The second section discusses the ways in which history (and therefore a claim based on a knowledge of the past) quickly became a dispensable resource in the definition of the language-nation. The next section outlines the simultaneous rise of a development agenda that relied on geography and an imagined future defined primarily in economic terms. By way of conclusion, I discuss the deployment of demography as a resource in defining the entitlements of Kannada language speakers against speakers of other languages within the finite boundaries of the state.

Linguistic Imaginings

Kannada language speakers were recognized by the SRC in 1955 as the most fragmented during the period of British rule. The commission took the community of language speakers as the natural basis for fashioning new administrative unities, with some notable exceptions, as in the region of Kolar.[20] Thus, because Kannada-speaking minorities were present in parts of Bombay, Madras, and Coorg, with a substantial minority in Hyderabad as well, they were to be converted into a majority of their own.[21] Geographical distance from the capitals of those provinces only heightened the sense of their being marginalized.

Karnataka's demand for a separate state, however, was primarily driven by Congress workers from North Karnataka, especially from Bombay Karnataka. Bombay Karnataka, Satish Deshpande has noted, is a cusp region, "an overlap zone, or a hybrid (or mixed) cultural space, where the transition from one 'pure' cultural identity to another can take place." Because it "straddles the cultural domain between 'north' and 'south' India, the Bombay Karnataka region marks both the southern boundary of northern culture as well as the northern boundary of the southern culture."[22] There were, in other words, marked cultural differences between this region and Old Mysore.

After the formal acceptance by Congress of the linguistic state principle in 1920, the pace of the demand for karnataka ekikarana quick-

ened. *The Karnataka Handbook*, brought out on the occasion of the 1924
Congress session, recognized that the physical boundaries of this new
entity were not quite firm, though it had already taken shape as a province in the Congress lexicon.[23] By 1937 the establishment of a Mysore
Pradesh Congress Committee, as distinct from the Karnataka Pradesh
Congress Committee (KPCC) set up in 1924, raised the possibility of two
states using the same language. Those attending meetings of the Kannada
Sahitya Parishat routinely mentioned the prospect of unification, but a
meeting devoted to ekikarana first took place only in 1946 at Davangere
and was attended by elected representatives from the British Presidencies
of Madras and Bombay.

In that year, a determined move was made to yoke the KPCC's demand for a linguistic state with Mysore's yearning for a "responsible
government." The pragmatic arrangements that could follow Indian
independence alarmed many young Mysore leaders, such as Kengal
Hanumanthaiya and H. C. Dasappa at the tenth Karnataka Ekikarana
conference held in Bombay in 1946. The writer Sriranga recalled that when
some important (North Karnataka) leaders said, "with Mysore if possible,
without Mysore if necessary," leaders from Mysore pleaded for the inclusion of their province.[24]

Questions of unification remained muted in Mysore and were somewhat confined even in the Bombay Karnataka region in the years following independence, though between 1947 and 1953 many calculations were
made of the potential strengths of Brahmans, Lingayats, or Vokkaligas in a
unified Mysore.[25] The possibility of two states strengthened as clear pref-
erences for joining Mysore were being made known in provinces such as
Kodagu, parts of Salem, and the Niligiris, while Bombay Karnataka leaders not only distanced themselves from "princely" Mysore but wanted to
relocate the state capital to Dharwad.[26]

The sudden gift of seven Bellary taluks from Madras Presidency to
Mysore by the first Partition Committee of 1949 made it clear that Mysore's
preference on the question of reorganization would count for nothing if
stronger claims, such as the one made by Andhra Pradesh, were to mate-
rialize. The Partition Committee, which consisted of Andhra and Tamil
leaders (but no Mysoreans), granted the inclusion of Bellary with neither
demands nor a struggle from the Mysore side. Kengal Hanumanthaiya
described the addition of Bellary to Mysore through the use of a filial

metaphor: "the return of the Bellary District to Mysore is like the calf returning to its mother."[27] The landfall quickened the debate on the possibility of a unified Karnataka.

The changes thrust on Mysore by the refashioning of other state boundaries altered the perceptions of unity considerably. In 1951, the KPCC warned that "formation of Andhra Province alone without Karnataka being simultaneously formed" was fraught with potential resentments.[28] Two years later, K. S. Gurusiddappa wrote to the prime minister that Karnataka had to be formed soon after the constitution of Andhra Pradesh.[29] Andhra had precipitated the demand for state reorganization in southern India, and there were significant differences in both the concerns and the paths chosen by each language region. The setting up of Andhra Sahitya Parishat in 1911 was quickly followed by the demand for an Andhra Province in 1912. Once this goal was achieved in 1953, it was linked to the movement in the Telengana region of Hyderabad by the demand for Vishal Andhra. The warmth between the literary realms and the realms of politics was less a feature of the Karnataka movement, in which the demand for unified statehood was slow to develop.[30] Kerala was a late developer on the question of a United (Aikya) Keralam, with firm steps taken in that direction only in the 1940s.[31] Tamil remained safely corralled within the erstwhile Madras Presidency, and the demand for a separate province was articulated only in 1938. According to K. V. Narayana Rao, the first official demand for Tamil Nadu was made as late as 1948.[32] Dilip Menon suggests, however, that the Dravidian movement conceived of southern India, at least since 1944, in racial terms, as Dravidanadu, its motto being "Divide on the basis of language, unite on the bases of race."[33]

Only in Karnataka was caste territorialized in a distinctive way. Although the struggle between the Kammas and Reddys for the control of regions (coastal Andhra and Rayalseema, respectively) subtended some of the discussions on unification and resistance to it, it never assumed the charge that questions of caste and territoriality attained in Mysore or Karnataka. Nor did such equations become possible in Tamil Nadu or Kerala.[34]

Nevertheless, by the 1950s it also became clear that the central government could make decisions that state governments could do little to oppose. The Dar Commission of 1948 firmly ruled out the necessity of linguistic states when a precarious stability had just been achieved on the subcontinent in the aftermath of partition, but a year later, the Congress

Party's Jawaharlal-Vallabhbhai-Pattabhi Sitaramayya Committee conceded the possibility of Andhra Pradesh. The appointment of the Fazl Ali Commission in 1954 after the formation of Andhra Pradesh was a breathtaking display of how centralized power could refashion the nation-space according to its priorities of unity and administrative rationalization. An anguished DVG lamented the command that the Congress Party had over its state governments. "I am greatly distressed by the way things are going on in our country. . . . The present provocation to me is the decision to kill Mysore. I am in grief because Mysore is to be wiped out from the map. To me it was a shining example of what Indian statesmanship could achieve in the modern age handicapped as it was."[35]

Mysore's response to the appointment of the commission was a hard-nosed assessment of the territories to be added using the criteria of the developmentalist state, taking account of the experience of the difficulties already posed by Bellary. Hanumanthaiya's own "discovery of Karnataka" in 1949 had persuaded him of the need to remain open to the addition of territory without necessarily precipitating such unity.[36] In 1954 Chief Minister Hanumanthaiya, who had virtually gagged dissenting congressmen by preventing them from appearing before the SRC in Mysore, appointed a committee headed by M. Seshadri, a professor of philosophy from Mysore University.[37] Appropriately named the Fact Finding Committee, it focused on gathering data relating to "the area and population of the Kannada speaking people in the states of Madras, Bombay, Hyderabad and Coorg" while assessing "the level of development in those areas particularly in the fields of Education, Medical and Public Health, Rural Development, Industries, Irrigation, and Power" and the "the availability of natural resources."[38]

The committee minced no words in declaring that these areas were decades behind the state of Mysore on practically all counts and would require massive doses of central government aid to integrate them into Mysore. The discussion of this report was the dress rehearsal for the discussion of the SRC Report, generating bitter debate about the appropriate grounds on which the proposed unity should be assessed, though arguments for economic well-being overshadowed the more sentimental grounds for unity.

The committee avoided any reference to caste and steered clear of the quicksands of popular sentiment. Instead, as B. K. Puttaramaiah, a vociferous opponent of the proposed state, said, the committee was appointed "to see whether the political costs of saying no to Karnataka were as high as saying yes to Karnataka," concluding "that saying no is not a problem."[39] T. Mariappa, however, pointed out that the "Seshadri Committee furnished a first class argument for the formation of [unified] Karnataka: we ourselves furnished . . . a handle to say [an independent] Karnataka is not financially viable."[40] By focusing on the compelling economic reasons *against* including these underdeveloped regions in the new state, the committee also laid the ground for invoking development goals rather than memories of a greater historical Karnataka in making a case for a linguistically unified state. It was to the benefits of liaison with the economically advanced region of Mysore that the All Karnataka Unification Sangha, for instance, pointed in its petition to the Dar Commission. The Sangha favored political unity as imperative to economic, and not just cultural, progress: "The State of Mysore which is smaller than union Karnataka and less favourably situated, has made wonderful strides in Agriculture, Industry and Mining. She has augmented her revenue by nearly four times than *[sic]* what it was in 1920 because she enjoyed independent administration."[41] The Sangha pointed out that although "the people of Karnataka [had] taken more initiative and invested larger capital in industries than the people of Mysore," in Mysore the state investment far exceeded private capital.[42]

Nevertheless, the actual decision to reorganize the state of Mysore to include areas from Bombay and Madras Presidencies, Coorg, Hyderabad, and several other small regions listed in the SRC report of 1955 officially brought together questions of caste and territory in Mysore's representative politics. To these questions the linguistic state was seen as a panacea:

It has been estimated that Lingayats or Veerashaivas constitute about 30 to 40 per cent of the population in the Kannada areas outside Mysore at present. The other important section of the Kannadigas namely the Vakkaligas *[sic]* similarly constitute a little less than 29 per cent of the population of Mysore. In the united Karnataka, it has been estimated that a little more than 20 per cent of the population may be Lingayats between 13 and 14 per cent Vakkaligas and about 17 to 18 per cent Harijans. It is clear therefore that no one community will therefore be dominant and any one section can be reduced to the status of a minority if other groups combine against it. . . .

Some of these minorities fear that one result of the political position which the Lingayats will occupy in the future Karnataka state may be the dominance or extension of Veershaivism at the cost of other religious faiths. However in the perspective of *the political and economic development of the Karnataka state which we have in view,* the importance of narrow communal jealousies should not be exaggerated.[43]

Lesiglative Council member M. P. L. Sastry was among those who pointed out that "the Commission has done a great injustice to the people and classes of Mysore by bringing in the question of caste."[44] But by this time the question of caste had become the indisputable common sense of administrative unification.

The Imagined Kannada Nation and the Limits of History

In his memoirs, Alura Venkatarao recalled that he had first raised hopes of a unified Karnataka in the journal *Vagbhushana* in 1903. The more influential term "Karnatakatwa" was historicized in *Karnataka Gatha Vaibhava,* first published in 1917. Signifying the love of country, "Karnatakatwa" was "that single word which was coined in my mint to describe the politics, dharma, history and art [of Karnataka]."[45] Widely circulated as the most important statement of Kannada and unmistakably Hindu pride, *Karnataka Gatha Vaibhava* strongly focused on history as a resource for remembering the achievements and the loss suffered by the Kannada people and their nation.[46]

As a political entity, Karnataka first found expression in 1923, a few years after Congress's acceptance of the Nagpur resolution on linguistic states. The effort of educating the Kannadiga in the contours of the new nation's history and geography, undertaken by Venkatarao, was joined by the 1924 publication of the *Karnatakada Kaipidi (Karnataka Handbook).* This handbook, or "ready reckoner," compiled by D. K. Bharadwaj, added not only a cartographic vision to writings by Mysoreans such as Thathacharya, with pictures and illustrations of the history of Karnataka "from the earliest times until the fall of Srirangapatna," but went further in providing demographic information on the slow growth and even decline of Kannada speakers in some British-ruled areas.[47]

The shuttling between history, especially of the medieval period, and

the discussion of injustices suffered by Kannadigas living under different administrations was not accidental. Throughout the debates on the
Andhra State Bill (1953), the Seshadri Fact Finding Committee Report
(1954), and the SRC Report (1955) in the Mysore legislature, the past was
used to build not love of country but a hard case for justice under the new
Indian dispensation. Hanumanthaiya, however, steered attention away
from history during the debate on the Andhra State Bill in 1953 when he
declared:

> We the people of Mysore are not ambitious territorially or even
> linguistically; we are here an administrative unit. It is history that
> has cemented our feelings into one administrative unit. It would
> be unwise to break up that administrative unity. . . . Mysore State
> is going to remain the administrative unit which it is today. The
> question next arises as to what we should do if some people of the
> neighbouring area express a wish to come to the Mysore State.
> To them we have decided to extend a hearty welcome. . . . Mysore
> state will not bring any pressure on these people to join Mysore
> state . . . we are not thinking in terms of Visala Mysore.[48]

By the end of 1955, Hanumanthaiya's idea of the "composite structure"
of Mysore became useful in advocating a complete change of political authority based on neither language nor its history but on the pragmatics of
power, of accommodating multiple languages and ethnicities for administrative and especially developmental convenience.[49] Drawing on H. G.
Wells's "theory of history," Hanumanthaiya said:

> Just as human beings have a life expectancy of 100–120 years, politi-
> cal regimes also have a life. . . . The Mysore kingdom developed as
> an independent kingdom from the time of Chamaraja Wodeyar in
> 1566. In the intervening 389 years, Mysore has waxed and waned.
> Even in this 389 year period, it did not remain stable. In the end,
> when Hyder and Tipu were the commanders . . . all of South India
> was joined to Mysore.[50]

By emphasizing the unstable contours of Mysore territory and the ever-
present possibility of changing regimes, Hanumanthaiya signaled the
end of Mysore as a remnant of a princely state. There was nothing worth

preserving about the rump state of Mysore (a mere 29,000 square miles carved out of 80,000 in 1799) even if the territory had remained stable for nearly 160 years. Yet it was precisely this latter-day stability and "improvement" under the auspices of a modernizing bureaucracy that the "no-changers" wished to preserve. M. P. L. Sastry emphasized the precious heritage of the "model state" of Mysore that had to be retained. Its urbanity, its educational achievements, and its famed gentility stood endangered by the inclusion of much less civilized regions.[51]

History served to compensate for the disincentives of adding underdeveloped regions: the symbolic gains of the Vijayanagar capital at Hampi were emphasized to counter the suspicion that the Bellary landfall was a result of Madras's refusal to retain this deficit region. J. Mohamed Imam declared the cultural gains important "since there are unmistakable proofs that Vijayanagara was absolutely 100 per cent Kannada country" and that Krishnadeva Raya was a Kannada Rajya Rama Ramana.[52] R. Ramaiah added, "Many auspicious monuments in the region of Bellary are intimately linked to Karnataka from Vijayanagar times," so "the fact that it joins Mysore is surely an act of god's grace."[53]

A consensus on the addition of Bellary was achieved within the houses, but although Hanumanthaiaya wished for a similar consensus on the SRC Report barely two years later, there was little hope that history could play this cementing role. If anything, his own minister for law and education, A. G. Ramachandra Rao, a vehement opponent of unification, declared that there had been no moment in history when Karnataka had been united. It had always been divided either between east and west or north and south: "The North Karnataka looked to the North and North east. The south Karnataka looked to the South and South east and there was no Karnataka kingdom comprising the entire area." *Neladaha* (a thirst for territory) only recalled the time of the paleyagaras, so he proposed support for two separate but robust states that were not haunted by the "ghost of linguism."[54]

From love of language and country to evocation of "the ghost of linguism": as Gopala Gowda had pointed out in 1953, there was a gulf between those (such as the littérateurs and poets) who understood the history of the language and its beauty and those who spoke in more practical but "squint-eyed" political terms. During the discussion on the Andhra State Bill, in 1953 he declared, "If we take our claims from history and entertain hopes of a new state there will be lots of obstacles. We have crossed that time, and we must make history ourselves: we must take the opportunity of the Andhra State Bill and argue for our own state from the centre."[55]

Hanumanthaiya himself returned to the pragmatic use of historical symbols in a moment of transition. He argued for the retention of the name Mysore, which he claimed would give "psychological satisfaction" to the people who spoke languages other than Kannada.[56] By this time, historical geography has lost its primacy as the basis for imagining the new nation, its place increasingly taken by a calculated interest in resources of the region.

Toward a Geography of National Resources

Forty-two pages of the Report of the Fact Finding Committee headed by Seshadri covered Karnataka's history from A.D. 550 to 1799.[57] Yet, as K. Shivarudrappa pointed out, "As soon as you read the facts and figures, you will conclude that Mysore will be destroyed by the addition of regions beyond where Kannada speaking people reside."[58] These aspects of Mysore or Karnataka's future were not just proportionately larger than appeals based on history but shifted the ground away from linguistic states to developmental strategies and their outcomes. There was, in other words, a distinct shift away from the cultural basis for imagining the nation to the realm of the economy. Modern rather than medieval or ancient Karnataka history was therefore pertinent to discussions of the potentialities for development in different regions of Mysore and the "model state" legacy considered worth preserving and extending. As G. A. Thimmappa Gowda said:

> This Mysore state from its earlier times was a unique and careful administration and is growing from strength to strength. This region is richer than the surrounding areas, and in education and urbanity it has reached a high level.... If other types of adjoining areas are joined to this developing state the economic status will decline.... "Enlightened self interest" is important for a nation's development.[59]

Several others who were also for the preservation of the advantages of a smaller constituent unit, who held that the ideal size was a population of ten million as opposed to the proposed Karnataka population of twenty-two million, faulted Hanumanthaiya for making no attempt to save the model state. Shivananjegowda, another outspoken critic of unification, commented on the prodigious outpourings of the Bombay Karnataka region on the demand for unification with Mysore on linguistic grounds. But "people of Mysore speak Tamil, Telugu, Urdu and are quite happy. Now on what principle they must join Karnataka?"[60] When the merger of seven taluks of the Bellary district was welcomed, despite the Rs 3 million annual deficit that it involved, hopes were pinned on the Tungabhadra River Valley project and its promise of bringing self-sufficiency to the area.[61] By 1954 it was clear that "Bellary had been an expensive addition."[62]

As Devaraj Urs said: "Without us saying we want these areas, without satyagrahas, without agitations, by themselves they [Bellary] have joined our Mysore Province."[63] This landfall, which should have brought joy and hope to the people of Mysore and welcomed as the first step toward the achievement of the linguistic state, stoked the fears of the Mysore leaders. Even more ignominious was the recommendation of the SRC in 1955 that Mysore return Bellary taluk to Andhra Pradesh on administrative grounds.[64]

Yet even this shared indignation did not unite the Mysore political leadership. "I have never heard in history," said R. Chennigaramaiah, "of a country that wants to expand being offered more territory and refusing to take it."[65] Even those supporting the idea of a united Karnataka were thus forced to make their arguments on new grounds that held out the promise of development. Aa Na Kru struck a pragmatic note, in contrast to his cultural arguments for unification, when he said:

> The gains and losses of a state are to be seen not only from the point of view of the present. . . . But the raw materials of North Karnataka and North Canara, the convenience of ports at Bhatkal, Kumta and Malpe, and the commercial co-operation of north Karnataka are vital for Mysore. If all these advantages of Mysore and other parts of Karnataka are combined, there will be no state as rich as Mysore.[66]

Unlike the supporters of Aikya Keralam, who saw little prospect for progress in the smaller units of the state, Aa Na Kru and others believed that

Mysore's vibrant self-sufficiency could be enhanced by unification. In the words of B. Madhavachar, "Mysore may be troubled but in the long run things will be fine."[67]

Partha Chatterjee has pointed out that "as early as the 1940s, planning had emerged as a crucial institutional modality by which the state would determine the material allocation of productive resources within the nation: a modality of political power constituted outside the immediate political process itself."[68] It is to this domain of political power that I believe the "pro-changers" were pointing, effecting another change of heart from their earlier opposition to the idea of a linguistically unified state to a more pragmatic embrace of a multilingual developmentalist state. Thus Hanumanthaiya enhanced the attractions of going beyond the pragmatics of administration: in 1953 he emphasized that the Tungabhadra project was three times larger than the Kannambadi (Krishnarajasagar in Mysore) dam project.[69] In 1955 he dwelt on what the new territory would add to Mysore: a two hundred–mile coastline to landlocked Mysore, three valuable harbors (Bhatkal, Malpe, and Karwar), new cities, crops, and the rivers and waterfalls of North Karnataka as potential hydroelectric dam sites. Nature had thus become a productive resource in the argument, subordinated to the demands of development and quite different from the Karnataka evoked in the poetry of Kuvempu. Indeed, an inventory of commodities had served as a crucial mnemonic device for the industrial achievements of the Mysore nation, invoking a regional topography of production and productive resources that imposed a patriotic duty on both the producer and the consumer. In the late 1930s, in a listing of Mysore's impressive state-owned industrial units, Mirza Ismail had famously declared:

> Mysoreans . . . wash themselves with Mysore soap, dry themselves with Mysore towels, clothe themselves in Mysore silks, ride Mysore horses, eat the abundant Mysore food, drink Mysore coffee with Mysore sugar, furnish their houses with Mysore furniture, light them with Mysore lamps, and write their letters on Mysore paper.[70]

That he was not merely being exhortatory was established by the *Indian Engineering* report of Mysore's first five-year plan for the Malnad regions, 1933–38: "Mysoreans are proud to point to these bridges [in Malnad] because they are constructed on most up to date and modern lines with local labour, local granite stones, local Chamundi brand cement, from Bhadravathi Iron Works, and Bhadravathi Steel for reinforced concrete decking of bridges."[71]

However, in the postindependence years, such regional patriotism reached its limits because, as Bjorn Hettne has shown, many of Mysore's state-run enterprises had become loss-producing units and there had been a distinct "ruralization" of the Mysore economy.[72] Hanumanthaiya was signaling an important shift in the development vision away from the resources of the state and toward an extended role for the power and resources of the central government. Three public-sector giants (Indian Telephone Industries, Hindustan Machine Tools, and Bharat Electronics Limited) had been established in Bangalore by this time to provide a way out of the state's impasse.[73] As Hanumanthaiya said:

All the capital we have invested is about Rs 5 crores [50 million]. All the dividend of income that we get runs to Rs 70 or to Rs 80 crores [700 to 800 million]. Much as we have progressed in the direction of industrialization, our industries are toy industries, they are merely token industries. We have to build bigger industries. There again we want Central assistance.[74]

However, the argument that unification enhanced Mysore's natural resources was turned into a convenient weapon by its opponents. Those who extolled the rich natural resources of the Bombay Karnataka, Coorg, and South Canara regions also provided their opponents with ready arguments for proposing a separate and equal Kannada-speaking state. Instead, what had to be questioned was the link between development and language, for, as T. M. Muddalagiri Gowda said, "Is the development of [Bombay and Hyderabad] regions contingent on them belonging to one linguistic province?"[75]

A strong argument based on the developmental prospects of the rich natural resources of the region served to repress the more difficult question of expanded populations and addressed even less the question of the people-nation in whose name the unification, or resistance to it, was being undertaken. In rare instances, it was the demographic advantages of the expansion that were brought to the foreground, once more by those on both sides of the argument. Some, such as H. V. Nanjundaiah, Veeranna, and G. A. Thimmappa Gowda, acknowledged the superiority of Mysore and said that it was the duty of the Mysoreans to educate the people of the north.[76] Mohamed Imam emphasized the virtue of sheer numbers when he said, "The bigger the state, the greater the scope for service, the greater the range for the selection of our leaders and ministers."[77] But to others the specter of being swamped by outsiders was easy to conjure up in a state that had long ago pioneered the techniques of keeping track of communal representations and vociferously kept the "outsiders" at bay.

However, it was in the very *lacks* of the people of Mysore that some legislators found a compelling reason for unification and for building up the resources for sustained development. Mohamed Imam drew attention to the Mysoreans' reputation for laziness and lack of entrepreneurship, which had left most of the industrial jobs within the state to Tamilians in Kolar Gold Fields, Bhadravathi, and Bangalore.[78] Gopala Gowda went further in discussing the relative lack of initiative among Mysoreans compared with the people of Dakshina Kannada:

> If you look at the people of Dakshina Kannada, they exert themselves in every task, and progress. Take schools, colleges, and other institutions, they have been set up with their own hard work. They are very hardworking people. . . . Since the lazy attitude is present here, the people of Dakshina Kannada come to work in the plantations and area plantations of Malnadu and for agriculture.[79]

The people of Dakshina Kannada would infuse Mysore with the fresh breath of enterprise, which would lead to the development of areas such as Malnad, the notoriously underdeveloped region of Mysore.[80]

At the end of the discussion on the SRC Report, hard-nosed calculations of economic benefit won the day over concerns that were expressed about the communal designs of the Lingayaths or even the dark fears about conversion that were thrown up by some representatives, such as Shivananjegowda.[81]

From State to Nation: Making Room for the Manina Maga (Son of the Soil)

It was a sentimental A. G. Ramachandra Rao, minister for law, labour, and education, who wrote a letter to the prime minister and president of India in October 1955:

Linguism as admitted by the Commission is a devitalizing force, in that it promotes conflicts in the body politic. . . . In the interests of Indian unity, linguism must be liquidated before it is too late. . . . Mysore should be enabled to decide about the continuance of their state and its head. Democratic policies and practices should not be denied to Mysore—the nursery of democracy in India. For these minor adjustments, Mysore, *like minorities,* prays for protection from your august hands to enable her to continue to pursue her progressive life.[82]

The minister's anguish was in vain, and the end of Mysore as it had been for nearly 160 years was quickly turned into cause for official celebration, despite his desperate attempt to appeal for central government "protection." Thus, in an official publication after unification, the Government of Mysore declared: "A cherished goal of the Kannadigas was achieved when on 1st November 1956, the New State of Mysore comprising [sic] of Kannada speaking areas was formed. From that date and *probably for the first time in history* these Kannada areas came under one administration."[83] An emphatically new state of 73,560 square miles containing 19.4 million people had been formed out of disparate and reluctant entities: this was indeed an unprecedented moment, both in Karnataka's history and in the brief history of the independent Indian nation-state.[84]

Within the legislature, the vote in 1955 on the SRC was 57 for and 3 against, and although a plea was made to count the abstentions (35), this was not conceded. Disillusionment was quick to set in among those who had anticipated the worst: DVG wrote to C. Rajagopalachari in 1958: "I have no first hand information about the results of the State's Reorganization elsewhere. But in Mysore, it has made conditions worse for everybody. Old Mysore, so homogenous, was a big enough charge for the kind and quality of Ministry we can hope to get in the present system. But New Mysore is heterogeneous . . . and the problems so much more complicated."[85] DVG's dissatisfactions may have been part of his deeper disillusionment with the workings of Indian democracy itself, but there were others who had been attentive to the significant gaps, silences, and repressions in the entire debate on unification. In discussions on territory and its relationship to language and caste, the question of democracy was left unspecified. Gopala Gowda was exceptional in bringing a reluctant assembly to reflect on who they represented. During the discussion of the Andhra State Bill, Devaraj Urs had said:

> Linguistic province is not an issue that concerns most people and therefore there is not much interest in it. Only *intelligent merchant class* is enthusiastic about this. . . . For the people of the country and the workers, if the linguistic province is not formed, their lives will not become worse. From this economic point of view, it is difficult to say that their lives will improve.[86]

He declared himself opposed to the idea of forming a linguistic state, though reorganization on other principles could be acceptable.

The remark of Devaraj Urs, though it sparked no debate, took the discussion of language and caste in a direction that anticipated developments for decades to come. By introducing the question of class and speaking of a figure that had largely been kept out of the discussion on unification, namely, the worker-citizen, Urs questioned the ways in which the "citizen" of Karnataka had been normed. In less than ten years' time, the figure and the issue around which the Kannada nation would crystallize were indeed the worker-citizen and his entitlements to livelihood within the finite boundaries of the Mysore or Karnataka state, and here the gendering of the subject or citizen as male was not accidental.[87] The SRC had warned against the growing trend in many states of confining job opportunities only to those who had been domiciled in the states. The meticulous scrutiny of demographic data so as to distribute public-service opportunities on communal lines was a method that had been perfected during Mysore's long engagement with the politics of reservation after 1918. In the wake of the massive expansion of the state sector, an increasing focus was on knowing Kannada as the qualification for jobs in the public sector. If the debates before and on the SRC Report engaged primarily with the dominance of Andhra Pradesh and its many claims on Mysore territory (Bangalore included), postunification discourse defined the Kannadiga in ways that excluded minorities such as Tamils and Muslims.

Yet throughout the discussions of 1953–55, some legislators, led by Hanumanthaiya, recalled the multilingual traditions of Mysore. H. S. Siddaiah reminded the house:

Neither in Mysore country nor in Karnataka country are there only Kannada speakers. If you take my Hassan District there are so many language speakers. The principle of building up a state on the basis of language alone is not correct. Lots of people from Madras have worked on our coffee estates and built their houses there. There are lakhs [hundreds of thousands] of people working on projects in Shimoga and Chikmagalur.[88]

Nevertheless, despite Hanumanthaiya's acknowledgment of the many "cusp cultures" of the state, Urdu was consistently ignored. H. R. Gaffar Khan pointed out this shocking silence by saying, "Even as the Chief Minister of Mysore, he [Hanumanthaiya] forgot that there are 8 lakhs [800,000] of people in the state of Mysore who speak Hindusthani and for whom thousands of Hindusthani schools are being managed by the Government."[89] In some ways, the identification of Kannada with Mysore or Karnataka and simultaneously with Hindu was to have serious consequences in the decades to come.[90]

Devaraj Urs and Lakshmi Devi Ramanna were among the earliest to point to another significant gap in the discourse on unification, namely, the castes that were sandwiched between the Big Two, the Vokkaliga and Lingayat castes.[91] The SRC Report itself hinted that the logic of representative democracy could render them subordinate roles in the dominant caste equations. What promises did the prospect of unification hold for the large numbers of minority castes that did not figure in the equation and could not be so easily territorialized? Demographically they constituted a good 5 million of the 7.3-million population of Mysore and represented forty-five castes.[92] There was, as G. Dugappa pointed out, no room for territorializing the *harijan* (member of a dominated caste), who was not confined to any one region of India.[93]

None of these critiques of the way in which the citizen-subject was being normed paid attention to the large and significant population that had remained invisible in all these decades of struggle and would remain thus until well into the 1980s. Only as a sign of the language itself, circulating as a feminized and captive icon of Kannada Bhuvaneswari or Kannada Thayi, did women enter into the discourse of language politics, whose supplicants and devotees were almost entirely male.[94] The hypermasculinism that surrounded the language protection movements of the region flared

into public view only when the *manina maga* (son-of-the-soil) movement
got underway, though the silencing of women had been a persistent feature from the unification movement's origins.

Conclusion

By insisting that the name of the new state remain Mysore, the Mysore
Legislature retained a symbolic continuity with the older monarchical
state and softened the blow to those who perceived the expanded state as
a loss of identity.[95] Hanumanthaiya declared that what was coming into
being was not a linguistic state but a composite one derived from Mysore's
unique history. In his speech to the legislative council in November 1955,
he noted, "It will bring great psychological satisfaction to people who
speak languages other than Kannada. It is with this view that I am advocating that the new State may be called MYSORE STATE."

The task of nation-building remained. Through the crucial years of the
early 1950s, there were attempts to construct a Karnataka aesthetic and
perhaps even define its unique elements within the well-known boundaries of the new Karnataka State. Litterateurs and writers such as R. R.
Diwakar and Kuvempu had knocked on the studio doors of Mysore's premier modern artist, K. Venkatappa, for help in defining a uniquely
Karnataka aesthetic. Shivarama Karanth similarly undertook something
of a pilgrimage around Karnataka to document and classify Karnataka's
artistic tradition and, more important, deployed folklore as a unifying cultural element.[96] The caste associational discourse of the Lingayats built up
a new vision of a pan-Karnataka identity as expressed in G. Halakatti's concept of "Karnatakastharu" in his brief statement on karnataka ekikarana.

However, these efforts were no match for the mass-mobilizing aspects
of cinema. As Madhava Prasad has argued in his analysis of the cinepolitics of southern India, in the aftermath of the linguistic reorganization of
states, cinematic icons in Tamil Nadu, Karnataka, and Andhra Pradesh
began to supplement the political life of the people in a parallel state form.
Indeed, "the national address that the cinema adopts as a marketing device
gives body to the linguistic nation more concretely than any other cultural
form."[97] The influence exerted by the literary or cultural imagination of the
Kannada language and people on the field of politics grew slighter with
the expansion of the cinematic field. By the 1970s, though the Kannada
nation was being mobilized through the parallel state form of cinepolitics,

one of the principal anchors of this mobilization was the question of jobs and the economy, for which demography became an invaluable resource.[98] The uses of history as a discourse for wresting away—or, more correctly, protecting—privilege had been dismissed by Abdul Gaffar during the debate on the SRC Report: "I think in the present set up . . . historic factors need not be given any consideration whatsoever. It is the facts that exist today that have got to be considered."[99] In 1973, Mysore was renamed Karnataka, thereby obliterating even the one small link with its long past.

By this time, it was the beleaguered minorities of Karnataka that were taking recourse to history as an explanation for their predicament. The movement away from the topography of Mysore products and resources, from the Mysorean as a "patriotic producer" to a focus on the "social origins" of the producer, soon occurred. Demands were vociferously made to restrict recruitment to the sons of the soil, both following and during direct attacks on linguistic minorities, which ignored the historical processes that had drawn them to Mysore. Despite several warnings against the dangers of narrowly defining Karnataka as a state for Kannadigas, the concept of the son of the soil became useful. Shivananjegowda's statement in the Assembly, which painted the image of a deprived son of the soil, became the war cry of Kannada nationalism in the years after unification.[100] It is precisely against such war cries that Hanumanthiaya had warned when he preached the virtues of compromise: "War cries have potency and force during times of war. We cannot use these cries and slogans in times of peace. They are unnecessary. In the same way, the war cries of Karnataka Matha ki Jai etc. must now be laid to rest, and they must come to this state with that approach of a happy compromise."[101]

Although the reference here was to the plight of the Vokkaligas, in its post-ekikarana version, this feeling of inadequacy was useful in getting the state to protect the sons of the soil from the claims of other language speakers rather than his dominant-caste counterparts. H. K. Veeranna Gowdh's dire predictions that a unified Karnataka was doomed to a short life and would lead to a struggle for two Karnatakas briefly flared into view but have thus far proved wrong, though his demand that "people's wishes" be given greater importance has been realized in unanticipated ways.[102]

Notes

Introduction

1. The best recent discussion of modernity in contemporary India is in Kaviraj, "An Outline of a Revisionist Theory of Modernity." Many arguments are being made for an Early Modern period in Indian history; see, for instance, Subrahmanyam, *Penumbral Visions*. Partha Chatterjee similarly outlines the many possibilities for the emergence of the modern that existed before the arrival of colonial modernity; in his scheme, Tipu Sultan represents the absolutist indigenous-modern. Chatterjee, "The Early Modern and Colonial Modern in South Asia" and "The Black Hole of Empire."

2. Mitchell, "The Stage of Modernity." On the limits to capitalism's universalizing and homogenizing ambitions, see Marx, *Grundrisse*, 410.

3. Kaviraj, "An Outline of a Revisionist Theory of Modernity," 517.

4. For this new way of conceiving Mysore's modernity, see chapter 8. According to Kaviraj, modernity could be theorized in two ways: the theory of *symmetry* assumes that the chief features of the modern are bundled together to become functionally dependent so that the existence of one feature, say capitalist economic relations, is supposed to produce the other characteristics, say individuation. Instead, the theory of *sequence* permits an unbundling of these features and allows attention to be given historical particularities. Kaviraj, "An Outline of a Revisionist Theory of Modernity," 509.

5. See Chakrabarty, *Provincializing Europe*, 32, 35. One of Mysore's many "exceptionalisms" singled out for approval was its relative insulation from "communal" riots, compared with other parts of India, such as Malabar or Hyderabad. On communalism in the south, see Kooiman, *Communities and Electorates*," and Chiriyankandath, "Communities at the Polls." David Washbrook has recently shown that colonial policies in Madras privileged the "local" in ways that were often at odds with Calcutta and London. Washbrook, "South India, 1770–1840."

6. Nair, "Beyond Exceptionalism."

7. According to him, Mysore's modern administrative history has passed through three important phases: (1) the growth of authority, 1700–1800; (2) the introduction of technique, 1800–1900; and (3) the development of policy, after 1900. He charts a steady and progressive growth from the administrative practices of the eighteenth century to those of the twentieth, so that colonialism is reduced to a set of techniques rather than a system of power and dominance. See Sastri, *An Introduction to the History of the Administration of Mysore*.

8. Ray, *Princely States and the Paramount Power*; Copland, *The British Raj and the Indian Princes*; Fisher, *Indirect Rule in India*. See also Copland, *The Princes of India in the Endgame of Empire*, and Ramusack, *The Indian Princes and Their States*.

9. Rangaswami, *The Story of Integration*. Manu Bhagwan compares Mysore and Baroda in *Sovereign Spheres*. An overview of nationalism in the southern region is in Chandrasekhar, *Colonialism, Conflict, and Nationalism*.

10. On Hyderabad, see Ray, *Hyderabad and British Paramountcy*, and Pernau, *The Passing of Patrimonialism*. On Mysore, see Hettne, *The Political Economy of Indirect Rule*, and Manor, *Political Change in an Indian State*. S. Chandrasekhar's volume of social history, *Dimensions of Socio-Economic Change*, marked out a different set of questions, though his focus, too, was on the late nineteenth and early twentieth centuries. On Kashmir, see Rai, *Hindu Rulers, Muslim Subjects*, and Zutshi, *Languages of Belonging*.

11. Dirks, *The Hollow Crown*.

12. Dirks says that Pudukkottai is "the final and only realization in the South Indian context of a state where ritual has been set apart on a stage with dramatic but ultimately only fictional power for an anonymous audience." Dirks, *The Hollow Crown*, 8. "If ever there was a theatre state in south India, this was it." Ibid., 355.

13. Price, *Kingship and Political Practice in Colonial India*, 6.

14. Bhagwan, *Sovereign Spheres*, 8, 176.

15. M. Shama Rao, *Modern Mysore*; Sastri, *The Administration of Sir Mark Cubbon*; C. Hayavadana Rao, *History of Mysore under the Wodeyar Dynasty*.

16. Hettne, *The Political Economy of Indirect Rule*; Manor, *Political Change in an Indian State*.

17. Chandrasekhar, *Dimensions of Socio-Economic Change* and *Colonialism, Conflict and Nationalism*; his more recent essays are in Chandrasekhar, *Adhunika Karnatakada Andolanagalu*. See also Bhagwan, *Sovereign Spheres*; Ramakrishnan, *Press and Politics in an Indian State*; Nair, *Miners and Millhands*.

18. Four recent studies (though by nonhistorians) have mapped out new understandings of an emerging modern Mysore public, associational practices and conflicts, and meanings of princely power under colonialism: Bairy, "Caste, Community and Association"; Boratti, "Narratives and Communities"; Shashikanth, "Carnatic Music, Kannada, and Kannadigas"; and Ikegame, "Royalty in Colonial and Post Colonial India."

19. Mahmud Khan Mahmud Banglori, *Tarikh-i-Sultanat-i-Khudadad*, 14. I am grateful to Raziuddin Aquil for his help in reading this text.

20. Stein, "State Formation and Economy Reconsidered," esp. 401.

21. See also Gopal, *Tipu Sultan's Mysore*. Purnaiya told the five-member British Commission that looked into the finances of Mysore that Tipu ordered a mosque to be built in each of six hundred taluks and was granted an annual allowance of 20 *pagodas* (gold coins); *mathas* were granted 20,000 Canteroy pagodas even in 1799. "Appendix, Proceedings of the Commission, Mad, Pol. Pro. 23 July 1799," in Gopal, *British Sources of the Economic, Political, and Social History of the Mysore State*, vol. 1, *1799–1812* (hereafter, Gopal, *British Sources, 1799–1812*), 402–3.

22. Sastri, *An Introduction to the History of the Administration of Mysore*, 5.

23. Bayly, "Hindu Kingship and the Origin of Community."

24. The most innovative reading is in Brittlebank, *Tipu Sultan's Search for Legitimacy*.

25. Salmond, *A Review of the Origin, Progress, and Result of the Decisive War with the*

Late Tippoo Sultaun in Mysore, Appendix D, no. 2, para. 63. As Mridu Rai shows, no such consideration about the majority Muslim subjects of Kashmir prevented the formation of Jammu and Kashmir under a Hindu Maharaja Gulab Singh in 1846, with long-term effects up to the present day. Rai, *Hindu Rulers,* 18–21.

26. Josiah Webbe to the Commissioners at Seringapatam, May 30, 1799, Brit. Mus. Add. MSS vol. 13667, in Gopal, *British Sources, 1799–1812,* 40. See also Kate Brittlebank, "Tales of Treachery."

27. As Michael Fisher shows, Purnaiya considered the company and not the Raja of Mysore his real employer. Fisher, *Indirect Rule in India.*

28. Buchanan, *A Journey from Madras through the Countries of Mysore, Canara, and Malabar,* 1:34.

29. Minutes of S. R. Lushington, Governor Fort St. George, July 4, 1831, For. Dept. Sec., October 7, 1831, no. 4-13, National Archives of India (NAI).

30. Dhondia Wagh was a soldier from Chennagiri, Shimoga, and was recruited by Haidar Ali in 1780. He attempted to establish himself independently in Shimoga in 1794. Though he briefly returned to Tipu's army, his repeated attempts to carve out an independent territory led to his imprisonment in Srirangapatna, from which he was freed when the city fell to British forces in 1799. Rajayyan, *South Indian Rebellion,* 102–3. Dhondia Wagh's declaration of power from Shimoga and the support that he quickly gathered from Chitradurga, Bellary, and Dharwad made him a serious threat to British control of Mysore. See Brittlebank "The White Raja of Srirangapattana," esp. 34. By the time of his eventual defeat in September 1800 by Wellesley's forces, he may have had up to seventy thousand armed followers.

31. Poorneah to the Governor, Ft. St. George, received April 22, 1802, Mad. Pol. Pro. April 23, 1802, in Gopal, *British Sources, 1799–1812,* 69; Mark Wilks, acting Resident to Chief Secretary, Fort St. George, Madras, October 4, 1805, and October 11, 1805, Mad. Pol. Pro. November 5, 1805, in Gopal, *British Sources, 1799–1812,* 101.

32. Mark Wilks, acting Resident to the Chief Secretary, Madras, November 17, 1806, Mad. Pol. Pro, February 13, 1806, in Gopal, *British Sources, 1799–1812,* 95.

33. Gopal, *The Finances of the Mysore State,* 32. See also Mark Wilks to Barry Close, January 1, 1803, Mad. Pol. Pro. August 31, 1802, in Gopal, *British Sources, 1799–1812,* 71. Mark Wilks to Governor Bentinck, Fort St. George, October 5, 1804, Ben. Sec. Cons. January 24, 1805 (no. 7a), in Gopal, *British Sources, 1799–1812,* 85.

34. Rice, *Mysore: A Gazetteer Compiled for Government* (hereafter, *Mysore Gazetteer*), 298.

35. Saki's is the most trenchant critique of colonial rule. Saki, *Making History,* 61–130.

36. Sastri, *The Administration of Mysore under Sir Mark Cubbon,* 232.

37. Stein, *Thomas Munro,* 103–4.

38. Memorandum, Mad. Pol. Pro. October 15, 1811, 379–412, in Gopal, *British Sources, 1799–1812,* 161.

39. Rajah of Mysore to Right Honourable Hugh Elliot, January 15, 1815, For. Misc., vol. 127, NAI.

40. Stein, *Thomas Munro,* 267.

41. Saki, *Making History,* 28.

42. Ikegame, "Royalty in Colonial and Post Colonial India," 209. For a more reflexive

conception of princely rule, see Mayer, "Perceptions of Princely Rule." See also Parayil, "Photography(s) in 20th Century Kerala."

43. Gopal, *The Finances of Mysore State*, 175.

44. For the form of "patrimonial bureaucracy" as opposed to the one rooted in legal domination that developed in Hyderabad, see Pernau, *The Passing of Patrimonialism*, 58, 60.

45. Governor General in Council, Fort William, to the Governor in Council, Fort St George, December 15, 1806, Mad. Pro. Pol. February 13, 1807, in Gopal, *British Sources, 1799–1812*, 93. The classic consideration of the way in which the king was conceptualized as having two bodies, the body natural and the body politic, in medieval Europe is Kantorowicz, *The King's Two Bodies*.

46. Chief Secretary, Fort St. George, Madras, to A. H. Cole, Resident, June 3, 1814, in Gopal, *British Sources of the Economic, Political, and Social History of the Mysore State*, vol. 2, *1813–1832* (hereafter, Gopal, *British Sources, 1813–1832*), 251.

47. Sastri recognizes this form of gift giving as the fulfillment of kingly dharma rather than as maladministration. Sastri, *An Introduction to the History of the Administration of Mysore*, 30. On gift giving more generally, see Mauss, *The Gift*.

48. Governor General William Bentinck to Rajah of Mysoor, September 5, 1831, Foreign Department Secret, October 7, 1831, NAI.

49. Gopal, *British Sources, 1813–32*, 456.

50. M. Shama Rao, *Modern Mysore*, 1:420.

51. *Report on the Origin, Progress, and Suppression of the Recent Disturbances in Mysore* (Bangalore: December 1833), 67 (hereafter, *Report on Disturbances in Mysore*). Lynd, "The Nagar Rebellion, 1830–1." For a reading of the Nagar rebellion as the result of an elite intrigue, see Chancellor, "Mysore."

52. J. A. Casamaijor, Officiating Resident to the Chief Secretary, Fort St. George, August 24, 1826, Mad. Sec. Pro. December 15, 1826, in Gopal, *British Sources, 1813–32*, 373.

53. In thinking through this formulation, I have found useful Ranciere, *The Politics of Aesthetics*.

54. Khureeta from H. H. the Maharaja of Mysore to H. E. the Rt. Honble John Lawrence, Viceroy and Governor General of India, April 1867, Further Papers Relating to Mysore in Continuation of no. 112 of [Parliamentary] Session, 1866, Box 28, Palace Papers, Karnataka State Archives.

55. Secretary of State in India to Governor General in Council, April 16, 1867. Further Papers relating to Mysore in Continuation of no. 112 of [Parliamentary] Session, 1866, Box 28, Palace Papers, KSA. See also Hayavadana Rao, "Krishnaraja Wodeyar III," esp. 44.

56. Hutchins, *The Illusion of Permanence*, 56.

57. Gopal, *The Finances of Mysore State*, 58. Among the improvements reported, the cultivation of coffee "took pride of place." Lieutenant General Mark Cubbon, Commissioner for Government of Mysore (hereafter GOM), to J. P. Grant, Secretary to Government of India (hereafter GOI), April 24, 1854, Foreign Political Department, 1854, May 19, no. 120-3, NAI.

58. Sastri, *The Administration of Sir Mark Cubbon*, 228. Sastri continues, "In the days of Hyder and Tippu, Mysore had been a Deccani power; Cubbon made it a Model State" (35).

59. List of Immovable Property Belonging to His Highness the Maharaja of Mysore, *Correspondence Relative to the Maharaja's Palace Affairs*, KSA (hereafter, *Elliot Report*); Muzrayi Memorandum, n.p., n.d. [1894?].

60. Chamarajendra Wodeyar's prolonged tutelage in the ways of the English aristocrat is well described in Singaraiyya, *Chamrajendra Wodeyaravara Charitre*. See also Hayavadana Rao "Krishnaraja Wodeyar III," 43–45.

61. Krishnaraja Wodeyar III enjoyed a stipend of 100,000 C.P., which amounted to about Rs 350,000, and one-fifth of the revenues of Mysore, together equaling about Rs 1.3 million. On the fluctuating incomes of the palace over the entire period, see Ikegame, "Royalty in Colonial and Post Colonial India," Table 5.2, 200.

62. Thomas Munro was remembered as having said of Mysore in 1799 that "the people of Mysore are not to be regarded as a distinct nation . . . but as a part of the great people who have sometimes been consolidated into extensive kingdoms of conquest but sometimes broken up . . . into petty states. . . . They . . . behold a change of rulers with indifference." For. Misc., no. 274, January–July, 1831, in Gopal, *British Sources, 1813–1832*, 456.

63. See Ikegame, "Royalty in Colonial and Post Colonial India," 158–66. I follow Barbara Ramusack's threefold classification of all princely states into the antique states (largely Rajput), the successor states of the Moghuls (Awadh, Hyderabad, Bengal) and the warrior states, to which category Mysore belonged. Ramusack, *The Indian Princes*, 12ff.

64. Parsons, *Mysore City* (London: Oxford University Press, 1930), 36. "In 1881, the Gandabherunda was officially adopted as the crest of Mysore state. A doubleheaded bird in front view was flanked by Sarabhas [elephant-headed lions] holding the crest, which was surmounted by a helmet. The motto of the Mysore kings was *satyam-evodharamyaham*—I uphold the truth." The Gandabherunda remained the crest after independence, and in 1950 the helmet was replaced by the lions of the Asoka column. In 1957, the motto was changed to *satyamevajayate*—may the truth always triumph. Stache-Rosen, "Gandabherunda," esp. 28.

65. Secretary of State, India Office, to C. C. Watson, Political Secretary to GOI, Simla, nineteenth January 1928, file no. GO-P of 1928, Confidential 1928, Sl. no. 69, ACC4, NAI.

66. Rangaswami, *The Story of Integration*, 25; also Ismail, *My Public Life*, 22. The largely ceremonial aspects of this assembly in its early stages are recounted in Elliot, *Gold, Sport, and Coffee Planting in Mysore*, 61ff.

67. Scott, "Colonial Governmentality," esp. 204.

68. On the notion of what the state was "obliged" to bring into being under the conditions of colonialism, see ibid., 193.

69. Hettne, *The Political Economy of Indirect Rule*; Gustafson, "The Making of a Model State"; Dushkin, "The Non-Brahmin Movement in Princely Mysore"; Chandrasekhara, *Dewan Rangacharlu*.

70. Ramusack, *The Indian Princes*; Ian Copland, *The Princes of India and the Endgame of Empire*; Fisher, *Indirect Rule*; Bhagwan, *Sovereign Spheres*.

71. Deshpande, "The Nation as an Imagined Economy," 56.

72. Ibid.

73. Kaviraj, "A Critique of Passive Revolution," 2430–31; Chatterjee, *Nationalist Thought in a Colonial World*, 47.

74. *Papers Relating to the Starting of an Automobile Company in Mysore* (Bangalore: Government of Mysore, 1942). On the "naturalization" of links between nation, economy, and territory, see Goswami, *Producing India*, 209ff.

75. On the concept of "political society" with reference to postindependence political practices as distinct from "civil society" of the restricted kind, see Chatterjee, "On Civil

and Political Society in Postcolonial Democracies"; for the distinct paths taken by colonial and postcolonial societies such as India, see Kaviraj, "In Search of Civil Society."

76. On the struggle in the late nineteenth century between the Madras and Mysore Brahmans, there is considerable discussion: Chandrasekhar, *Dimensions of Socio-Political Change in Mysore, 1918–40*; Hettne, *The Political Economy of Indirect Rule*, 72–74.

77. Bairy, "Caste, Community, and Association," esp. 80–87; see also Pandian, *Brahman, Non-Brahman*; Vivek Dhareshwar, "Caste and the Secular Self."

78. *Report of the Committee Appointed to Consider Steps Necessary for the Adequate Representation of Communities in the Public Service* (1918) (hereafter, *Miller Committee Report*).

79. Rangaswami, *The Story of Integration*, 253n93.

80. Ismail, *My Public Life*, 33.

81. See Nair, *Miners and Millhands*, esp. 17–22, for a brief introduction to the economic policies of Mysore in the twentieth century.

82. Princely states were ranked according to size and contribution to the colonial state's exchequer. Mysore was among the top five, meriting a twenty-one-gun salute at large imperial gatherings or meetings with the viceroy and other state heads. The other twenty-one-gun states were Hyderabad, Kashmir, Baroda, and Gwalior.

83. File no. 42 of 4-41, CB 181-40-1, KSA. See also Mirza, *My Public Life*, 139. For a different view of the reasons for Mirza's resignation, see Copland, *The Princes of India in the Endgame of Empire*, 171.

84. On the concept of the legal form, see Pashukannis, *Law and Marxism*, 42, 45. Sudipta Kaviraj uses the Gramscian model of "passive revolution" to analyze the composition and character of the postindependence Indian state. I believe the seeds were sown in the bureaucratic functioning of princely Mysore. See Kaviraj, "A Critique of Passive Revolution," 2430–31.

85. The limits to the schematic understanding of the "nationalist resolution of the women's question," as advanced by Partha Chatterjee, are made clear by the case of Mysore. See Chatterjee, "The Nation and Its Women."

86. Kasturbhai Lalbhai, *Report on the State-Owned and State-Aided Industrial Concerns in Mysore* (Delhi: Government of India, 1951).

87. Gustafson, "The Making of a Model State," 312.

88. Ibid., 83, 66–67; Rangachar and Rao, "A Brief Life Sketch," 318. See Visvesvaraya's "rule of citizen efficiency" included in his celebrated *Planned Economy for India*, 264.

89. Kaviraj, "On the Structure of Nationalist Discourse," 327. Although Kaviraj here refers to the Nehruvian moment, early twentieth-century Mysore's development agenda clearly anticipated the economic vision of the independent Indian state. Consider, for instance, the statistics for the circulation of newspapers in Ramakrishnan, *Press and Politics in an Indian State*, 165–66, which shows that between 1903 and 1936 the circulation of the Kannada newspaper with the largest readership increased from 4,810 (1903) to 5,100 (1917), then declined sharply to 4,000 (1936). Needless to say, there were many more contenders in the field by that time, none of whose circulation figures exceeded 3,000.

90. Vanaja Rangaswami notes that the anti-"foreign Brahmin" movement was common to Mysore, Travancore, and Cochin states. Rangaswami, *The Story of Integration*, 31.

91. T. Ramachandra Rao, "Nanna Alilu Seve," 70; Nair, *Miners and Millhands*; Nair, "Contending Ideologies."

92. The term *community association* has been used as a way of distinguishing caste institutions from the institutions of the public sphere. Devika and Mukherjee, "Reforming Women in Malayalee Modernity."

93. The "population" emerged as the entity to which these policies were addressed, and the "economy" in the sense defined by Foucault came to take the shape of a bounded, recognizable category. Foucault, "Governmentality," 92.

94. Thimmaiah, *Power, Politics, and Social Justice.* The most systematic acknowledgement of the "communal frame" of Mysore politics is in Hettne, *The Political Economy of Indirect Rule.*

95. Compare Thimmaiah, *Power, Politics, and Social Justice,* for the ways in which such a rethinking of caste is already under way. See also Rege, *Writing Caste, Writing Gender.*

96. Aya Ikegame says that the Ursu caste (from which the ruling family sprang) was a far-from-stable identity even in the twentieth century, containing within that unified description at least three and possibly five subcastes stratified primarily on class lines and only partially bound by the rules of clan (and *gotra,* or lineage) exogamy. Ikegame, *Royalty in Colonial and Post Colonial India,* 64–105.

97. Ibid., 106–48.

98. Ibid. On the bitter and sometimes violent conflicts between Brahmans and Lingayats in the twentieth century, see Bairy, "Caste, Community and Association," 168 ff. See also Boratti, "Narratives and Communities."

99. Dushkin, "The Non-Brahmin Movement in Princely Mysore," 183.

100. Sood, "The Matha State."

101. Nair, *Miners and Millhands,* 208–9.

102. *Miller Committee Report;* Visvesvaraya, *Memoirs of My Working Life,* 87.

103. Thimmaiah, *Power, Politics and Social Justice,* 45.

104. *Miller Committee Report,* 3.

105. Manor, *Political Change in an Indian State,* 64; Chandrasekhar, *Dimensions of Socio-Political Change,* 81; more generally see Thimmaiah, *Power, Politics and Social Justice,* 73 ff.

106. Manor, *Political Change in an Indian State.*

107. Mirza to Thumboo Chetty, April 10, 1936, file no. 14/1936, Dasara, Mysore Divisional Archives, KSA.

108. Nair, *Women and Law in Colonial India,* 204–11.

109. *Proceedings of the Mysore Representative Assembly* (hereafter, *PRAM),* 1928, October–November, 336.

110. *Report of the Committee Appointed by the Government of Mysore: Women's Rights under Hindu Law* (Bangalore: Government Press, 1930), 3.

111. *Proceedings of the Mysore Legislative Council* (hereafter, *PMLC),* December 1932, 411–12.

112. *PRAM,* 1912, 53; *PRAM,* 1921, 15–70, 216; *PRAM,* 1936, 26–27.

113. DVG, "A Gentleman to the Press Too," 112.

1. Tipu Sultan's War Colors and the Battle for Perspective

1. M. S. Rao, *Modern Mysore,* 1:3.

2. Beatson, *A View of the Origin and Conduct of the War with Tippoo Sultaun,* 139.

3. Wilks, *Historical Sketches of the South of India*, 3:451. MMDLT [Monsieur De La Tour] noted the resemblance of these events to Edward Gibbon's 1784 account of the defeat of Constantine Paleologus, the last Greek emperor of the east, by the Turks under Muhammad II in the siege of Constantinople. MMDLT, *The History of Hyder Shah alias Hyder Ali Khan Bahadur and of his son, Tippoo Sultaun;* Gibbon, *The History of the Decline and Fall of the Roman Empire*, 1052.

4. I have considered some precolonial modes of historical writing in "Eighteenth Century Passages to a History of Mysore."

5. Edney, *Mapping an Empire*, 13.

6. Jay, "Scopic Regimes of Modernity."

7. Crary, *Techniques of the Observer*, 38.

8. See the Introduction. Brittlebank, "Srirangapatnam Revisited," esp. 144–45.

9. Metcalf, *An Imperial Vision*, 10–11.

10. Kate Brittlebank has departed from the polarized readings of Tipu Sultan as either India's first secular-modern monarch or the tyrannical enemy of the Hindus, Christians, and even the Kannada language. Tipu's search for legitimacy as a Muslim monarch at the helm of a predominantly Hindu people, says Brittlebank, drove him to evolve a symbolic regime that drew on both Hindu and Islamic notions of power that were current in eighteenth-century India. Brittlebank, *Tipu Sultan's Search for Legitimacy.*

11. Gleig, *The Life of Sir Thomas Munro*, 1:25, as cited in Hasan, *History of Tipu Sultan*, 15. See also Buddle, *The Tiger and the Thistle*, 15.

12. The estimates of the force vary greatly in each historical source. These details are taken from Hasan, *History of Tipu Sultan*, 13–15.

13. Kirkpatrick, *Select Letters of Tippoo Sultan to Various Public Functionaries* (hereafter *Select Letters*), 392.

14. Cannon, *Historic Record of the Seventy First Regiment*, as cited in Buddle, *The Tiger and the Thistle*, 16.

15. See Moienuddin, *Sunset at Srirangapatam after the Death of Tipu Sultan*, 24–40. According to an eyewitness account, "The carnage on this occasion is greatly to be lamented. . . . Many of our soldiers, both natives and Europeans, without much ceremony, possessed themselves in a few hours after entering the town, of very valuable effects in gold and jewels; the houses of the chief sirdars, as well as of the merchants and shroffs (or bankers) being completely pillaged." *Narrative Sketches of the Conquest of Mysore*, 74–75.

16. On memorial stones, see Settar and Sontheimer, *Memorial Stones.*

17. Narasimhan, *Karnataka Bhitthi Chitra Parampara*, 112–13. Narasimhan's is the only work that discusses Karnataka's mural traditions at some length (110 ff). See also Kramrisch, *A Survey of Painting in the Deccan*, 141.

18. Howes, *The Courts of Pre-colonial South India*, 94.

19. Mittal, "Paintings of Hyderabad School."

20. Although it has been claimed that it was so named to commemorate his victory extending to the seas, here *dariya* may simply refer to the Cauvery River. In *Haidar Nama*, written shortly after the death of Haidar Ali in 1782, the author, Nallappa, refers more than once to the landing of Haidar's troops at the Mahanavami Mantapa of Srirangapatna; could this have formed the site of the new palace? Nallappa speaks of the establishment of the

two gardens (Lal Bagh and Dariya Daulat) and the building of two palaces on these sites, though the completion of the latter was definitely after Haidar's death. Constance Parsons claims, though without citing her sources, that the Dariya Daulat was built on the site of the Mahanavami Mantapa, from which the Mysore kings were seen during the Dasara celebrations. Parsons, *Seringapatam*, 98. Guidebooks available at Dariya Daulat today also make this claim. However, no Kannada source, not even the official *Mysore Samsthanada Prabhugalu: Srimanmaharajara Vamshavali* (hereafter *Srimanmaharajara Vamshavali*) mentions any such correlation.

21. Ramachandra Rao ("Punganuri"), *Memoirs of Hyder and Tippoo, Rulers of Seringapatam*, esp. section 2, paragraph 51, and section3, paragraph 18.

22. Information provided by M. Moienuddin, personal communication.

23. Although there were many French artisans who were employed by Tipu—for instance, cannon makers, watchmakers, and metalworkers—there is no evidence that they included fine artists. See Lafont, *Indika*. Of course, it is also likely that fine art was not the monopoly of the trained artist and that many artisans tried their hand at painting.

24. The album consisted largely of portraits of renowned Indian Sufis and appears to have been commissioned in 1796.

25. Buchanan, *A Journey from Madras through the Countries of Mysore, Canara, and Malabar*, 1:73–74.

26. Wilks, *Historical Sketches of South India*, 1:416.

27. As cited in Parsons, *Seringapatam*, 111. It is not clear whether subsequent renovations of the painting altered these representations or whether these descriptions were in fact exaggerations.

28. Bowring, *Eastern Experiences*, 56. See also George B Malleson, *Seringapatam*.

29. Bowring, *Eastern Experiences*, 120.

30. Bull, *Romantic Seringapatam*, 30–31; Parsons, *Seringapatam*, 113.

31. Karanth, *Karnataka Painting*, 85; C. Hayavadana Rao, *Mysore Gazetteer*, 5:819.

32. Archer, *Company Painting*, 70. Mysore produced only a small body of Company-style paintings (69).

33. Shekhar, "Dhariya Daulat Bagh Paintings."

34. On the many levels at which some Indian images have circulated and with varying connotations of sacral or temporal power, see Davis, *The Lives of Indian Images*.

35. Malleson, *Seringapatam Past and Present*, Appendix, 7.

36. R. H. Campbell, "Tippoo Sultan, the Fall or Seringapatam, and the Restoration of the Hindu Raj," esp. 28.

37. Valentia, *Voyages and Travels to India*, 366–67, my emphasis.

38. Wilks, *Historical Sketches*, 1:416.

39. See Brittlebank, "Tales of Treachery," 195–211.

40. Bowring, *Eastern Experiences*, 56.

41. Malleson, *Seringapatam*, Appendix.

42. In 1869, it was reported that the Dariya Daulat "was repaired, repainted and put in thorough order at a cost of a little exceeding Rs 50,000." Colonel Wilkinson, Officiating Secretary to Commissioner of Mysore, to Secretary, Public Works Department, GOI, For. Dept. Pol. A Jan. 1869, no. 344/51, NAI.

43. *Administration Report of the Public Works Department Mysore Province for the year 1887–88, KSA.*

44. Stephen Basappa, *A Guide to Seringapatam and Its Vicinity, Historical and Traditional,* 23.

45. Painting Works at Dariya Daulat, Srirangapatna, file no. 21 of 1916, Sl. no. 190, Maramath, Mysore Divisional Archives, KSA.

46. For instance, Colley, *Captives,* esp. 269–307.

47. Zebrowski, *Deccani Painting,* 7, 8.

48. Ibid., 10.

49. Howes, *The Courts of Pre-colonial South India,* 111.

50. Rice, *Epigraphia Carnatica,* vol. 2, part 1, 36.

51. Brittlebank, "The White Raja of Srirangapattina," 23–35.

52. Kramrisch, *A Survey of Painting in the Deccan,* 141.

53. Zebrowski, *Deccani Painting,* 183.

54. Kramrisch, *A Survey of Painting in the Deccan,* 141. See also Koch, *Mughal Art and Imperial Ideology,* 137, in which the author suggests that Jahangir was depicted in pure profile in contrast with Akbar, who was shown in the preferred three-quarters style. In his discussion of the late sixteenth-century portrait of Burhan Nizam Shah II of Ahmadnagar, Douglas Barrett has noted the first appearance of the three-quarters portrait in Deccani painting. Barrett, *Painting of the Deccan,* 14. In the context of the Srirangapatna mural, however, this hierarchy appears to have been reestablished.

55. Koch, *Moghul Art and Imperial Ideology,* 138. On the "peculiarity of [Deccani] portraiture setting figures in profile against a flat background," see Archer and Archer, *Indian Painting for the British,* 76.

56. On the question of the verisimilitude of Moghul paintings, see Verma, "Elements of Historicity in the Portraits of the Mughal School."

57. Gulammohammed Sheikh, *Contemporary Art in Baroda,* 32.

58. Bull, *Romantic Seringapatam,* 27.

59. Kirmani, *The History of Hydur Naik,* 390.

60. This has been interpreted by Linda Colley as a visual emasculation of the British. Colley, *Captives,* 269. However, British soldiers are portrayed as emphatically clean shaven in several contemporary British representations. See, for instance, Colebrooke, *Twelve Views of Places in the Kingdom of Mysore.*

61. Sheikh, *Contemporary Art in Baroda,* 32.

62. Howes, *The Courts of Pre-colonial South India,* 96.

63. Karanth, *Karnataka Painting,* 87.

64. This painting has been wrongly identified as *Raja Sarabhoji of Tanjore* in Archer, *Company Painting,* 59.

65. Mittal, "Paintings of Hyderabad School," 44, 45.

66. Among the books that note Tipu's religious and secular concerns and visions, see Habib, *State and Diplomacy under Tipu Sultan;* Hussain, *The Dreams of Tipu Sultan;* Habib, *Confronting Colonialism;* Khan, "State Intervention in the Economy," esp. 67. There is a large body of texts, now housed at the Asiatic Society Library, that have not been analyzed; a partial list would include *Muayyidu'l Mujahidin* (a collection of *khutbas,* or Friday sermons at a mosque), *Jawahirul Quran* (a commentary on portions of the Quran), *Majmua*

(dealing with the prophet's food and drink), *Fatawa-i-Muhammadi* (on jihad and kafirs, or unbelievers in Islam), *Fakhrush Shuyukh* (an exposition of the Muslim religious system written in 1786 by Ali Razaq Shaif), *Fiqh-i-Muhammadi* (on Muhammadan jurisprudence), and *Za'adul Mujahidin* (on jihad), in addition to texts on following Sunni Islam, marriage rituals, and so on. Among Tipu's orders to the Mir *asafs,* Order 34 is an injunction that the children of the officers and soldiers in the forts should be taught from "Zad al Mujahidin [on jihad] and Murid al Mujahidin [Disciple of the Holy Warriors]" and further that the *qazi* (a Muslim judicial officer administering towns according to Sharia law) should "ensure the lighting of the lamps," presumably of Islam. See Khan, "State Intervention in the Economy," 76.

67. MMDLT, *The History of Hyder Shah alias Hyder Ali Khan Bahadur,* 246.

68. Wilks, *Historical Sketches,* 3:140.

69. A large number of eyewitness accounts were written by British prisoners held in Hyder and Tipu's prisons and published in the late eighteenth century, and these formed an important historical source for both writers and history painters. For an analysis of these captivity narratives, see Colley, *Captives.* On the growing importance of India in the British press between 1790 and 1792, see Marshall, "Cornwallis Triumphant," esp. 58.

70. Another cartoon, by Cruikshank, titled *How to Gain a Compleat Victory and Say You Got Safe out of the Enemy's Reach,* was also issued in 1791. See Constance McPhee, "Tipu Sultan of Mysore and British Medievalism in the Paintings of Mather Brown."

71. Marshall, "Cornwallis Triumphant," 59.

72. Allen, "From Plassey to Seringapatam," esp. 31, 32.

73. Narayani Gupta appears to have overlooked this genre of work in her brief summary of the prelude to representations of the mutiny in "Pictorialising the 'Mutiny' of 1857." However, she argues that the "mutiny" heralded the extensive use of photography as an *aide-mémoire.*

74. An Impartial Observer, *A Letter to a Member of Parliament on the Conclusion of the War with Tippoo Sultaun,* 39. It is likely, as Marshall suggests, that wars (such as those against Mysore) that aimed at territorial expansion rather than the "preservation of commerce in East India" led to public alarm that had to be swiftly contained. Marshall, "Cornwallis Triumphant," 65.

75. Marshall, "Cornwallis Triumphant," 72.

76. Allen, "From Plassey to Seringapatam," 29.

77. Home, *Select Views in Mysore,* 30.

78. *Authentic Memoirs of Tippoo Sultaun.* See also Wilks, *Historical Sketches,* 2:277.

79. Mildred Archer has identified hostage paintings produced by James Northcote, Edward Bird, George Carter, Robert Smirke, Mather Brown, and Henry Singleton, all working in Britain, whereas Home and Devis alone were actually present in India. Archer, *India and British Portraiture.*

80. Rohatgi, "From Pencil to Panorama."

81. Ibid., 47.

82. McPhee, "Tipu Sultan of Mysore," 202–3. McPhee suggests that these paintings deliberately invoked memories of British villains such as Richard II or Henry VII (210).

83. McPhee, "Tipu Sultan of Mysore," 204.

84. Archer, *India and British Portraiture,* 423.

85. Ramachandra Rao ("Punganuri"), *Memoirs of Hyder and Tipoo, Rulers of Mysore*, book 4, paragraph 34.

86. Meer Husain Ali Khan Kirmani, *History of Tipu Sultan*, 104.

87. Rohatgi, "From Pencil to Panorama," 47.

88. Sen, *Distant Sovereignty*, xxi.

89. The parallels with Gibbon's description of the identification of the slain body of Constantine are once more striking. Gibbon says, "Yet [Muhammad's] mind was not satisfied nor did the victory seem complete till he was informed of the fate of Constantine, whether he had escaped or been made prisoner or had fallen in the battles. Two janizaries [elite Ottoman bodyguards] claimed the honour and reward of his death, the body under a heap of slain was discovered by the golden eagles embroidered on his shoes; the Greeks acknowledged with tears the head of their late emperor, and after exposing the bloody trophy Mahomet bestowed on his rival the honours of a decent funeral." Gibbon, *The History of the Decline and Fall of the Roman Empire*, 1057.

90. Some sent him to Mecca and others to Pondicherry! An Impartial Observer, *A Letter to a Member of Parliament*, 39, Appendix. In December 2003, an actual identification "drama" was enacted on television screens worldwide: U.S. forces "dug" the former president of Iraq, Saddam Hussein, out of his hiding place and examined him, in the full glare of television cameras, to establish his identity.

91. Beatson, *A View of the Origin and Conduct of the War with Tippoo Sultaun*, 136, my emphasis.

92. Kirmani, *History of Tipu Sultan*, 28.

93. Beatson, *A View of the Origin and Conduct of the War with Tippoo Sultaun*, 101 Annexure, no. 33.

94. The most important reading of this painting is in Rohatgi, "From Pencil to Panorama," 49. See also, Teltscher, *India Inscribed*, 253–55.

95. *Narrative Sketches of the Conquest of Mysore*.

96. Oettermann, *The Panorama*, 125.

97. *Narrative Sketches of the Conquest of Mysore*. An advertisement for the book on its inside cover read: "The materials from which these sketches have been produced were collected to assist the design and regulate the execution of an extensive Historical Painting, . . . *Storming of Seringapatam* painted by R. K. Porter."

98. Archer , *British Portraiture in India*, 428.

99. Oettermann, *The Panorama*, 116. Ker Porter's portrayal of the campaigns against Napolean won him the offer of a job as painter at the court of the Russian tsar.

100. Oettermann, *The Panorama*, 115.

101. On the emergence of genre (history) painters in an entirely different setting and the structure of meanings in their painting, as history and as comment, see the paintings by Tshibumba Kanda Matulu in Fabian and Matulu, *Remembering the Present*.

102. See Neil Larsen's excellent discussion of the achievements of this painting alongside his critique of its place in art history in *Modernism and Hegemony*, 32–48.

103. Archer, *India and British Portraiture*, 431–33. The current display at Dariya Daulat equally lionizes Tipu Sultan and Arthur Wellesley in an uncritical postindependence retention of colonial awe and reverence for the Duke of Wellington's later military achievements.

104. In 1929, Charles Todhunter, private secretary to the Maharaja, arranged a "number of engravings and other articles illustrative of the history of Mysore." Almost all of them had to do with the fall of Srirangapatna. Charles Todhunter to Edmund Bull, October 7, 1929, File no. 2/1929, Dasara Exhibition, MDA, KSA.

105. Crary, *Techniques of the Observer*, 38.

106. Berger, *Ways of Seeing*, 109.

107. Kirmani, *History of Tipu Sultan*, 82–83.

108. Lewis, "Chitradurga in the Early 1800s," 5, 7.

109. Home, *Select Views in Mysore*; Hunter, *Picturesque Scenery in the Kingdom of Mysore*; Colebrooke, *Twelve Views of Places in the Kingdom of Mysore*. There were three hundred subscribers to Colebrooke's prints, signs of a robust British interest in these themes.

110. Allen and Wells, *A Collection of Views in the Mysore Country*.

111. Edney, *Mapping an Empire*, 55, my emphasis.

112. Ibid., 72, my emphasis.

113. Svetlana Alpers, *The Art of Describing*; Jay, "Scopic Regimes of Modernity."

114. For the fate of "atemporal, decorporealised and transcendental" perspectivalism in late nineteenth-century France, however, see Jay, *Downcast Eyes*, 149–209.

115. Subramanyan, *The Living Tradition*, 78.

116. Nochlin, *Realism*, 33, 45.

117. Karanth, *Karnataka Painting*, 85.

118. Ibid., 87.

119. Ibid., 85.

120. These were installed only in the twentieth century, and the result is a noticeable faded lower portion compared with the rich, dark colors above. *Administration Report of the PWD [Public Works Department] Mysore State for the Year 1920–26*, 7, KSA.

121. I am grateful to Ghulammohammed Sheikh for drawing my attention to this work while I was on a visit to Vadodara in September 2005. Thanks also to Deeptha Acharya and Sneha Raghavan for the images.

2. An Illusion of Permanence

1. Havanur, *Hosagannadada Arunodaya*, 162–63. One may note that Havanur judges the greatness of the Karnataka past solely from the point of view of the patronage of Kannada literature. Karnataka's significant political and cultural heritage that may be traced to the Bahmani Sultans or Tipu Sultan are thus denied a place in such an account.

2. Ibid., 163; Shashikant, "Carnatic Music, Kannada, and Kannadigas." The Veena maestro Venkatasubbaiya accumulated not only honor but extraordinary power within the Mysore court and was the recipient of several village *inams*, in addition to assuming administrative power to become the *moosahib*, or counselor of the king, in 1819 (n7). This degree of political influence was attained by no other musician even in the twentieth century. See also S. K. R. Rao, *Mysore Chitramala* and *Mummadi Krishnaraja Wodeyara Sritatvanidhi*.

3. Peterson, "Portraiture at the Tanjore Maratha Court" and "Facing the Modern in Nineteenth Century Tanjavur."

4. Aitken, "The Practiced Eye," 153.

5. Stein, "Notes on 'Peasant Insurgency' in Colonial Mysore"; Saki, *Making History*, 183–247; *The Origin, Progress, and Suppression of the Recent Disturbances in Mysore* (Bangalore, December 12, 1833); Lynd, "The Nagar Rebellion."

6. The distinctions between representational and aesthetic strategies is in Rancière, *The Politics of Aesthetics*, 10, 21.

7. Aiya, *Travancore State Manual*, 263–64. Textual sources for the provenance of the earlier period are few and far between compared with the relatively more detailed diaries and letters of palace artists, as well as records of their output and their wages in the early twentieth century. Apart from S. K. R. Rao's *Mummadi Krishnaraja Wodeyara Sritatvanidhi*, I have found few references even in Kannada sources to the commissioning of the portraits or murals. On the other hand, there is a series of (self-?) portraits of artists both in the volumes and on the walls of the Rang Mahal.

8. In early British correspondence, the king was referred to as the "Rajah of Mysoor," although the subsidiary treaty refers to him as the "Maharaja of Mysore." An example of the exaggerated importance of Krishnaraja Wodeyar III is the description of his establishment of the Chamarajeswara temple at Chamarajanagar taluk in 1828: "The rajadhiraja-raja parameswara, praudhapratapa, unequalled hero, champion over those who say they have titles, sole hero of the world, a moon in raising the tide of the Yadukula having the emblem of the conch, the discus, the elephant god, the axe, the crocodile, the fish, the sarabha, the salva, the gandabherunda, the bear that raised the earth, Hanumanta, Garuda, and the lion, adorned with these and many titles, Krishna Raja Wodeyar, having created Chamarajanagara, created the Chamarajeswara temple." Lewis, *Epigraphia Carnatica*, 4:10.

9. For instance, Gopal, *British Sources, 1813–1932*, 378.

10. List of Immovable Property Belonging to His Highness the Maharaja of Mysore, *Elliot Report*.

11. S. R. Rao and Sastry, *Traditional Paintings of Karnataka*, 5.

12. Ibid., 20.

13. S. K. R. Rao, *Mysore Chitramala*, 7–14. Rao is less confident about the stress on continuity when he uses the word "traditional" in quotes (18) and describes the Dariya Daulat murals as "transitionally traditional" (19).

14. S. K. R. Rao, *Mysore Chitramala*, 20.

15. Suggesting that the Mysore style represents "a miniature continuation (if also a noteworthy deviation) of the Vijayanagar murals, incorporating Deccani influences," Rao says that "this transitional style was crystallized in and around Mysore during the reign of the Wodeyar rulers (1371–1947)." At once "decorative, aristocratic and popular," he continues, "it is a royal school of painting which found favour among the people at large." Ibid., 33–34. He thus renders the term too supple to be of any critical use.

16. Zebrowski, *Deccani Painting*, 245, 272; Mittal, "Paintings of Hyderabad School."

17. S. K. R. Rao, *Mummadi Krishnaraja Wodeyara Sritatvanidhi*, 44, 62.

18. Ibid. Although Rao mentions one thousand line drawings and paintings, the number of illustrations varied from copy to copy. Robert Del Bontà, personal communication, February 20, 2009.

19. Del Bontà, "A Bhagavata Purana Manuscript from Mysore," esp. 470n9.

20. See also del Bontà, "See Krsna Run."

21. *Annual Administration Report of the Archaeological Department* (Bangalore: Government Press, year as indicated) (hereafter, *Mysore Archaeological Report*), 1943, 39–40.

22. Peterson, "Portraiture at the Tanjore Maratha Court," 2, and "Facing the Modern in Nineteenth Century Tanjavur," 4.

23. Aiya, *Travancore State Manual*, 1906, 4:263.

24. Aitken, "The Practiced Eye," 69.

25. Thakurta, *The Making of a New "Indian" Art*.

26. S. K. R. Rao, *Mummadi Krishnaraja Wodeyara Sritatvanidhi*, Appendix 1. See also Del Bontà, "See Krsna Run," 101. Several excellent reproductions are to be found in S. K. R. Rao, *Mysore Chitramala*, 56–62.

27. Pinney, *Photos of the Gods*, 123–38.

28. Arthur Wellesley to Earl of Mornington, June 30, 1799, in Salmond, *A Review of the Origin, Progress, and Result of the Decisive War*, Appendix D, II, enclosure no. 15.

29. These are the words of Francis Buchanan on the young Raja in 1801. Buchanan, *A Journey from Madras through the Countries of Mysore, Canara and Malabar*, 1:68; Lord Valentia, describing his visit to India in 1803, similarly reported his encounter with the poised young Raja. Campbell, "Tippoo Sultan," 15.

30. This portrait is reproduced in Parsons, *Mysore City*, frontispiece.

31. Jagdish Mittal notes that the prodigious output of the Hyderabad school in Nizam Ali's period reveals a deliberate emphasis on themes of princely leisure, such as listening to music, rather than action, such as fighting on the battlefield or hunting. Mittal, "Paintings of Hyderabad School," 44. See also Zebrowski, *Deccani Painting*, 7, which speaks of the escapist mood of the Deccani courts, "where the Sultauns took more interest in leisure and the arts than in government or conquest" (8). Zebrowski also notes the Deccani obsession with princely portraits compared with hunts, court ceremonials or rituals (as in the Rajasthani miniatures), or historical events (as in the Mughal paintings); the portraits themselves became sterile with political stability.

32. Peterson, "Portraiture at the Tanjore Maratha Court," 3.

33. Barrett, *Painting of the Deccan*, 14. As in the Dariya Daulat mural, discussed earlier, Stella Kramrisch points out that the difference between Persian- and Deccani-style portraiture is the use of three-quarters views in the artistic practice of the former and the use of strict profiles in the latter. Kramrisch, *A Survey of Painting in the Deccan*, 146. Del Bontà, however, terms the continued use of profile for portraits in contemporaneous murals of Sravanabelagola "old fashioned," though he does not date the usage of such profiles. Del Bontà, "A Bhagavata Purana Manuscript from Mysore," 469n8. See also Aitken, "The Practiced Eye," 99.

34. Peterson, "Facing the Modern in Nineteenth Century Tanjavur," 12.

35. Ibid., 16.

36. Aitken, "The Practiced Eye," 197, 204.

37. The portrayal of the aging monarch is even used to date the paintings, as in Del Bontà, "A Bhagavata Purana Manuscript from Mysore," 466. Following C. S. Pierce, Pinney says that of the three types of signs—the symbolic, the iconic, and the indexical—symbols are arbitrary and conventional, while iconic signs have a relationship to their referents. "Those signs are indexical which have some natural relationship of contiguity with their

referent." Pinney, *Camera Indica,* 20. It was precisely its indexicality that established photography's superiority over other systems of signs.

38. C. A. Bayly, "From Company to Crown," 132.

39. See, for instance, Gopal, *The Finances of the Mysore State,* 56–60, on the extractive nature of Purnaiya's regime. See also Saki, *Making History,* 100 ff.

40. See S. K. R. Rao, *Mysore Chitramala,* 44–45.

41. In his comparison of the western and Indian modes of spectation and his explanation of the relative failure of Indian popular images to address beholders indifferently, which led to the emergence of a new theatrical or "corpothetic" image, Christopher Pinney leaves out of consideration the growing genre of portraiture in Europe, which also unequivocally acknowledged the viewer's presence. See Pinney, *Photos of the Gods,* 22–23. Peterson has provided a very similar reading of the Tanjore portraits, arguing that Serfoji II's gesture of salutation and worship was adapted to address a wider colonial public sphere. Peterson, "Facing the Modern in Nineteenth Century Tanjavur," 18. Apart from the suggestion that the portraits circulated widely, there is no other evidence offered of the "public" that evolved in most other parts of southern India, if only in the latter part of the nineteenth century. See, for instance, Price, *Kingship and Political Practice in Colonial India,* 132 ff.

42. Chancellor, "A Picture of Health."

43. C. A. Bayly suggests that the Indian courts were unable to afford the British painters, but the deliberately cultivated Indian painterly practice at Mysore is not explained by this. Bayly, "From Company to Crown," 132.

44. *Mysore District Gazetteer.* Serfoji II was far more eclectic in his choices; he even commissioned two European-style sculptures. Peterson, "Portraiture at the Tanjore Maratha Court," 5.

45. Correspondence Relative to the Re-establishment of a Native Government in Mysore, Palace Papers, KSA, 77; Copies of Extracts of Correspondence between the Secretary of State for India and the Governor General Regarding Re-establishment of a Native Government by the Time the Maharaja Shall Come of Age (in continuation of Parliamentary Papers, Session 1867), Palace Papers, KSA.

46. C. Elliot to L. B. Bowring, Commissioner of Mysore, October 31, 1868, *Elliot Report.*

47. Schama, "The Domestication of Majesty," 155. Although informal portraits were being executed as early as the mid-seventeenth century, they were not extended to images of the royal family until the mid-nineteenth, especially in England. Ibid., 169.

48. Issar, *Royal City,* 10.

49. Ikegame, "Royalty in Colonial and Post Colonial India," 92. This was achieved only with the active assistance of the Residents and political agents of the Rajputana states.

50. Ravi Varma was willing to represent mythological figures such as Rama in blue rather than using a fleshy tint. See Ravi Varma to Raghavendra Rao, Assistant Private Secretary, March 22, 1905, in *Selections from the Records of the Mysore Palace,* 238.

51. Ravi Varma visited Mysore with the intention of securing a major commission from the newly installed king. Plans were also made for a series of thirteen paintings for the Amba Vilas, a series eventually assigned to K. Venkatappa. Correspondence between Ravi Varma and Raghavendra Rao, Assistant Private Secretary to His Highness the Maharaja,

November 12, 1904, Maramath, sl. no. 8, 1904–14, KSA, in *Selections from the Records of the Mysore Palace*, 235–36.

52. K. Keshavaiah to His Highness Sri Krishna Rajendra Wodeyar Bahadur, July 2, 1903, Maramath, File no. 19, 1903–14, in *Selections from the Records of the Mysore Palace*, 247–48.

53. "A Memo of My Case," K. Keshavaiah to Huzur Secretary (?), June 6, 1925, Maramath, sl. no. 19, 1914–38, in *Selections from the Records of the Mysore Palace*, 256–58.

54. S. K. R. Rao, *Mysore Chitramala*, 7. Rao has surmised that they were in wide circulation, though neither the numbers in which they were produced nor the people to whom they were distributed are known.

55. Shekar, *Mural Paintings of Sibi, Keladi and Bangalore*, 52; Narasimhan, *Karnataka bhitti chitra parampare*.

56. Pinney, *Camera Indica*, 20.

57. Zebrowski, *Deccani Painting*, 245, 272.

58. Parayil, "Photography(s) in 20th Century Kerala," 103–82.

59. See, for instance, Pinney, *Camera Indica*, 72–92.

60. Peterson, "Facing the Modern in 19th Century Tanjavur," 2, 22.

61. File no. 306-15, sl. nos. 20–112, General Miscellaneous, KSA.

62. File no. 306-15, sl. nos. 48 and 56, General Miscellaneous, KSA; file no. 306-15, sl. nos. 1–122, General Miscellaneous, KSA.

63. Diary, Keshavaiah, file no. 14 of 1910, sl. no. 56 (A), entries for July 18, 1911, and January 1, 1913, Mysore Divisional Archives, Mysore.

64. S. Venkatesh. *K. Keshavayya*, 27.

65. *Mysore Samsthanada Prabhugalu*, part 2, 133–37; *Mysore Archaeological Report*, 1938, 64–5.

66. Singaraiyya, *Chamrajendra Wodeyaravara Charitre*, 135ff.

67. Rangaswami, *The Story of Integration*, 49, 50. Permission was granted, however, only after his speech was approved by the British regime. Iyer, *Modern Mysore*, 11.

68. Parayil, "Photography(s) in 20th Century Keralam," 185–86.

69. Del Bontà, "A Bhagavata Purana Manuscript from Mysore," 473. Recognizable features of the Old Residency (later called the Government House) of Mysore, among the earliest of the colonial buildings, are to be seen in the paintings, as well as lavish use of European-style chandeliers. See also S. K. R. Rao, *Mysore Chitramala*.

70. Del Bontà, "A Bhagavata Purana Manuscript from Mysore," 470n9.

71. Ibid., 478.

72. Gole, *Indian Maps and Plans*, 25.

73. *Mysore Archaeological Report*, 1920, 2 ff.

74. *Sri Subbaraya Dasaru Prathinama Sri Gopaldasaru artharth Sri Gopala Wodeyaravara Charitre*, 115; *Mysore Samsthanada Prabhugalu*, part 1. No details of the commission or its execution are given here.

75. Both local legend and the hagiography of Subbaraya Dasa mention the close relationship he shared with Krishnaraja Wodeyar III, who patronized at least three pilgrimages by Subbaraya Dasa, to Tirupati in 1828, to Kasi from 1829 to 1835, and to Tirupati again in 1842. Indira Peterson has discussed the pilgrimage to Banares undertaken by Serfoji II from 1820 to 1822, primarily to collect religious and scientific manuscripts, in order to impress the

colonial masters. Peterson, "Subversive Journeys?" as cited in Ramusack, *The Indian Princes and Their States*, 127.

76. See Kramrisch, *A Survey of Painting in the Deccan*, 160.

77. Archer, *Company Painting*, 11.

78. *Srimanmaharajaravara Vamshavali*, 2:173–75.

79. Thippanna supposedly lived until 1856, making the attribution of the picture to him doubtful, because it definitely refers to the events of 1866.

80. See S. R. Rao and Sastry, *Traditional Paintings of Karnataka*.

81. *Sri Gopala Wodeyaravara Charitre*, 115.

82. The small chitramantapa, which has today fallen into disrepair, was supposedly where Krishnaraja Wodeyar III often went to play chess with Subbarayadasa. For the details of the genealogies on the doors, see *Mysore Archaeological Report*, 1920, 2.

83. Alexander Beatson dated the founding of the dynasty, as opposed to the family, to 1610, when Raja Wodeyar moved to Srirangapattana and assumed "the ceremony of sitting on the throne." Beatson, *A View of the Origin and Conduct of the War with Tippoo Sultaun*, 229.

84. "As the crown in Travancore," says Lewis Rice in the revised *Mysore Gazetteer*, "so the throne is the peculiar emblem of royalty in Mysore." *Mysore: A Gazetteer Compiled for Government*, 279. S. K. R. Rao, *Mysore Chitramala*, 52.

85. An attempt to write the period's history from the perspective of the *dalavais* is in the manuscript on the dynasty of Kalale written about 1800. The purpose was to set out the achievements of the Kalale chiefs, so the *dalavais* were shown as the principal military chiefs and the kings as figureheads. Although the first *dalavai* was appointed only in 1616, *dalavais* were made to appear in battles even earlier. Thus, during the period of Wodeyar rule for 190 years (reckoned from the time of Raja Wodeyar, 1610), Mysore was ruled by fourteen kings and nine *dalavais*. *Mysore Archaeological Report*, 1942, 78–99.

86. Rice, *Mysore Gazetteer*, 69.

87. Ibid., 70.

88. Jaganmohan Palace Chitrasala, Mysore, *Gallery of Historical Portraits*.

89. C. H. Rao, *Mysore Gazetteer*, vol. 2, part 1 (1930), 336–38. Murals were executed during the nineteenth century at different sites in Mysore, such as the durbar scenes on a Jain temple at Chamarajanagar.

90. Constance Parsons describes it as "the western older building." Parsons, *Mysore City*, 38. The *Gazetteer* describes a lofty building "intended by the Raja as an ornament to the town and a place of amusement for the European visitors." Rice, *Mysore Gazetteer*, 69. The *Elliot Report* lists it as a large bungalow (see Introduction, note 59).

91. According to Constance Parsons, "They are very much in the style of those on the walls of the Daria Daulat, at Seringapatam." Parsons, *Mysore City*, 42. See also, "Mural Paintings at the Jaganmohan Palace," in *Mysore Archaeological Report*, 1938, 46–71.

92. S. R. Rao and Sastry, *Traditional Paintings of Karnataka*, 39.

93. Resident J. A. Casamaijor to Commission for the Government of Mysore, September 1, 1832, For. Dept. Secret., October 15, 1832, 22–23, NAI; Smollett to Casamaijor, September 18, 1832, For. Dept. Secret., October 15, 1832, 22–23, NAI.

94. For a detailed written description, see "Mural Paintings at the Jaganmohan Palace,"

Mysore Archaeological Report, 1938, 46–71. For the most part, my focus will be on the procession itself.

95. The portraits appear to have been drawn from a wide range of pictorial sources, including portraits from the court of the Nizam of Hyderabad and reproductions of Ranjit Singh and Sher Singh in Eden, *Up the Country.* I am grateful to Robert Del Bontà for sharing this information.

96. Jennifer Howes discusses the battle fresco on the walls of the Ramnad Palace, which shows the Setupati and the Maratha king using bows and arrows to invoke memories of epic battles. Howes, *The Courts of Pre-colonial South India,* 90 ff.

97. See Kantorowicz, *The King's Two Bodies.*

98. Del Bontà discusses a folio in the Bhagavata Purana in which Krishnaraja Wodeyar III is looking at the god Krishna leaving the city. Del Bontà, "A Bhagavata Purana Manuscript from Mysore," 482, pl. 141. In another instance, there is an obverse of this trope, which depicts the god Krishna mounted on an elephant, bearing a striking resemblance to representations of Krishnaraja Wodeyar III in the Rang Mahal. Ibid., 477n17.

99. The only visual reference to the Englishman is to a mounted soldier in a hat, leading a company of bandsmen.

100. For a description of the phenomenon in England, see Schama, "The Domestication of Majesty."

101. I am grateful to Gautam Bhadra for suggesting that I clarify this difference.

102. On Mirza Ismail's desire to instruct spectators, see his instructions to Venkatappa in chapter 5.

103. E. W. Thompson minced no words when he said, "The Indian Prince, far from being, as most suppose an impressive survival from antiquity . . . is the creation of Lord Wellesley in his half dozen years of daemonic activity." Thompson, *The Making of the Indian Princes,* 140. Later Thompson added that the British quest was for a "safety valve," "a form that would admit of freer action, undisturbed by a succession of wars" (287).

104. *Gallery of Indian Paintings,* 4.

105. Constance Parsons, for instance, refers to the "quaint and interesting mural paintings" but deplores the representation of the state cows in the Rang Mahal as "crude paintings." Parsons, *Mysore City,* 42–3, 187.

106. Balibar "The Nation Form," esp. 101–2.

3. Srirangapatna

1. This is John Leyden's 1805 translation of a Kannada poem, "The Dirge of Tippoo Sultaun," whose original version has been lost. From *The Poetical Remains of the Late Dr. John Leyden,* 64. I am grateful to Rosinka Chaudhuri for sharing this poem with me. The poem was translated back into Kannada by L. Gundappa in 1945. See Halemane, *Dhira Tipuvina Laavanigalu,* 25. See also C. Hayavadana Rao, *Mysore Gazetteer,* vol. 2, part 1, 457.

2. Leyden, *The Poetical Remains of the Late Dr. John Leyden,* 64.

3. Banglori, *Tarikh-i-Sultanat-i-Khudadad,* 17.

4. Nandalal Bose included Tipu Sultan in the pantheon of twenty-two mythical and historical "heroes" he used to illustrate the Indian Constitution in 1950. Since then,

assessments of Tipu Sultan's legacy have been more ambiguous, particularly in contemporary Karnataka. In September 2006, Lingadevaru Halemane's script for a sound and light program at the Mysore palace was prevented from being used in the upcoming Dasara celebrations by a descendent of the Wodeyar family, Srikantadatta Wodeyar, because it celebrated a history of Mysore, not just the reign of the Wodeyars. According to recent reports, the script is likely to be used in Dasara programs. "Sound and Light show to be revived" *Hindu*, June 11, 2007.

5. "Bi-Centenary Celebration of Tipu Sultan" *Islamic Voice*, http://www.Islamicvoice. com/June99/tippu/htm (accessed July 25, 2007). The state-sponsored commemoration scheduled for May 4, 1999, was postponed due to threats from the Bajrang Dal and was finally held in a more subdued manner on May 6 and 15, 1999. In 2006 Karnataka's higher education minister, G. H. Shankaramurthy (BJP), deplored the excessive emphasis on Tipu Sultan in textbooks. "Shankaramurthy on the Offensive against Tipu Sultan," *Hindu*, September 20, 2006. See also "Historians Protest Remarks against Tipu," *Hindu*, September 26, 2006.

6. The most recent tribute to the Mysore Wodeyars is in Sampath, *Splendours of Royal Mysore*.

7. Satara State was the only other case of a "territory carved out of conquest and given to the descendent of those who formerly reigned in the same region." *Selections from Parliamentary Debates (House of Commons) in 1867 re: The Restoration of Mysore to the Maharajah*, intervention of Viscount Cranbourne, 837. See also Ramusack, *The Indian Princes*, 81–82.

8. See E. W. Thompson, *The Making of the Indian Princes*, 140.

9. "In short, the Kalale Family had come to assert itself and become the arbiter of the destiny of the Kingdom of Mysore." C. H. Rao, *History of Mysore*, 2:66.

10. Banglori, *Tarikh-i-Sultanat-i-Khudadad*, 8–9.

11. From the Mysore Commissioners to the Governor General, June 30, 1799, in Salmond, *A Review of the Origin, Progress, and Result of the Decisive War*, Appendix (D), no. II, no. 15.

12. As cited in Parsons, *Mysore City*, 158–59.

13. Salmond, *A Review of the Origin, Progress, and Result of the Decisive War*, Appendix (D), no. II, no. 16.

14. Governor General to the Court of Directors, August 3, 1799, in Salmond, *A Review of the Origin, Progress and Result of the Decisive War*, paragraph 63.

15. Moienuddin, *Sunset at Srirangapatam after the Death of Tipu Sultan*, 35. The gold medal was designed by C. H. Kushler in 1799 and presented to Lord Cornwallis in 1800. Davis, *The Lives of Indian Images*, 148.

16. Rice, *Mysore Gazetteer*, 298.

17. Governor General to the Court of Directors, August 3, 1799, in Salmond, *A Review of the Origin, Progress, and Result of the Decisive War*, paragraph 63.

18. In the words of G. B. Malleson, "Seringapatam under its later Hindu sovereigns has never been aggressive, but under its two Mahommedan rulers the English in Madras had learned to speak of it with respect, whilst in Trichnapali and in Madura, in Trevandrum and Kochin, its name was never mentioned but with awe." Malleson, *Seringapatam*, 22.

19. As cited in Moienuddin, *Sunset at Srirangapatam*, 26. Arthur Wellesley was given the

command of the Mysore troops even though General Baird not only had a stronger claim but had led the storming of the fort. Wellesley was clearly amplifying his role in the pacification of Srirangapatna. See Parsons, *Seringapatam*, 17–20.

20. Davis, *Lives of Indian Images*, 156–57.

21. Ibid., 156.

22. Ibid.

23. Brittlebank, "The White Raja of Srirangapattana," 23–35.

24. Mornington to the Commissioners of Mysore, June 4, 1799, in Salmond, *A Review of the Origin, Progress, and Result of the Decisive War*, paragraph 63.

25. Rice, *Mysore Gazetteer*, 298.

26. Mark Wilks, Acting Resident, to N. B. Edmondstone, Chief Secretary Fort St. George, December 25, 1804. For. Misc. 1805, Dept. Pol. Cons., April 25, no. 12, in Gopal, *British Sources, 1799–1812*, 86.

27. Buchanan, *A Journey from Madras through the Territories of Mysore, Canara, and Malabar*, 1:66.

28. Rice, *Mysore Gazetteer*, 81.

29. Bowring, *Eastern Experiences*, 55; Stephen Basappa, *A Guide to Seringapatam and Its Vicinity*, 1. According to another estimate, the population was 12,744 in 1851–52, while revenue collection had absolutely declined. Sastri, *The Administration of Mysore under Sir Mark Cubbon*, 199.

30. Bowring, *Eastern Experiences*, 58.

31. Ibid., 12.

32. Rice, *Mysore Gazetteer*, 78.

33. C.S Raghunatha Rao, *Mysore*, 196.

34. Malleson, *Seringapatam*, 51; Basappa, *A Guide to Seringapatam*, 12.

35. Rice, *Mysore Gazetteer*, 78.

36. Buchanan, *A Journey from Madras through the Territories of Mysore, Canara and Malabar*, 1:69.

37. Valentia, *Voyages and Travels to India*, 358–59.

38. Beatson, *A View of the Origin and Conduct of the War with Tippoo Sultan*, 234. Mark Cubbon to Secretary, GOI, Pol. Dept., August 25, 1841; For. Pol Pro. October 4–11, 1843, 903, NAI.

39. Cubbon to Secretary, Government of India, For. Pol. Pro. October 4–11, 1843, 903; For. Pol. Pro. October 4–11, 1843, NAI.

40. Cubbon to Secretary, GOI, Pol. Dept., August 25, 1841; For. Pol. Pro. October 4–11, 1843, 903, NAI.

41. Cubbon to Resident at Mysore, August 15, 1841, For. Pol. Pro. October 4–11, 1843, 903; For. Pol. Pro. October 4–11, 1843 NAI.

42. Montgomery to Secretary to Commissioner of Mysore, September 3, 1841, For. Pol. Pro. October 4–11, 1843.

43. Cubbon to Secretary, GOI, For. Pol. Pro. October 4–11, 1843, 903, NAI.

44. Maddock to Commissioner of Mysore, October 4, 1841, For. Pol. Pro. October 4–11, 1843, 903; For. Pol. Pro. October 4–11, 1843, NAI.

45. *The Mysore Gazetteer,* 78.

46. Buchanan, *A Journey from Madras through the Territories of Mysore, Canara and Malabar,* 1:73.

47. Home, *Select Views in Mysore,* 17.

48. Wilks, *Historical Sketches,* 3:238. "Beautiful," as Wilks was obliged to explain in a footnote, "according to the ancient taste of our own country, when it had not begun to abhor straight lines, and imitate nature." See also E. W. Thompson, *The Last Siege,* 74.

49. *Authentic Memoirs of Tippoo Sultaun,* 3.

50. Home, *Select Views in Mysore,* 18.

51. Mark Wilks, Acting Resident, to N. B. Edmondstone, Chief Secretary Fort St. George, December 25, 1804, For. Misc. 1805, Dept. Pol. Cons., April 25, no. 12, in Gopal, *British Sources, 1799–1812,* 86.

52. Moienuddin, *Sunset at Srirangapatam,* 39; CSI St. Stephan's Church, Ootacamund, Niligiris, *175th Anniversary Souvenir,* 1830–2005, souvenir booklet, 6. I am grateful to Anvar for providing this reference.

53. Beatson, *A View of the Origin and Conduct of the War with Tippoo Sultan,* 144.

54. Bowring, *Eastern Experiences,* 56.

55. Malleson, *Seringapatam,* Appendix.

56. On museums as forms of "practical memory," see Benjamin, *The Arcades Project.* The layout of the exhibition at Dariya Daulat is a case in point. The visitor enters the south-facing building through displays of engravings by Robert Orme (after the Mather Brown painting showing the taking of Tipu Sultan's sons as hostages), Henry Singleton's representation of the last effort of Tipu in defense of the portals of Seringapatam, and the storming or siege of Seringapatam by Robert Ker Porter. A panel then introduces both Tipu Sultan and the Duke of Wellington, the latter credited with restoring the palace and renovating the city. The inner halls house the portraits of Tipu's sons by Hickey, along with innumerable British engravings of the forts of Tipu Sultan.

57. *Report on the Administration of the Public Works Department in Mysore for 1886–87; Administration Report of the PWD Mysore State,* 1919–20, 12.

58. Governor General to the Court of Directors, August 3, 1799, in Salmond, *A Review of the Origin, Progress, and Result of the Decisive War,* Appendix (D), no. II, no. 18.

59. Parsons, *Seringapatam,* 18.

60. Ibid., 19–20; Rice, *Mysore Gazetteer,* 299n1.

61. Malleson, *Seringapatam,* vii.

62. Bowring, *Eastern Experiences,* 55.

63. H. S. S. Lawrence, *St. George's Cathedral, Diocese of Madras, Church of South India,* 5. I am grateful to Anvar for this reference.

64. Bowring, *Eastern Experiences,* 12, 55.

65. Wilks, Acting Resident, to Chief Secretary, Fort St. George, October 4, 1805, Mad. Pol. Pro. November 5, 1805, in Gopal, *British Sources, 1799–1812,* 101.

66. Poorneah to the Governor General, August 15, 1809, Ben. Pol. Cons. February 20, 1810 (no. 7), in Gopal, *British Sources, 1799–1812,* 137; Malleson, *Seringapatam,* 60.

67. J. L. Pearse, Superintendent Ashtagram to the Secretary, to Commissioner of Mysore, September 30, 1863, For. Dept. Gen. A, Dec. 1863 51/54, NAI.

68. Bowring, *Eastern Experiences,* 54, 57. When Ghulam Mohamed, the eighth son of

Tipu Sultan who had been exiled to Calcutta, wrote a memorial to the government in 1863 reporting that the tombs of Tipu Sultan and Haidar Ali were being neglected, the Mysore Commissioner, Bowring, was asked to inspect and reply. The tone of his response echoed that of the Superintendent of Ashtagram, Captain J. L. Pearse, who said that "it would [not] be possible to find any other set of buildings in Mysore or Seringapatam whether public or private, so well kept or watertight, and well preserved as those." J. L. Pearse to Secretary for the Commissioner of Mysore, September 22, 1863, For. Dept. Gen. A, December 1863, 51/54, NAI.

69. C. H. Rao, *Mysore Gazetteer,* vol. 5, part 2 (i), 820.

70. Bull, *Romantic Seringapatam,* 27.

71. Ibid., 38.

72. Ibid., 32–33.

73. C. H. Rao, *Mysore Gazetteer,* vol. 5, part 2 (i), 822.

74. Malleson, *Seringapatam,* 10.

75. Thompson, *The Last Siege of Seringapatam,* 7.

76. *Mysore Archaeological Report,* 1935, 55.

77. Campbell, "Tippoo Sultan," 36.

78. Anonymous, *A Visit to Seringapatam* (n.p., n.d.), 18.

79. *Mysore Archaeological Report,* 1935, 155.

80. See also C. H. Rao, *Mysore Gazetteer,* vol. 5, part 2 (i), 811–15.

81. *Mysore Archaeological Report,* 1935, 61.

82. Josiah Webbe, Resident, to Governor, Fort St. George, August 27, 1802, Mad. Pol. Pro. August 31, 1802, in Gopal, *British Sources, 1799–1812,* 1:70.

83. Parsons, *Seringapatam,* 161.

84. File no. 9 of 1914, sl. no. 120, Maramath, KSA.

85. C. H. Rao, *Engravings at Government House,* 14.

86. *Indian Engineering,* 78 (February 20, 1926): 108–9.

87. Bull, *Romantic Seringapatam,* Introduction.

88. Parsons, *Seringapatam,* 162. Even more damning were the words of M. Shama Rao, who called it "a city of ruined ramparts and dilapidated houses with rank vegetation making the place malarial and unhealthy." M. Shama Rao, *Modern Mysore,* 1:5.

89. Thompson, *The Last Siege of Seringapatam,* 74; C. H. Rao, *Mysore Gazetteer,* 2:456.

90. File no. 9 of 1924, Maramath, Mysore Divisional Archives, KSA.

91. Thompson, *The Last Siege of Seringapatam,* 11–14, 60.

92. *Mysore Archaeological Report,* 1935, 60.

93. Leyden, *The Poetical Remains of the Late Dr. John Leyden,* 66.

94. C. H. Rao, *Mysore Gazetteer,* vol. 5, part 2 (i), 808.

95. *Mysore Archaeological Report,* 1912, 2. This assertion was repeated in several subsequent reports and the *Mysore Gazetteer* to give it a sense of authenticity and a claim to truth.

96. Parsons, *Seringapatam,* 60.

97. C. H. Rao, *Engravings at Government House.*

98. Nora, "Between Memory and History," 8–9.

99. Ibid., 9.

100. T. S. Satyan recalls in his memoirs: "My father was a fan of Vishakanta Rao. He had

learnt his lines by heart and would recite them when he was in a relaxed mood or when he was ill and lay in bed with a fever. When he was in a delirious condition, he would begin singing about Tipu Sultan. My siblings and I would stand beside his bed and hear him singing with eyes closed. The louder he sang the higher was his temperature. Or so we thought. When he got better we used to congratulate him on his singing prowess but he would get angry and chastise us for concocting stories." Satyan, *Alive and Clicking*, 14.

101. From *Javid-Namah* (Lahore, 1932), in Persian; excerpted by Macquarie University, Sydney, Australia, at http://www.lib.mq.edu.au/digital/seringapatam/other/iqbal.html (accessed August 27, 2008).

102. *Monuments of Srirangapatna* (New Delhi: Archaeological Survey of India, n.d. [1997?]). See also *Tipu Sultan Museum, Srirangapatna*, brochure, n.d.

4. The Museumized Cityscape of Mysore

1. Brit. Mus. Add. MSS vol. (?), Letter/report from Lt. Col. Kirkpatrick to the Governor General, June 8, 1799, in Gopal, *British Sources, 1799–1812*, 47.

2. Bowring, *Eastern Experiences*, 54. The transformation of an irregular fort (*hudevu*, a circular bastionlike structure of stones to provide rudimentary protection) into a regular fortification (inner enclosure wall, or *valasuttinakote*) occurred in the time of Chamaraja Wodeyar II (1515–53). At that time there were only three temples, a Someswara temple from Chola times, a Bhairava temple, and one to Lakshmi Narayanaswami. C. H. Rao, *History of Mysore under the Wodeyar Dynasty of Kings*, 2:35–36. Even after the shift of the capital to Srirangapatna, Mysore was not ignored, and considerable expansion of the fort of Mysore and its inhabitants occurred in the time of Kantirava Narasaraja Wodeyar I (1638–59) and Chikkadevaraja Wodeyar (1673–1704). Ibid., 176, 388–89. In the time of Haider Ali, Mysore City stood "as the historical capital of the kingdom, by itself with its old fort and its famous temple on the hill closeby." Ibid., 3:515. It was used as an armory by Haider Ali in 1767 against the Marathas. Ibid., 2:26. Devachandra mentions the destruction of Mysore and the construction of Nazarabad by Tipu. Sannaiah, *Rajavali Kathasara*, 307, 353–54.

3. C. H. Rao, *Mysore Gazetteer*, vol. 5, part 2 (i), 753.

4. *Mysore Archaeological Report*, 1909, 26.

5. *Srimanmaharajara Vamshavali*, 2:139–40. Srimushna, near Chidamabaram, South Arcot District, is one of the *ashta swayambhu kshetras*, or eight venerated sites, of Vishnus form, of which one form is Bhuvarahaswami.

6. Ibid.

7. *Mysore Archaeological Report*, 1912, 20.

8. Davis, *Lives of Indian Images*, 76.

9. There is no mention of this traveling idol in *Tirumalarya's Chikadevaraya Vamshavali*, ed. M. A. Ramanuja Iyengar (Mysore, 1933), which was written by Tirumala Iyengar himself in about 1670. The genealogy focuses largely on Dodda Devaraja Wodeyar.

10. According to some accounts, Srirangaraya abdicated his position due to illness and retired to Talakkad. In other accounts, Srirangapatna was won by Raja Wodeyar.

11. A contemporary account by the "descendents" of the Mysore *pradhans* (first coun-

cilors or ministers of the king) claims Tirumala Iyengar as a descendent of Anantachar, who was the first to receive an auspicious grant of eight villages *(ashtagram)* from Vishnu-vardhana Ballala in A.D. 1117. In this narrative, the capital of Mysore had already moved to Srirangapatna in 1421. Iyengar and Char, *The Mysore Pradhans,* 1, 3.

12. *Srimanmaharajara Vamshavali,* 1:133.

13. Ibid., 135–36. C. Hayavadana Rao identifies three phases in the adoption of Srivaish-navism: from 1673 to 1680, Saivism and Jainism flourished alongside one another; from 1686, Srivaishnavism was more pronounced, and from 1693 *purohits* (priests) and scholars began wearing the Srivaishnava marks. C. H. Rao, *History of Mysore under the Wodeyar Dy-nasty of Kings,* 1:36off.

14. *Srimanmaharajara Vamshavali,* 2:140. Mark Wilks noted that the "bigotry led [Tipu] to the extinction of Hindoo worship, and the confiscated funds of the temples were intended to compensate and would if well administered in a great degree have bal-anced the tax on intoxicating substances; the measure commenced in an early period of his reign and the extinction was gradual but in 1799, *the temples within the fort of Seringa-patam* alone remained open throughout the extent of his dominions." Wilks, *Historical Sketches of the South of India,* 2:573–74, my emphasis. The demolition of *gopuras* is not mentioned. This has been repeated by C. H. Rao, *History of Mysore under the Wodeyar Dynasty of Kings,* 3:925.

15. Sannaiah, *Rajavali Kathasara,* 311.

16. Desikacharya, *The Origin and Growth of Sri Brahmatantra Parakala Mutt,* 12.

17. Ibid., 13.

18. Ibid., 17.

19. Ibid., 42.

20. Wilks, *Historical Sketches of the South of India,* 3:468.

21. The Trineshwaraswami temple had been in existence since at least the sixteenth century, when the Mysore fort walls were expanded to include it. *Srimanmaharajara Vam-shavali,* 1:70.

22. C. H. Rao, *History of Mysore under the Wodeyar Dynasty of Kings,* 1:173.

23. Ikegame "The Capital of Rajadharma."

24. Ikegame, "Royalty in Colonial and Post Colonial India," 188–233.

25. Compare, for instance, the descriptions of Srirangapatna and Mysore in C. H. Rao, *History of Mysore under the Wodeyar Dynasty of Kings,* 1:173–80, 388–89.

26. Campbell, "Tippoo Sultan," 25.

27. Bentinck to Lushington, September 6, 1831, For. Dept. Secret, October 7, 1831, NAI.

28. *Mysore District Gazetteer,* 69.

29. Ibid., 67.

30. Bowring, *Eastern Experiences,* 59.

31. *Palace Administration Report,* 1868–1918, 5.

32. Among other things, he feared being slighted by those who might wear shoes while riding in front of his *sowaree* (public procession). Stokes to J. H. Maddock, Secretary to GOI, July 15, 1841, For. Pol., August 2, 1841, no. 127, NAI.

33. Cubbon to Secretary, GOI, August 9, 1841, For. Pol., NAI.

34. J. D. Stokes, Resident of Mysore, to Secretary, GOI, July 23, 1841, For. Pol., NAI.

35. Stokes to Cubbon, July 23, 1841, For. Pol., NAI.

36. Cubbon to Maddock, August 14, 1841, For. Pol. Proceedings, October 4–11, 1841, For. Dept . Pol., NAI.

37. Cubbon to Secretary, GOI, Political Dept., August 2, 1841, For. Pol., NAI.

38. Acting Superintendent Montgomery to Secy to Commissioner for the Territories of Govt of Mysore, August 27, 1841, For. Pol., NAI.

39. From the Commissioner for the Government of the Territories of His Highness the Maharajah of Mysore to the Secretary to the GOI, *Elliott Report,* September 5, 1868, KSA.

40. Ibid.

41. The Commissioner for Mysore to Secretary, GOI, November 10, 1868, *Elliott Report.* For the details on the expansion of this civil list, see chapter 1.

42. List of Immovable Property Belonging to His Highness the Maharaja of Mysore, *Elliott Report,* KSA. There were several other palaces (or large bungalows) for the use of the royal family scattered across southern Mysore, two at Srirangapatna and one each at Chamundi Hills, Melkote, Chamarajnagar, and Allanhalli.

43. Viceroy and Governor General to His Highness the Maharaja of Mysore, August 21, 1876, Palace Papers, 97/30, KSA.

44. Singaraiyya, *Chamarajendra Wodeyaravara Charitre,* 136–46. "In this way, Sri Chamarajendra Wodeyar saw the important temples, world famous waterfalls, unparalleled hills, high mountains, beautiful and dangerous forests, historic old towns, and other important places, understood the woes and pleasures of his people, earned their praise" (146).

45. *Correspondence Relating to Native Government in Mysore.* There were proposals to bring the prince to study in Bangalore and remove him from the adverse influence of the palace. C. B. Saunders, Officiating Commissioner, Mysore, to Secretary, GOI, For. Dept., July 2, 1867; Officiating Secretary to Chief Commissioner of Mysore, to Secretary to GOI, For. Dept., November 12, 1873.

46. Singaraiyya, *Chamrajendra Wodeyaravara Charitre,* 85

47. Ibid. Almost identical efforts were made in the nineteenth century by his Travancore counterparts, Uthram Thirunal Marthanda Varma and Ayilyam Thirunal. *Travancore Administration Report,* 1936–37, 249.

48. Manu Bhagwan has shown that the Maharaja of Baroda also adopted many of the signs of modernity and won the praise of his British masters, until he defied the protocols of the imperial durbar of 1911. Baroda's modernity was thus a form of resistance to the colonial order. Bhagwan, *Sovereign Spheres,* 8.

49. Rice, *Mysore Gazetteer,* 277.

50. *Indian Engineering,* August 18, 1894.

51. Ibid.

52. C. H. Rao's comments were similarly disparaging: he called the style that had evolved from the mingling of western norms and Indian interpreters a "mongrel" style, singling out only the new guest mansion (the new palace) then under construction for praise. See C. H. Rao, *Mysore Gazetteer,* 2:378–79.

53. See, for instance, Issar, *The Royal City,* 60–61.

54. Ismail, *My Public Life,* 34.

55. Ibid., 59, my emphasis.

56. Ikegame, "The Capital of Rajadharma," 18–19.

57. Ibid.

58. On the evolution of conceptions of kingship in European history, see Kantorowicz, *The King's Two Bodies.*

59. Bennett, "The Exhibitionary Complex"; Greenberg, Ferguson, and Nairne, *Thinking about Exhibitions,* 84.

60. Ibid., 95.

61. Price, *Kingship and Political Practice in Colonial India,* 158.

62. Sandria Freitag develops the term "public arena" in preference to Jürgen Habermas's term "public sphere" to include, for the Indian subcontinent, not only "Habermas' communication / surveillance functions . . . but also cultural expression of this knowledge in public." The term "public arena" encompasses the print media as well as performance, architecture, etc. Freitag, "More than Meets the (Hindu) Eye," 95. See also Freitag, *Collective Action and Community.*

63. Pvt. Secy to Maharaja to Dewan Krishnamurti, February 10, 1904, file no. 73, 1904, sl. no. 1-7, Mysore Residency, NAI.

64. N. Krishnamurti to Bourdillon, February 12, 1904, file no. 73, 1904, sl. no. 1-7, Mysore Residency, NAI.

65. Ibid.

66. As cited in Issar, *The Royal City,* 46–47.

67. *Palace Administration Report from 1868 to 1918,* 5.

68. Commissioner to Secretary of State for India, September 28, 1868, *Correspondence Relating to the Native Government in Mysore,* 52.

69. Dewan's Office Files, 1897, KSA.

70. *Indian Engineering,* April 10, 1897, and October 1, 1898. H. C. Irwin (1841–1922), a student of the "founder" of the Indo-Saracenic as an architectural style in India, Robert Chisholm, used Indian design elements, in particular the dome and arch, for a series of public buildings in Madras, such as the university, state bank, post office, and law courts. Metcalf, *An Imperial Vision,* 58, 82–85.

71. On the development of the Indo-Saracenic style in the latter half of the nineteenth century, see Metcalf, *An Imperial Vision,* 55–104.

72. *Indian Engineering,* December 3, 1910.

73. C. H. Rao, *Mysore Gazetteer,* vol. 5, part 2 (1), Mysore District, 764.

74. *Madras Mail,* June 2, 1909, in *Selections from the Records of the Mysore Palace,* 2:211.

75. Ismail, *My Public Life,* 49–50.

76. Mysore City Inspection by the Dewan on the 23rd October 1916, in *Selections from the Records of the Mysore Palace,* 2:26.

77. Proceedings of the Government of His Highness the Maharaja of Mysore, in *Selections from the Records of the Mysore Palace,* 2:194–95.

78. C. H. Rao, *Mysore Gazetteer,* vol. 5, part 2 (1), Mysore District, 741.

79. File no. 315 of 1906, sl. no. 87/91, General Miscellaneous, KSA. Krumbiegal had had an apprenticeship in the royal gardens at Pillnitz and the fruit gardens at Schwerine

in Germany and also acquired experience working at Hyde Park and Kew Gardens in England in the late nineteenth century. At first employed in Baroda, where he looked after thirty gardens, Krumbiegal joined the Mysore government in 1908.

80. Krumbiegal, "Mysore," 57.

81. File no. 19, 1918, vol. 4, Krumbiegal to Mirza, October 24, 1918, in *Selections from the Records of the Mysore Palace*, 2:126.

82. James Holston's *The Modernist City*, 119–26, has the most systematic exposition of the transformation of city space in Brasília, and particularly of the new relationship between figure and ground that was forged there.

83. Parsons, *Mysore City*, 136.

84. Marginal notes, Executive Engineer to Huzur Secretary, December 18–19, 1919, file no. 14.1919, Maramath, Mysore Divisional Archives, KSA.

85. C. H. Rao, *Mysore Gazetteer*, vol. 5, part 2 (1), Mysore District, 746.

86. Ibid., 746–47.

87. *Administration Report for the Mysore Public Works Department, 1906–07*, 15.

88. C. H. Rao, *Mysore Gazetteer*, vol. 5, part 2 (1), Mysore District, 747.

89. Krishnamurti to Machonochie, September 3, 1904, file no. 3 of 1904, sl. no. 24, Maramath, Mysore Divisional Archives, KSA.

90. Raghavendra Rao to K. Subbaroyer, March 9, 1907, file no. 3 of 1904, sl. no. 24, Maramath, Mysore Divisional Archives, KSA.

91. E. Machonochie to Madhava Rao, August 7, 1907, file no. 3 of 1904, sl. no. 24, Maramath, Mysore Divisional Archives, KSA.

92. Order no. R 1564-7/L-R-11507-1, Bangalore, August 24, 1907, file no. 53, 1910–12, vol. 2, Mysore Divisional Archives, KSA.

93. M. Visvesvaraya to Mirza Ismail, file no. 13 of 1913, sl. no. 9, Maramath, Mysore Divisional Archives, KSA.

94. Lakshmi Kantharaj Urs to Raghavendra Rao, Huzur Secretary, August 12, 1912, file no. 18/1916, sl. no. 53, Maramath, Mysore Divisional Archives, KSA.

95. M. G. Krishnaswami Rao, Vice President, City Municipal Council, to M. Lakshmi Kantharaj Urs, August 10, 1912, file no. 9 of 1912, sl. no. 66, Maramath, Mysore Divisional Archives, KSA.

96. M. Visvesvaraya to Mirza Ismail, September 13, 1913, file no. 13 of 1913, sl. no. 9, Maramath, Mysore Divisional Archives, KSA.

97. Mirza Ismail to M. Visvevaraya, November 29, 1913, file no. 13 of 1913, sl. no. 9, Maramath, Mysore Divisional Archives, KSA.

98. J. Govinda Row, Secretary to Dewan, to Raghavendra Rao, Huzur Secretary to Maharaja, July 15, 1912, file no. 9 of 1912, sl. no. 66, Maramath, Mysore Divisional Archives; General Order no. Mily [Military], 1359-63/221-09-8, April 25, 1911, file no. 1 of 1910, Maramath, Mysore Divisional Archives, KSA.

99. V. R. Thyagaraja Iyer, Secretary to Government, Revenue Department, to H. Ramakrishna Rao, Palace Controller, June 10, 1916, file no. 26 of 1914, Maramath, Mysore Divisional Archives, KSA.

100. Mirza Ismail to M. Visvesvaraya, July 24, 1914, file no. 25 of 1914, sl. no. 136, Maramath, Mysore Divisional Archives, KSA.

101. V. R. Thyagaraja Iyer, Secretary to Government, Revenue Department, to H. Rama-

krishna Rao, Palace Controller, June 10, 1916, file no. 26 of 1914, Maramath, Mysore Divisional Archives, KSA; note on letter dated June 29, 1917, from Sirdar Lakshmi Kantharaj Urs, file no. 18/1916, sl. no. 53, Maramath, Mysore Divisional Archives, KSA. For a similar ruling against Venkatappa, see chapter 5.

102. File no. 18/1916, sl. no. 53, Maramath, Mysore Divisional Archives, KSA.

103. Lakshmi Kantharaj Urs to Mirza, April 21, 1919; Mirza to Lakshmi Kantharaj Urs, April 23, 1919, file no. 18/1916, sl. no. 53, Maramath, Mysore Divisional Archives, KSA.

104. Krumbiegal to Thumboo Chetty, August 12, 1918, file no. 18/1916, sl. no. 53, Maramath, Mysore Divisional Archives, KSA.

105. H. V. Bapat, Assistant Engr., Palace Maramath, November 18, 1927, file no. 34/1928, Mysore Divisional Archives, KSA.

106. Cannadine, *Ornamentalism*, 48.

107. Mirza asked Krumbiegal to redesign the corners of the Jaganmohan palace wall, including the removal of "ugly elephants." Mirza to Krumbiegal, July 8, 1913, file no. 27/1913, Mysore Divisional Archives, KSA.

108. Edwin Woollaston Fritchley was born of poor Anglo-Indian parents and worked his way up as an architect until he secured a junior partnership with a firm in Bombay, which he left shortly afterward to start a firm of his own. His association with the Mysore palace began around 1910 and continued until his death in the 1920s. *Daily Post,* March 24, 1926. Fritchley's continuous renegotiation of his terms and his attempt to get the Mysore government to guarantee him all new buildings in Mysore exasperated Mirza on more than one occasion. The establishment of the Mysore Palace Division to undertake the building of the Mysore palace in the late nineteenth century, and that of the Architects' Division in 1917, headed by S. H. Lakshminarasappa, helped the palace to remain self-reliant, often taking only the drawings from architects elsewhere and leaving the supervision to the palace employees themselves. Karpur Srinivas Rao to Mirza, September 6, 1917, file no. 25/1917, Mysore Divisional Archives, KSA.

109. E. W. Fritchley to Raghavendra Rao, January 3, 1910, file no. 1 of 1903, sl. no. 22, Fort Palace Construction Works, Maramath, Mysore Divisional Archives, KSA.

110. Frtichley to Mirza, October 15, 1918, file no. 5 of 1910, Maramath, Mysore Divisional Archives, KSA.

111. Fritchley to Mirza, January 15, 1917 and Mirza to Fritchley, January 19, 1917, file 1916 to 35–52, sl. no. 106, Maramath, KSA. The Kapurthala palace was designed by French architect M. Marcel, who "combined elements from Fontainebleu and the Louvre to create a vision of a French chateau on the plains of the Punjab." The decorations were from France, and the Kapurthala prince Jagatjit Singh played out his dreams of being a sun king like Louis XIV, after whom the reception hall was named. Metcalf, *An Imperial Vision,* 121.

112. File no. 34/1916, sl. no. 5, Correspondence with E. W Fritchley, vol. 1, Maramath, Mysore Divisional Archives, KSA.

113. Fritchley to Mirza, June 29, 1917, file no. 143/4, Maramath, Mysore Divisional Archives, KSA.

114. As, for instance, in Fritchley's decision to include a "winter garden," which was vetoed by Krumbiegal. Krumbiegal to Mirza, April 12, 1918, file no. 1, sl. no. 1, Correspondence with Mr. E. W. Fritchley, vol. 2, Maramath, Mysore Divisional Archives, KSA.

115. Mirza to Krumbiegal, June 13, 1919, sl. no. 3, 1919, New Mansion Construction, vol. 4, Maramath, Mysore Divisional Archives, KSA.

116. Mirza to Krumbiegal, March 28, 1918, sl. no. 12, New Mansion: Mr. Fritchley, 1918–19, Maramath, Mysore Divisional Archives, KSA.

117. Dewan's Office Files, 1897, KSA.

118. See chapter 2.

119. See Dirks, *The Hollow Crown*, 390–1.

120. *Indian Engineering*, October 1, 1898. In 1903, the *Times of India* had already anticipated that it would be "among the modern architectural triumphs of India." *Times of India*, August 5, 1903. The report described the palace grounds at the time of the construction as "a huge technical school, where a thousand to 1,200 people were learning skills in chiseling stone, making screens, carving wood and inlaying ivory in wooden panels."

121. *Palace Administration Report from 1868 to 1918*, 21.

122. Raghavendra Rao to Govinda Rao, July 26, 1910, Maramath, in *Selections from the Records of the Mysore Palace*, 2:12.

123. *Administration Report for the PWD*, 1916–17, 7; 1920–21, 7.

124. Ikegame, "The Capital of Rajadharma," 35. Palace temples came under the care of the Muzrai Department.

125. Stein, "Idiom and Ideology in Early Nineteenth Century South India," esp. 40.

126. Note on the Construction of the Permanent Durbar Hall and the Method of Financing the Same, file no. 11 of 1930, sl. no. 522, Maramath, Mysore Divisional Archives, KSA. Emphasis added.

127. Ibid.

128. Ikegame, "The Capital of Rajadharma," 33.

129. T. Thumboo Chetty to Mirza Ismail, October 19, 1936, file no. 14/1936, Dasara, Mysore Divisional Archives, KSA.

130. File no. 14/1936, Dasara, Mysore Divisional Archives, KSA. A senior (non-Brahman) bureaucrat, A. V. Ramanathan, reminded the committee that the Dasara Durbar was a state and not a religious occasion. Brahman members proposed various degrees of concession: the historian M. Shama Rao pleaded that the Dasara Durbar was historically a political ceremony with no religious significance, but Adi Karnatakas were prohibited because they were "passionate" and "crude." Others recommended that entry of Adi Karnatakas be restricted to the nonreligious ceremonies or, alternatively, that religious ceremonies not be carried out before the public durbar.

131. Thamboo Chetty to Mirza Ismail, October 19, 1936, file. no. 14/1936, Dasara, Mysore Divisional Archives, KSA.

132. Price, *Kingship and Political Practice in Colonial India*, 159.

133. DVG, "A Gentleman to the Press Too,"115.

134. In 1894, *Indian Engineering* opined, "Neither durability not architectural effect have been secured by the State Engineer, in the design and execution of buildings, notwithstanding the expenditure of enormous sums of public funds." *Indian Engineering*, August 18, 1894. By 1927 a writer for the journal said, "The Mysore City is also studded all over with stately buildings, well designed unlike the monotonous piles built at Delhi by the European Architects. I was particularly struck by the design and situation of the new Guest

House they are building to the east of the city, which was designed by Mr. Pritchery [sic; Fritchley] and is estimated to cost Rs 3.0 million. It is not as ornate as the palaces at Mysore and Baroda, but it is certainly more comfortable." *Indian Engineering*, July 23, 1927.

135. Note on the construction of the Permanent Durbar Hall and the Method of Financing the Same, file no. 11 of 1930, sl. no. 522, Maramath, Mysore Divisional Archives, KSA.

136. To the Chief Secretary, no date, file no. 4 of 1929, sl. no. 501, Maramath, Mysore Divisional Archives, KSA. Lakshminarasappa was a Liverpool-trained architect who returned to Mysore in 1917 and was made the head of the new Architects' Division at the palace. He later moved to Bangalore to become, first, head of the engineering college and then the chief architect of the Mysore government. Karpur Srinivas Rao to Mirza, September 6, 1917, file no. 25/1917, Mysore Divisional Archives, KSA. See also file no. 17 of 1917, vol. 11, sl. no. 31, Maramath, Mysore Divisional Archives, KSA.

137. Note on the Design of the New Durbar Hall, January 11, 1933, in *Selections from the Records of the Mysore Palace*, 2:69.

138. Instructions of His Highness Conveyed through the Kille Cutcherry Bakshi, on November 19, 1932, in *Selections from the Records of the Mysore Palace*, 2:70, 72, 73.

139. Palace Engineer to Huzur Secretary, April 5, 1941, file no. 5/1940, Maramath, Mysore Divisional Archives, KSA.

140. File no. 31 of 1932, sl. no. 576, Maramath, Mysore Divisional Archives, KSA. The invitation to the competition specified that the designs should conform to the *shilpasastras*.

141. Proceedings of the Durbar Hall Committee Meeting Held on Friday the 11th of May 1934, file no. 2, 1934, Maramath, Mysore Divisional Archives, KSA.

142. Letter to Chief Secretary, Government of Mysore, December 27, 1929, file no. 4 of 1929, Maramath, Mysore Divisional Archives, KSA, my emphasis.

143. File no. 3 of 1949, sl. no. 845, Maramath, Mysore Divisional Archives, KSA.

144. Ikegame suggests that the reorientation of temples to face the palace in the fort complex was done in order to symbolically emphasize the king as the focus of the dharmic order. Ikegame, "Royalty in Colonial and Post Colonial India," 235, 261 ff. However, this does not explain the other liberties taken in certain aspects of fort and temple construction.

145. Krumbiegal to Mirza, 222/October 24, 1918, in *Selections from the Records of the Mysore Palace*, 2:126.

146. Ibid.

147. Ibid.

148. File no. 31 or 1932, sl. no. 576, Maramath, Mysore Divisional Archives, KSA.

149. *Palace Administration Report for the Year 1927–28*, 3.

150. Metcalf, *An Imperial Vision*, 80.

151. Sennett, *The Conscience of the Eye*, 178, my emphasis.

152. Ikegame, "The Capital of Rajadharma," 31–32.

153. Ibid., 31. I briefly discussed a similar logic that underlay the building of the Malleswaram and Basavangudi extensions in Bangalore at the turn of the twentieth century in Nair, *The Promise of the Metropolis*, 50–53.

154. Memorandum of K. Seshadri Iyer, Dewan of Mysore, August 3, 1897, file no. 1 of 1897, Jagan Mohan Palace, vol. 1, Maramath, Mysore Divisional Archives, KSA.

155. Palace Controller to V. Anjanswami Iyer, Exec. Engineer, Palace Division, September 27, 1898, Maramath, Mysore Divisional Archives, KSA.

156. It is tempting to find a parallel here between the search for a Rajputana family connection and the choice of Rajputana domes for the main palace!

157. M. Visvesvaraya to Raghavendra Rao, April 22, 1912, in *Selections from the Records of the Mysore Palace*, 2:142.

158. S. P. Rajagopalachari (for Huzur Secretary) to Executive Engineer, Special Division, Mysore, May 5, 1926, Maramath, in *Selections from the Records of the Mysore Palace*, 2:149. Palace Controller [?] to Hiriyannaiya, Secretary to Dewan of Mysore, July 17, 1917, Maramath, Mysore Divisional Archives, KSA.

159. File no. 2 of 1913, sl. no. 80, Maramath, Mysore Divisional Archives, KSA.

160. Cousins and Cousins, *We Two Together*, 415; Chitrasala, "Mysore," 76. See also, Cousins to Thumboo Chetty, July 3, 1924, file no. 30, vol. 5, Mysore Divisional Archives, KSA.

161. *Palace Administration Report (PAR)*, 1927–28, 22; *PAR*, 1931–32, 33; *PAR*, 1932–33, 26; *PAR*, 1934–35, 21; *PAR*, 1943–44, 24; *PAR*, 1945–46, 31.

162. See chapter 2.

163. What follows is an extremely abbreviated version of a full-length article on the Mysore Dasara Exhibition. "Mysore's Wembley? The Dasara Exhibition's Imagined Economies" (forthcoming).

164. Progs. of the GOI in For. Pol., April 26, 1878, file no. 22 of 1876, sl. no. 1-20, General Miscellaneous, KSA.

165. File no. 366 of 1905, sl. nos. 1 and 2, General Miscellaneous, KSA; Progs. of the Government of Mysore, file no. 535-05, sl. nos. 1 and 9, October 1905, General Miscellaneous, KSA.

166. Dewan N. Krishnamurti to Resident Williams, September 3, 1905, Williams to Krishnamurti, September 16, 1905, and Krishnamurti to Williams, September 24, 1905, file no. 535-05, sl. nos. 1 and 9, October 9, 1905, General Miscellaneous, KSA.

167. President's Address, Mysore Dasara Agricultural and Industrial Exhibition, and arrangement of lectures for Raiyats and Artisans, file no. 1/1907, sl. no. 11, Dasara, Mysore Divisional Archives, KSA.

168. Ibid.

169. Dr. Palpu, Office of the Sanitary Commissioner with Government of Mysore, to Raghavendra Rao, October 25, 1909, file no. 2/1909, Dasara, Mysore Divisional Archives, KSA.

170. Kantharaja Urs to Mirza Ismail, March 15, 1920, file no. 9/1919, Dasara, Mysore Divisional Archives, KSA.

171. *Mysore Information Bulletin*, 1939–1941 (selected issues).

172. *Mysore Information Bulletin* 3, no. 11 (November 1940): 339.

173. Sreenivasan, *The Last Mysore Pradhan*, 107–29.

174. Ibid., 113–14.

175. Ibid., 124.

176. *Palace Administration Report for 1947–48*, 10.

177. See Nair, *The Promise of the Metropolis*, 200–33.

178. Trouillot, *Silencing the Past*, xix.

5. K. Venkatappa and the Fashioning of a Mysore Modern in Art

1. K. Venkatappa Diary (hereafter Diary), June 2, 1916, K. Venkatappa Private Papers (hereafter KVPP), KSA.

2. Raghavendra Rao, Private Secretary to the Maharaja of Mysore, to Raghavalu Naidu, Electrical Engineer, Palace Division, June 12, 1905, KVPP, KSA.

3. Thakurta, *The Making of a New "Indian" Art.*

4. Venkatachallam, *Contemporary Indian Painters,* 21, 65; Jaya Appasamy says he represented "an unsophisticated and indigenous aspect of the Bengal School." Appasamy, "He Created a New Indian Style," 71. P. R. Rao, *Modern Indian Painting,* 12; Mitter, *The Triumph of Modernism.* Mitter classifies Venkatappa as a regional expression of academic naturalism, moving from "orientalist historicism" to a "very personal form of naturalism" and finally shedding his allegiance to oriental art altogether to embark on a "careful empirical exploration of nature" (65).

5. Bourdieu, *The Field of Cultural Production,* 54.

6. This article only briefly discusses Venkatappa's works, focusing instead on the conditions of artistic production.

7. Kapur, "When Was Modernism in Indian Art?"

8. Venkatachalam, *Contemporary Indian Painters;* S. K. R. Rao, *K. Venkatappa;* Subrahmanyam, *Venkatappa.* Even critics who are more willing and able to demystify this artist usually do so through an evaluation of his art work alone. Kasi, "Odedha Kannadi," 42.

9. Bourdieu, *The Field of Cultural Production,* 40.

10. Tagore, "The Three Forms of Art," 393. A. K. Coomaraswamy delivered a similar indictment of the artist who longed to be "hung" or "shown" in a museum, "for things are made normally for certain purposes and certain places to which they are appropriate and not simply for exhibition because whatever is custom made, i.e., made by an artist for a consumer is controlled by certain requirements and kept in order." Coomaraswamy, *Christian and Oriental Philosophy of Art,* 7.

11. V. Sitaramaiah, *K. Venkatappa,* i; S. K. R. Rao, *K. Venkatappa,* 13; Sundar, *Patrons and Philistines,* 113.

12. Memo, file no. 33, Chitrasala Department, Mysore Divisonal Archives, KSA.

13. Aiyer, "Indian Arts and Crafts," 58. Indeed, E. B. Havell expressed dismay over the dilution of caste as a marker of tradition when he wrote that "students not belonging to the weaving caste" used the Serampore Central Weaving College as a passport to work in Swadeshi factories. Havell, *Artistic and Industrial Revival in India,* 136.

14. Today at Shashwati Museum, NMKRV College, Bangalore.

15. Ravi Varma and his brother asked for music from the finest at the Mysore Palace School of Music. Sl. no. B 190, 1904, Chitrasala Department, Mysore Divisional Archives. Even his son, Rama Varma, was able to turn his father's reputation to his advantage when he received Rs 1,000 as payment for the painting of *Harishchandra* in 1914. Palace Memo 8.2.194, in *Selections from the Records of the Mysore Palace,* 246.

16. Thakurta, *The Making of a New "Indian" Art,* 277–84; see also Indian Society for Oriental Art, *Special Issue on Abanindranath Tagore.*

17. "Exhibition at the Government School of Art," 76.

18. K. Keshavaiah to Maharaja of Mysore, July 22, 1903, in *Selections from the Records of the Mysore Palace*, 247.

19. Mitter, *Art and Nationalism in Colonial India*, 55, 318. Suniti Kumar Chatterjee similarly noted that neither the Calcutta School nor Santiniketan drew students belonging to the hereditary artisan castes or guilds. Chatterjee, "The Revival of Indian Art and the Lucknow School of Arts," 404.

20. Thakurta, *The Making of a New "Indian" Art*, 270.

21. Mitter, *Art and Nationalism in Colonial India*, 313.

22. Nivedita and Coomaraswamy, *Myths of the Hindus and Buddhists*; Tagore, "Indian Iconography"; Diary, February 13, 1914, March 8, 1920, and June 21, 1920, KVPP, KSA. It is not quite clear whether Venkatappa was a member of the team that accompanied Lady Herringham to the Ajanta caves in 1910–11, but see Mitter, *Art and Nationalism in Colonial India*, 305. Contrast Thakurta, *The Making of a New "Indian" Art*, 278.

23. JDW, "The India Society," 161. See also Coomaraswamy, *Art and Swadeshi*, 132–33, for an appreciation of Venkatappa's early work.

24. N. Vyasa Ram, "The New Spirit in Indian Art," 298.

25. Diary, July 27, 1923, KVPP, KSA.

26. Diary, May 15, 1914, KVPP, KSA.

27. Diary, May 31, 1916, KVPP, KSA.

28. Venkatappa to Inspector General of Education in Mysore, December 13, 1916; Percy Brown to Private Secretary, Maharaja of Mysore, February 17, 1916, KVPP, KSA; Diary, July 8, 1916. This was later interpreted as the Mysore government's reluctance to risk "a great loss to the art world" by sending Venkatappa to a war-torn Europe. See "Veeneya Hucchu Chitra Parichaya," *Prabuddha Karnataka* 10, no. 1 (1928): 5–12, quote on 6. His colleagues from the Calcutta school, Asit Haldar and Promode Kumar Chatterjee, both went to Europe in the 1920s, and Haldar came back, in Abanindranath's words, "perfectly cured of foreign ideas." Abanindranath Tagore to E. B. Havell, September 5, 1925, as cited in S. K. R. Rao, *K. Venkatappa*, 104.

29. Diary, January 24, 1918, and January 30, 1918, KVPP, KSA. See also Cousins, *The Music of the Orient and Occident*, 150.

30. Diary, August 16, 1916, KVPP, KSA; Diary, March 31, 1917, KVPP, KSA.

31. Diary, February 14, 1918; see also June 26, 1918, KVPP, KSA.

32. Diary, June 4, 1916, KVPP, KSA; Diary, July 8, 1916, KVPP, KSA.

33. Diary, February 14, 1918, KVPP, KSA. Similarly, Keshavaiah was asked to paint a portrait of Dewan Purnaiah for the Victoria Memorial. File no. 30, 1899–1913–1927, Jagan Mohan Palace and Chitrasala, 6-8-1905, Mysore Divisional Archives, KSA.

34. Venkatesh, *K. Keshavayya*, 10–11.

35. Petition of K. Keshavaiah, June 6, 1925, in *Selections from the Records of the Mysore Palace*, 257.

36. Letter dated July 22, 1903, and letter dated June 6, 1925, in ibid., 257.

37. See Thakurta, *The Making of a New "National" Art*, 276.

38. D/O no. 163/1, List, July 30, 1917, in *Selections from the Records of the Mysore Palace*, 251.

39. Keshavaiah to Darbar Bakshi, October 11, 1928, in ibid., 259.

40. S. Shankar Raju to Huzur Secretary, November 24, 1943, Chitrasala Department, Mysore Divisional Archives, KSA.

41. B. Ramkrishna to Thamboo Chetty, October 20, 1916, file no. 8, sl. no. 4, box 17, Chitrasala Department, Mysore Divisional Archives, KSA.

42. S. Raghavulu Nayudu, Executive Engineer, Palace Division, Recommendation, December 16, 1908, file no. 1/1908, Maramath Department, Mysore Divisional Archives, KSA.

43. Maramath Department to Officer in Charge of Palace Establishment, June 18, 1911, file no. 1/1908, Maramath Department, Mysore Divisional Archives, KSA; Memo, Assistant Engineer, HQ Range 1916, file no. 1/1908, Maramath Department, Mysore Divisional Archives, KSA.

44. See chapter 1, "Perspective on a Decisive Battle." File no. 21 of 1916, sl. no. 1-90, Maramath Department, Mysore Divisional Archives, KSA.

45. Lakshman Krishna to Assistant Engineer, Palace Maramath Department, July 4, 1917, file no. 1/1908, Maramath Department, Mysore Divisional Archives, KSA.

46. *PAR,* 1934–43.

47. Ramakrishna Rao to Thumboo Chetty, June 10, 1916, and July 5, 1916, file no. 30, vol. 3, Jagan Mohan Palace and Chitrasala, Mysore Divisional Archives, KSA.

48. Diary, August 11, 1916, KVPP, KSA.

49. Diary, February 3, 1918, KVPP, KSA.

50. Diary, January 2, 1924, KVPP, KSA.

51. On April 9, 1924, he went to a public library to consult the New International Dictionary for "the exact difference between artisan and artist." Diary, April 9, 1924, KVPP, KSA. The word *craftsman* was heavily crossed out in Venkatappa's copy of Venkatachalam, *Contemporary Indian Painters,* 39. Curiously, Venkatappa seems to have either missed or ignored P. R. Rao's even more damning indictment that he was "unresponsive to his milieu [and] his output has an archaic quality which is informed, at his best, with delicacy and charm." P. R. Rao, *Modern Indian Painting,* 20. G. Venkatachalam referred to him as "a skilled craftman, with a supreme command over his technique," and as a "colorist of the first order." Venkatachalam, *Contemporary Indian Painters,* 39.

52. Venkatappa to Tiger Varadachari, November 15, 1935, KVPP, KSA.

53. S. K. R. Rao, *K. Venkatappa,* 30.

54. Ibid., 31; Kasi, "Odedha Kannadi," 34; M. S. Nanjunda Rao, "Varnamaya Baduku," 38.

55. Kasi, "Odedha Kannadi," 34.

56. Venkatachalam, *Contemporary Indian Artists,* 41.

57. Diary, September 28, 1922, KVPP, KSA.

58. Venkatappa to Cousins, June 4, 1928, KVPP, KSA.

59. A. Coomaraswamy, "About Pictures," 523.

60. An anonymous article suggested that he be given a chair of fine arts at Calcutta University. "Indian Art at the Calcutta University," 34.

61. Sen, "The Rise and Decadence of Art in India," 602.

62. Ramanand, "The Fine Arts in India," 97.

63. AC, "Indian Art and Art Critics," 132.

64. The words were Surendranath Mallik's, spoken during a debate in the Bengal Legislative Assembly. "Indian Art," 402.

65. See Thakurta, "Westernisation and Tradition in South Indian Painting," 191.

66. See, for instance, the report on Mr. Solomon's speech at Bombay, calling for the

careful cultivation of bourgeois patrons. "Mr. Solomon on Indian Art," *Rupam* 2, no. 8 (1921): 36.

67. Mitter, *Art and Nationalism in Colonial India*, 64; report no. 62/20/21, 948, from officer-in-charge Chitrasala, Chitrasala Department, Mysore Divisional Archives, KSA.

68. JDW, "The India Society," 161; Sen, "The Exhibition of Oriental Art," 438; Venkatappa to Huzur Secretary, December 6, 1935, KVPP, KSA.

69. "James H. Cousins," *Modern Review* 59, no. 1 (1936): 110.

70. Cousins and Cousins, *We Two Together*, 260–61.

71. See Cousins, *The Renaissance in India, Aesthetical Necessity in Life*, and *The Social Value of Arts and Crafts*.

72. Diary, September 16, 1923, KVPP, KSA.

73. Diary, September 28, 1923, KVPP, KSA; Cousins to Venkatappa, September 21, 1923, KVPP, KSA; Cousins and Cousins, *We Two Together*, 415; *Gallery of Indian Paintings*, 76. See also Cousins to Thumboo Chetty, July 3, 1924, file no. 30, vol. 5, Mysore Divisional Archives, KSA. Cousins to Venkatappa, September 3, 1924, KVPP, KSA.

74. *Gallery of Indian Paintings*, 75, my emphasis.

75. Cousins to Venkatappa, August 31, 1927, KVPP, KSA; S. Fyzee Rahamin, Society for Encouragement of Indian Art, to Venkatappa, July 29, 1927, KVPP, KSA. A diary entry records that Rs 630 was received as payment from Cousins for the two paintings bought by the yuvaraja after the 10 percent commission. Diary, August 6, 1924, KVPP, KSA; Diary, February 14, 1923, March 15, 1923, April 27, 1923, and May 26, 1923, KVPP, KSA.

76. Abanindranath to Venkatappa, no date, KVPP, KSA.

77. Tagore to Venkatappa, March 24, 1922, KVPP, KSA. Indeed, it is more than likely that the theme suggested itself to Venkatappa after he received Abanindranath's letter telling him that "painting was his first wife" and music only "his second." Abanindranath to Venkatappa, November 2, no year, KVPP, KSA.

78. Treasurywalla to Venkatappa, March 3, 1922; Diary, October 27, 1922, KVPP, KSA.

79. Diary, February 4, 1923, KVPP, KSA.

80. *Gallery of Indian Paintings*, 76.

81. Cousins to Venkatappa, November 25, 1929, KVPP, KSA.

82. Venkatachalam to Venkatappa, June 7, 1927, July 1, 1927, July 8, 1927; August 2, 1927, February 14, 1930, July 19, 1934, August 27, 1944, and August 22, 1950, KVPP, KSA.

83. Cousins to Venkatappa, February 19, 1928, KVPP, KSA.

84. These are evident from the seals on the letters preserved by Venkatappa; the actual details of the two cases are not known.

85. Ram, "The New Spirit in Indian Art," 303.

86. Venkatappa to Cousins, June 4, 1928, KVPP, KSA.

87. See, for instance, Karanth, *Bharatiya Chitra Kala*, 45.

88. *The Karnataka Handbook*, 165.

89. *Gallery of Indian Paintings*, 77.

90. Venkatappa to Cousins, August 3, 1938, KVPP, KSA.

91. Venkatappa to Cousins, October 7, 1926, KVPP, KSA; G. Venkatachalam to Venkatappa, October 26, 1925, KVPP, KSA.

92. Cousins to Venkatappa, December 23, 1925, KVPP, KSA.

93. He wanted Rs 3,000 for the portrait in ivory, Rs 1,500 for the bust on paper, and Rs 2,500 for a full-length portrait.

94. Diary, August 25, 1924, KVPP, KSA.

95. Diary, July 14, 1926, KVPP, KSA.

96. Diary, October 19, 1923, and June 8, 1924, KVPP, KSA.

97. Venkatachalam to Venkatappa, January 29, 1925, and August 16, 1925, KVPP, KSA.

98. Treasuryvalla to Venkatappa, May 21, 1920; Diary, May 22, 1920, KVPP, KSA.

99. Treasuryvalla to Venkatappa, June 25, 1921, KVPP, KSA.

100. Treasuryvalla to Venkatappa, July 20, 1921, KVPP, KSA.

101. Treasuryvalla to Venkatappa, December 26, 1923, KVPP, KSA.

102. Diary, September 18, 1924, September 21, 1924, September 27, 1924, September 29, 1924, and October 2, 1924, KVPP, KSA.

103. Khusru Jung to Venkatappa, March 28, 1925, and July 16, 1925, KVPP, KSA. The mythology of Venkatappa has it that he finally refused to alter "the drunkard's nose." Venkatachalam, "The Artist with Strong Character," 57.

104. Diary, September 8, 1924, KVPP, KSA; Diary, April 11 and April 24, 1926, KVPP, KSA; Diary, July 14, 1926, KVPP, KSA.

105. Diary, September 9, 1924; *Amba Vilas Durbar Hall, Mysore,* brochure of text and drawings at Venkatappa Art Gallery, Bangalore.

106. Undated memo, Subjects for Paintings on the Wall of Amba Vilas by Venkatappa, KVPP, KSA.

107. Venkatachalam to Venkatappa, August 9, 1927, KVPP, KSA.

108. Diary, December 17, 1928, KVPP, KSA; Diary, January 2, 1929, KVPP, KSA; file no. 33, sl. no. 11, Office Order dated January 30, 1929, Chitrasala Department, Mysore Divisional Archives, Mysore.

109. *PAR,* 1928–29, 20.

110. The annual *Palace Administration Reports* between 1928–29 and 1944–45, for instance, give us an indication of the enormous output of the palace artists. Venkatappa's communications with A. V. Subrahmanyaraj Urs are a case in point; see May 15, 1931, and November 11, 1933, KVPP, KSA.

111. *PAR,* 1938–39, 18; 1941–42, 18; 1942–43, 17.

112. Venkatappa to Maharaja, August 6, 1940, KVPP, KSA.

113. Diary, September 23, 1940, KVPP, KSA.

114. Diary, September 25, 1940, KVPP, KSA.

115. Diary, September 20, 1943, KVPP, KSA.

116. *Venkatappa v. The Mysore Palace,* October 28, 1946, in *Mysore High Court Reports,* 51:486–527. Venkatappa submitted a set of documents, probably as proof of his agreement with the palace, but regrettably these records are untraceable. More surprising is the fact that all papers relating to the case are missing from Venkatappa's private papers as well.

117. *Hindu,* October 30, 1946; *Indian Express,* November 1, 1946, KVPP, KSA, commenting on the decision that the Mysore palace is not a legal entity, said, "Some of the State Congress leaders would prefer a judgment declaring the occupant of the premises in question as a legal nullity."

118. Despite knowledge of his aversion to exhibitions, there were several requests.

Bratindranath Tagore to "Appa Saheb," November 16, 1935, R. R. Diwakar to Venkatappa, October 10, 1927, and Venkatachalam to Venkatappa, July 21, 1934, KVPP, KSA.

119. Gangoly, "Indian Society of Oriental Art," 99.

120. As cited in Mitter, *Art and Nationalism in Colonial India,* 350; see also Thakurta, *The Making of a New "Indian" Art,* esp. 274–84.

121. Cousins, "The Future of Indian Art,"46.

122. Venkatachalam to Venkatappa, August 9, 1927, and August 2, 1927; Cousins to Venkatappa, November 25, 1929, KVPP, KSA.

123. In 1931 he sought permission to photograph his work for international journals. Venkatappa to A. V. Subrahmanyaraja Urs, May 15, 1931; reply to Venkatappa, May 17, 1931, KVPP, KSA.

124. For instance, on January 1, 1926, four photos were sent to E. W. Edwards, Hardwicke College, Mysore. Diary, KVPP, KSA; R. R. Diwakar to Venkatappa, October 10, 1927, KVPP, KSA.

125. Diary, February 14, 1926, KVPP, KSA.

126. "Veeneya Hucchu Chitra Parichaya," *Prabuddha Karnataka* 10, no. 1 (1928): 5–12.

127. Bourdieu, *The Field of Cultural Production,* 47.

128. Diary, August 21, 1933, KVPP, KSA.

129. Venkatappa to Shivarama Karanth, August 10, 1933, KVPP, KSA.

130. Letter protesting against the poor reproduction of *Nocturne* (no date, no place), KVPP, KSA.

131. Draft letter, no date, no place, KVPP, KSA; B. Srinivas to Venkatappa, October 8, 1930, KVPP, KSA.

132. A. R. Krishna Sastri to Venkatappa, October 11, 1930, and October 17, 1930, KVPP, KSA.

133. V. Sitaramaiah to Venkatappa, September 29, 1930; Venkatappa to Sitaramaiah, October 9, 1930, October 31, 1930, and November 6, 1930, KVPP, KSA. See Sitaramaiah, *Githagalu,* which contains illustrations by both Venkatappa and Nandalal Bose.

134. Benjamin, *Illuminations,* 221.

135. Thakurta, "Visualising the Nation," 31–35.

136. *Udbodhan,* Ashwin 1342, Puja Special Number (1935): 473, 497.

137. Venkatappa to Huzur Secretary, December 6, 1935, KVPP, KSA.

138. Ibid.

139. *Udbodhan,* 1342 (1935).

140. Reports of Important Decisions of the Calcutta High Court and of the Judicial Committee of the Privy Council on Appeal from India, in *The Calcutta Weekly Notes,* vol. 41 (November 1937–December 1938): 1046.

141. The first case he filed was in 1920 at the Mysore magistrate's court against a person who stole coconuts from his trees, for which the convicted thieves were caned. Diary, November 19, 1920, KVPP, KSA. The judge, while appreciating Venkatappa's work as an artist, did his best to discourage the artist from litigious behavior and hoped he would become a great man. But Venkatappa, having drawn blood, developed a taste for courtroom battles. Although we do not know the details of all cases, he successfully fought at least three other legal battles before the *Udbodhan* case and threatened several recalcitrant buyers and pa-

trons with legal action. Diary, March–April 1924, September 3, 1932, and January 1933. See also S. K. R. Rao, *Venkatappa,* 86–87.

142. *Statesman,* April 7, 1938, 13.

143. *Calcutta Weekly Notes,* 1047.

144. Diary, April 16, 1938, KVPP, KSA; *Calcutta Weekly Notes,* 1051.

145. Diary, April 8, 1938, KVPP, KSA.

146. Percy Brown to Private Secretary, Maharaja of Mysore, 1916, KVPP, KSA.

147. In 1951 he told O. C. Gangoly that he did not believe in attending lectures on art. Diary, September 11, 1951, KVPP, KSA. In 1949 he spurned the young Rumale Chennabasavaiah's offer to arrange for Karnataka congressmen such as Hardekar, T. Siddalingaiah, and K. C. Reddy to visit his studio. Diary, April 5, 1949, and April 3, 1951, KVPP, KSA.

148. Abanindranath's reply was simply to reassert what he had said in the article on Indian iconography: "You must know that the sastras were made after the statues were made by artists." Abanindranath to Venkatappa, February 11, 1937, KVPP, KSA. The bas relief finally depicted Shiva with two hands.

149. Nandalal Bose was at Santiniketan, A. K. Haldar at Lucknow, Samarendranath Gupta at Lahore, Sailendranath Dey at Jaipur, Sarada Ukil at Delhi, Promode Chatterjee at Machilipatnam, and D. P. Roychoudhry at Madras; although P. R. Rao claimed that Venkatappa "taught at Mysore," this was not the case. P. R. Rao, *Modern Indian Painting,* 12.

150. Diary, April 16 and 17, 1920, KVPP, KSA; Diary, April 24, 1928, KVPP, KSA.

151. Srinivas Row to Venkatappa, March 19, 1926, June 1, 1926, and September 23, 1926, KVPP, KSA.

152. Letter, no date (1931?), no place, KVPP, KSA.

153. Diary, January 27, 1942, KVPP, KSA; Sitaramaiah, *Savi Nenapu,* 14; Diary, July 6, 1948, KVPP, KSA; see also Balarama Kulkarni to Venkatappa, December 20, 1946, KVPP, KSA; Abanindranath to Venkatappa, May 31, 1928, KVPP, KSA.

154. Subrahmanya Raju, *Savi Nenapu,* 20.

155. Diary, February 7, 1949; March 21, 1952; October 12, 1954; September 8, 1956, KVPP, KSA.

156. Karanth, *Bharatiya Chitra Kala,* 45.

157. Kasi, "Odedha Kannadi," 34–42.

158. Coomaraswamy, "Why Exhibit Works of Art?" 7.

159. R. R. Diwakar to K. Venkatappa, October 15, 1928, KVPP, KSA.

160. H. J. Bhabha to Venkatappa, February 27, 1940, KVPP, KSA.

161. Venkatappa to Secretary, Dasara Exhibition Committee, September 21, 1950, KVPP, KSA.

162. Venkatappa to Srikrishna Kumar Singhji, Governor, Madras, September 12, 1951, KVPP, KSA.

163. R. R. Diwakar to Venkatappa, October 10, 1927, KVPP, KSA.

164. S. V. Ramaswamy Mudaliar to Venkatappa, November 19, 1927, December 17, 1927, January 2, 1928, and February 14, 1928, KVPP, KSA.

165. Diary, April 14, 1928, KVPP, KSA.

166. Diary, November 14, 1946, KVPP, KSA; Diary, May 24, 1944, KVPP, KSA.

167. Diary, November 20, 1946, KVPP, KSA.

168. Diary, November 23–25, 1946, KVPP, KSA.

169. Diary, November 20, 1946, KVPP, KSA.

170. Superintendent, Government Museum Madras, to Venkatappa, May 17, 1954, KVPP, KSA.

171. Kamaladevi to Venkatappa, September 2, 1954; Venkatappa to Kamaladevi, October 7, 1954, KVPP, KSA.

172. Venkatappa to Kamaladevi, September 27, 1954, KVPP, KSA.

6. The Illicit in the Modern

1. Bagchi, "Colonialism and the Nature of Capitalist Enterprise."

2. Sarkar, "Rhetoric against Age of Consent,"1870.

3. Chatterjee, "The Nationalist Resolution of the Women's Question."

4. See, for instance, Rege, *Writing Caste, Writing Gender;* Kodoth, "Courting Legitimacy or Delegitimising Custom?"; Kodoth, "Shifting the Ground of Fatherhood"; Devika, *Her Self;* Devika, *Engendering Individuals;* G. Arunima, *There Comes Papa;* Sinha, *Specters of Mother India,* 152 ff.

5. Groups formed in Mysore and Bangalore to encourage widow remarriage, for example, rarely survived beyond their first few meetings. Gustafson, "Mysore 1881–1902," 2. Members of the Representative Assembly and Legislative Council never failed, however, to summon the specter of an English-style suffrage movement in discussions on women's rights. *PMRA,* 1921, 68. For a good overview of the social reform and feminist movements, see Kumar, *The History of Doing.*

6. Jamuna, "Social Change in Mysore with Special Reference to Women," 75.

7. I have discussed the intersecting discourses on health and morality as they were revealed in the operations of the Contagious Diseases Acts and the legislation to curb prostitution in "Imperial Imperatives."

8. Sangari and Vaid, "Introduction," 17.

9. "Notes and Comments," *Stri Dharma* 13 (March 1930): 217.

10. "Mrs. Dr. Muthulakshmi, Reddi's Address," *Stri Dharma* 13, nos. 1–2 (December 1929).

11. At the National Social Conference of 1927 in Madras, Reddi even urged the British government to follow the footsteps of the native states. See Sinha, *Specters of Mother India,* 168.

12. "Annual Report of the All India Women's Conference, 1929," *Stri Dharma* 13 (March 1930): 217.

13. Letter of Governor-General Bentinck, September 6, 1831, as cited in Sastri, *An Introduction to the History of the Administration of Mysore,* 26.

14. Ibid., 28.

15. Appadurai and Breckenridge, "The South Indian Temple."

16. Ibid., 50–52.

17. C. H. Rao, *Mysore Gazetteer,* 4:139, 140, 146.

18. Stein, *Thomas Munro,* 103.

19. In this, says Stein, the British ironically drew on and extended a process that had been initiated by Tipu Sultan. Ibid., 103–4.

20. *Muzrayi Memorandum* (n.p., n.d. [1894?]), 1.

21. In 1835, Governor-General William Bentinck issued instructions to Superintendents in Mysore: "All the ancient usages and institutions of the country especially those of a religious nature shall be respected and maintained inviolate." Sastri, *An Introduction to the History of the Administration of Mysore*, 141. This principle was stated afresh in the Despatch from the Court of Directors, April 21, 1847, in *Muzrayi Memorandum*, 5. For Madras, see Arjun Appadurai, *Worship and Conflict under Colonial Rule;* see also Presler, *Religion under Bureaucracy.*

22. *Muzrayi Memorandum*, 7.

23. Ibid., 10.

24. Ibid., 11.

25. Ibid., 12.

26. Address of the Dewan of Mysore to the Representative Assembly, October 4, *PMRA*, 1892, 19.

27. C. H. Rao, *Mysore Gazetteer*, 4:686–89.

28. Address of the Dewan, *PMRA*, 1892, 19.

29. *Proceedings of the Government of Mysore*, February 8, 1892, Muzrai.

30. Amrit Srinivasan, "Reform and Revival: The Devadasi and Her Dance," 1873. Nautch parties were troupes of dancing and singing women who were frequently engaged for the entertainment of upper-class Indian patrons and, in the early stages of British rule, for East India Company officials as well.

31. R. R. Diwakar, *Karnataka through the Ages*, 877–88.

32. *Vrittanta Chintamani*, October 14, 1891, Native Newspaper Reports (NNR), Tamil Nadu State Archives (TNSA).

33. Derrett, *Religion, Law and State in India*, 452; Kumar, *The History of Doing*, 34–37.

34. File no. 186 of 1898–99, "Revision of the Tasdik Patti of the Sri Srikanteshvara Temple at Nanjangud," Muzrai Department, KSA.

35. *Proceedings of the Government of Mysore*, April 1909, Muzrai.

36. Spivak, "Feminism and Decolonisation," 153.

37. Story, *Nityasumangali*, 47.

38. Parasher and Naik, "Temple Girls of Medieval Karnataka," esp. 66–67.

39. Ibid., 64.

40. Ibid., 67, 76. See also L K Ananthakrishna Iyer, *The Mysore Tribes and Castes*, 1:217; for the Tamil region, see Anandhi "Representing Devadasis."

41. Parashar and Naik, "Temple Girls of Medieval Karnataka," 70. See also Talbot, "Temples, Donors and Gifts."

42. Srinivasan, "Reform and Revival," 1870.

43. Ibid. Discussions of women's donations to temples do not delineate the spaces within medieval social formations where some women of independent means other than devadasis must have existed if they had control of land they could gift away.

44. Diwakar, *Karnataka through the Ages*, 879.

45. *Census of India, 1891*, vol. 25, part 1, Report, Mysore (1893), 242.

46. *Census of India, 1901*, vol. 24, part 1, Report, Mysore (1902), 539.

47. Ibid.

48. *Census of India, 1911*, vol. 21, part 1, Mysore (1912), 172.

49. Parkar, "'A Corporation of Superior Prostitutes.'"

50. Iyer, *Mysore Tribes and Castes,* 4:422.

51. Ibid., 423.

52. Ibid., 427.

53. Both Amrit Srinivasan and Veena Talwar Oldenburg view the relative freedoms of sex workers, whether devadasis or courtesans, as an indication of the spaces within patriarchy that were free. See Srinivasan, "Reform and Revival," and Oldenburg, "Lifestyle as Resistance." Contrasting views on the position of devadasis in Tamil Nadu and Andhra Pradesh are found in Anandhi, "Representing Devadasis," and Priyadarshini Vijaisri, *Recasting the Devadasi.*

54. Iyer, *Mysore Tribes and Castes,* 2:214.

55. Parkar, "A Corporation of Superior Prostitutes"; Jordan, *From Sacred Servant to Profane Prostitute.*

56. Ibid., 43.

57. Ibid., 43–46.

58. Ibid., 47.

59. As cited from the *Journal of the Anthropological Society of Bombay* in Iyer, *Mysore Tribes and Castes,* 4:214.

60. "Notes and Comments," 217.

61. See also Srinivas, *Marriage and Family in Mysore,* esp. 177–84, where the inheritance rights of basavis are mentioned only in passing.

62. File no. 8 of 1898–99, Muzrai Department, KSA. Resumption refers to the reversal of donations of land to a temple on the grounds that the services for which it had been granted were improperly performed. Presler, *Religion under Bureaucracy,* 18.

63. Deputy Commissioner of Kolar to Muzrai Superintendent, November 18, 1898, file no. 8, 1898–99, Muzrai Department, KSA.

64. *Karnataka Prakasika,* January 16, 1893, and June 26, 1983, NNR, TNSA.

65. *Vrittanta Patrike,* May 21, 1896, NNR, TNSA.

66. File no. 2 of 1900–1901, sl. no. Sect V, Muzrai Department, KSA.

67. Srinivasacharlu to S. M. Fraser, October 31, 1900, file no. 2, 1900–01, Muzrai, KSA.

68. File no. 124, sl. nos. 1–3, July 1905, Muzrai Department, KSA.

69. File no. 84, 1905, Petition no. 2104, November 13, 1905, Muzrai Department, KSA.

70. Ibid.

71. In 1927, the devadasis of the Madras Presidency presented similar memorials on the eve of the introduction of legislation prohibiting devadasi dedication. See Jordan, *From Sacred Servant to Profane Prostitute,* 127 ff. The female entertainers of Shanghai waged a similar battle against the efforts of authorities to legally classify them as prostitutes along with women employed in tea houses, inns, and hotels, arguing that they were singing girls who sold only their voices and not their bodies. Gronewald, "Beautiful Merchandise."

72. Note of Dewan, November 10, 1906, file no. 84, 1905, Muzrai, KSA.

73. The *agamasastras* are texts that outline all temple rituals; however, the Shaiva Agamas are the sole authorities for the Shaivite temples, the Pancaratra and Vaikhanasa agamas for the Vaishnavite temples. Siva Chariyar, *Kamikagamaha.* The agamiks referred to both sets of texts.

74. Memo no. 2104, dated November 13, 1905, file no. 84, 1905, Muzrai, KSA.

75. Muzrai superintendent's note, file no. 84, 1905, Muzrai, KSA.

76. Memo no. 2675, dated December 9, 1905, file no. 84, 1905, Muzrai, KSA.

77. The chief features of this dystopia as summarized by Sumit Sarkar are "oppressive *mleccha* (alien and impure) kings, Brahmans corrupted by too much rational argument, overmighty *shudras* (lower castes), expounding the scriptures and ceasing to serve the *brahmans*, girls choosing their own partners, and disobedient and deceiving wives having intercourse with menials, slaves and even animals." Sarkar, "Kaliyuga, Chakri, and Bhakti," 1549.

78. Note of the muzrai superintendent, November 21, 1906, file no. 84 of 1905, Muzrai Department, KSA.

79. *Proceedings of the Government of Mysore,* April 1909, Muzrai Department.

80. Note of the muzrai superintendent, November 21, 1906, file no. 84 of 1905, Muzrai Department, KSA.

81. File no. 718-16, Muzrai, KSA.

82. File no. 56-19, sl. nos. 1–15, 1919, Muzrai Department, KSA.

83. File no. 364-28, sl. nos. 1–6, Muzrai Department, KSA.

84. File no. 369-29, sl. nos. 1–4, Muzrai Department, KSA.

85. Vijaisri, *Recasting the Devadasi.*

86. Although the extension of the Contagious Diseases Acts in England was resented as a threat to virtuous women by members of the contagious diseases campaign, it did not have the same impact that the violation of family and community honor by alien authorities appeared to have had in colonial India. See Walkowitz, *Prostitution and Victorian Society,* 110.

87. Price, *Kingship and Political Practice in Colonial India,* 155.

88. Perhaps the most striking instance of the dissociation of the nationalist elite from disreputable women was Gandhi's refusal to allow nearly two hundred prostitutes from Barisal to participate in the noncooperation movement until they publicly renounced their profession. See Kishwar, "Gandhi on Women."

89. See, for instance Anandhi, "Representing Devadasis," 740. "Presidential Address, Andhradesa Kala Vanthula Conference," *Stri Dharma* 15, no. 11 (September 1932): 609.

90. Tharu and Lalita, *Women Writing in India,* 1–9.

91. See Law Commission of India, *Sixty-fourth Report on the Suppression of Immoral Traffic Act in Women and Girls 1956* (1975), 5; *Towards Equality: Report of the Committee on the Status of Women in India,* Delhi, 1974, 92.

92. Note that women from the devadasi tradition largely survived in the reformed social order as singers, not as dancers. Amrit Srinivasan argues that the revival of the dance and musical forms of the devadasis in a suitably puritanical form was enabled by recasting it as high brahmanic culture, which it was now safe, even desirable, for women of upper-caste families to acquire. See Srinivasan, "Reform and Revival." See also Subramanian, *From the Tanjore Court to Madras Music Academy.*

93. Diwakar, *Karnataka through the Ages,* 880.

94. See, for example, several articles in *Stri Dharma,* especially the issue of January 1930, 79 ff.

95. Iyer, *Mysore Tribes and Castes,* 4:423.

96. See N. G. Sanjivaiah's intervention, *PMRA,* October 1934, 126.

97. Gundappa, *Kelavu Mahaniyaru,* 166–78. I am grateful to Tejaswini Niranjana for this reference.

98. DVG himself, as a member of the Legislative Council, vigorously opposed the passage of the Suppression of Immoral Traffic Act on the grounds that it was a ploy of missionaries to gain converts from among the rescued women. *PMLC,* December 18, 1935, 177.

99. Ba Na Sundara Rao, *Bengalurina itihasa,* 420.

7. The Licit in the Modern

1. Dewan's Address to the Mysore Representative Assembly, *PMRA,* 1893.

2. Dewan's Address to the Mysore Representative Assembly, *PMRA,* 1932.

3. Ranajit Guha first used the phrase "state's emissary" to signify "law" in "Chandra's Death." Upendra Baxi further distinguishes between "state law" and other nonstate lawways. Baxi, "The State's Emissary: The Place of Law in Subaltern Studies."

4. File no. 47-95, sl. nos. 25, 26, 29, and 32, Police, KSA.

5. For a full text of the regulation, see *Mysore Gazette,* September 13, 1894. The term *marriage* was used in colonial Indian official discourse to signify not just the condition of conjugality but the event or ceremony itself. I retain this term to serve both senses throughout this article. Similarly, the Mysore use of the term *infant* for all children under age eight is puzzling but presumably was chosen over *child* because cradle marriages were a common practice.

6. File no. 47-95, sl. nos. 25, 26, 29, and 32, Police, KSA.

7. We must remind ourselves here that Chambar Ganga's defiant voice has already been organized, even produced, by the multiple mediations of the machinery of the state in detecting criminality in what had been until then a civil act. What did the "alias" before "Chavaluga" signify, and was it recognized by the community? The dilemmas presented by such sources are thus inescapable.

8. For instance, Manor, *Political Change in an Indian State,* 30–31.

9. C. H. Rao, *Mysore Gazetteer,* 4:115.

10. Smith, "Rule-by-Records and Rule-by-Reports," esp. 154.

11. Cohn, *An Anthropologist among the Historians and other Essays.* At least until the 1950s, local forms of dispute settlement were quite common. See Epstein, *Economic Development and Social Change in South India.* For an account of the effects of later political developments in the same region, see Epstein, Suryanaryana, and Thimmegowda, *Village Voices.*

12. Cohn, *An Anthropologist among the Historians,* 588.

13. File no. 47-95, sl. nos. 25, 26, 29, and 32, Police, KSA.

14. File no. 53 of 1897, sl. nos. 21, 26, 38, and 39, Police, KSA.

15. File no. 53 of 1896–97, sl. nos. 34, 36, 46, and 50, Police, KSA.

16. Dewan's Address to the Mysore Representative Assembly, *PMRA,* 1893, 21.

17. Panigrahi, *Social Policy and British Rule in India;* Pakrasi, *Female Infanticide in India.*

18. Law Commission of India, *Eighty First Report on Hindu Widows Remarriage Act of 1856* (Delhi: Government of India, 1979), 15.

19. Gidumal, *The Status of Women in India,* 149. Responding to Malabari's "Notes on Infant Marriage," one person from the Bombay Presidency said: "Without going to the

length of charging all young widows with wicked conduct, I can safely say that a large number of them go astray, and the consequences are horrible. Attempts at procuring abortions, which in some cases terminate in death, and murder of pregnant widows by their relatives are the results."

20. Ibid., 169.

21. Iyer, *Mysore Tribes and Castes,* 1:212; Srinivas, *Marriage and Family in Mysore.*

22. Iyer, *Mysore Tribes and Castes,* 1:35 and 48.

23. Inspector General of Police to General Secretary of the Mysore Government, April 10, 1896, file no. 47-95, sl. nos. 25, 26, 29, and 31, Police, KSA.

24. Ibid.

25. Government of India, *Report of the Age of Consent Committee* (Calcutta, 1929), 10.

26. *PMRA,* 1891, 36.

27. *PMRA,* October 1893, 46.

28. Ibid., 48.

29. *PMRA,* 1891, 38.

30. Ibid., 37.

31. Sarkar, *Hindu Wife, Hindu Nation,* 218.

32. *Vrittanta Chintamani,* January 1891, NNR, TNSA.

33. Forbes, "Women and Modernity," esp. 410. See also Sarkar, *Hindu Wife, Hindu Nation;* Chandra *Enslaved Daughters;* Chakravarti, *Rewriting History.*

34. *Karnataka Prakasika,* February 2, 1891, NNR, TNSA.

35. *Karnataka Prakasika,* February 16, 1891, NNR, TNSA.

36. Engels, "The Limits of Gender Ideology," esp. 427–29.

37. Chandra, *Enslaved Daughters;* Chakravarti, *Rewriting History.*

38. "Rakhmabai's 'Reply' to Dadajee's 'Exposition,'" in Chandra, *Enslaved Daughters,* 241.

39. McGinn, "The Age of Consent Act (1891) Reconsidered," esp. 102; Chandra, *Enslaved Daughters,* 162–63.

40. Ramabai, *The High Caste Hindu Woman,* 67. For a similar instance of a dilution of the colonial state's commitment to social reform when faced with nationalist opposition in another part of the empire, Kenya, see Pedersen, "National Bodies, Unspeakable Acts."

41. Gustafson, "Mysore 1881–1902," 222–26.

42. *PMRA,* October 1892, 19.

43. On the generalization of the legal form, see Pashukannis, *Law and Marxism.*

44. Dirks, *Castes of Mind,* esp. 127–227.

45. Cohn, *An Anthropologist among the Historians,* 224–54. For a detailed discussion of Colin Mackenzie's surveys, particularly in northern Mysore, see Dirks, *Castes of Mind,* 81–106.

46. *Census of India, 1891,* vol. 25, Mysore, part 1, Report, 131.

47. Ibid., 132–33.

48. *PMRA,* October 1893, 48.

49. Appendix B2, *PMRA,* 1893, 187.

50. Appendix B, *PMRA,* 1893, 186.

51. *Mysore Gazette,* September 13, 1894, 9.

52. Gidumal, *The Status of Women in India,* 297.

53. *PMRA,* October 1893, 49.

54. File no. 47-95, sl. nos. 43, 44, 47, and 48, Police, KSA.

55. Feminists in the Madras Presidency realized that exactly such a strategy was being followed by those who were likely to be prosecuted under the Child Marriage Restraint Act of 1929: they reported that the secretary of the Vyshya Seva Sangha of Visakhapatnam had said that even when people were convicted, the fines were so slight that it "encouraged people to quietly defy the Act and provide in the marriage expenses for the fine in the prospective criminal cases." "The Sarda Bill," *Stri Dharma* 15, no. 11 (September 1932).

56. *Vrittanta Patrike*, August 1, 1895, NNR, TNSA.

57. File no. 47-95, sl. nos. 2, 3, 16, 17, 22, 23, and 24, Police, KSA. Thus when the seven-year-old daughter of Naranappa was married to the twenty-three-year-old son of Visveswaraiah, the two men pleaded ignorance of the law but did not escape prosecution, along with the groom himself. File no. 47-95, sl. nos. 39 and 42, Police, KSA.

58. File no. 53-97, sl. nos. 9, 11, 44, and 48, Police, KSA.

59. File no. 53 of 1897, sl. nos. 21, 26, 38, and 39, Police, KSA.

60. File no. 53 of 1896–97, sl. nos. 4 and 10, Police, KSA.

61. File no. 53 of 1896–97, sl. nos. 22, 24, 28, and 32, Police, KSA, in which both the shanbogue and the patel of Ramagondanahalli Village warned Tiglars against conducting a child marriage; file no. 53 of 1896–97, sl. nos. 34, 36, 46, and 50, Police, KSA, in which the priest and the patel of Mangasandra Village warned Agasas against violating the law; file no. 53 of 1896–97, sl. nos. 47, 51, 63, and 69, Police, KSA, in which the patel and the shanbogue of Muthukur Village warned Holeyas against performing infant marriage; file no. 53 of 1896, sl. nos. 70 and 74, Police, KSA, in which Patel Lakshmappa of Akkamanahalli warned Kurubas against marriage; and file no. 31-97, sl. nos. 9, 12, 25, and 28, Police, KSA, in which Left-Hand (Madigas?) castes were warned by the patel of Beechagondanahalli.

62. For instance, see file no. 31-97, sl. nos. 4, 5, 18, and 22, Police, KSA, for details of the patel of Jalamangala Village in Closepet Taluk who married his nine-year-old son to five-year-old Timmi, inviting prosecution, which ended in a hefty fine of Rs 51 for each of the accused, including the grandfather of the groom and the uncle of the bride. Also, file no. 53 of 1897, sl. nos. 15, 19, 41, and 43, Police, KSA, has details of the case in which Patel Nanjunda Gowda of Kenadanahalli in Sidlaghata Taluk was prosecuted with his relatives for celebrating the marriage of his six-year-old niece in his house.

63. *Census of India, 1911*, vol. 25, Mysore, part 1, report, 97; Government of India, *Report of the Age of Consent Committee*, 346–47.

64. Gustafson, Mysore 1881–1902, 225.

65. Engels, "The Limits of Gender Ideology," 427.

66. *Tamil Nadu*, April 7, 1932; *Dravidian*, July 13, 1932; *Desabhaktan*, July 16, 1932; *Tamil Nadu*, December 19, 1933; *India*, December 19, 1933; *Chetti Nadu*, July 12, 1934; *Tamil Nadu*, July 5, 1934, NNR, TNSA.

67. Basu, *Hindu Women and Marriage Law*, 51. See also Judy Whitehead's discussion of motherhood myths and archetypes of the report of the Age of Consent Committee. Whitehead, "Modernising the Motherhood Archetype."

68. Gowda, *Infant Marriages of post 1894 in the Princely State of Mysore*, 26, 27.

69. For some of the other legal problems presented by the relatively autonomous status of Mysore, see Gustafson, "The Making of a Model State," 273–74.

70. File no. 67, sl. nos. 17–22, Police, KSA.

71. Balibar "The Nation Form."

72. File no. 26 of 1894–95, sl. nos. 5, 9, 11, 12, 14, and 16, Police, KSA; file no. 31-97, sl. nos. 3, 6, 8, 10, 45, and 47, Police, KSA; file no. 67, sl. nos. 3, 4, 7, 32, and 35, Police, KSA.

73. File no. 47-95, sl. nos. 27, 28, and 36, Police, KSA.

74. Nair, "The Emergence of Labour Politics in South India."

75. DC to IGP, March 30, 1897, file no. 53 of 1897, sl. nos. 52, 55, 62, and 66, Police, KSA.

76. File no. 31-97, sl. nos. 7, 11, 24, and 27, Police, KSA.

77. File no. 53 of 1896–97, sl. nos. 4 and 10, Police, KSA.

78. Bourdieu, *Outline of a Theory of Practice,* 34.

79. File no. 47-95, sl. nos. 2, 3, 16, 17, 22, 23, and 24, Police, KSA; file no. 47-95, sl. nos. 27, 28, 36, and 41, Police, KSA.

80. File no. 47–95, sl. nos. 27, 28, 36, and 451, Police, KSA; file no. 53 of 1897, sl. nos. 12, 13, 17, and 23, Police, KSA.

81. On South Indian kinship systems, see Karve, "The Kinship Map of India," and Trautmann, "The Study of Dravidian Kinship."

82. File no. 53 of 1897, sl. nos. 21, 26, 38, and 39, Police, KSA; file no. 67, sl. nos. 8, 9, 30, and 33, Police, KSA.

83. File no. 20-17, sl. nos. 5 and 6, Police, KSA.

84. File no. 3 of 1902, sl. nos. 1, 3, 10, 14, 21, and 22, Police, KSA.

85. File no. 31-97, sl. nos. 13, 15, 29, and 31, Police, KSA.

86. File no. 20-17 of 1917, sl. nos. 1–4, Police, KSA.

87. File no. 56 (B) of 1901, sl. nos. 1–2, Courts, KSA.

88. Foucault, *The History of Sexuality,* 110–11.

89. Sambasiva Iyer, *Mysore, Industrial and Commercial,* 1:11.

90. *Stri Dharma* 14, no. 7 (May 1931); see also *Kistna News,* August 15, 1893, and *Prabhavati,* March 22, 1897, NNR, TNSA, which asked the Government of India to prohibit marriages on the lines of the Mysore regulation rather than having a minimum age of consent.

91. *Karnataka Prakasika,* January 10, 1898, and February 7, 1898, NNR, TNSA.

92. See, however, McGinn, "The Age of Consent Act (1891) Reconsidered."

93. Forbes, *Women in Modern India;* Everett, *Women and Social Change In India;* Nair, *Women and Law in Colonial India.*

94. Sinha, *Specters of Mother India,* 152 ff, esp. 176. Recent feminist arguments that have revisited the nationalist period in the light of the reservation issues and in response to critiques that the Indian feminist subject is normed as upper-caste, upper-class, and urban have suggested that such "unities" may have strategically, and with lasting impact, sealed irreducible differences between Indian women. See John, "Alternate Modernities?" and Menon, "Elusive 'Women.'" In such an argument, the acknowledgement of difference functions to democratize rights discourse rather than dilute it.

95. *PMRA,* Dewan's Address, 1893.

96. *PMRA,* Dewan's Address, 1932, 30–31.

97. "Balya Vivahada Sastartha," in A. Shankar Collection, Private Papers, KSA.

98. Ismail, *My Public Life,* 22–3.

99. Sarkar, *Hindu Wife, Hindu Nation,* 191–225.

100. *PMRA,* 1932, 120.

101. See Lotika Sarkar's discussion of the persistent reluctance of lawmakers to address the question of either outlawing prostitution or making it legal. Sarkar, *National Specialised Agencies and Women's Equality Law Commission of India,* 49.

102. *PMRA,* 1895, 37.

103. File no. 44-22, Legislation, KSA; *PMRA,* 1922, 29; *PMRA,* 1922, 29.

104. File no. 16-30, Notes, Legislature, KSA.

105. *PMRA,* 1932, 103.

106. Ibid., 100–102.

107. *PMRA,* 1928, Dasara Session, 336ff. On Bhashyam's career as a labor leader, see Nair, "The Emergence of Labour Politics in South India," chaps. 5–7.

108. *PMRA,* 1932, 114.

109. Ibid., 125.

110. *Stri Dharma* 8, no. 6 (April 1925); *Stri Dharma* 9, no. 4 (February 1926).

111. *Stri Dharma* 14, no. 7 (1931).

112. *PMRA,* 1932, 99.

113. Ibid., 118.

114. *Saraswathi* 9, no. 12 (1930).

115. *PMRA,* 1932, 121.

116. Hosakoppa Krishna Rao, *PMRA,* 1932, 125.

117. *Saraswathi* 9, no. 2 (December 1929).

118. *Saraswathi* 9, no. 3 (December 1929).

119. *Saraswathi* 10, no. 1 (1930).

120. Mass Awakener's Union, Special Branch Reports of Meetings, 20/7/1937 to 14/7/39, Police, KSA. See also Meetings in Bangalore District, 10/1/39 to 18/5/39, Police, KSA. Bhashyam cited a number of cases in which the question of ruling on women's rights had come up: "In Mysore we have had it explicitly laid down by more decisions than one that sex is no ground of disqualification for inheritance." *PMRA,* Dasara Session, October–November 1928, 340.

121. Balibar, "The Nation Form," esp. 101–2.

122. This paragraph is based on my article "Contending Ideologies," 62–63.

8. Giving the State a Nation

1. Thambanda, *Conflicting Identities in Karnataka,* and *Adhunika Kodagu.* A High Power Committee headed by D. M. Nanjundappa for redressal of regional imbalances (2002) recommended investments of up to Rs 310 billion and a series of other measures, such as choosing at least 50 percent of the cabinet of ministers from the region.

2. For instance, DVG to C. Rajagopalachari, March 29, 1958, DVG Private Papers, KSA; see also B. K. Puttaramaiah, *Mysore Legislative Council Debates* (hereafter *MLCD*) 7 (1955): 771; M. P. L. Sastry, *MLCD* 7 (1955): 595.

3. The literature is huge and growing: among some of the recent statements are V. N. Rao, *Kannadathana Mattu Bhaaratheeyathe;* Ramachandrappa, *Kannadaabhimana;* Murthy, "Kannadada Samasyegalu." K. V. Narayana offers a different optic on the predicament

of Kannada today, which draws attention to the homogenization of Kannada that has already been violently achieved. Narayana, "What Should We Address?"

4. H. S. G. Rao, *Karnataka Ekikarana Itihasa,* 315.

5. Ibid., 18; A. V. Rao, *Karnataka Gathavaibhava.* A newer version of the attempt to instill "pride," though without making an overt plea for territorial claims, is Murthy, *Bhasika Bruhat Karnataka.*

6. Nair, "'Memories of Underdevelopment'"; see, however, Tarikere, *Karnatakada Sufigalu.*

7. Halappa, *History of the Freedom Movement in Karnataka,* 419–26.

8. S. Chandrasekhar, "Mysuru Mattu Ekikruta Karnatakada Rachane," 93–104; King, *Nehru and the Language Politics of India; Manor, Political Change in an Indian State,* 84–85, and "Karnataka." Nijalingappa, *My Life and Politics,* 62 provides a brief and telling account of the late development of karnataka ekikarana: "This drive to unify Kannadigas had begun in 1915, when the first conference of Kannadigas was organized by the Karnataka Sahitya Parishad in Bangalore. Subsequently it held its meetings in different parts of the Kannada speaking areas from year to year. While this kept people thinking of a unified Karnataka state, it had no political clout. It was only after Congress took up this unification work from 1945 that it began to influence the All India Congress and its working committee."

9. *States Reorganisation Commission Report* (Government of India, 1955), 91 hereafter, *SRC Report.*

10. Among the earliest to suggest that all the linguistic movements were in fact masks for other agendas was Harrison, *India.*

11. President's speech by D. V. Gundappa at the Karnataka Sangha Rajathotsava, Bangalore Central College, January 16, 1944.

12. Here it must be remembered that the term *communal* in administrative terminology referred to the two dominant caste groups of Mysore, Lingayats and Vokkaligas.

13. S. Gopala Gowda, *Mysore Legislative Assembly Debates* (hereafter *MLAD*) 13, no. 15 (1955): 873.

14. Deshpande, *Contemporary India,* 48–73.

15. For instance, A. Thimmappa Gowda, *MLAD* 13, no. 20 (1955): 1295.

16. Chatterjee, "Development Planning and the Indian State."

17. Ibid., 276.

18. Hettne, *The Political Economy of Indirect Rule,* 341.

19. Deshpande, *Contemporary India,* 71.

20. *SRC Report,* 93.

21. H. S. G. Rao, *Karnataka Ekikarana Itihasa,* lists the nineteen administrations under which Kannada speakers beyond Mysore were found.

22. Deshpande, *Contemporary India,* 158.

23. "The boundary of Karnataka," it said with respect to the map that was included, "marked by thin straight lines, may only be taken as approximately marking the limits of the Kannada speaking people. It does not follow the Congress Division. Suggestions for rendering it accurate will be thankfully received." *Karnataka Handbook,* note on map in preface.

24. H. S. G. Rao, *Karnataka Ekikarana Itihasa,* 67. Before the Congress session of 1946 at Birur, Mysore's congressmen, such as T. Channaiah, T. Siddalingaiya, A. G. Bandi Gowda,

K. G. Wodeyar, T. Subrahmanyam, and others raised the question of forming Karnataka with the Maharaja as the constitutional head. J. Mohamed Imam, *MLAD* 12, no. 11 (March 1955): 646. For a discussion of B. R. Ambedkar's position on the relevance and necessity of linguistic states, see Sarangi, "Ambedkar and the Linguistic States." See also King, *Nehru and the Language Politics of India*, 71 ff.

25. H. S. G. Rao, *Karnataka Ekikarana Itihasa*, 146.

26. Ibid., 155.

27. Hanumanthaiya, *MLAD* 9, no. 37 (1953): 2499.

28. Letter no. 604 dated October 12, 1951, from General Secretary, KPCC, Hubli, to the Chief Secretary, Government of Mysore, file no. 24 (13) PA/51, 1951, Ministry of States, Political A Branch, NAI.

29. K. S. Gurusuddappa to Prime Minister, 5/9/1953, file no. F.2 (8)-PA/53, 1953, Ministry of States, Political A Section, sl. nos. 1–2, NAI.

30. H. S. G. Rao, *Karnataka Ekikarana Itihasa*.

31. Devika, "The Idea of Being Malayali." Many of Devika's observations on Kerala have helped me to conceptualize in comparison the debates in Karnataka. See also Menon, "Being Brahman the Marxist Way," 82.

32. K. V. N. Rao, *The Emergence of Andhra Pradesh*, 202.

33. Menon, "Being Brahman the Marxist Way," 62–63.

34. One might say that the territorialization of caste in Tamil Nadu occurred well after the moment of independence, with alliances between sets of castes in northern and southern Tamil Nadu.

35. DVG to C. Rajagopalachari, November 21, 1955, DVG Private Papers, KSA.

36. Hanumanthaiya was accompanied by J. Mohamed Imam on the tour of the regions of North Karnataka when, according to Imam, he was moved by the predicament of the people in those regions.

37. Others included T. Singaravelu, a High Court judge; V. L. D'Souza, vice chairman of Mysore University; H. R. Guruve Reddy; and lawyer O. Veerabasappa.

38. *Report of the Fact Finding Committee* (States Reorganisation) (Bangalore, 1954), 1.

39. B. K. Puttaramaiah, *MLCD* 7, no. 18 (1955): 772.

40. T. Mariappa, *MLAD* 13, no. 20 (1955): 1269.

41. "Replies by All Karnataka Unification Sangha to the Questionnaire Issued by the Linguistic Provinces Commission," September 9, 1948, National Library, Kolkata (mimeo).

42. Thus, although "union Karnataka" had invested Rs 60 million, with private capital adding another Rs 49 million, the Mysore state had invested Rs 199.1 million, with private capital contributing another paltry Rs 16.7 million. Ibid., 28.

43. *SRC Report*, 91, my emphasis. The idea of the linguistic state being a panacea to the irritants of caste were echoed within the assembly as well by R. Ramaiah among others. See also *Karnataka Handbook*, 130.

44. M. P. L. Sastry, *MLCD* 7 (October 10–December 1, 1955): 595.

45. H. S. G. Rao, *Karnataka Ekikarana Itihasa*, 72.

46. Alura proposed that festivals similar to Maharashtra's Ganeshotsava be organized to honor Karnataka's heroes: Kannada poets such as Pampa and Kumara Vyasa; Vidyaranya, the intellectual guide of Vijayanagar kings; and Basaveswara, the twelfth- century reformer.

47. *Karnataka Handbook*, 1, 7–8.

48. Hanumanthaiya, *MLAD* 9, no. 38 (1953): 2716.

49. "People who speak Kannada, people who speak Telugu and people who speak Tamil . . . these three form what is called the constituents of the state of Mysore. . . . The *composite character* of this portion of India has been there probably for several thousands of years. . . . It [Mysore] was not only one set of people talking one language who constituted the unit." Hanumanthaiya, *MLCD* 7 (October 10–December 1, 1955): 583, my emphasis; *MLAD* 8, no. 13 (1955): 791.

50. Ibid.

51. Sastry, *MLCD* 7 (October 10–December 1, 1955): 594.

52. J. Mohamed Imam, *MLAD* 9, no. 43 (1953): 2546.

53. R. Ramaiah, *MLAD* 9, no. 43 (1953): 2509–10.

54. A. G. Ramachandra Rao, *MLAD*, 13, no. 14 (1955): 880.

55. Gopala Gowda, *MLAD* 9, no. 37 (1953): 2556.

56. K. Hanumanthaiya, *MLCD* 7 (October 10–December 1, 1955): 585.

57. Shivananjegowda, *MLAD* 12, no. 1 (1955): 606–7.

58. H. K. Shivarudrappa, *MLAD*, 13, no. 15 (1955): 570.

59. G. A. Thimmappa Gowda, *MLAD* 9, no. 39 (1953): 2782.

60. Shivananjegowda, *MLAD* 12, no. 1 (1955): 606–7.

61. Address of His Highness the Rajapramukh, *MLAD* 10, part 1 (January 11, 1954): 2–3.

62. Srinivasa Gowda, *MLAD* 12, no. 1 (1955): 607.

63. Devaraj Urs, *MLAD* 9, no. 37 (1953): 2708.

64. File no. 58/2/55-SR, 1955, Ministry of Home Affairs, GOI, SR Section, NAI; file no. 16/1/55-SR, 1955, Ministry of Home Affairs, GOI, SR Section, NAI.

65. Chennigramaiah, *MLAD* 12, no. 1 (1954): 668.

66. Aa Na Kru, *Karnataka Ekikarana Kaipidi,* as cited in H. S. Gopala Rao, *Karnataka Ekikarana Itihasa,* 15.

67. B. Madhavachar (Bhadravathi), *MLAD* 12, no. 6 (1955): 577.

68. Chatterjee, *State and Politics,* 276.

69. Hanumanthaiya, *MLAD* 9, no 38 (1953): 2499.

70. Cited in Ismail, *Speeches,* 2:361.

71. "Mysore Roads and Bridges," *Indian Engineering* 105 (September 1939): 95. It was certainly far more inspiring an aide-mémoire than the comparison between a unified Karnataka and a left foot proposed by R. B. Kulkarni in *Kannadigana Sarvasva* in 1924! H. S. Gopala Rao, *Karnataka Ekikarana Itihasa,* 80.

72. Hettne, *The Political Economy of Indirect Rule,* 345.

73. Ibid., 346.

74. Hanumanthaiya, *MLAD* 13, no. 13 (1955): 797.

75. T. M. Muddalagiri Gowda, *MLAD* 12, no. 2 (1955): 666.

76. *MLAD* 7, no. 3 (1955): 787.

77. Imam, *MLAD* 7, no. 2 (1955): 654.

78. Imam, *MLAD* 13, no. 14 (1955): 870.

79. Gopala Gowda, *MLAD* 13, no. 12 (1955): 622.

80. Ibid., 623. Gowda complained that the people of Malnad had been referred to as "blanket wearing bears" but their development on new lines was possible with the available energies of unification. "Simply saying 'Mysore is ours' will not fill our stomachs" (624).

81. Shivananjegowda, *MLAD* 12, no. 1 (1955): 606–7.

82. A. G. Ramachandra Rao, Minister for Law Labour and Education, to Mr. President and Mr. Prime Minister, October 25, 1955, box 22, Palace Papers, KSA, my emphasis.

83. *Mysore on the March: 24 October 1947 to 26th January 1950* (Bangalore: Principal Information Officer, Mysore, n.d.) 220, my emphasis.

84. Here I am not taking up the very serious questions about the modalities of representative democracy that were thrown up during these debates. Briefly, some opponents of unification wanted a form of direct democracy, a plebiscite (on Kashmir lines) to be held in Mysore, suggesting that this was a question that the representative of the people alone could not decide; others wanted a "simple 2/3 majority vote in the houses," and yet others wanted a postponement of the issue of unification until the next election, when it could be a platform to contest the elections. Some others, such as Madhavachar, declared that decisions might have to be taken even against the opinion of the people when it was for their good. Legislators such as H. K. Veeranna Gowdh insisted on taking the issue to the electorate.

Hanumanthaiya firmly denied the need for a plebiscite, a two-thirds majority vote, a referendum, or even a postponement of the decision of unification until the next elections. In his long lecture on the history and merits of representative democracy he displayed a rare literary flourish, and he hoped for a consensual approach on the lines of the resolution to accept Bellary.

85. DVG to C. Rajagopalachari, March 29, 1958, DVG Private Papers, KSA, Bangalore.

86. Urs, *MLAD* 9, no. 37 (1953): 2708, my emphasis.

87. On the norming of the citizen as male, see Tharu and Niranjana, "Problems for a Contemporary Theory of Gender."

88. H. S. Siddaiah (Representative from Belur, Scheduled Castes), *MLAD* 13 (1955): 993.

89. The speech by Velluri in Urdu was not even translated! H. R. Abdul Gaffar (Teachers' Constituency), *MLCD* 7 (October 10–December 1, 1955): 839.

90. The identification of Kannada with Hindu, which was already clear in the writing of Alura Venkatrao, became even stronger in the 1940s. The organizers of a National Language Convention in New Delhi, who wished to introduce Hindi in Nagari script, invited a group of eminent linguists, writers, and leaders of regional language associations in order to strengthen the case for Hindi: "The leaders of the Bangiya Sahitya Parishat, the Kannada Sahitya Parishat and the great South Indian writers Vallathol and Kunhan Raja were among those who joined this convention (no date: late 1940s Constituent Assembly period). They had invited mostly those intellectuals whose sympathy for Hindi was well known and who were by no means representative of the language views of their regions." Das Gupta, *Language Conflict and National Development*, 135. For a recent espousal of "Kannadathana" as a quality that has endured the rise and fall of dynasties, fluctuating economic fortunes, war, and peace, see Narayana, *Kannadathana mattu Bharatiyate*, 15. Narayana says that the splintering of people into regions that spoke other languages occurred with the destruction of Vijayanagar, while unity was restored by the ekikarana movement and lost once more thereafter (43).

91. Devaraj Urs, *MLAD* 9, no. 37 (1953): 2708.

92. Lakshmi Devi Ramanna (Anekal-Hoskote), *MLAD* 13, no. 20 (1955): 1259.

93. G. Duggappa (Holalkere, Scheduled Caste), *MLAD* 13, no. 17 (1955): 1049.

94. For Tamil, see Ramaswamy, *Passions of the Tongue,* esp. 79–134. See also Niranajana, "Reworking Masculinities."

95. K. Hanumanthaiya to G. V. Pant, Minister for Home Affairs, 5/12/1955, sl. no. 1, D.O. letter no. K.K.1558 dated 5/18 December 1955 from the Chief Minister, Mysore State, GOI, Ministry of Home Affairs, S.R. Section, NAI.

96. Karanth, *Karnataka Painting.*

97. Prasad, "Cinema as a Site of Nationalist Identity," 80.

98. Joseph, "Politics of Recruitment in Public Sector Undertakings."

99. H. R Abdul Gaffar, *MLCD* 7, no. 13 (1955): 838.

100. Shivananjegowda, *MLAD* 13, no. 16 (1955): 981.

101. Extempore Speech delivered by Sri K. Hanumanthaiya on the 30th of November 1955, on the floor of the Legislative Council while moving an amendment to the Official resolution of seventeenth November 1955, file no. 16/2/55-SR 1955, GOI, Ministry of Home Affairs, S.R. Section, NAI.

102. B. K. Veeranna Gowdh, *MLAD* 13, no. 18 (1955): 1109.

Glossary

Words that are not defined here or in the text are found in current English dictionaries.

achara	types of conduct or behaviors
Adi Dravida	an original inhabitant of the Tamil region; adopted in the 1920s by dominated castes as self-description
Adi Karnataka	an original inhabitant of Karnataka; adopted in the 1920s by dominated castes as a self-description
agamasastras	scriptures relating to temple practices and rituals
agamik	a scholar well versed in agamasastras
agnihotra	the offering of oblations to fire
aksharabhyasa	literacy
amildari	a right to the revenue collected from a taluk
amildars	under Tipu Sultan, a revenue officer in charge of a taluk
aparigraha	refusal to posses wealth in excess of one's needs; noncovetousness
archaka	officiating priest of a temple
asaf	a provincial governor under Tipu Sultan
ashtagram	eight villages
ashta swayambhu kshetras	eight venerated Vaishnavite sites with images of "self-born" deities, i.e., idols that are not made by humans
babri	a stylized tiger stripe
banajiga	a member of a merchant class or sect
basavi	a lower-caste woman dedicated to temple service who could resort to prostitution
bhadralok	the emergent Bengali middle class
brahmacharya	the observance of celibacy
bungaroo	a royal concubine
Canteroy pagoda	derived from Kantirava varaha or pagoda; a type of gold coin, struck over a long period of time by various dynasties and trading companies, reissued in Mysore in the early nineteenth century; in the mid-nineteenth century, equal to approximately three rupees
chattram	a resting place for pilgrims or travelers
chattri	a decorative canopy
chiks	window blinds
chitragara	a member of an artist community
chitramantapa, chitramandira	a picture gallery

crore	unit of 10 million
cutcherry	an office
daffedar	a head peon in charge of ten or more persons
dalavai	a hereditary commander of military forces
darshan	the sight of a sacred or royal figure
Dasara	a ten-day festival commemorating the triumph of truth over evil; commemorates the victory of the epic hero Rama over Ravana
devadasi	a dancer-prostitute dedicated to the temple
devadaya	a land grant for performance of service to the temple
Dewan	a chief minister
dharma	righteousness; moral or suasive power
dharmadarsi, dharmakartha	a manager or superintendent of a religious institution
durbar	a royal assembly or court
Durga	a Hindu goddess; in Mysore, also referred to as Chamundeswari
ekikarana	unification
gandharva	a heavenly musician
ganjifa	richly decorated playing cards
gita	a song
gopi	a milkmaid
gopura	a tower over the gate of a South Indian temple
gruha pravesham	a housewarming
harijans	"children of god"; Mohandas K. Gandhi's name for those of the "untouchable" castes
hudevu	a circular, bastionlike structure of stones to provide rudimentary protection
inam	a revenue-free land grant
jambusavari	an elephant procession
janmamantapa	a structure commemorating a birthplace
jatakam	a horoscope
jharoka	a balcony
kafir	an unbeliever (in Islam)
kaikolas	members of a hereditary group of performers
kala vaishmaya	the corruptions of the (present) time
kalyani	a temple pond
karanji	a large tank
khillat	a royal honor/gift
khutba	a Friday sermon at a mosque
khyreat	a missive of well-being
killedar	a commander of a fort
koota	a gathering
koti	a store or warehouse
kudike	a form of widow remarriage among some non-Brahman castes
kula devata	a clan or family deity
lagna patrika	a wedding invitation

lakh	unit of 100,000
lavani	a folk ballad
Lingayat	a member of a Shaivite sect in Karnataka
Maharajakumari	a princess
mahathayi	a noble or great woman
manina maga	a son of the soil
mantapa	a structure or canopy
matha, mutt	a sectarian monastic institution, usually Brahman, Jain, or Lingayat
mathadhipathi	a head of a monastic institution
mitakshara	a legal text and system of family law
mleccha	non-Indian; a barbarian
moosahib	a counselor of the king
musnad	a throne
muzrai	a state grant for a religious or charitable purpose
nartaki	a female dancer
natuva	a member of a community of dancing masters or musicians
nautch	dance
neladaha	a thirst for land
nityasumangali	an ever-auspicious woman
nritya	dance
pagoda	a gold coin
paleyagara	a warrior chieftain
panchayat	a court of arbitration, usually consisting of five members
pandal	a tent
patel	a village headman
patra	the role of singer or dancer
patta	a term denoting a reign of twelve years; also means a deed to property
peta	a turban
pettah, pete	an emporium or market town
pradhan	the first counselor or minister of the king
prayaschitta	atonement
purana	a sacred text of Hinduism
qazi	a Muslim judicial officer administering towns according to Sharia law
ragini	a melodic structure personified as a woman in illustrations
ragmala	literally, a garland of melodic forms; a poetic genre that seeks to evoke the mood of classical melodic structure, frequently the subject of illustration
rajadharma	kingly duty
rishi	a sage
ryots	peasants
sampradaya	a system of religious doctrines; customs or usage
samstanam	a small regional court or estate
sanatana dharma	literally, "an unbroken tradition"; a set of ethical rules in Hinduism
santanambuja	a genealogy represented in the form of a lotus
sanyasi	a Hindu ascetic; a renouncer of the world

sastra	a preceptual text
satyagraha	nonviolent resistance, based on an insistence on truth
satyagrahi	a volunteer for nonviolent action
sejje	an extended front porch of a palace
setti, yajaman	a village or caste headman
shanbogue	a village accountant
shilpasastras	classical treatises on the making of the arts
shirti muchalika	revenue farming
shradhum	oblations for the dead in Hinduism
sowaree	horses, camels, and elephants that form part of the public procession of the Maharaja
sudra	fourth and last in the hierarchy of "touchable" castes
sule	a prostitute
tafe	dancing service
taluk	an administrative division consisting of a group of villages
tasdik patti	a list of sanctioned expenditures in temples
thera	bride price in the Malnad region of Mysore
upadesha	advice
vachana	a Kannada poetic form dating from the twelfth century
vakeel	a representative or ambassador
valasuttinakote	an inner enclosure wall
vamsavali	a genealogy
vamsavatarana vaibhava	the "wealth" of a family (ancestors and descendents)
vamsa vriksa	a genealogical tree
varnashilpi	an honorific title meaning "sculptor of colors"
varnashrama achara	the observance of caste customs
vasanthotsava	a spring festival, the festival of color
vimana	"sky caressing," or the topmost tower of a temple
virakallu	hero stones
yajaman	a caste or community headman
yugapurush	a man of the age
yuvaraja	a younger brother of the Maharaja
zamindari	a large landholding

Bibliography

Aa Na Kru. *Karnataka Ekikarana Kaipidi*. Vol. 1. Dharwad, 1947.

AC. "Indian Art and Art Critics." *Modern Review* 39, no. 1 (1926).

Aitken, Molly Emma. "The Practiced Eye: Styles and Allusions in Mewar Painting." Ph.D. diss., Columbia University, New York, 2000.

Aiya, V. Nagam. *Travancore State Manual*. Trivandrum: Travancore Government Press, 1906.

Aiyer, V. Aiyaswami. "Indian Arts and Crafts." *Quarterly Journal of the Mythic Society* 3, no. 1 (1916).

Allen, A., and J. Wells. *A Collection of Views in the Mysore Country*. London, 1794.

Allen, Brian. "From Plassey to Seringapatam: India and British History Painting, c. 1760–1800." In *The Raj: India and the British, 1600–1947*, ed. C. A. Bayly, 26–37. London: National Portrait Gallery, 1990.

Alpers, Svetlana. *The Art of Describing: Dutch Painting in the Seventeenth Century*. Chicago: University of Chicago Press, 1983.

Anandhi, S. "Representing Devadasis: 'Dasigal Mosavalai' as a Radical Text." *Economic and Political Weekly* 26, nos. 11–12 (March 1991): 739–54.

Appadurai, Arjun. *Worship and Conflict under Colonial Rule: A South Indian Case*. Cambridge, England: Cambridge University Press, 1981.

Appadurai, Arjun, and Carol Breckenridge. "The South Indian Temple: Authority, Honours and Redistribution." *Contributions to Indian Sociology* 10 (1984): 187–211.

Appasamy, Jaya. "He Created a New Indian Style." In *K. Venkatappa: Savi Nenapu*, ed. S. N. Chandrasekhara. Bangalore: Karnataka Lalit Kala Academy, 1987.

Archer, Mildred. *Company Painting*. London: Victoria and Albert Museum, with Mapin, Ahmedabad 1992.

———. *India and British Portraiture, 1770–1825*. Delhi: Oxford University Press, 1979.

Archer, Mildred, and W. G. Archer. *Indian Painting for the British*. Oxford, England: Oxford University Press, 1955.

Archer, Thomas. *Pictures and Royal Portraits Illustrative of English and Scottish History: From the Introduction of Christianity to the Present Time: Engraved from Important Works by Distinguished Modern Painters and from Authentic State Portraits, with Descriptive Historical Sketches*. London, Glasgow, and Edinburgh: Blackie and Son, n.d.

"Art and Art Critics in India." *Modern Review* 513 (1932).

Arunima, G. "Multiple Meanings: Changing Conceptions of Matrilineal Kinship in 19th and 20th Century Malabar." *Indian Economic and Social History Review* 33 (1996): 283–308.

———. *There Comes Papa: Colonialism and Transformation of Matriliny in Malabar, c. 1850–1940.* Hyderabad: Orient Longman, 2004.

Authentic Memoirs of Tippoo Sultaun, including His Cruel Treatment of English Prisoners; Account of His Campaigns with the Mahrattas, Rajahs, Warren Hastings, etc., esq. Lord Cornwallis and Lord Mornington; Plunder, Captures and Intrigues, and Secret Correspondence with France as Laid before the House of Commons. Also Descriptions of Eastern Countries, Hitherto Unknown, Palaces, Gardens, Zenanas, &c &c with a Preliminary Sketch of the Life and Character of Hyder Ally Cawn. By an officer in the East India Service. Calcutta: Mirror Press, 1819.

Bagchi, A. K. "Colonialism and the Nature of Capitalist Enterprise." *Economic and Political Weekly* 23, no. 31 (July 30, 1988): PE 38–49.

Bairy, T. S. Ramesh. "Caste, Community, and Association: A Study of the Dynamics of Brahmin Identity in Contemporary Karnataka." Ph.D. diss., University of Hyderabad, 2003.

Balibar, Etienne. "The Nation Form: History and Ideology." In *Race, Nation, Class: Ambiguous Identities,* ed. Etienne Balibar and Immanuel Wallerstein, 86–106. London: Verso, 1991.

Banglori, Mahmud Khan Mahmud. *Tarikh-i-Sultanat-i-Khudadad.* Bangalore: Matbua Kansar, 1934.

Barrett, Douglas. *Painting of the Deccan: XVI–XVII Century.* London: Faber and Faber, 1958.

Basappa, Stephen. *A Guide to Seringapatam and Its Vicinity, Historical and Traditional.* 3rd ed. Revised and enlarged. Bangalore, 1897.

Basu, Monomoyee. *Hindu Women and Marriage Law: From Sacrament to Contract.* Delhi: Oxford University Press, 2004.

Baxi, Upendra. "The State's Emissary: The Place of Law in Subaltern Studies." In *Subaltern Studies 7,* ed. G. Pandey and Chatterjee, 247–63. Delhi: Oxford University Press, 1992.

Bayly, C. A. "From Company to Crown: Nineteenth Century India and Its Visual Representation." In *The Raj: India and the British, 1600–1947,* ed. C. A. Bayly. London: National Portrait Gallery, 1990.

Bayly, Susan. "Hindu Kingship and the Origin of Community: Religion, State and Society in Kerala, 1750–1850." *Modern Asian Studies* 18, no. 2 (1984): 177–213.

Beatson, Alexander. *A View of the Origin and Conduct of the War with Tippoo Sultaun, Comprising a Narrative of the Operations of the Army under the Command of Lt. General George Harris and of the Siege of Seringapatam.* London: W. Bulmer, 1800.

Benjamin, Walter. *The Arcades Project.* Trans. Howard Eiland and Kevin McLaughlin. Cambridge, Mass., and London: Belknap Press of Harvard University Press, 1999.

———. *Illuminations.* Trans. Harry Zohn. New York: St. Martin's Press, 1985.

Bennett, Tony. "The Exhibitionary Complex." In *Thinking about Exhibitions,* ed. Reesa Greenberg, Bruce W. Ferguson, and Sandy Nairne, 81–112. London and New York: Routledge, 1996.

Berger, John. *Ways of Seeing.* London: BBC, 1972.

Bhagwan, Manu. *Sovereign Spheres: Princes, Education, and Empire in Colonial India.* Delhi: Oxford University Press, 2003.

Boratti, Vijaykumar. "Narratives and Communities: A Study of Select 'Literary' Controversies in Karnataka." Ph.D. diss., University of Hyderabad, 2004.

Bourdieu, Pierre. *The Field of Cultural Production*. Cambridge, England: Polity Press, 1993.

―――. *Outline of a Theory of Practice*. Cambridge, England: Cambridge University Press, 1977.

Bowring, Lewin Bentham. *Eastern Experiences*. London: Henry S. King, 1871.

Brittlebank, Kate. "Srirangapatnam Revisited: History as Experience Rather than Event." In *State and Diplomacy under Tipu Sultan: Documents and Essays*, ed. Irfan Habib. Delhi: Tulika, 2001: 140–50.

―――. "Tales of Treachery: Rumour as the Source of Claims That Tipu Sultan was Betrayed." *Modern Asian Studies* 37, no. 1 (2003): 195–211.

―――. *Tipu Sultan's Search for Legitimacy: Islam and Kingship in a Hindu Domain*. New Delhi: Oxford University Press, 1997.

―――. "The White Raja of Srirangapattana: Was Arthur Wellesley Tipu Sultan's True Successor?" *South Asia: Journal of South Asian Studies*, n.s. 26, no. 1 (2003): 23–35.

Buchanan, Francis. *A Journey from Madras through the Countries of Mysore, Canara, and Malabar*. 3 vols. London: T. Cadell and W. Davies. 1807. Rpt. Delhi: Asian Educational Services, 1988.

Buddle, Anne, with Pauline Rohatgi and Iain Gordon Brown. *The Tiger and the Thistle: Tipu Sultan and the Scots in India, 1760–1800*. Edinburgh: National Gallery of Scotland, 1999.

Bull, Edmund. *Romantic Seringapatam: A Supplementary Guide Book to Seringapatam Fort and Its Surroundings*. Mysore: Government Press, 1927.

Campbell, R. H. "Tippoo Sultan, the Fall of Seringapatam, and the Restoration of the Hindu Raj." *Quarterly Journal of the Mythic Society* 10, no. 1 (1919): 12–40.

Cannadine, David. *Ornamentalism: How the British Saw Their Empire*. London: Allen Lane, Penguin, 2001.

Cannon, R. *Historic Record of the Seventy First Regiment*. London, 1852.

Carroll, Lucy. "Law, Custom and Statutory Social Reform: The Hindu Women's Remarriage Act of 1856." In *Women in Colonial India*, ed. J. Krishnamurthy, 1–26. Delhi: Oxford University Press, 1989.

Chakrabarty, Dipesh. *Provincializing Europe: Postcolonial Thought and Historical Difference*. Delhi: Oxford University Press, 2000.

Chakravarti, Uma. *Rewriting History: The Life and Times of Pandita Ramabai*. Delhi: Kali for Women, 1998.

Chancellor, Nigel. "Mysore: The Making and Unmaking of a Model State." *South Asian Studies* 13 (1997): 109–26.

―――. "A Picture of Health: The Dilemma of Gender and Status in the Iconography of Empire: India c. 1805." *Modern Asian Studies* 35, no. 4 (2001): 769–82.

Chandra, Sudhir. *Enslaved Daughters: Colonialism, Law and Women's Rights*. Delhi: Oxford University Press, 1998.

Chandrasekhar, S. *Adhunika Karnatakada Andolanagalu*. Belegere: Tiptur, 2002.

―――. *Colonialism, Conflict and Nationalism*. Delhi: Wishwa, 1995.

―――. *Dimensions of Socio-Economic Change*. Delhi: Ashish, 1985.

―――. "Mysuru Mattu Ekikruta Karnatakada Rachane, 1937–1956." In *Adhunika Karnatakada Aandolanagalu*, ed. S. Chandrasekhar, 93–104. Belegere: Tiptur, 2002.

Chandrasekhara, N. S. *Dewan Rangacharlu.* Delhi: Publications Division, 1977.

Chatterjee, Partha. "The Black Hole of Empire." Staff seminar, Centre for Studies in Social Sciences, Calcutta, June 11 and 12, 2007.

———. "Development Planning and the Indian State." In *State and Politics in India,* ed. Partha Chatterjee, 271–98. Delhi: Oxford University Press, 1997.

———. "The Early Modern and Colonial Modern in South Asia: A Proposal for a Distinction." Staff seminar, Centre for Studies in Social Sciences, Calcutta, July 12, 2004.

———. "The Nation and Its Women." In *The Nation and Its Fragments: Colonial and Postcolonial Histories,* 116–134. Princeton, N.J.: Princeton University Press, 1993.

———. "The Nationalist Resolution of the Women's Question." In *Recasting Women: Essays in Indian Colonial History,* ed. Kumkum Sangari and Sudesh Vaid, 233–53. New Brunswick, N.J.: Rutgers University Press, 1990.

———. *Nationalist Thought in a Colonial World: A Derivative Discourse?* Delhi: Oxford University Press, 1986. Rpt. Minneapolis: University of Minnesota Press, 1992.

———. "On Civil and Political Society in Postcolonial Democracies." In *Civil Society: History and Possibilities,* ed. Sudipta Kaviraj and Sunil Khilnani, 165–78. Delhi: Foundation, 2002.

———, ed. *State and Politics in India.* Delhi: Oxford University Press, 1997.

Chatterjee, Suniti Kumar. "The Revival of Indian Art and the Lucknow School of Arts," *Modern Review* 41, no. 4 (1927).

Chiriyankandath, James. "Communities at the Polls: Electoral Politics and the Mobilisation of Communal Groups in Travancore." *Modern Asian Studies* 27, no. 3 (1993): 643–65.

Cohn, Bernard. *An Anthropologist among the Historians and Other Essays.* Delhi: Oxford University Press, 1987.

Colebrooke, Robert Hyde. *Twelve Views of Places in the Kingdom of Mysore, the Country of Tippoo Sultan, from Drawings Taken on the Spot.* London: Thomson, 1793–94.

Colley, Linda. *Captives: Britain, Empire, and the World, 1600–1850.* London: Jonathan Cape, 2002.

Coomaraswamy, Ananda. "About Pictures." *Modern Review* 8, no. 5 (1910).

———. *Art and Swadeshi.* Madras, 1912.

———. *Christian and Oriental Philosophy of Art.* Mineola, N.Y.: Dover Publications, 1956.

———. "Why Exhibit Works of Art?" In *Christian and Oriental Philosophy of Art.* Mineola, N.Y.: Dover Publications, 1956.

Copland, Ian. *The British Raj and the Indian Princes: Paramountcy in Western India, 1857–1930.* Delhi: Orient Longman, 1982.

———. "Communalism in Princely India: The Case of Hyderabad, 1930–40." *Modern Asian Studies* 22, no. 1 (1988): 783–814.

———. *The Princes of India in the Endgame of Empire, 1917–47.* Cambridge, England: Cambridge University Press, 1997.

Cousins, James H. *Aesthetical Necessity in Life.* Allahabad, 1944.

———. "The Future of Indian Art." *Rupam* 5, no. 17 (1924).

———. *The Renaissance in India.* Madras, 1918.

———. *The Social Value of Arts and Crafts.* Bangalore, 1925.

Cousins, James, and Margaret Cousins. *We Two Together.* Madras, 1950.

Cousins, Margaret E. *The Music of the Orient and Occident: Essays towards Mutual Understanding.* Madras, 1938.

Crary, Jonathan. *Techniques of the Observer: On Vision and Modernity in the Nineteenth Century.* Cambridge, Mass.: MIT Press, 1999.

Das Gupta, Jyotirindra. *Language Conflict and National Development: Group Politics and National Language Policy in India.* Bombay: Oxford University Press, 1970.

Davis, Richard. *The Lives of Indian Images.* Delhi: Munshilal Manoharlal, 1999.

Del Bontà, Robert J. "A Bhagvata Purana Manuscript from Mysore: A Preliminary Analysis." In *Sri Nagaabhinandanam Dr. M. S. Nagaraja Rao Festschrift: Essays on Art, Culture, History, Archaeology, Epigraphy and Conservation of Cultural Property of Indian and Neighbouring Countries,* 2 vols., ed. L. K. Srinivasan and S. Nagaraju, 2:465–93. Bangalore: Dr. N. Rao Felicitation Committee, 1995.

———. "See Krsna Run: Narrative Painting for Mummadi Krsnaraja Wodeyar." *Ars Orientalis,* Supp. 1, 2000.

Derrett, J. D. M. *Religion, Law, and State in India.* 1968. Rpt. Delhi: Oxford University Press, 1999.

Deshpande, Satish, ed. *Contemporary India: A Sociological View.* Delhi: Viking, 2003.

———. "The Nation as an Imagined Economy." In *Contemporary India: A Sociological View,* ed. Satish Deshpande, 48–73. Delhi: Viking, 2003.

Desikacharya, N. *The Origin and Growth of Sri Brahmatantra Parakala Mutt.* Bangalore: Bangalore Press, 1949.

Devika, J. *Engendering Individuals: The Language of Re-forming in Early Twentieth Century Keralam.* Delhi: Orient Longman, 2006.

———. *Her Self: Early Writings on Gender by Malayalee Women, 1898–1938.* Kolkata: Stree, 2005.

———. "The Idea of Being Malayali: The Aikyakeralam Movement of the Mid-Twentieth Century." Mimeo held by the author.

Devika, J., and Avanti Mukherjee. "Reforming Women in Malayalee Modernity: A Historical Overview." In *The Enigma of the Kerala Woman: A Failed Promise of Literacy,* ed. Swapna Mukhopadhyay, 112–30. New Delhi: Social Science Press, 2007.

Dhareshwar, Vivek. "Caste and the Secular Self." *Journal of Arts and Ideas* 25–26, (1993): 115–26.

Dirks, Nicholas. *Castes of Mind: Colonialism and the Making of Modern India.* Delhi: Permanent Black, 2001.

———. *The Hollow Crown: Ethnohistory of a South Indian Little Kingdom.* Princeton, N.J.: Princeton University Press, 1989.

Diwakar, R. R. *Karnataka through the Ages: From Prehistoric Times to the Day of the Independence of India.* Bangalore: Government Press, 1968.

Dushkin, Lelah. "The Non-Brahmin Movement in Princely Mysore." Ph.D. diss., University of Pennsylvania, Philadelphia, 1974.

DVG [D. V. Gundappa]. "A Gentleman to the Press Too." In *"M.V.": A Birth Centenary Commemoration Volume,* 110–20. Bangalore: Visvesvaraya Centenary Celebrations Committee, 1960.

Eden, Emily. *Up the Country: Letters Written to Her Sister from the Upper Provinces of India.* 2 vols. London, 1866.

Edney, Matthew H. *Mapping an Empire: The Geographical Construction of British India, 1765–1843.* Chicago and London: University of Chicago Press, 1997.

Elliot, R. H. *Gold, Sport, and Coffee Planting in Mysore.* Westminster: Archibald Constable, 1898.

Engels, Dagmar. "The Limits of Gender Ideology: Bengali Women, the Colonial State, and the Private Sphere, 1890–1930." *Women's Studies International Forum* 12, no. 4 (1989): 425–37.

Epstein, T. S. *Economic Development and Social Change in South India.* Manchester, England: Manchester University Press, 1962.

Epstein T. S., A. P. Suryanaryana, and T. Thimmegowda. *Village Voices: Forty Years of Rural Transformation in South India.* Delhi: Sage, 1998.

Everett, Jana. *Women and Social Change In India.* New York: St. Martin's Press. 1979.

"Exhibition at the Government School of Art." *Rupam* 3, no. 11 (1922).

Fabian, Johannes, and Tshibumba Matulu. *Remembering the Present: Painting and Popular History in Zaire.* Berkeley and Los Angeles: University of California Press, 1996.

Fisher, Michael H. *Indirect Rule in India: Residents and the Residency System, 1764–1857.* Delhi: Oxford University Press, 1991.

Forbes, Geraldine. "Women and Modernity: The Issue of Child Marriage in India." *Women's Studies International Quarterly* 2, no. 3 (1979): 407–19.

———. *Women in Modern India.* Delhi: Foundation Books, 2000.

Foucault, Michel. "Governmentality." In *The Foucault Effect: Studies in Governmentality,* ed. Graham Burchell et al., 87–104. London: Harvester, 1991.

———. *The History of Sexuality.* Vol. 1, *An Introduction.* New York: Vintage, 1980.

Freitag, Sandria. *Collective Action and Community: Public Arenas and the Emergence of Communalism in North India.* Delhi: Oxford Univesity Press, 1990.

———. "More than Meets the (Hindu) Eye: The Public Arena as a Space for Alternative Visions." In *Picturing the Nation: Iconographies of Modern India,* ed. Richard Davis, 92–116. Hyderabad: Orient Longman, 2007.

Gallery of Indian Paintings: Catalogue, with an Historical Introduction and Explanatory Notes. Mysore, [1924?].

Gangoly, O. C. "Indian Society of Oriental Art." In *Abanindranath Tagore: Golden Jubilee Number.* Calcutta: Indian Society of Oriental Art, 1961.

Gibbon, Edward. *The History of the Decline and Fall of the Roman Empire.* Edited and annotated with an introduction by Anthony Lentin and Brian Norman. London: Wordsworth, 1998.

Gidumal, Dayaram. *The Status of Women in India or the Handbook for Hindu Social Reformers.* Delhi: Publications India, 1989.

Gleig, G. R. *The Life of Sir Thomas Munro.* 2 vols. London, 1830.

Gole, Susan. *Indian Maps and Plans: From Earliest Times to the Advent of European Surveys.* Delhi: Manohar, 1989.

Gopal, M. H. *British Sources of the Economic, Political and Social History of the Mysore State.* Vol. 1, *1799–1812.* Bombay: Popular Prakashan, 1993.

————. *British Sources of the Economic, Political and Social History of the Mysore State*. Vol. 2, *1813–1832*. Bombay: Popular Prakashan, 1993.

————. *The Finances of the Mysore State, 1799–1831*. Hyderabad: Orient Longman, 1960.

————. *Tipu Sultan's Mysore: An Economic Study*. Bombay: Popular Prakashan, 1971.

Goswami, Manu. *Producing India: from Colonial Economy to National Space*. Delhi: Permanent Black, 2004.

Gowda, Sanna Nanje. *Infant Marriages of Post 1894 in the Princely State of Mysore*. Bangalore: Karnataka State Archives, 1979.

Greenberg, Reesa, Bruce W. Ferguson, and Sandy Nairne. *Thinking about Exhibitions*. London and New York: Routledge, 1996.

Gronewald, Sue. "Beautiful Merchandise: Prostitution in China, 1860–1936." *Women and History* 1 (Spring 1982): 51–66.

Guha, Ranajit. *An Indian Historiography of India: A Nineteenth-Century Agenda and Its Implications*. Calcutta: K. P. Bagchi and Sons, 1988.

————. "Chandra's Death." In *Subaltern Studies 5*, ed. Ranajit Guha, 135–65. Delhi: Oxford University Press, 1987.

Gundappa, D. V. *Kelavu Mahaniyaru*. Bangalore: Gokhale Institute of Public Affairs, 1987.

Gupta, Narayani. "Pictorialising the 'Mutiny' of 1857." In *Traces of India: Photography, Architecture, and the Politics of Representation, 1850–1900*, ed. Maria Antonella Pelizzari. New Haven, Conn.: Yale Centre for British Art, 2003.

Gustafson, D. F. "Mysore 1881–1902: The Making of a Model State." Ph.D. diss., University of Wisconsin, Madison, 1969.

Habib, Irfan. *Confronting Colonialism: Resistance and Modernisation under Haidar Ali and Tipu Sultan*. Delhi: Tulika, 2001.

————, ed. *State and Diplomacy under Tipu Sultan: Documents and Essays*. Delhi: Tulika, 2001.

Halappa , G. S. *History of the Freedom Movement in Karnataka*. Vol. 2. Bangalore: Government of Mysore, 1964.

Halemane, Lingadevaru, ed. *Dhira Tipuvina Lavanigalu*. Mysore: Samvahana, 2003.

Harrison, Selig. *India: The Most Dangerous Decades*. Princeton, N.J.: Princeton University Press, 1960.

Hasan, Mohibbul. *History of Tipu Sultan*. Calcutta: World Press, 1971.

Havanur, Srinivasa. *Hosagannadada Arunodaya*. Mysore: Mysore Vishwavidyalaya, Kannada Adhyayana Samsthe, 1974.

Havell, E. B. *Artistic and Industrial Revival in India*. 1912. Rpt. Delhi, 1986.

Hettne, Bjorn. *The Political Economy of Indirect Rule: Mysore, 1881–1947*. Delhi and Malmo: Curzon, 1978.

Hobsbawm, E. J., and Terence Ranger, eds. *The Invention of Tradition*. Cambridge, England: Cambridge University Press, 1983.

Holston, James. *The Modernist City: An Anthropological Critique of Brasilia*. Chicago and London: University of Chicago Press, 1989.

Home, Robert. *Select Views in Mysore, the Country of Tippoo Sultan from Drawings on the Spot Taken by Home with Historical Descriptions*. 1808. Rpt. Delhi: Asian Educational Services, 2000.

Howes, Jennifer. *The Courts of Pre-colonial South India: Material Culture and Kingship.* London and New York: Routledge Curzon, 2003.

Hunter, James. *Picturesque Scenery in the Kingdom of Mysore.* London: J. Hunter, 1805.

Hussain, Mahmud. *The Dreams of Tipu Sultan.* Karachi: Pakistan Historical Society, 1952.

Hutchins, Francis G. *The Illusion of Permanence: British Imperialism in India.* Princeton, N.J.: Princeton University Press, 1967.

Ikegame, Aya. "The Capital of Rajadharma: Modern Space and Religion in Colonial Mysore." *International Journal of Asian Studies* 4, no. 1 (2007): 15–44.

———. "Royalty in Colonial and Post Colonial India: A Historical Anthropology of Mysore from 1799 to the Present." Ph.D. diss., University of Edinburgh, 2007.

An Impartial Observer. *A Letter to a Member of Parliament on the Conclusion of the War with Tippoo Sultaun.* London: T. Cadell, 1792.

"Indian Art." *Modern Review* 32, no. 3 (1922): 216–39.

Indian Society for Oriental Art. *Special Issue on Abanindranath Tagore.* Calcutta, 1916.

Ismail, Mirza. *My Public Life: Recollections and Reflections.* London: George Allen and Unwin, 1954.

———. *Speeches by Amin-Ul-Mulk, Sir Mirza M. Ismail, Dewan of Mysore.* Vol. 2, *January 1931 to January 1936.* Bangalore: Government Press, 1937.

Issar, T. P. *Royal City: A Celebration of the Architectural Heritage and City Aesthetics of Mysore.* Bangalore: Marketing Consultants and Agencies, 1991.

Iyengar, M., A. Narayana, and M. A. Sreenivasa Char. *The Mysore Pradhans.* Mysore: Brahmavadin Press, 1992.

Iyengar, M. A. Ramanuja, ed. *Tirumalarya's Chikadevaraya Vamshavali.* Mysore, 1933. Original written by Tirumala Iyengar c. 1670.

Iyer, A. Padmanabha. *Modern Mysore: Impressions of a Visitor.* Trivandrum: Sridhara, 1938.

Iyer, L. K. Ananthakrishna. *The Mysore Tribes and Castes.* Vols. 1–4. Mysore, 1928–1935.

Iyer, Sambasiva. *Mysore, Industrial and Commercial, Being a Preliminary Sketch of the Resources, Industries, Trade, and Commerce of the Mysore State.* 3 vols. Bangalore: Vokkaligara Sangha, 1914.

Jaganmohan Palace Chitrasala, Mysore. *Gallery of Historical Portraits: Catalogue: With Short Sketches of the Indians and the Europeans in the Portraits.* 2nd revised ed. Bangalore: Bangalore Press, 1942.

Jamuna, M. "Social Change in Mysore with Special Reference to Women." Ph.D. diss., Bangalore University, 1990.

Jay, Martin. *Downcast Eyes: The Denigration of Vision in Twentieth-Century French Thought.* Berkeley and Los Angeles: University of California Press, 1994.

———. "Scopic Regimes of Modernity." In *Modernity and Identity,* ed. Scott Lash and Jonathan Friedman, 178–95. Oxford: Blackwell, 1992.

JDW. "The India Society." *Modern Review* 8, no. 2 (1910): 161.

John, Mary E. "Alternate Modernities? Reservations and Women's Movement in 20th Century India." *Economic and Political Weekly* 35, nos. 43–44 (October 28, 2000): WS 22–29.

Jordan, Kay. *From Sacred Servant to Profane Prostitute: A History of the Changing Legal Status of the Devadasis in India, 1857–1947.* Delhi: Manohar, 2003.

Joseph, T. M. "Politics of Recruitment in Public Sector Undertakings: A Study of the Nativist Movement in Bangalore." Ph.D. diss., Institute for Social and Economic Change, Bangalore, 1994.

Kannabiran, Kalpana. "Judiciary Social Reform and Debate on 'Religious Prostitution' in Colonial India." *Economic and Political Weekly* 32, no. 43 (October 28, 1995): 59–71.

Kantorowicz, Ernst H. *The King's Two Bodies: A Study in Medieval Political Theology.* Princeton, N.J.: Princeton University Press, 1957.

Kapur, Geeta. "When Was Modernism in Indian Art?" In *When Was Modernism? Essays on Contemporary Cultural Practice in India,* ed. Geeta Kapur, 297–324. New Delhi: Tulika, 2000.

Karanth, Shivarama. *Bharatiya Chitra Kala.* Puttur: Shivarama Karanth, 1930.

———. *Karnataka Painting.* Mysore: Prasaranga, 1973.

The Karnataka Handbook. Printed and published for the Editorial Board of the Karnataka Provincial Congress Committee. Bangalore, 1924.

Karve, Irawati. "The Kinship Map of India." In *Family Kinship and Marriage in India,* ed. Patricia Uberoi, 50–73. Delhi: Oxford University Press, 1993.

Kasi, Ravikumar. "Odedha Kannadi." *Sanchaya* 8, no. 1 (1996).

Kaul, Rekha. *Caste, Class, and Education: Politics of the Capitation Fee Phenomenon in Karnataka.* Delhi: Sage, 1993.

Kaviraj, Sudipta. "A Critique of Passive Revolution." *Economic and Political Weekly,* special issue (November 23, 1988): 2429–43.

———. "In Search of Civil Society." In *Civil Society: History and Possibilities,* ed. Sudipta Kaviraj and Sunil Khilnani, 282–320. Delhi: Foundation, 2002.

———. "On the Structure of Nationalist Discourse." In *State and Nation in the Context of Social Change,* 2 vols., ed. T. V. Satyamurthy, 1:315–40. Delhi: Oxford University Press, 1994.

———. "An Outline of a Revisionist Theory of Modernity." *Journal of European Sociology* 46, no. 3 (2003): 497–526.

Khan, I. G. "State Intervention in the Economy: Tipu's Orders to Revenue Collectors, 1792–97; A Calendar." In *State and Diplomacy under Tipu Sultan: Documents and Essays,* ed. Irfan Habib, 66–81. Delhi: Tulika, 2001.

King, Anthony. *Colonial Urban Development: Culture, Social Power, and Environment.* London: Routledge and Kegan Paul, 1976.

King, Robert. *Nehru and the Language Politics of India.* Delhi: Oxford University Press, 1997.

Kirkpatrick, William. *Select Letters of Tippoo Sultan to Various Public Functionaries.* London, 1811.

Kirmani, Meer Husain Ali Khan. *The History of Hydur Naik.* Translated from the Persian by Col. W. Miles. London: Oriental Translation Fund, 1862.

———. *History of Tipu Sultan, Being a Continuation of Nishan I Hyderi.* Trans. from the Persian by Col. W Miles. 1864. Rpt. Calcutta: Sushil Gupta, 1958.

Kishwar, Madhu. "Gandhi on Women." *Economic and Political Weekly* 20, nos. 40 (October 5, 1985) and 41 (October 12, 1985): 1691–1702, 1753–58.

Koch, Ebba. *Mughal Art and Imperial Ideology: Collected Essays.* Oxford, England: Oxford University Press, 2001.

Kodoth, Praveena. "Courting Legitimacy or Delegitimising Custom? Sexuality, Samband-
ham, and Marriage Reform in Late Nineteenth Century Malabar." *Modern Asian Studies* 35, no. 2 (2001): 349–84.

———. "Shifting the Ground of Fatherhood: Matriliny, Men, and Marriage in Early Twentieth Century Malabar." Working Paper Series 359. Centre for Development Studies,
Trivandrum, 2004.

Kooiman, Dick. *Communities and Electorates: A Comparative Discussion of Communalism in
Colonial India.* Amsterdam: V. U. University Press, 1995.

Kramrisch, Stella. *A Survey of Painting in the Deccan.* New Delhi: Oriental Books, 1983.

Krumbiegal, G. H. "Mysore: Its Horticulture and Gardens." In *Mysore: Ruling Chiefs of
India,* ed. C. Raghunatha Rao, 54–58. Ser. 2. Madras: S. Kristnan, 1908.

Kumar, Radha. *The History of Doing: An Illustrated Account of Movements for Women's Rights
and Feminism in India.* Delhi: Kali for Women, 1993.

Lafont, Jean Marie. *Indika: Essays in Indo-French Relations, 1630–1976.* Delhi: Manohar,
2000.

Lallahai, Kasturbhai. *Report on the State-Owned and State-Aided Industrial Concerns in Mysore.* Delhi, 1951.

Larsen, Neil. *Modernism and Hegemony: A Materialist Critique of Aesthetic Agencies.* Minneapolis: University of Minnesota Press, 1990.

Lewis, Brian. *Chitradurga in the Early 1800s: Archaeological Interpretations of Colonial Drawings.* Bangalore: Indian Council of Historical Research, Southern Regional Centre, 2006.

Leyden, John. *The Poetical Remains of the Late Dr. John Leyden with Memoirs of His Life by
the Reverend James Morton.* London, 1819.

Lynch, Kevin. *The Image of the City.* Cambridge, Mass.: MIT Press, 1960.

Lynd, Kyrre Magnus. "The Nagar Rebellion, 1830–1: Administration and Rule in an Indian
Native State." M.A. thesis, University of Oslo, 2004.

Mahabaleswarappa, B. C. "Quit India Movement in Isoor." Research project, Gulbarga
University, Karnataka, India, 1998. Mimeo.

Malleson, George B. *Seringapatam: Past and Present, a Monograph.* Madras: Higginbothams, 1876.

Mani, Lata. *Contentious Traditions: The Debate on Sati in Colonial India.* Berkeley and Los
Angeles: University of California Press, 1998.

Manor, James. *Political Change in an Indian State: Mysore, 1917–1955.* New Delhi: South Asia
Books, 1978.

Marshall, J. "Cornwallis Triumphant: War in India and the British Public in the Late Eighteenth Century." In *Studies on the Rise of British Dominance in India,* 51–74. London:
Varorium, 1993.

Marx, Karl. *Grundrisse: Foundation of the Critique of Political Economy.* Trans. with a fore-
word by Martin Nicklaus. Harmondsworth, England: Pelican, 1973.

Mauss, Marcel. *The Gift: The Form and Reason for Exchange in Archaic Societies.* London:
Routledge, 1990.

Mayer, Adrian C. "Perceptions of Princely Rule: Perspectives from a Biography." In *Meth-
odology and Fieldwork,* ed. Vinay Kumar Srivastava, 288–306. Delhi: Oxford University
Press, 2004.

McGinn, Padma Anagol. "The Age of Consent Act (1891) Reconsidered: Women's Perspectives and Participation in the Child Marriage Controversy in India." *South Asia Research* 12, no. 2 (1992): 100–18.

McPhee, Constance. "Tipu Sultan of Mysore and British Medievalism in the Paintings of Mather Brown." In *Orientalism Transposed: The Impact of the Colonies on British Culture,* ed. Julie F. Codell and Dianne Sachko Mcleod, 202–19. London: Ashgate, 1998.

Menon, Dilip. "Being Brahman the Marxist Way: E. M. S. Namboodiripad and the Pasts of Kerala." In *Invoking the Past: The Uses of History in South Asia,* ed. Daud Ali. Delhi: Oxford University Press, 1999.

Menon, Nivedita. "Elusive 'Women': Feminism and Women's Reservation Bill." *Economic and Political Weekly* 35, nos. 43–44 (October 28, 2000): WS 35–44.

Metcalf, Thomas R. *An Imperial Vision: Indian Architecture and Britain's Raj.* London and Boston: Faber and Faber, 1989.

Mitchell, Timothy. "The Stage of Modernity." In *Questions of Modernity,* ed. Timothy Mitchell, 1–34. Minneapolis: University of Minnesota Press, 2000.

Mittal, Jagdish. "Paintings of Hyderabad School." *Marg* 16, no. 2 (March 1963): 43–56.

Mitter, Partha. *Art and Nationalism in Colonial India: 1850–1922.* Cambridge, England: Cambridge University Press, 1994.

———. *The Triumph of Modernism: India's Artists and the Avant-garde, 1922–47.* London: Reaktion Books, 2007.

MMDLT [Monsieur De La Tour]. *The History of Hyder Shah alias Hyder Ali Khan Bahadur and of His Son, Tippoo Sultaun, Revised and Corrected by His Highness Prince Gholam Mohammed the Only Surviving Son of Tippoo Sultaun.* London: W. Thacker, 1855.

Moienuddin, Mohammed. *Sunset at Srirangapatam after the Death of Tipu Sultan.* Hyderabad: Orient Longman, 2000.

Moor, Edward. *A Narrative of the Operations of Captain Little's Detachment and of the Mahratta Army Commanded by Parseram Bhow during the Late Confederacy in India against Nawab Tippoo Sultan Bahadur.* London, 1794.

Murthy, Chidananda M. *Bhasika Bruhat Karnataka.* Bangalore: Sapna, 2005.

———. "Kannadada Samasyegalu." In *Kannada-Kannadiga-Karnataka Kannada Shakti,* ed. Ra Nam Chandrasekhar. Bangalore: Kannada Shakthi Kendra, 1996.

The Mysore District Gazetteer. Bangalore, 1869.

Mysore Samsthanada Prabhugalu: Srimanmaharajara Vamshavali (Annals of the Mysore royal family). Parts 1 and 2. Mysore, 1916, 1922.

Nair, Janaki. "Beyond Exceptionalism: South India in the Modern Historical Imagination." *Indian Economic and Social History Review* 43, no. 3 (2006): 323–47.

———. "Contending Ideologies: The Mass Awakeners' Union in Mysore, 1936–1942." *Social Scientist* 22, nos. 7–8 (July–August 1994): 42–63.

———. "Eighteenth Century Passages to a History of Mysore." In *History in the Vernacular,* ed. Raziuddin Aquil and Partha Chatterjee, 66–106. Delhi: Permanent Black, 2008.

———. "The Emergence of Labour Politics in South India: Bangalore, 1900–1947." Ph.D. diss., University of Syracuse, Syracuse, N.Y., 1991.

———. "'Imperial Imperatives,' National Honour, and New Patriarchal Compacts in Early Twentieth Century India." *History Workshop Journal* 66 (2008): 208–26.

———. "'Memories of Underdevelopment': The Identities of Language in Contemporary Karnataka." *Economic and Political Weekly* 21, no. 42 (October 12, 1996): 2809–16.

————. *Miners and Millhands: Work, Culture, and Politics in Princely Mysore*. New Delhi: Sage, 1998.

————. *The Promise of the Metropolis: Bangalore's Twentieth Century*. Delhi: Oxford University Press, 2005.

————. "The Troubled Relationship between Feminism and Indian Historiography." *Economic and Political Weekly* 43, no. 43 (October 25–31, 2008): 57–65.

————. *Women and Law in Colonial India: A Social History*. Delhi: Kali for Women, 1996.

Narasimhan, Aa La. *Karnataka bhitthi chitra Parampara*. Karnataka Lalith Kala Akademy, 1998.

Narayana, K. V. "What Should We Address? Kannada Cause or the Kannada Hegemony?" *Journal of Karnataka Studies* 2, no. 1 (May 2–April 5, 2006): 257–64.

Narrative Sketches of the Conquest of Mysore Effected by the British Troops and Their Allies in the Capture of Seringapatam and the Death of Tippoo Sultaun, May 4, 1799, with Notes Descriptive and Explanatory. 2nd ed. London, 1800.

Nijalingappa, S. *My Life and Politics: An Autobiography*. Delhi: Vision Books. 2000.

Niranjana, Tejaswini. "Reworking Masculinities: Rajkumar and the Kannada Public Sphere." *Economic and Political Weekly* 3, no. 47 (November 18–24, 2000): 4147–50.

Nivedita, Sister, and Ananda Coomaraswamy. *Myths of the Hindus and Buddhists*. London, 1920.

Nochlin, Linda. *Realism*. New York and Baltimore: Penguin, 1976.

Nolan, J. H. *The Illustrated History of the British Empire in India and the East, from the Earliest Times to the Suppression of the Sepoy Mutiny in 1859*. London: James S. Virtue, n.d. [1860].

Nora, Pierre. "Between Memory and History: Les lieux de memoire." *Representations* 26 (Spring 1989): 7–24.

Oettermann, Stephen. *The Panorama: History of a Mass Medium*. Trans. Deborah Lucas Scheider New York: Zone, 1997.

Oldenburg, Veena. "Lifestyle as Resistance: The Case of the Courtesans of Lucknow." *Feminist Studies* 16, no. 2 (Summer 1990): 259–89.

Pakrasi, Kanti B. *Female Infanticide in India*. Calcutta, 1971.

Pandian, M. S. S. *Brahman, Non-Brahman*. Delhi: Permanent Black, 2007.

Panigrahi, Lalita. *Social Policy and British Rule in India*. Delhi: Munshilal Manoharlal, 1972.

Parasher, Aloka, and Usha Naik. "Temple Girls of Medieval Karnataka." *Indian Economic and Social History Review* 23, no. 1 (1986): 63–91.

Parayil, Sujith Kumar. "Photography(s) in 20th Century Kerala." Ph.D. diss., Manipal University, Manipal, India, 2007.

Parkar, Kunal. "'A Corporation of Superior Prostitutes': Anglo Indian Legal Conceptions of Temple Dancing Girls, 1800–1914." *Modern Asian Studies* 32, no. 3 (1998): 559–633.

Parsons, Constance. *Mysore City*. London: Oxford University Press, 1930.

————. *Seringapatam*. London: Oxford University Press, 1931.

Pashukannis, Evgeny. *Law and Marxism: A General Theory*, 1929. Trans. Barbara Einhorn. Worcester, Mass.: Pluto, 1989.

Pedersen, Susan. "National Bodies, Unspeakable Acts: The Sexual Politics of Colonial Policy Making." *Journal of Modern History* 63 (1991): 647–80.

Pernau, Margrit. *The Passing of Patrimonialism: Politics and Culture in Hyderabad, 1911–48.* Delhi: Manohar, 2000.

Peterson, Indira Vishwanathan. "Facing the Modern in Nineteenth Century Tanjavur: Frontality as a Sign in Maratha Royal Portraits." Paper presented at the conference The Art of Exchange: Circulation of Visual Culture in Colonial India, Columbia University, New York, October 2008. Mimeo.

———. "Portraiture at the Tanjore Maratha Court: Toward Modernity in the Early 19th Century." Mimeo held by the author.

———. "Subversive Journeys? Travel as Empowerment in King Serfoji II of Tanjore's 1820–22 Pilgrimage to Benares." Paper presented at the New England Conference of the Associations for Asian Studies, Brown University, Providence, R.I., September 30, 2000.

Pinney, Christopher. *Camera Indica: The Social Life of Indian Photographs.* Chicago: University of Chicago Press, 1997.

———. *Photos of the Gods: The Printed Image and Political Struggle in India.* Delhi: Oxford University Press, 2004.

Poonacha, Vijaya Thambanda. *Adhunika Kodagu.* Hampi, India: Prasaranga, Kannada University, 2000.

———. *Conflicting Identities in Karnataka: Separate State and Anti–Separate State Movements in Coorg.* Hampi, India: Prasaranga, Kannada University, 2004.

Prasad, Madhava. "Cinema as a Site of Nationalist Identity." *Journal of Karnataka Studies* 1 (November 1, 2003–April 2004): 60–85.

Presler, Franklin. *Religion under Bureaucracy: Policy and Administration for Hindu Temples in South India.* Cambridge, England: Cambridge University Press, 1987.

Price, Pamela. *Kingship and Political Practice in Colonial India.* Cambridge, England: Cambridge University Press, 1996.

Rai, Mridu. *Hindu Rulers, Muslim Subjects: Islam, Rights, and the History of Kashmir.* Delhi: Permanent Black, 2004.

Rajayyan, K. *South Indian Rebellion: The First War of Independence, 1800–01.* Mysore: Rao and Raghavan, 1971.

"Rakhmabai's 'Reply' to Dadajee's 'Exposition.'" In Chandra, *Enslaved Daughters: Colonialism, Law, and Women's Rights,* Appendix D. Delhi: Oxford University Press, 1998.

Ram, N. Vyasa. "The New Spirit in Indian Art." *Quarterly Journal of the Mythic Society* 17, no. 4 (1927): 294–308.

Ramabai, Pandita. *The High Caste Hindu Woman.* Philadelphia: J. B. Rodgers, 1887.

Ramachandrappa, Bargur. *Kannadabhimana.* Bangalore: Ankita Pustaka, 2002.

Ramakrishnan, R. *Press and Politics in an Indian State, 1859–1947.* Channarayapatna, India: Swabhimana Prakashana, 1997.

Ramanand, P. "The Fine Arts in India." *Modern Review* 21, no. 1 (1917).

Ramaswamy, Sumathi. *Fabulous Geographies, Catastrophic Histories: The Lost Land of Lemuria.* Delhi: Permanent Black, 2005.

———. *Passions of the Tongue: Language Devotion in Tamil Nadu, 1891–1970.* Delhi: Munshiram Manoharlal, 1998.

Ramusack, Barbara. *The Indian Princes and Their States.* Cambridge, England: Cambridge University Press, 2004.

Rancière, Jacques. *The Politics of Aesthetics: The Distribution of the Sensible*. Trans. with an introduction by Gabriel Rockhill. New York: Continuum, 2004.

Rangachar, H., and Kodanda Rao. "A Brief Life Sketch." In *"M.V.": A Birth Centenary Commemoration Volume*, 293–334. Bangalore: Visvesvaraya Centenary Celebrations Committee, 1960.

Rangaswami, Vanaja. *The Story of Integration: A New Interpretation in the Context of the Democratic Movements in the Princely States of Mysore and Travancore*. Delhi: Manohar, 1981.

Rao, Alura Venkata. *Karnataka Gathavaibhava*. 1917. Rpt. Bangalore: Kannada Sahitya Parishat, 1982.

Rao, Ba Na Sundara. *Bengalurina Itihasa*. Bangalore, 1985.

Rao, C. H.. *Engravings at Government House, Mysore*. Bangalore, [1933?].

———. *History of Mysore under the Wodeyar Dynasty of Kings, 1399–1799*. 3 vols. Bangalore: Government Press, 1943–46.

———. "Krishnaraja Wodeyar III." *Quarterly Journal of the Mythic Society* 6, no. 1 (1915–16): 43–45.

———. *Mysore Gazetteer*. 5 vols. Bangalore: Government Press, 1929–34.

Rao, H. S. Gopala. *Karnataka Ekikarana Itihasa*. 1996. Rpt. Bangalore: Navakarnataka, 2004.

Rao, K. V. Narayana. *The Emergence of Andhra Pradesh* (Bombay: Popular Prakasham, 1973), 202.

Rao, M. Shama. *Modern Mysore*. Vol. 1, *From the Beginnings to 1868*. Bangalore: Higginbothams, 1936.

———. *Modern Mysore*. Vol. 2, *From 1868 to the Present*. Bangalore: Higginbothams, 1936.

Rao, M. S. Nanjunda. "Varnamaya Baduku." In *K. Venkatappa: Savi Nenapu*, ed. S. N. Chandrasekhara, 32–40. Bangalore: Karnataka Lalit Kala Academy, 1987.

Rao, P. Ramachandra. *Modern Indian Painting*. Madras, 1953.

Rao, P. V. Narayana. *Kannadathana Mattu Bhaaratheeyathe*. Belgavi, India: Kannada Jagruti Pustaka Male, 2000.

Rao, Ramachandra ("Punganuri"). *Memoirs of Hyder and Tippoo, Rulers of Seringapatam*. Trans. from the Marathi by C. P. Brown. Madras: Simkins, 1842.

Rao, S. K. Ramachandra. *K. Venkatappa: The Man and His Art*. Bangalore: Government of Karnataka, 1988.

———. *Mummadi Krishnaraja Wodeyara Sritatvanidhi*. Vol. 1, *Swara Chudamani*. Hampi, India: Kannada Vishwavidyalaya, 1993.

———. *Mysore Chitramala: Traditional Paintings*. Bangalore: Karnataka Chitrakala Parishat, 2004.

Rao, S. R., and B. V. K. Sastry. *Traditional Paintings of Karnataka*. Bangalore. Eastern Press, 1990.

Rao, T. Ramachandra. "Nanna Alilu Seve." In *Karmayogi*, ed. M. N. Jois. Bangalore: Mysore, 1974.

Rao, V. Narayana. *Kannadathana Mattu Bhaaratheeyathe*. Belgavi, India: Kannada Jagruti Pustaka Male, 2000.

Ray, Bharati. *Hyderabad and British Paramountcy, 1858–1883*. Delhi: Oxford University Press, 1988.

Ray, Mihir Kumar. *Princely States and the Paramount Power, 1858–1876*. New Delhi: Rawat, 1981.

Rege, Sharmila. *Writing Caste, Writing Gender: Dalit Women's Testimonios*. Delhi: Zubaan, 2006.

Rice, Lewis. *Epigraphia Carnatica*. Vol. 2, *Inscriptions of the Mysore District*, Part 1. Bangalore: Government Press, 1894.

———. *Epigraphia Carnatica*. Vol. 4, *Inscriptions in the Mysore District*, Part 2. Bangalore: Mysore Government Press, 1898.

———. *Mysore: A Gazetteer Compiled for Government*. Vol. 2, *Mysore, by Districts*. London: Archibald Constable, 1897.

Rohatgi, Pauline. "From Pencil to Panorama: Tipu in Pictorial Perspective." In *The Tiger and the Thistle: Tipu Sultan and the Scots in India, 1760–1800*, ed. Anne Buddle with Pauline Rohatgi and Iain Gordon Brown, 39–52. Edinburgh: National Gallery of Scotland, 1999.

Saki. *Making History: Karnataka's People and Their Past*. Vol. 2, *Colonial Shock, Armed Struggle, 1800–1857*. Bangalore: Vimukthi Prakashana, 2004.

Salmond, James. *A Review of the Origin, Progress, and Result of the Decisive War with the Late Tippoo Sultaun in Mysore*. London: T. Cadell et al., 1800.

Sampath, Vikram. *Splendours of Royal Mysore: The Untold Story of the Wodeyars*. New Delhi: Rupa, 2008.

Sangari, Kumkum, and Sudesh Vaid. "Introduction." In *Recasting Women: Essays in Indian Colonial History*, ed. Kumkum Sangari and Sudesh Vaid, 1–26. New Brunswick, N.J.: Rutgers University Press, 1990.

Sannaiah, B. S., ed. *Rajavalli Kathasara, Devachandra Virachita*. Mysore: Mysuru Vishwavidyalaya Prasaranga, 1988.

Sarangi, Asha. "Ambedkar and the Linguistic States: A Case for Maharashtra." In *Economic and Political Weekly* 41, no. 2 (January 14–20, 2006): 151–57.

Sarkar, Lotika. *National Specialised Agencies and Women's Equality Law Commission of India*. Delhi: Centre for Women's Development Studies, 1988.

Sarkar, Sumit. "Kaliyuga, Chakri, and Bhakti: Ramakrishna and His Times." *Economic and Political Weekly* 27, no. 29 (July 27, 1992): 1548–50.

———. *Modern India*. Delhi: Macmillan, 1982.

Sarkar, Tanika. *Hindu Wife, Hindu Nation: Community, Religion, and Cultural Nationalism*. Delhi: Permanent Black, 2000.

———. "Rhetoric against Age of Consent: Resisting Colonial Reason and the Child Wife." *Economic and Political Weekly* 28, no. 36 (September 4, 1993): 1869–78.

Sastri, K. N. Venkatasubba. *The Administration of Sir Mark Cubbon, 1832–1864*. Bangalore: Higginbothams, 1936.

———. *An Introduction to the History of the Administration of Mysore*. Mysore: Wesley, 1937.

Satyan, T. S. *Alive and Clicking: A Memoir*. New Delhi: Penguin, 2005.

Schama, Simon. "The Domestication of Majesty: Royal Family Portraiture, 1500–1850." *Journal of Interdisciplinary History* 18, no. 1 (1986): 155–83.

Scott, David. "Colonial Governmentality." *Social Text* 43 (Fall 1995): 191–200.

Selections from the Records of the Mysore Palace. Vol. 1, *Musicians, Actors, and Artists*. Mysore: Mysore Divisional Archives Office, 1993.

Selections from the Records of the Mysore Palace. Vol. 2, *Palaces and Mansion of the Royal Family*. Bangalore: Department of Archives, 1997.

Sen, Arun. "The Exhibition of Oriental Art." *Modern Review* 13, no. 4 (1913).

———. "The Rise and Decadence of Art in India." *Modern Review* 11, no. 6 (1912).

Sen, Asok. "A Pre-British Economic Formation in India of the Late Eighteenth Century: Tipu Sultan's Mysore." In *Perspectives in Social Sciences: Historical Dimensions,* ed. Barun De. Vol. 1, 46–115. Delhi: Oxford University Press, 1977.

Sen, Sudipta. *Distant Sovereignty: National Imperialism and the Origins of British India.* New York and London: Routledge, 2002.

Sennett, Richard. *The Conscience of the Eye.* New York: W. W. Norton, 1992.

Settar, S., and Gunther Dietz Sontheimer. *Memorial Stones: A Study of their Origin, Significance and Variety.* Dharwad, India, and Heidelberg: Institute of Indian Art History and South Asia Institute, University of Heidelberg, 1982.

Sharma, Thi Tha, ed. *Charitrika Dakhalegalu.* Bengaluru, India: Kannada Sahitya Parishat, 1999.

Shashikanth, K. "Carnatic Music, Kannada, and Kannadigas: Certain Moments from Princely Mysore." Mimeo held by author.

Sheikh, Gulammohammed. *Contemporary Art in Baroda.* Delhi: Tulika, 1997.

Shekhar, Veena. "Dhariya Daulat Bagh Paintings: A Study." M.F.A. thesis, Chitrakala Parishat, Bangalore, 1995.

———. Mural Paintings of Sibi, Keladi, and Bangalore, India. Keladi: Museum and Historical Research Bureau; Bangalore: International Centre for Indian Art and Cultural Studies, 1999.

Singaraiyya, M. *Chamrajendra Wodeyaravara Charitre.* 4th ed. Revised and enlarged. Bangalore: Government Press, 1927.

Sinha, Mrinalini. *Specters of Mother India: The Global Restructuring of an Empire.* Durham, N.C.; London: Duke University Press, 2006.

Sitaramaiah, V. *Githagalu.* Karnataka: Karnataka Sahitya Prakatana Mandira, 1931.

———. *K. Venkatappa.* Delhi: Lalit Kala Academy, 1980.

Siva Chariyar, Swaminatha. *Kamikagamaha.* Madras: Dakshina Bharata Archaka Sangha, 1975.

Smith, Richard Saumarez. "Rule-by-Records and Rule-by-Reports: Complementary Aspects of the British Imperial Rule of Law." *Contributions to Indian Sociology* 19, no. 1 (1985): 153–76.

Sood, Aditya Dev. "The Matha State: Kinship, Asceticism, and Institutionality in the Public Life of Karnataka." Ph.D. diss., University of Chicago, 2006.

Spivak, Gayatri. "Feminism and Decolonisation." *Differences* 3, no. 3 (1991): 139–70.

Sreenivasan, M. A. *The Last Mysore Pradhan: The Memoirs of M. A. Sreenivasan.* Bangalore: Drone Quill, 2005.

Srinivas, M. N. *Marriage and Family in Mysore.* Bombay: New Book Co., 1942.

Srinivasan, Amrit. "Reform and Revival: The Devadasi and Her Dance." *Economic and Political Weekly* 20, no. 44 (November 2, 1985): 1869–76.

Sri Subbaraya Dasaru Prathinama Sri Gopaldasaru Artharth Sri Gopala Wodeyaravara Charitre. Mysore: Sri Subbaraya Dasara Marimakkalu, 1967.

Stache-Rosen, Valentina. "Gandabherunda." *Quarterly Journal of the Mythic Society* 67, nos. 1–4 (January–December 1976): 1–24.

Stein, Burton. "Idiom and Ideology in Early Nineteenth Century South India." In *Rural*

India: Land Power and Society under British Rule, ed. Peter Robb, 23–58. London: Curzon, 1983.

———. "Notes on 'Peasant Insurgency' in Colonial Mysore." In *Institutions and Ideologies: A SOAS South Asia Reader,* ed. David Arnold and Peter Robb, 186–200. Surrey, England: Curzon, 1993.

———. "State Formation and Economy Reconsidered." *Modern Asian Studies* 19, no. 3 (1985): 387–413.

———. *Thomas Munro: The Origins of the Colonial State and His Vision of Empire.* Delhi: Oxford University Press, 1989.

Story, Saskia Kersenboom. *Nityasumangali.* Delhi: Motilal Banarsidass, 1987.

Subbarayappa, D. C. "He Stood by Merit." In *"M.V.": A Birth Centenary Commemoration Volume,* 156–64. Bangalore: Visvesvaraya Centenary Celebration Committee, 1960.

Subrahmanyam, K. V. *Venkatappa: Samakaleena Punaravalokana.* Bangalore: Chitrakavya Prakashana, 1980.

Subrahmanyam, Sanjay. *Penumbral Visions: Making Politics in Early Modern South India.* Delhi: Oxford University Press, 2001.

Subramanian, Lakshmi. *From the Tanjore Court to Madras Music Academy: A Social History of Music in South India.* Delhi: Oxford University Press, 2006.

Subramanyan, K. G. *The Living Tradition: Perspectives on Modern Indian Art.* Calcutta: Seagull, 1987.

Sundar, Pushpa. *Patrons and Philistines: Arts and the State in British India.* Delhi: Oxford University Press, 1995.

Tagore, Abanindranath. "Indian Iconography." *Modern Review* 15, no. 3 (1914).

———. "The Three Forms of Art." *Modern Review* 1, no. 6 (1907).

Talbot, Cynthia. "Temples, Donors, and Gifts: Patterns of Patronage in 13th Century South India." *Journal of Asian Studies* 50, no. 2 (May 1991): 308–40.

Tarikere, Rahmat. *Karnatakada Sufigalu.* Hampi, India: Prasaranga, Kannada University, 1998.

Teltscher, Kate. *India Inscribed: European and British Writing on India, 1600–1800.* Delhi: Oxford University Press, 1985.

Thakurta, Tapati Guha. *The Making of a New "Indian" Art: Artists, Aesthetics, and Nationalism in Bengal, c. 1850–1920.* Cambridge, England: Cambridge University Press, 1992.

———. "Visualising the Nation." *Journal of Arts and Ideas,* nos. 27–28 (1995): 7–41.

———. "Westernisation and Tradition in South Indian Painting: The Case of Raja Ravi Varma, 1848–1906." *Studies in History,* n.s. 2, no. 2 (1986).

Thambanda, Vijaya Poonacha. *Adhunika Kodagu.* Hampi, India: Prasaranga, Kannada University, 2000.

———. *Conflicting Identities in Karnataka: Separate State and Anti-separate State Movements in Coorg.* Hampi, India: Prasaranga, Kannada University, 2004.

Tharu, Susie, and K. Lalita. *Women Writing in India.* Vol. 1. New York: Feminist Press at the City University of New York, 1991.

Tharu, Susie, and Tejaswini Niranjana. "Problems for a Contemporary Theory of Gender." In *Subaltern Studies,* ed. Shahid Amin and Dipesh Chakrabarty. Vol. 9, *Writings on South Asian History and Society,* 232–260. Delhi: Oxford University Press, 1996.

Thimmaiah, G. *Power, Politics, and Social Justice: Backward Castes in Karnataka.* Delhi: Sage, 1993.

Thompson, E. J. *The Last Siege of Seringapatam.* 1923. Rpt. New Delhi: Asian Educational Services, 1990.

Thompson, E. W. *The Making of the Indian Princes.* Oxford, England: Oxford University Press, 1943.

Trautmann, Thomas. "The Study of Dravidian Kinship." In *Family Kinship and Marriage in India,* ed. Patricia Uberoi, 74–90. Delhi: Oxford University Press, 1993.

Trouillot, Michel Rolph. *Silencing the Past: Power and the Production of History.* Boston: Beacon Press, 1995.

Valentia, Viscount George. *Voyages and Travels to India, Ceylon, the Red Sea, Abyssinia, and Egypt in the Years 1802–1806.* Vol. 1. London: F. C. and J. Rivington, 1811.

Venkatachalam, G. "The Artist with Strong Character." In *K. Venkatappa: Savi Nenapu,* ed. S. N. Chandrasekhara. Bangalore: Karnataka Lalit Kala Academy, 1987.

———. *Contemporary Indian Painters.* 1927. Rpt. Bombay: Nalanda, 1947.

Venkatesh, S. *K. Keshavayya.* Bangalore: Karnataka Lalit Kala Akademi, 2004.

Verma, S. P. "Elements of Historicity in the Portraits of the Mughal School." *Indian Historical Review* 9, nos. 1–2 (July 1982–January 1983): 63–73.

Vijaisri, Priyadarshini. *Recasting the Devadasi: Patterns of Sacred Prostitution in Colonial South India.* New Delhi: Kanishka, 2004.

Visvesvaraya, M. *Planned Economy for India.* Bangalore: Bangalore Press, 1934.

Walkowitz, Judith. *Prostitution and Victorian Society: Women, Class and the State.* New York: Cambridge University Press, 1989.

Washbrook, David. "South India, 1770–1840: The Colonial Transition." *Modern Asian Studies* 38, no. 3 (2004): 479–516.

Whitehead, Judy. "Modernising the Motherhood Archetype: Public Health Models and the Child Marriage Restraint Act of 1929." In *Social Reform, Sexuality, and the State,* ed. Patricia Uberoi, 187–210. New Delhi: Sage, 1996.

Wilks, Mark. *Historical Sketches of the South of India in an Attempt to Trace the History of Mysoor from the Origin of the Hindoo Government of that State to the Extinction of the Mohammedan Dynasty in 1799.* Vols. 1–3. London: Longman, Hurst Rees, and Orme, 1810.

Zebrowski, Mark. *Deccani Painting.* New Delhi: Roli, 1983.

Zutshi, Chitralekha. *Languages of Belonging: Islam, Regional Identity, and the Making of Kashmir.* Delhi: Permanent Black, 2003.

Index

JANAKI NAIR is professor at the Centre for Historical Studies, Jawaharlal Nehru University. Her previous books include *The Promise of the Metropolis: Bangalore's Twentieth Century, Women and the Law in Colonial India,* and *Miners and Millhands: Work, Culture, and Politics in Princely Mysore.*